Reconstructing Teacher Education:
Teacher Development

Edited by

John Elliott

The Falmer Press

(A member of the Taylor & Francis Group)
London • Washington, D.C.

UK   The Falmer Press, 4 John St, London WC1N 2ET
USA   The Falmer Press, Taylor & Francis Inc., 1900 Frost Road, Suite 101,
           Bristol, PA 19007

First published 1993

**A catalogue record of this publication is available from the
British Library**

ISBN 0 75070 127 7 cased
ISBN 0 75070 128 5 paperback

**Library of Congress Cataloging-in-Publication Data are
available on request**

Jacket design by Caroline Archer

Typeset in 9.5/11 pt Garamond by
Graphicraft Typesetters Ltd., Hong Kong

*Printed in Great Britain by Burgess Science Press, Basingstoke
on paper which has a specified pH value on final paper
manufacture of not less than 7.5 and is therefore 'acid free'.*

Contents

v

Contents

Synopses of Chapters

INTRODUCTION
John Elliott

PART 1 COHERENCE AND CONTINUITY IN TEACHER EDUCATION: PERSPECTIVES AND ISSUES

CHAPTER 1 Three Perspectives on Coherence and Continuity in Teacher Education: John Elliott

This chapter establishes a framework which informs the organization of the book as a whole. It opens with a discussion of the problem of establishing a National Curriculum for teacher education and argues that coherence and continuity in such a curriculum will depend upon the philosophical perspective informing its construction. Three different possible perspectives, their key principles, and implications for teacher education are briefly described.

CHAPTER 2 The Assault on Rationalism and the Emergence of the Social Market Perspectives: John Elliott

The chapter opens with an analysis of the New Right attack on higher education-based teacher education. This attack is portrayed as a conflict between a system based on rationalist assumptions and the emerging social market perspective. An account is then provided of what 'coherence' and 'continuity' mean in the context of this latter perspective, and is contrasted with what they mean from a platonic or rationalist perspective.

The chapter concludes with a detailed analysis of the Hargreaves proposals for teacher education, and locates them unambiguously in the social market perspective.

CHAPTER 3 Evaluation, Economics and Performance Indicators: Nigel Norris

As the previous chapter suggested, the construction and use of performance indicators as measures of quality is a central feature of educational processes when they are viewed from the social market perspective as production-consumption technologies.

Norris locates the emergence of the idea of performance indicators in the 'political imperative for more effective and efficient public services' and argues that they constitute a device for constructing 'essentially an economic calculus' on which to base policy decisions. The idea is a symptom of the attempt to transform education by the importation of business and industrial values.

The rest of the chapter consists of a comprehensive and succinct review of the major methodological and political problems which confront attempts to construct and use performance indicators and concludes that the basic purpose underpinning the appeal to economics and business values is to 'reduce the influence of service professionals and subsume professional authority under managerial authority'. Such a conclusion throws light on the New Right's attack on teacher education in higher education (see chapter 2).

CHAPTER 4   *One in a Million? The Individual at the Centre of Quality Control: Saville Kushner*

Drawing on data from his evaluation of an innovatory course for student musicians in a conservatoire, the author argues that attempts to discover standardized measures of benefit is a largely futile exercise. Quality, he argues, 'is a feature of professional practice that is nurtured by freedom and discretion but compromised by restraint and standardization'. There is, he claims, a tension between quality and control when control is perceived as a function of systems. Whereas judgments which serve external control render the individual accountable to the system, those which save the development of quality render the system accountable to the individual. In order to assess quality we need to portray how features of systems — projects and programmes — influence the personal development of individuals rather than assess the extent to which they succeed in adapting individuals to the requirements of the system. Projects and programmes need to be set in the context of the unfolding biographies of individual practitioners. The author suggests that emerging systems of quality control will divorce the culture of educational practice from the culture of educational politics. He is pessimistic about the possibility that we shall live to see a quality control process which is sensitive to the needs and experience of individuals, and therefore sceptical of the feasibility of what is proposed in the next chapter.

CHAPTER 5   *Are Performance Indicators Educational Quality Indicators?: John Elliott*

This chapter opens by reiterating the conclusion drawn by Norris in chapter 3, but goes on to argue that a concern for quality has also emerged from within the teaching profession. However, it has taken a different form to the construction and use of performance indicators. It is manifested in the emergence of 'a reflective professional culture' from the destabilization of the traditional craft culture; Elliott later goes on to explain how this new culture can be understood as a quest for qualitative indicators of quality. He locates it in the process model of curriculum development implicit in the school-initiated curriculum reforms of the 60s and 70s and the spread of educational action-research as a medium of continuing professional learning for experienced teachers. However, the chapter also takes a look at the Labour Party's position on performance indicators, and identifies some ambiguities in its quality control proposals, which stem from it taking on board certain aspects of the social market perspective.

The chapter generally develops a distinction between *quality* and *performance* indicators. The former are constructed in the reflective judgments of educational practitioners rather than operating as predefined and externally imposed control devices. As such the idea of quality indicators is consistent with Kushner's contention that quality is nurtured by conditions of freedom and discretion as opposed to those of restraint and standardization (see chapter 4).

CHAPTER 6 Professional Education and the Idea of a Practical Educational Science: John Elliott

This chapter elaborates a paradigm of educational inquiry which is derived from the hermeneutic perspective and embraces such ideas as 'teachers as researchers', 'educational action research', 'action inquiry', and 'reflective practitioners'. This practical science paradigm provides the context in which the identification and use of qualitative quality indicators, as opposed to performance indicators, is rendered intelligible. Such a paradigm of inquiry constitutes a search for situational understanding and involves a mode of reflection 'which supports wise and intelligent decisions in particular, complex, and fluid practical situations'.

The chapter draws on the work of Dreyfus on the development of situational understanding and associates of McBer and Company on generic professional competencies to formulate a developmental model of professional learning within the practical science paradigm. Although it is competency-based it employs a reconstructed account of the nature of teacher competence to the behaviourist account which has tended to dominate the development of competency-based education and training systems in the past.

Proposals are developed for an experiential learning curriculum in the area of initial teacher education, entailing close collaboration and partnership between schools and institutions of higher education.

The chapter concludes with a discussion of the role of higher education-based schools of education in reconstructing educational practice as a practical science.

CHAPTER 7 A Common-sense Model of Professional Development of Teachers: David Hargreaves

Hargreaves argues that his proposals for teacher training are not underpinned by a social market ideology and that my inferences to this effect are distorted, biased, and emotively expressed in a manner which is designed to render his position unattractive. He believes that his position is consistent with my practical science model, and that our respective views of teacher professional development have more in commmon than I care to admit.

In the second part of chapter 7 Hargreaves offers an account of teacher professional development which is grounded in an analysis of *what* teachers need to learn and when. He argues that the professional development model he outlines is compatible with my own, but that I have emphasized processes of professional learning and neglected the content of that learning. According to Hargreaves my 'process model' can be applied to each segment of the professional learning content he describes. Such segments can be progressively ordered. He concludes that 'a coherent model of professional development embraces both continuity and progression and matches process to content. Elliott's practical science model falls short of this ideal'.

PART 2 SCHOOL-BASED TEACHER EDUCATION: FOUR STUDIES OF INNOVATION

CHAPTER 8 A Case Study of School-based Training Systems in New Zealand Secondary Schools: R.G. Munro

This ethnographic study looks at two school-based initial training innovations established at the Secondary Teachers' College, Auckland: A mathematics/science programme and a history/social studies programme. Its focus was 'on identifying those influences which most affected the dispositions and behaviour of the trainees during the period of training', and it attempts to locate its findings in a broader range of theoretical and research literature about teacher training in the northern hemisphere.

Munro pin-points the significance of students' biographical experiences as pupils in shaping their basic perspective on the teaching role which he describes as a 'preoccupation with control'. Moreover, his data suggested that college and school-based trainers were limited in their ability to address this preoccupation 'for fear they might themselves be thought to be inadequate in the classroom or, alternatively, in the hope that it will be assumed that they have no difficulties in managing classes'. Citing Van Maanen (1979) he locates discussion of control issues as a 'taboo-violating activity' which is something to be avoided.

The history/social studies programme generated skill and resource-based routines which were relatively effective in diminishing the intensity of students' preoccupation with control. Munro points out that this programme in contrast to the other one had established a strong partnership between college staff and associate tutors in the schools. In the mathemetics/science programme the absence of such partnerships resulted in students modelling their teaching 'on that of their associates and on remembrances of their own schooling'. College inputs became less and less credible and useful. The partnership context of the history/social studies programme also encouraged students to attach greater credibility to educational theory inputs.

Munro found little evidence of reflective practice developing amongst trainees in either programme, and concludes that this is 'less a function of structural deficiencies in training' than 'simple neglect'. What evidence of reflective practice was discerned appeared to be the result of personal biography. Munro argues that recent recommendations that initial teacher training should promote 'self-reflective' and 'self-analytical' approaches to teaching fail to note the 'preoccupation with the rigours of initial survival in the classroom'.

In spite of some differences between the two programmes Munro argues that students in both gave greater credibility to their school rather than their college experience. This was reinforced by students' perceptions of differential status in college and school contexts; between that of 'student' and that of being 'very nearly a real teacher'. Such a status differential enhanced rapid self-socialization into the occupational culture of teaching; a process which appeared to inhibit trainees' reflective capacities. According to Munro 'they were aware that to act in a reflective manner was often inconsistent with what was regarded as professionally acceptable in the schools . . .'

Munro reports that 'oppositional' and 'resistant' conduct on the part of trainees, which deviates from the values, assumptions and norms of the prevailing occupational culture was minimal. In spite of claims made by the programmes to link theory and practice Munro concludes that the issue 'remains unresolved'.

One interesting contrast between the two programmes was that the history/ social studies one adopted a competency-based approach which enabled the college tutors to control trainees' practical learning experiences in schools. This stood in marked contrast to the maths/science programme which created an apprenticeship learning mode characterized by dependency on teacher associates. This perhaps suggests that in the former programme students were effectively initiated into a *technology* of education, rather than into the traditional craft culture.

The final part of the paper looks at the implications of the study reported for 'future trends' in secondary school teacher training. Munro is sceptical that current 'proposals' for reform in the UK will do nothing more than reinforce the conservative values and power structures already evidenced in the contemporary practice of schooling. Moreover, he argues that they will do little to radically reconstruct the theory-practice relationship and the roles of school and higher education-based trainers.

Munro points out that his findings basically support MacDonald's radical proposals for research-based programmes of initial training which neither support the traditional model of higher education-based training nor the trend towards an apprenticeship model. In doing so he supports MacDonald's contention that research-based initial training can provide the basis for a new vision of continuity and coherence in teacher education as a whole. However, he is sceptical about the extent to which this option will be politically endorsed by policy-makers in either the UK or New Zealand for the forseeable future.

CHAPTER 9   Capital T Teaching: Les Tickle

The focus of this study is on beginning teachers involved in innovatory induction programmes designed by the author and aimed at developing them as 'reflective practitioners' (see Schon, 1983). Tickle acknowledges that he was uncertain about the applicability of Schon's ideas to new teachers because 'there is only a very limited repertoire of experiences to draw upon' in assessing the complex and unstable circumstances which confront them. Yet paradoxically the intensity with which beginning teachers experienced their practice as highly problematic suggested that the induction period 'involves extensive reflection'. So Tickle sets out to explore through his own second-order action research the relationship between the kind of reflective thought and action beginning teachers tend to engage in, and the construct of 'reflective practice' embodied in his programme aims.

Tickle argues that the beginning teachers in his samples reflected continuously, if not systematically, about a plethora of concerns. Amongst them the question of teaching strategies predominated. Yet this reflective activity was largely engaged in isolation from others without any forms of personal and professional support. Teachers were up to work out things for themselves as best they could.

According to Tickle the new teachers reflected to establish control over the situations they handled: to simplify the complex, to render the unpredictable

predictable, and to stabilize what is essentially unstable. Reflection was non-systematic and orientated to 'getting it right' by eliminating the problematics of practice and establishing routinized solutions for them. 'Capital T' status implied the experience of mastery and control through the 'deproblematizing' of teaching. According to Tickle this form of reflection was at best only a partial success: '. . . such deproblematization was hardly possible . . . Security was both an interest and an illusion'. The more the beginning teachers constructed their 'capital T' identities the more their practices became non-reflective and habituated. The outcome of their reflection was non-reflection. Tickle becomes aware of a discrepancy between this form of security orientated reflection and Schon's theory which posits reflection as a means of overcoming 'selective inattention' and habitual practice through a continuous willingness to reframe problems and to test new solutions.

Tickle finds that his teachers were engaged in a kind of reflection which reduced problems to their technical aspects and ignored questions about ends and values. And he finds Schon's theory insufficient to clearly differentiate a purely technical and clinical mode of reflection from the 'broader, deeper and more rigorous use of reflection and action' he alludes to.

The chapter concludes with an attempt to define this deeper level of reflection. Tickle argues from his data that as teachers achieve technical mastery some develop a different level of concern which focusses on ways of realizing personal values in their teaching. Although they do not articulate and consciously reflect about their values, Tickle argues, they are implicit in the way these teachers begin to define their practical problems. He then develops an account of a *reflexive* practice which subordinates technical reflection to reflection which aims at the transformation of self. In the light of this account Tickle questions the extent to which his induction programmes have supported this deeper level of reflection, but is convinced that such support is essential to 'the education of new entrants'.

*CHAPTER 10   The Development of Teachers' Thinking and Practice:
Does Choice Lead to Empowerment?: Christopher Day*

Under the Local Management of Schools (LMS) provisions of the Education Reform Act of 1988, local education authorities in the UK are devolving financial resources for in-service education to the schools. This chapter is based on an evaluation study the author carried out for an English LEA on a pilot experiment in financial devolution of responsibility for INSET to schools. One of the claims enshrined in such experiments is that it empowers teachers at the 'chalk face', and gives them 'ownership' over their own professional development.

Day's findings are strikingly consistent with those of Munro in New Zealand (chapter 8) with respect to school-based initial training, and of Tickle with respect to the school-based induction of beginning teachers; namely, that teachers 'increased their content and pedagogical knowledge without reexamining the situational assumptions or moral and ethical contexts for their work'. In other words the dimension of critical self-reflection was missing as a mode of professional self-development.

One of the effects of school managed INSET was an increased provision for peer learning through the sharing of experience and collaborative planning. Less emphasis was placed on course attendance outside the school context, i.e. mounted by the LEA or local higher education institutions. A variety of reasons were given for this including mismatches between provision and perceived needs and the irrelevance of theory. However, some teachers felt there were problems about restricted access to external courses in terms of their potential to 'renew thinking', 'foster self-development' and enabling them to transcend to danger of parochialism.

Day argues that in spite of the value of self-generated and serviced on-site INSET evidenced in his interviews with heads and teachers there was also evidence that the lack of investment in longer externally-led courses was implicitly preventing teachers 'from moving to deeper levels of reflection' and thereby in the longer term likely to have a negative effect on 'the maintenance and enhancement of motivation, experience and knowledge' among school teachers.

In the second part of his chapter Day examines the school culture as a context for teacher development. He compares his evaluation findings with a variety of studies of the influence of school culture or ethos on the professional motivation and development of teachers. His data indicated a shift in some schools towards the development of more collaborative and less hierarchical organizational cultures which made individuals feel they had 'a voice' in determining their own professional development. In other schools teachers felt that access to, and opportunities for, professional growth were managerially manipulated to satisfy institutional needs. However, in schools with a collaborative ethos Day also discerned a tension between institution-focussed and person-focussed provision which required sensitive leadership to handle in ways which made individuals feel valued.

Even within the collaborative cultures Day notes that developments in classroom pedagogy and teacher collegiality were largely reinforcements of ongoing work, and operating below the level of significant and radical changes in customary practice.

In summarizing the second part of this chapter Day argues that 'power of choice over the management of finance for teacher development should not be confused with teacher empowerment. This must relate to the nature of the learning processes themselves and to such factors as leadership and school culture which create conditions for teacher development . . .' But the establishment at an organizational level of a collaborative culture is, he argues, a necessary but not sufficient condition of high quality professional development. He supports Rudduck (1987) in raising doubts about 'the intellectual rigour of self-created learning opportunities'.

In the final section of his chapter Day generates an account of the 'deeper levels' of professional development which is highly consistent with those provided earlier in this book by Elliott and Tickle. In conclusion he argues that empowering teachers to take responsibility for their professional learning is not simply a matter of changing the organizational culture of schooling. It is also a matter of developing their capacities to critically self-reflect about 'the moral and ethical implications of pedagogy and of social structures and concepts', about the ends as well as the technical means of education.

*CHAPTER 11   Chronicles: Doing Action Research: The Stories of Three
                       Teachers: Richard Davies*

This chapter assembles three teachers' stories about their experience of the PALM project, which was based in CARE at the University of East Anglia and provided support for classroom action research by teachers into promoting autonomous learning in pupils through the use of microcomputers. The project's pedagogical aim was to foster in teachers that level of self-reflection and analysis which Munro, Tickle and Day found to be a missing dimension in the school-based learning of students, beginning and experienced teachers.

Jane's story is of a teacher who wants to work in a collaborative school culture and is continuously frustrated by its apparent absence. She concluded that 'my school was not the right school physically, socially or educationally for the project'. It appears to have contributed little to whole school development. Yet in spite of this, involvement in the project appears to have contributed considerably to Jane's own professional development. What Jane found personally valuable about the experience exemplifies the very thing Tickle found absent amongst his beginning teachers. She discovered that development and change are the result of remaining open to the problematics and uncertain aspects of practice and re-fusing to retreat into the safety of customary ways of coping. Action research involved her breaking through into that deeper level of reflection described by Tickle and Day. It was 'psychologically useful . . . It made me reassess myself . . . It widened and deepened my understanding of the parameters of education'. Jane's story suggests that individual teachers can radically change their practices and grow professionally in spite of an unsupportive school culture, providing they have access to an alternative culture which supports and sustains a high level of reflection and self-analysis.

Daphne was a deputy head and close to retirement after thirty years of teaching and on her own admission somewhat resistant to change, in a school where it appears other teachers welcomed it. Although she cites no radical changes she testifies to a relaxed confidence which action research enabled her to achieve in the face of the uncertainties and complexities introduced by a microcomputer in her classroom. In the area of information technology she came to feel that action research had been more effective than other INSET strategies in helping teachers to cope with change.

Helen's story testifies to the power of systematically gathered data to radically change teachers' self-understanding of their practices, rather than simply to re-inforce ongoing work. It made her aware of the mismatch between her practice and her educational values, and resulted in the insight that the 'only way I could encourage more independent learning in the classroom was by letting go of the reins'. But the insight depressed her because she came to feel that 'everything I had done in the past was wrong . . . It was contrary to what I believed in but couldn't-find the method to let go'. At this point 'I would have done anything to get out of teaching'. But she persisted in collecting data and discovered that 'the more you look, the more you see, the more you change; round and round'. In the end she realized 'There is no success or failure' — no Capital T Teacher that Tickle's beginning teachers were trying to construct as a professional identity for themselves — but 'there is only development. You learn how to ask questions. You don't have to please anybody. The only thing you have to do is please your-self'. Through action research Helen learned more about herself as a teacher and a person, and what she learned was that 'you get more control over yourself and less control over others. You've got to create a different type of environment for that to happen. You've got to have organized chaos'.

PART 3 RESEARCHERS AND TEACHERS: CHANGING ROLES AND RELATIONSHIPS

CHAPTER 12 Through the Looking Glass: The Use of Associative Methods to Enhance Teacher Thinking: Michael Schratz

Schratz opens his chapter with a review of change strategies aimed at reforming teaching and learning in schools. Drawing on a range of literature from the USA and Europe he concludes that little progress has been made. What has been neglected he argues is the problem of creating a learning culture amongst teachers which enables them to articulate and reconstruct the implicit practical theories that underpin their practices. 'Changing teaching', he argues, 'always means changing one's "practical theory" of teaching'.

The rest of the chapter describes a number of 'associative methods' which that author has successfully used as a teacher educator to help teachers develop their insights into the practical theories which structure their practice. Each method requires teachers to represent their experience in an imaginative form and to use such representations as a basis for reflective dialogue with peers.

The chapter provides practical illustrations of collaborative research into teachers' thinking which cannot be separated from the process of teacher development. It is therefore very consistent with the position Elliott argues in an earlier chapter.

CHAPTER 13 Academics and Action-Research: The Training Workshop as an Exercise in Ideological Deconstruction: John Elliott

Support for a practical science paradigm of professional learning in higher education requires the reconstruction of the professional culture of academic educationalists. This chapter describes in detail the way the rationalist and objectivist assumptions which underpin this culture were challenged through a training workshop mounted for Venezuelan educational researchers and teacher educators. The account contained in this chapter is an illustration of what the author calls 'second-order' action research, i.e. a reflective inquiry into his own practice as a facilitator of action research. He shows how such 'second order' reflection based on data contributes to the development of his own theorizing about the nature of action research as a mode of professional learning.

CHAPTER 14 The Relationship Between 'Understanding' and 'Developing' Teachers' Thinking: John Elliott

The chapter begins with two teachers' accounts of their professional learning through a research-based MA course operating within the practical science paradigm. They are compared and contrasted with theories of reflection developed by Schon, Carr and Kemmis, and Louden, and used to critique them as a basis for constructing a more comprehensive account of the reflective dimensions of professional learning. Issues surrounding the validity of this account are then discussed and their implications for research into teachers' thinking generally. Finally, it is argued that such research itself constitutes a form of practical science and that a separation of processes, aimed at 'understanding' and the 'development' of teachers' thinking respectively is methodologically undesirable.

PART 4   PORTRAYING TEACHERS' DEVELOPMENT

CHAPTER 15   The Development of Primary School Teachers' Thinking about the Teaching and Learning of Science: Peter Ovens

This detailed study of the development of two teachers' thinking about their practice was carried out in the context of an award-bearing in-service course in primary science. The course involved teachers undertaking action research into their own teaching of science. The author had been running the course for ten years and as he points out at the beginning his research was not motivated by 'the desire to know about teachers' thinking . . . to gain knowledge for its own sake, but to understand teachers' professional development in order to foster it more wisely'. In other words the research constitutes a piece of second-order action research aimed at improving the course tutor's own pedagogical practice.

The study maps out in some detail, in relation to each teacher, the ways in which their reflections interact with their practices, so that the reader is able to see how reflection leads to the development of practice, and how the latter influences the quality of reflection. The author also examines his own role as the course tutor and the impact of his interventions on the learning experiences of teachers.

CHAPTER 16   Thinking and Being in Teacher Action Research: Marion Dadds

Through a case study of the professional development of a single, but not untypical, teacher (undertaking an MA course in Applied Research in Education), the author shows how action research-based professional learning implies a distinctive paradigm of educational inquiry in which the identities of teacher and researcher are inextricably fused. She demonstrates the significance of the teacher's personal values, attitudes and biographical formation in the development of insight and understanding, and argues that these aspects of self cannot be dissociated from cognition as tends to be assumed in more objectivist paradigms of research.

Dadds also shows how the action research-based learning of an individual can influence whole school development, and provides evidence of the process by which this influence is exerted, not simply through the persuasive logic of arguments and evidence but through insights that are mediated by certain personal qualities manifested in relationships with peers.

Dadds' chapter provides data which empirically and comprehensively grounds the hermeneutic perspective on teacher education and the practical science paradigm of educational practice, as these are elaborated in the early chapters of the book.

If some previous chapters tend to treat professional learning as largely a matter of changing teachers' cognitions this contribution reminds us that cognitions arise from historically conditioned and socially situated selves, and that the development of understanding implies the transformation of self.

CHAPTER 17   Importance of an Articulated Personal Theory of Professional Development: Christine O'Hanlon

This chapter again arises from a study of teacher professional development in the context of an action research-based award-bearing course for experienced teachers on which the author served as a tutor for many years. She argues that action research enables teachers to develop an articulated personal theory of their professional development by reflecting about the relationship between their personal values and the professional practices which are shaped by institutional roles. Her case study of Jo demonstrated how personal values and theories about how to realize them within the teacher's professional role, are reintegrated through reflection on practice, and about how professional roles are in turn reintegrated in the light of these developing personal theories.

O'Hanlon's study draws out the implications of this reflexive interaction between persons and roles, for the form of reports teachers produce on their professional learning. She demonstrates how teachers' public accounts of learning tend to focus on content rather than process and therefore mask and hide the personal theories of professional change and development which tacitly informed their construction. However, she also shows that the journal and diary entries in which the data was originally represented actually depict the personal processes of learning. Such 'private' records therefore constitute personal theories of professional development.

O'Hanlon's conclusion is that in order to achieve the status of a fully functioning occupant of their professional role teachers must be helped to reflexively develop through action research an explicit personal theory of their own professional development.

Introduction

John Elliott

The material in this book has all mostly been written during a period when 'teacher trainers' in the UK have been under attack from the New Right, and government policy-makers have been sufficiently influenced by its ideas to threaten the very existence of higher education-based teacher training. At the time of writing we are awaiting the publication of a Government White Paper for teacher training, which the Secretary of State for Education and Science, Kenneth Clarke, has already revealed will recommend the devolution of 80 per cent of initial teacher training time for secondary school teachers to the schools from September 1992.*

The attack on teacher training from the New Right has been very much directed towards theory-based training which is accused of promoting progressive theories that are politically biased in favour of a left-wing egalitarian ideology. The overall effect, it is argued, is a failure to raise standards.

Broadly speaking, the New Right, aided and abetted by the tabloid press, wants to see the removal of teacher training from higher education, and for it to be unambiguously located in the schools, where it can be linked to the 'theory-free' development of practical skills.

This book does not contain a 'defence' of current practice in higher education-based teacher education and training. But it does provide a rationale for a continuing role for higher education while at the same time endorsing a move towards more experientially-based professional learning. In doing this it articulates in some detail a perspective which transcends the polar opposites that the New Right and the present Government want to couch the current debate in. On the one hand we have a theory-based and impractical form of training emanating from higher education and on the other hand we want a more realistic practically based form of training based in the schools.

This book embraces neither 'the bogey' of the New Right nor the 'baby' it is trying to give birth to in the form of a school-based training which fosters the acquisition of on-the-job technical skills. It argues that the practice of teaching is neither a matter of applying ideas derived from theory rather than experience nor simply a matter of applying instrumental technical skills, learned on-the-job, to

* Following the consultation period after the publication of the White Paper, Clarke's successor as Secretary of State, John Patten, reduced the proportion of school-based training from 80 per cent to 66 per cent.

produce standardized and measurable end-products. Rather it argues that teaching is best viewed as a practical science in which the relationship between theory and practice is interactive. Practical skills are not simply technical in character. They are structured by values and understandings of how to act consistently with them. Such values and understandings constitute 'practical educational theories' which inform practice with varying degrees of explicitness. When teachers monitor their own practices they bring such theories into a conscious realm of reflection which enables them to test and modify them through further experimental action. In this way theory is derived from practice and in turn informs its further development.

Part 1 of this book (chapters 1–7) attempts to develop a coherent and unified account of a process of teacher education which takes into account the issues at stake in the current debate, but hopefully transcends the terms in which they are couched, for example, 'theory' v. 'practice', 'knowledge' v. 'competence', 'professional' v. 'public' control.

The opening chapter briefly sketches three perspectives on teacher education: platonic rationalism; the social market philosophy; and the hermeneutic. The former constitutes the basis of the traditional rationale for the higher education base, and 'the bogey' of the New Right. The second constitutes the philosophy of education which informs the New Right critique and the third the perspective which underpins the practical science paradigm.

Chapter 2 locates the current debate in a detailed account of 'the social market' assumptions which underpin the New Right's attack on teacher education, and of 'the platonic rationalist assumptions' which underpin the position attacked. Although I argue that the attack is based on certain myths about the current state of the art in higher education, there is an element of truth in it, inasmuch as the organization of teacher training in higher education still reflects the platonic/rationalist perspective.

The second part of chapter 2 involves an exposition and critique of David Hargreaves' detailed and radical proposals for reform in teacher education and training. I argue that in spite of Hargreaves' espousal of a non-partisan political stance one can squarely locate his proposals within the social market perspective. One of the key implications of this perspective for teacher education is that it is the school within a deregulated market system that constitutes the unit of benefit with respect to teacher training as opposed to individual teachers. The Hargreaves proposals in my view unambiguously subordinate the needs of individual teachers to the needs of the system construed as a number of atomized and competing production-consumption units.

The next three chapters (3, 4 and 5) constitute a critique of the quality control implications of the social market perspective on education generally and teacher education in particular. This critique focusses on the construction and use of performance indicators as measures of quality. Norris' chapter locates the idea of performance indicators in 'the political imperative for more effective and efficient public services' and argues that they essentially provide the basis for an economic calculus concerned with 'minimizing inputs to achieve the same level of output, or maximizing outputs with the same level of input'. In doing so they subordinate educational values to business values.

The chapter summarizes very cogently the major methodological and political problems which are raised by the construction and use of performance indicators: 'data overload', 'measuring change', 'corruption of the processes they are intended to monitor', 'standards fixing', 'validity and reliability'. Norris concludes that performance indicators fail to achieve their central purpose of providing simple and unambiguous measures of quality, and therefore should be abandoned. However, he is well aware of the non-rational ideological purposes they serve politically; namely, to replace the values of professional educators with the possessive individualism which underpins all production-consumption systems. Rational considerations alone are unlikely to lead policy-makers to abandon performance indicators since they are integral to the whole control ideology they espouse. One cannot abandon performance indicators without also abandoning the social market perspective on education.

Although Kushner's chapter draws on data gathered during an evaluation of an innovatory training programme for student musicians, it has enormous implications for teacher training, which is why it has been included in this book. On the basis of his evaluation data Kushner argues that the search for quality in education is fruitless if we measure the performance of individuals against standardized indicators of effectiveness. Such indicators limit and constrain the freedom and discretion of professional practitioners, which are the very conditions in which quality is nurtured. There is a tension between the ideas of *quality* and *control.*

Kushner suggests that whereas most *quality control* procedures view the individual as accountable to the system, one needs an evaluation process which views the system as accountable to individual practitioners. This is because the quality of educational practice resides in the personal qualities people bring to, and develop within, their professional roles. Such a position is antithetical to the assumptions of the social market perspective concerning the relationship between individual practitioners and the systems they operate. From the latter perspective the practitioner is a functionary of the system and the quality of his/her performance depends on the acquisition of skills which are derived from an analysis of the functional requirements of the role. From Kushner's perspective the quality of an individual's performance depends on what he/she brings as a person from their own biographical history and is able to develop further through the professional role. In other words, the quality of a system's performance is more likely to be enhanced by fostering the personal development and growth of the individuals who perform in it, than by pushing them through training programmes which largely focus on the acquisition of technical skills. The latter may be necessary conditions for the achievement of excellence but excellence as such is not constituted by it.

Kushner sees an increasing divide emerging between a culture of educational politics permeated with social market assumptions and a culture of educational practice that nurtures quality in education. He is pessimistic about the political possibility of constructing an alternative form of quality assurance which manifests a culture of educational practice. At best he thinks educational practitioners may be able to use the rhetoric of performance indicators, competencies, etc. as a protective smokescreen while developing 'undercover' a culture of practice which nurtures quality in education.

In chapter 5 I, more optimistically, set about the task of elaborating an alternative form of quality assurance and accountability which is consistent with the hermeneutic perspective and a practical science paradigm of educational practice. Central to this alternative is the idea that the quality of teaching and schooling resides not so much in its instrumentality in effecting certain measurable outputs, but in its ethical consistency with educational values. The idea is not original. Over twenty years ago R.S. Peters argued that 'aims' in education are not extrinsic outcomes of educational processes. Rather they are conceptions of value which are manifested and realized in the processes themselves. They constitute criteria for judging what is to count as an *educative* process. Stenhouse constructed his 'process model' of curriculum design around the idea, and exemplified it in the Humanities Project. And it was in the context of the latter that the 'teachers as researchers' movement emerged in the UK. The focus of such research was how to develop a teaching-learning process which was consistent with educational values. Teachers collected evidence as a basis for making judgments about the extent to which their values and practices were consistent with each other. In other words they searched for evidence about the educational quality of their practices. In chapter 5 I have called such evidence *quality indicators* and contrasted it with the kind of evidence we now call *performance indicators*.

Performance indicators are essentially quantifiable data which measure the effectiveness and efficiency of technologies of production. Quality indicators on the other hand are essentially manifestations of values being realized in practice. They are constituted by qualitative judgments rather than quantitative measurement, and are always contestable and open to debate.

From an ethical, rather than technological, perspective educational practices are interpretations of values. Educational values are defined by judgments and decisions about appropriate courses of action in a situation. Quality indicators constitute the database for an evaluative discourse about those judgments and decisions. Whereas performance indicators pronounce closure on public dialogue, quality indicators open it up. Such dialogue does not support 'consumer choice' by providing fixed and unambiguous benchmarks against which to evaluate quality. Rather it provides a context of improving the quality of educational judgments and decisions. From a 'social market' perspective establishing conditions for high quality reflective dialogue between teachers and their public may not appear to be a very appropriate form of quality assurance. But from a hermeneutic perspective on education it is the only appropriate form. In the final analysis the quality of teachers' educational practices depends on the development of a form of public discourse which supports, rather than undermines, wise and intelligent professional judgment.

Chapter 6 provides a detailed elaboration of the 'practical science' paradigm of educational inquiry and spells out its implications for a coherent and continuous process of teacher education aimed at the development of capacities for situational understanding. It explores the relevance of Dreyfus' five-stage model of the development of situational understanding for describing phases of teacher development and curriculum design. It also uses the research of McBer and Company on Generic Professional Competencies to clarify those dimensions of professional competence involved in the idea of the teacher as a practical scientist.

Having mapped out what I consider to be a coherent view of teacher development I make an attempt to construct an experiential learning curriculum for initial teacher training which establishes a foundation for later reflective practice and avoids an overrapid immersion of student teachers into an occupational culture which defines 'the realities' of teaching and schooling for them. Such a curriculum I argue should be based on field-research and only allow for a gradual and controlled immersion into direct practical experience. Support for this position can, I believe, be found in the studies reported by Munro, Tickle and Day in Part 2 of the book. All testify in different contexts to the power of the occupational culture in schools to limit, circumscribe and restrict the development of personal capacities for in-depth reflection about practice. They support my argument that the central role of higher education in teacher training is to protect, foster and develop the reflective capacities of teachers. This gives higher education a key role in competency-based teacher training when the latter is conceived not in terms of behaviourally defined functional skills but in terms of those personal abilities which are generic conditions of all reflective educational practice.

The final section of chapter 6 looks at the implications of my account of teacher education for the organization of roles and relationships in departments of education within the higher education sector. My account not only requires the transformation of professional and organizational cultures in schools. It also demands the transformation of professional and organizational cultures in higher education. I argue for a greater integration of research and teaching so that the teacher educator becomes a practical scientist who does not divorce his or her teaching from research. Although I support the development of specialized discipline-based research in education, I want to see it less dissociated from the problematics of practice, as these are investigated within the more general scope of a practical educational science conducted by teachers and academics working collaboratively to improve the quality of teaching and schooling. Specialized researchers need to collaborate with teacher educators and teachers in schools to define the questions which need to be addressed and to decide how 'the answers' can best be disseminated to maximize their usefulness to the 'practical scientist'.

In the concluding chapter in Part 1 (chapter 7) Hargreaves argues that his proposals for teacher training are not underpinned by a social market ideology and that my inferences to this effect are distorted, biased, and emotively expressed in a manner which is designed to render his position unattractive. He believes that his position is consistent with my practical science model, and that our respective views of teacher professional development have more in common that I care to admit.

Hargreaves offers three examples of what he considers to be invalidly inferred assumptions, including 'the remarkable inference that the professional training needs of the individual teacher are now to be subservient to making the school more efficient and effective'.

In the second part of chapter 7 Hargreaves offers an account of teacher professional development which is grounded in an analysis of *what* teachers need to learn and when. He argues that the professional development model he outlines is compatible with my own, but that I have emphasized processes of professional learning and neglected the content of that learning. According to Hargreaves my 'process model' can be applied to each segment of the professional learning content he describes. Such segments can be progressively ordered. He concludes that 'a coherent model of professional development embraces both continuity and progression and matches process to content. Elliott's practical science model falls short of this ideal'.

In his model Hargreaves renders practical common-sense knowledge in the areas of classroom management and pedagogy as basic to any further progression in professional learning. In doing so, he draws on Shutz's phenomenological account of practical knowledge in everyday life, and thereby attempts to establish consistency between his current thinking and the phenomenological/symbolic interactionist perspective which informed his earlier educational research and writing.

I am happy to leave the reader to judge whether Hargreaves succeeds in dissociating his proposals from the ideological underpinnings I inferred from them and in articulating a professional development model which is consistent with the symbolic-interactionist perspective that did indeed, as he claims, inform his earlier writing and research. All those educationalists who, rightly or wrongly, have come to feel that there are discrepancies between the perspectives underpinning Hargreaves' earlier and later educational writings, will be grateful to him for this attempt to demonstrate the continuity of his ideas.

All I want to do in this introduction is alert the reader to an issue I feel may be at stake between Hargreaves and myself. Hargreaves appears at points to doubt whether my process model of professional development is consistent with his content model. In which case the latter is not simply a neglected aspect onto which the process model can be grafted. This may be because the process model implies a certain view of the content of professional learning which is inconsistent with Hargreaves' attempt to specify progression in learning in terms of his content analysis. On my account of professional learning, 'classroom management', 'pedagogy', 'curriculum', and 'school structures' are all aspects of professional situations which need to be considered in relation to each other at every phase of development.

Underpinning Hargreaves' model is the assumption that development implies a process of progression through segmented content components. Underpinning my model is the assumption that development implies a transition between different forms of holistic understanding with respect to practical situations. What appears to be at stake between Hargreaves and myself are two rather different understandings of the process of teacher development, namely, 'development' as a process of unfolding forms of professional learning versus development construed as a process of progression through different content domains. In whose favour the issue should be resolved I am happy for the reader to judge.

Part 2 (chapters 8–11) consists of studies of school-based teacher development programmes which are relevant to the phases of experiential learning I mapped out in chapter 6. Rae Munro's chapter is based on a very substantial and detailed piece of research into the learning experiences of student teachers on PGCE programmes in New Zealand. The two programmes he studied had very substantial school-based components. Munro found that immersion into 'the realities of teaching' did very little to foster reflective practice. Rather his evidence strongly suggested that the rapid and extensive socialization which occurred primarily involved the learning of coping and survival strategies. Student teachers, he argues, were overwhelmingly preoccupied with questions of control that impeded any reflective consideration of children's learning needs. Mentoring in the schools appeared to reinforce rather than militate against socialization into habitual and routinized practice, and the higher education staff were powerless to counteract it. Only biographical factors appeared to be significant in determining the extent to which students maintained a capacity for intelligent reflection about their experience of direct immersion in the 'realities' of practice. Munro concludes by proposing a more gradual and controlled immersion process which begins by training students to become 'critical and reflective' observers of the 'realities' of contemporary schooling. In other words he proposes that premature and rapid socialization into bad practice can only be overcome if student teachers are trained as educational field-researchers before they are required to have any extensive direct practical experience of teaching. This is not an invitation to return to the old theory-based training. Field-research enables students to construct and develop their own insights into children's experiences of schooling from first-hand observational evidence. If some theories prove to be useful as a basis for understanding and making sense of this evidence then this is something that the students will have judged for themselves. Munro argues that the programmes he studied did little to link theory and practice. His radical alternative suggests that the missing link can be found in the mediating role of field-research.

In chapter 6 my proposals for a basic training curriculum take Munro's findings seriously and provide a structure of learning activities which enable a gradual immersion into direct practical experience while at every point remaining closely in touch with it.

Tickle's chapter constitutes a study of his own attempts to promote reflective practice through school-based induction programmes for recently qualified teachers (what I have described as Advanced Beginners). He argues that although reflection takes place, it is limited and constrained by the same preoccupation with control cited by Munro. Each of the teachers he provides evidence about, to varying degrees see the outcome of reflection as a state of secure and certain mastery and control over the situations they experience on a daily basis. Once they believe they have achieved this state their behaviour becomes more routinized and non-reflective.

Tickle's data prompts him to re-examine the adequacy of his concept of reflective practice, and to develop it in ways which are highly congruent with the practical science paradigm I outline in chapter 6. He warns of the dangers of seeing reflection purely as an instrumental mode of thinking aimed at the development of clinical and technical competencies alone. Reflection which solely aims to deproblematize practice and to achieve the security of certain and stable knowledge is, according to the evidence provided by Tickle, the pursuit of an illusion. The more his teachers constructed for themselves a professional identity based on technical control and mastery, the more they were unable to respond to unanticipated events and challenges. Their capacity to question the assumptions embedded in the strategies they had evolved in a quest for security, certainty and control appeared to decrease. Any experienced emotional turbulence tended to be resented rather than reflectively examined.

Tickle also sees the achievement of the illusion of mastery as an obstacle to the development of the teacher as a person within his/her professional role. This involves developing a personal educational philosophy and the competence to increasingly match one's practice to it. The illusion of technical mastery, according to Tickle, splits the professional from the personal identity and alienates teachers in their role from a sense of themselves as persons who are aware of where their values lie and how they stand in relation to them. It is reflection which achieves the level of thinking jointly about the relationship between one's personal educational values and one's practices which establishes the conditions for continuing personal growth and change. How such reflection operates to integrate the professional and personal dimensions of teacher development is the subject of the concluding chapter in the book by O'Hanlon.

Day's study of the devolution of responsibility for the in-service training of experienced teachers to the schools suggests that school cultures tend not to support the development of reflective capacities amongst teachers. School-based INSET which is school-controlled tends not to empower teachers. Day's study reinforces the findings of Munro and Tickle. Certainly he doesn't present us with an image of school culture which is capable of supporting the development of teachers' reflective capacities in any depth. Like Tickle he suggests that professional learning and practical improvements are largely confined to the technical aspects of practice. Day argues that teacher development in the deeper sense of an increased ability to realize one's educational values in practice, and to clarify those values in the light of that practice, requires some form of external intervention from 'beyond' the system itself, for example, from LEA advisers or higher education staff.

The chapters by Munro, Tickle and Day enable us to clarify and reformulate the issue between the present Government in the UK and teacher educators. It is not so much an issue of 'barmy theory' — to quote Kenneth Clarke — v. practical competence. Rather, perhaps, the issue revolves around the fact that the power of the emerging 'practical science' paradigm in teacher education threatens the transformation of education into a technology of production and consumption. And what is at stake here is not so much the quality of learning in schools — since this in itself becomes ideologically defined in terms of standardized product specifications — as the costs of public education. The Government's ideologically framed conception of standards is simply a legitimation for severe reductions in resources. And the problem contemporary teacher education presents to policy-makers is its potential for spreading ideological disenchantment amongst teachers by transforming their professional culture into that of a practical science. So it does indeed make 'political sense' for a Secretary of State to attempt to 'turn back the clock' by preventing higher education from having any significant influence on teachers and thereby reinforcing those aspects of their culture which are conservative and unreflective. Rather than a recipe for increasing the quality of children's learning, the present Government's teacher training proposals are simply a strategy of ideological protection.

Richard Davies' chapter tells three stories of professional development in the teachers' own words. They suggest the potential of on-the-job learning which is structured by an externally coordinated programme of action-research into an area of practical concern. In this case the programme was collaboratively supported by both higher education and LEA advisory staff. Even the teacher operating in an unsupportive school climate is able to change and develop personally and professionally through involvement in the programme. Davies' accounts of how 'action-research' fostered changes in practice by changing the teachers' understandings of themselves in relation to their values, illustrate the development of a depth and level of reflection which Munro, Tickle and Day found to be largely missing from the school-based learning they studied.

However, I am not naive enough to believe that higher education institutions are unambiguously the kind of reflective cultures which can support the development of teachers as practical scientists in schools. It is the task of higher education institutions to protect and nurture the growth of reflective intelligence in society. However, the model of reflective intelligence embedded in academic cultures has tended, as I argue in this book, to be a highly rationalist one. Knowledge is viewed as a certain and secure foundation for rational practice, and by implication something to be generated independently by experts who have mastered the techniques of knowledge production in particular fields. Intelligent and reflective practice from the perspective of such a model involves the application of 'rational principles' or 'theories' generated by academic experts. The contexts of knowledge generation and that of knowledge application are viewed as quite separate. The former is contemplative and detached from practical concerns while the latter is action orientated and 'passionate'. It is this view of knowledge that the Conservative Government has attacked in its 1992 proposals for reforming teacher training. Unfortunately it appears to be unaware of the cultural transformation that has been going on over the past decade and a half in higher education-based teacher training.

The rational model of reflective intelligence has itself been increasingly challenged by researchers and scholars working inside the 'academic disciplines'. Knowledge of principles and theories is increasingly viewed as provisional and open to continuing revision in the light of new evidence. No longer can it be viewed as a sure and certain foundation for practice and a source of solutions that renders the practice less and less problematic. Moreover, the academic knowledge-generators have increasingly acknowledged that the questions they ask and the answers they come up with cannot be dissociated from the interests and 'biases' which are embedded in the everyday practices of people in the host society. For example, some historians of ideas have argued that the generation of 'psychological knowledge' about the distribution of certain abilities and aptitudes amongst people is motivated by a search for a rational foundation on which to base discriminatory social practices. Knowledge generation is increasingly viewed as a reflexive activity in which researchers have an obligation to bring the biases and assumptions which condition their inquiries to conscious awareness as objects for critical reflection.

Thus the shift within academic cultures has been from an objectivist view of knowledge as fixed and certain to a view where it is regarded as provisional, open to question, and socially constructed. On this view the development of knowledge depends not so much on the capacity of researchers to dissociate the process of inquiry from their practical interests as human beings, but on their capacity to reflect critically about the way in which these interests condition their inquiries. The result of such reflection is not the abolition of bias but rather its continuous modification in ways which open up new questions and issues to be addressed.

This shift of view about the nature of knowledge in academic cultures has implications for the relationship between theory and practice which are now particularly reflected in the ways 'professional schools' in higher education generate and disseminate knowledge. The development of theory and practice is increasingly viewed as an interactive process, as dimensions of a single and unified enterprise. The reflective development of practice poses questions and issues for theoretical investigation, the answers to which help practitioners to redefine the practical problems which confront them and their 'solutions'. The reflective implementation of these 'solutions' in turn pose further questions and issues for theoretical inquiry, and so it goes on. The development of educational theory is dependent on the reflective development of practice in schools, and the latter on the former. Theoretical inquiry is continually redefining its 'agenda' and 'findings' in the light of the problematics of practice, and those problematics are in turn being continuously informed by theoretical inquiry. This view of the interdependency between the development of theory and practice does indeed imply a collaborative process in which academic specialists and practitioners operating as 'practical scientists' in schools are engaged in a continuing dialogue with each other as equal partners in a mutually dependent relation.

In chapter 12 Michael Schratz describes a number of methods which he and colleagues at the University of Innsbruck have used to enhance teachers' capacities to reflect about their practices. They involve helping teachers to reflexively articulate and reconstruct the frameworks of belief ('practical theories') which underpin their practices. Schratz and his colleagues in the University used pedagogical strategies to enhance that 'deeper level of reflection', which Day noted was largely absent in school-based INSET programmes that were internally controlled and managed, and involved little external support.

It seems to me entirely appropriate for higher education to play a major role in enhancing reflective practice in schools since this is a condition for the kind of interaction between the development of theory and of practice which I have outlined. It is interesting that Schratz's chapter is not only concerned with the development of the reflective capacities of school teachers. One of the 'methods' he illustrates focusses on the development of reflective practice amongst university teachers.

I would certainly want to argue, with respect to teachers of teachers in higher education, that their ability to support reflective practice in schools is dependent upon the extent to which they operate as reflective practitioners themselves. Teacher education is itself a form of 'second-order' practical science.

In chapter 13 I describe a workshop I conducted for academic educationalists in Venezuela. It involved a number of practical exercises aimed at helping participants to deepen their methodological understanding of action-research. I try to illustrate the ways in which the workshop exposed and challenged the rationalist and objectivist assumptions which have prevailed in academic cultures, and enabled participants to explore an alternative epistemology and its methodological implications.

This chapter constitutes a reflexive account, inasmuch as I show how my own thinking about educational research, as well as that of participants, is developed through the workshop. It illustrates how, by treating a training workshop in action research as an object for second-order action research, one can use it to further develop one's theory of theory and practice.

The use of second-order action research by teacher educators to develop theories of theory and practice is further illustrated in chapter 14. I use two teachers' accounts of their professional learning on an MA course in Applied Educational Research to critique major theories of reflective practice developed by Schon, Carr and Kemmis, and Louden. In doing so I attempt to construct a more comprehensive account of the dimensions of reflective practice.

Chapter 14 also addresses the issue of how one validates a theory generated from action research, since the latter rejects the objectivist assumptions which have underpinned traditional educational research methodology. I argue that such theories are necessarily personally constructed and that there are no incontestable benchmarks for assessing the extent to which they constitute valid representations of reality. But this does not imply that questions about the validity of theories are pointless. The view that there are not theoretical certainties does not negate the possibility of theory development. It is possible to justify an idea in comparison with others by showing how it provides a more comprehensive and unified account of the available evidence. And this is precisely what I attempt with respect to my account of teacher reflection in relation to those of Schon, Carr and Kemmis, and Louden.

I conclude chapter 14 by arguing that the epistemological transformation of academic cultures no longer renders attempts to separate the processes of 'understanding' and 'developing' teachers' thinking intelligible. To persist with the attempt is to endorse a developmentally 'primitive' paradigm of inquiry. The shift towards a practical science paradigm of inquiry into teachers' thinking in which the aims of 'understanding' and 'developing' reflective thinking are fused is, I argue, indicative of a transformation in the culture of academic educationalists to a higher level. The final chapters by Ovens, Dadds and O'Hanlon in Part 4 of this book constitute evidence of this transformation occurring. All three authors draw on case data they have collected in researching their own practice as teacher educators, operating in the practical science paradigm, to construct their own theories of professional learning and development. All three chapters make a significant contribution to our understanding of the implications of the practical science paradigm for the professional development of teachers.

Ovens presents data to show the links between reflection and action as these are manifested in the development of two teachers undertaking an action research-based in-service course in primary science. In doing so he shows how certain 'established' academic models of the relation between reflection and action in the action-research process constitute a constraint on, rather than support for, reflective teaching. Dadds' case data enables her to examine the role of the biographically conditioned and socially situated 'self' in shaping the development of understanding and insight through action research. She argues that this 'self' is not detached and dissociated from the search for understanding but an integral part of it. Personal values, attitudes and biographical formation significantly influence the practical inquiry undertaken by the teacher in this study. The chapter challenges the assumption which underpins the traditional rationalist paradigm of educational research, which assumes that detachment from 'the passions' of the self (biases) is a condition for developing insight and understanding. Dadds' case study of Julie constitutes a powerful argument for reconstructing educational research as a form of passionate inquiry, in which cognition is inextricably bound up with the quest for self-realization, and none the worse for being so 'biased'.

O'Hanlon's chapter seemed to me to take up and develop an aspect of Dadds' study; namely, the role of the personal self in professional development. Drawing again on a case study of a teachers' development through an action research-based in-service course, O'Hanlon shows how a teacher develops his/her professional role by reflecting about the relationship between his/her personal values and the practices which are shaped by the role. In order to achieve consistency between practice and the personal self, the teacher reflectively reconstructs his/her role in the light of his/her values and reinterprets his/her values in the light of the role. This process of continuously reconstructing the professional role through self-reflection inevitably makes the teacher aware of, and able to articulate, a process of development which is both 'professional' and 'personal'.

All of the papers in Part 4 challenge the traditional assumptions which underpin the idea of 'research' in higher education. Within the framework of these assumptions the action research reported in these chapters would be rendered biased and invalid. What the three authors illustrate is an increasing capacity on the part of academic institutions to reconstruct educational research as a form of hermeneutic practical science, which integrates the search for understanding with the professional development of teachers. All the authors of Part 4 emphasize the point Kushner made earlier in this book that the quality of professional practice depends not so much on adapting the individual to a system defined role but of enabling the individual to develop as a person within a role. The practical science paradigm implies a vision of development which integrates the 'personal' and 'professional' as aspects of a single and unified learning process. This is a far cry from the assumption underpinning the social market model of education; namely, that the individual is primarily a functionary in a technology of production and consumption.

Part 1

Coherence and Continuity in Teacher Education: Perspectives and Issues

Chapter 1

Three Perspectives on Coherence and Continuity in Teacher Education

John Elliott

Teacher education would appear to be currently lacking in coherence and continuity. Some argue that only a National Curriculum in teacher education covering initial, induction and in-service education will provide coherence and continuity. Well it may but there is a problem here.

The present muddle exists because there are at least three quite distinct philosophies of teacher education underpinning current practice. Each philosophy furnishes basic principles that in themselves have implications for coherence and continuity. The problem with a National Curriculum is that it is likely to be grounded in one of these philosophies to the exclusion of the others. Not that this is so much of a problem if the philosophical basis of such a curriculum has been clearly articulated and widely debated in relation to its alternatives, so that it comes to represent a broad spectrum of agreement and endorsement by all the relevant interest groups.

However, one of these philosophies is heavily endorsed by the state, and if the National Curriculum in schools is anything to go by, a teacher education system grounded in this philosophy is unlikely to be developed and implemented in a context of free and open discussion of its basic ideas and principles.

The problem about a National Curriculum for teacher education essentially lies in the conditions under which it is likely to be constructed. So the question is whether or not conditions can be established which will enable all relevant parties to participate in its construction. Certainly teacher educators in higher education ought to be more proactive than they appear to be in articulating together a shared vision of the future. Hargreaves (1990) has mapped out a set of detailed proposals for radical change which in my view are very coherent and imply principles of continuity in teacher education. The problem for me with his proposals is that they constitute a reasonably detailed working out of the perspective and principles which the present Government is likely to endorse, and perhaps also the opposition parties will find them attractive. In fact Hargreaves has done a much better job than the Hillgate Group in fully articulating the implications of a particular philosophical perspective which may also be embraced more widely across the political party spectrum in the future.

Unfortunately a comparable job is not being done with another philosophical perspective that has underpinned a considerable amount of change in teacher education over the past two decades, particularly the education of serving teachers: but also increasingly initial teacher education.

I will now briefly outline the three philosophical perspectives which are currently in contention, the basic principles which underpin them, and their implications for teacher education as a continuing process. This framework will be articulated more fully in subsequent chapters.

The Platonic or Rationalist View of Teacher Education

This view is embedded in the traditional pattern of higher education based teacher education. It emphasizes the image of the teacher as a *rational-autonomous* professional. Underpinning this image is the basic principle of rationalism; namely, that good practice transcends the biased and prejudiced practical cultures of everyday living when it is derived from a theoretical understanding of educational values and principles. This principle entails that good practice consists of consciously applying theory, and indeed is derived from it.

From this perspective a pattern of teacher education emerges in which the initial phase can be sharply differentiated from the continuing education of serving teachers. Firstly, it implies that the initial education phase gives priority to the development of theoretical understanding, and opportunities to demonstrate an ability to apply them appropriately in practice. The idea of school-based components or 'school practice' is quite consistent with the rationalist perspective on initial teacher education.

The rationalist aim for the initial phase is the development of the rationally-autonomous professional. As Hargreaves points out this is a highly individualistic image of the teacher.

Once this rationally-autonomous professional has been developed at the initial phase (s)he can then be left to self-direct future professional learning. Rationalism in professional education implies a volunteristic pattern of in-service provision. Any prescription would be inconsistent with its image of the rational-autonomous teacher. And of course this volunteristic pattern has prevailed for over thirty years in higher education institutions (although it is now in serious trouble).

One would not expect rationalist teacher educators to welcome a National Curriculum which secured continuity of learning by prescribing learning experiences of qualified teachers.

The platonic perspective gives little significance to an *induction phase* in teacher education, which is perhaps why, given the dominance of this perspective in the past, it has been neglected. The increasing emphasis on the importance of induction reflects an increasing disenchantment with rationalist assumptions.

The 'Social-Market' View of Teacher-Education as a Production/Consumption System

This view applies the production-consumption systems which prevail in the economic sphere of Western democracies to the cultural/social sphere of the public services; including education. With respect to teacher education the outcomes of professional learning are construed as quantifiable products which can be clearly pre-specified in tangible and concrete form. In other words learning outcomes are conceived as behavioural, with an emphasis placed on the atomistic specification of discrete practical skills (competences).

Products have to have markets and consumers. From a 'social market' perspective schools conceived as individual consumers of the products of teacher education are the market. And since these products are behavioural outcomes in the form of practical skills schools also become the main sites for training activities at all phases (from this perspective professional learning is an outcome of training rather than education).

If teacher educators in higher education have a role in this scenario it is in a purely service function, for which they must compete against other training agencies. Professional development expertise from the 'social market' perspective is transferred from higher education to senior staff in schools. It is the latter who identify 'training needs' and essentially control and monitor its provision. Basically teacher trainers from higher education become part-time technical operatives of a training technology which is designed and managed by schools.

The basic principle entailed by this 'social market' perspective is that of behaviourism, with its implication that the significance of theoretical knowledge in training is a purely technical or instrumental one. Knowledge belongs to the realm of inputs rather than outputs. Its introduction can only be justified if it is a necessary condition for generating the desired behavioural outcomes of learning. From this 'social market' perspective the initial training phase constitutes induction. It need not take very long because from this perspective people can identify a few basic behavioural skills which are sufficient to assure the organization that the trainee is able to function within it. The continuing education phase is concerned with progressively developing higher level skills, and this of course may be a more prolonged process. It is certainly not viewed as a volunteristic process. An individual's training needs are identified by the school which also controls the provision for them. There is not much room for the rationally-autonomous professional in this scenario.

The most articulate working out of the implications of this perspective for the future of teacher education in this country is in my view contained in David Hargreaves' 1990 Hockerill Lecture. But it also underpins the Government's Licensed Teacher Scheme, the DES interest in competency-based teacher education and the increasing involvement of the NCVQ in matters of teacher training.

The Hermeneutic View of Teacher Education as a Practical Science

This perspective has become increasingly adopted by in-service teacher educators in higher education as an alternative to the Platonic view. It is now also making inroads into initial teacher education, where in my view it is more problematic. Its manifestation in the in-service field has been the adoption of classroom and school-focussed action-research approaches which highlight the role of 'teachers as researchers' in effecting improvements in practical situations construed as complex, ambiguous and unpredictable.

At the level of initial training this perspective has tended to manifest itself by the adoption of Donald Schon's account of professional learning as 'reflective practice': in my view a softer, more privatized and individualized notion than that of educational action-research.

From the hermeneutic perspective one does not derive practice from theory as rationalism suggests. Nor does one reduce theory to practice as behaviourism suggests. The basic principle which underpins the hermeneutic perspective is that of *situational understanding*. This principle implies that practice is grounded in interpretations of particular situations as a whole and cannot be improved without improving these interpretations. Moreover, such interpretations are not 'objective' in the rationalist sense of detached from the biases and prejudices of everyday practical cultures. From the hermeneutic perspective bias is a condition of situational understanding because all interpretation is shaped by a practical culture i.e. a system of value and belief which is conditioned by practical concerns. The hermeneutic understanding of situations is improved not by detachment from one's biases but by being open to aspects of the situation which may render them problematic in some respects as a basis for interpretation. In order to arrive at an understanding in these circumstances one has to accommodate the discrepant data by modifying one's initial biases. Situational understanding is improved not by eliminating bias but by modifying it.

The hermeneutic perspective also differs from the Platonic perspective in another, not unrelated respect. Situational understanding cannot solely be reduced to theoretical understandings of particular elements and aspects of a situation. The latter involves abstracting parts from wholes, while the former is constituted by the grasp of a concrete situation as a total entity. And this is not simply a matter of adding up the sum of the parts which have been abstracted, for situational understanding grasps a meaning which is more than such a sum.

Theory may play an important role in improving situational understanding but it is subordinate to the latter. A theoretical analysis of particularly problematic aspects of a situation, that one is trying to understand as a whole, is often an important episode in the development of a new synthesis. The relevance and use of theoretical ideas are, from the hermeneutic perspective, conditioned by the experience of a problem in accommodating certain aspects of the situation to the interpretative framework one brought to it in the first place. And so from the hermeneutic perspective one does not derive situational understanding from a prior theoretical analysis of all its aspects. Rather, theoretical analyses are episodes in an overall attempt to arrive at a holistic understanding of a situation.

The hermeneutic perspective implies the dependence of behaviour on situational understanding. Intelligent responses in a practical situation often cannot be specified in advance of it. Such situations are very complex and unpredictable in the way they develop. Judgments about what to do and how to respond in them have to be made *in situ*. Hence the practical significance of situational understanding. Good practice is not a matter of reproducing pre-programmed responses but responding intelligently and wisely to a situation as it unfolds on the basis of discernment, discrimination and insight. Moreover, the relationship between understanding and action is an interactive one. One does not first understand and then act. Understanding is developed through actions in the situation, and those actions are themselves improved as understanding develops. Hence, from the hermeneutic perspective I have outlined, the activity of teaching constitutes a kind of 'practical science'.

Teacher education becomes largely a matter of facilitating the development of teachers' capacities for situational understandings as a basis for wise judgment and intelligent decisions in complex, ambiguous and dynamic educational situations.

I will conclude by suggesting that the hermeneutic perspective and its basic principle of situational understanding has implications for a teacher education curriculum, and continuity and progression in professional learning, which we have hardly begun to fully articulate and explore. In my view this is an urgent matter if we want to generate an innovatory alternative vision of teacher education to the rapidly emerging and politically endorsed vision from the 'social market' perspective. And we should want to do this if we think higher education has an important role to play in the education of teachers. If the 'social market' perspective becomes the sole basis for articulating a radical alternative to a now discredited rationalism, then we can effectively kiss 'goodbye' to any significant higher education involvement in teacher education.

References

DREYFUS, S.E. (1981) *Formal Models v. Human Situational Understanding: Inherent Limitations on the Modelling of Business Expertise*, US Air Force Office of Scientific Research, Contract No F49620-79-C-0063, University of California, Berkeley.

HARGREAVES, D. (1990) *The Future of Teacher Education, Hockerill Lecture 1990*, Hockerill Educational Foundation, Frinton-on-Sea, Essex, CO13 9NQ.

Chapter 2

The Assault on Rationalism and the Emergence of the Social Market Perspectives

John Elliott

We have a messy, fragmentary, provision for teacher education. Prior to various government initiated changes one might argue that it had a sort of coherence; namely:

— a period of higher education-based initial training in the form of either the one-year PGCE for graduates or the four-year BEd degree for under-graduates;
— an induction period in school (the probationary year) for the beginning teacher supported by an internal mentor and sometimes by special external provision organized through the LEA;
— voluntary attendance by experienced teachers on LEA based or higher education-based award-bearing in-service courses.

As Hargreaves (1990) has pointed out, this pattern is heavily resourced at the level of initial training and very weakly resourced at the induction and in-service levels. What gives this pattern coherence is that it is basically underpinned by *the principle of rationalism*: the view that good practice is derived from a theoretical under-standing of educational principles. Teacher training in this view is, in addition to the basic content the student teacher will be qualified to teach, essentially a matter of establishing the theoretical foundations on which to base rational practices. Of course, no initial training programme has simply left student teachers to apply the theoretical principles of education after subsequent entry into the profession. If rational professional practices are derived from a theoretical understanding of educational principles then practice provides an opportunity for demonstrating such understanding, and the ability to deduce right courses of action from it.

There is a sense then in which a weakly resourced period of subsequent induction is an implication of rationalism. If students are able to demonstrate an ability to apply educational theory in practice during the initial training period then the induction period is easily seen as a 'safety net' for the weaker ones; an additional opportunity for borderline cases to make the grade. No wonder then that the Government has recently announced its intention to abolish the probationary year. It is the weaker element in the rationalist system of teacher education and therefore the logical point at which to embark on dismantling it.

The voluntaristic provision of in-service training is also an implication of rationalism at the level of initial training. Its ideal product is the rational/ autonomous professional: the individual who regulates his/her own professional development in the light of universal educational values and principles.

Any exercise of control over such a teacher's choice of professional development opportunities with respect to both teaching methods and extending his/her roles and responsibilities in the educational system is viewed as an infringement of rational autonomy.

The pattern outlined above, particularly with respect to the initial training level, has been the subject of considerable attack from the 'New Right' of the Conservative Party; an attack which has received concrete political expression in the form of the Licensed Teacher Scheme with its emphasis on two years of school-based on-the-job training as the entry point into teaching. The New Right's attack effectively collapses the distinction between initial training and induction and implies the removal of the former from the control of higher education; at best the latter is given a minor service role. It is hostile to educational theory in a very ambiguous way. In one respect it views the contemporary practice of teaching to be derived from the ideas of progressive theorists such as John Dewey. In doing so it attributes great power to theory in shaping concrete practice, and appears to be attacking only a particular kind of theory. The attack on 'theory' is therefore in this respect ideologically based. In another respect the New Right's attack appears to be more philosophically based viewing theoretical understanding of any kind as largely irrelevant to teacher training, and emphasizing the primacy of practical experience and modelling as the sources of practical skills.

This ambiguity in the New Right's attack is at the root of an apparent contradiction in their proposals. On the one hand they argue that standards in schools are low because teaching methods have become contaminated with the progressive theories of teacher educators. Yet on the other hand they propose to base teacher training on this contaminated system of schools. Of course, it could be argued that once one removes teacher training from higher education its contaminating influence will diminish in time. But this is hardly a basis for recommending a radical policy change in the short term, unless it is coupled with a high degree of optimism about the power of LMS, the National Curriculum and consumer accountability to rapidly transform the occupational culture of teachers. And, of course, it is this coupling which enables the New Right to escape from the charge of contradiction, and which gives its teacher training proposals a degree of ideological coherence. Underpinning them is the principle of the *social market* in which education is conceived as a commodity produced by schools for citizens (parents) cast in the role of consumers. Within the framework of this ideology there is little room for rationalism in the sense of deriving educational practice from a coherent set of objective values and principles governing the development of human potentials.

Coherence and Continuity from the Social Market Perspective

Education is essentially viewed as a production technology governed by 'product specifications' in the form of tangible and measurable targets, and accountable for its effectiveness in matching those specifications to individual consumers who have the right to exercise choice over which products they buy. Within the framework of the market ideology there is no space for rational minds to grasp objective educational values and principles. The aims of education are simply conceived as whatever sorts of commodities are valued by consumers in the social market place. The value of such commodities — knowledge, understanding, skills — simply resides in their utility for consumers: pupils, parents, employers. If they lack utility as social commodities they are valueless.

Questions about methods in education, seen as a production technology, are dissociated from educational theorizing. Whether a particular method is consistent with educational theory is a redundant question. The question about methods is simply a technical one about its efficient and effective functioning in the production system. Rationality in teaching is purely instrumental reasoning, and has no intellectual foundations. From the New Right perspective learning to teach is a matter of learning the technical skills which enable individuals to function effectively in the production system of education. As the production system changes to improve its productivity so individuals will need to amend and improve their skills through continuing training; the need for which can be identified at the school level through the staff appraisal system.

In the context of the educational reforms — LMS, consumer accountability, the National Curriculum, and appraisal — the mechanisms of the social market which are so established give the teacher training proposals of the New Right tremendous ideological coherence, which in turn provides a basis for viewing on-the-job teacher training as a continuum of experiences throughout a teacher's career.

Reinforcing the New Right attack on rationalism in teacher education is the competency-based training movement (CBT), emphasizing the pre-specification and standardization of job-functional skills. Under the auspices of the National Council for Vocational Qualifications the movement is attempting to make inroads into the professional occupations and exploring ways of applying jobs/functions analysis to derive detailed specifications of their skill-requirements. These 'competencies' can then provide a basis for identifying training needs, the design of training programmes, and the assessment of their outcomes.

This emphasis on performance-outcomes rather than theoretical understanding has met with some resistance in professional education circles on the grounds that it ignores the importance of theoretical knowledge as a foundation for intelligent professional practice. The sophisticated response to this defence of rationalism in professional education is that CBT does not deny the significance of theoretical knowledge but neither does it have to accommodate it in specifying the outputs of training. Theoretical knowledge is conceived as a learning input, but in assessing professional competence one need only take account of behavioural outputs.

The rationalist professional educator will be far from happy with this, arguing that one cannot identify what constitutes right performance independently of a theoretical grasp by a rational autonomous mind of the objective values and principles which make it right. But as we have seen there is no space for this argument within the ideological framework of the social market. Educational thinking within it is governed by the principle of *behaviourism.* If rationalism subordinates *knowing how* to *knowing that* then behaviourism reverses the relationship and subordinates *knowing that* to *knowing how.* Performance is not the outcome of the theoretical operations of rational autonomous minds. It has no theoretical foundations in the human mind. Rather performance is a behavioral response of an organism to certain pre-existing stimulus conditions, and knowledge — construed as information or data — is simply one of those conditions.

It is easy to see how the *principle of behaviourism* which underpins competency-based approaches to professional education is based upon the negation of Plato's idea of the rational autonomous mind which has persisted for so long in Western societies as the fundamental concept underpinning professional education. Later I shall argue that we need to move beyond these bipolarities in conceptualizing a coherent view of professional training. The truth of behaviourism lies in its denial of a mind which can detach itself from the body and its behaviour to contemplate an objective reality which exists independently of that behaviour. The fallacy of behaviourism lies in its implicit assumption that the idea of a reflective consciousness, capable of theorizing about its actions in the world, necessarily implies the rationalist construct of consciousness as the detached contemplation of independently existing objective and universal truths. It is then easy to draw the conclusion that one should focus on the performance outcomes of learning processes.

The CBT model offers the prospect of strengthening the ideological coherence of the New Right's training proposals. It provides teacher training with a production technology for commodifying professional learning for consumption at those points within the school organization where it is needed. As such it represents a means for rationalizing the use of scarce resources. CBT offers the promise of being able to specify minimal competences as a basis for qualifying individuals as teachers. These will be derived from an analysis of certain basic tasks and functions teachers have to carry out in classrooms. Other functions related to curriculum planning and evaluation, the assessment of learning, and school organization can be catered for through competency-based training provision at later stages.

The social market ideology bestows coherence on recent changes in teacher education, namely the movement through the Licensed Teacher Scheme towards school-based training in the context of LMS and consumer accountability, the implementation of teacher appraisal as a mechanism for identifying inservice training needs, and the specification of functional competencies as the basis for designing on-the-job training programmes and assessment systems. The fact that such changes have been initiated in a piecemeal manner gives the appearance of fragmentation and incoherence, particularly when they are still operating alongside a pattern of training which is sustained through Education Departments in the higher education system who continue to 'lock up' a considerable amount of Government resources.

The social market ideology also gives new meaning to the idea of 'continuity' in professional development. From a rationalist perspective 'continuity' of professional learning is the responsibility of rationally-autonomous individual practitioners. From the perspective of the social market ideology 'continuity' is the responsibility of the 'production-unit' i.e. the school.

Naturally Education Departments in HE are on the defensive. The educators who operate from them feel that the attack from the New Right misrepresents what they do and fails to take into account significant changes in teacher training over the past decade. For example, they argue that they have strengthened the school-based components of initial training and established greater collaboration with teachers in supervising and assessing the performance of student teachers. Departments of Education point to the CATE requirement that tutors working in initial training now have to have 'recent and relevant experience' of teaching in schools. All of which points to the strengthening of practical experience as a basis for professional learning. Morever, some Departments of Education are developing competency-based approaches as a basis for profiling student-development through school-experience.

Even at the in-service level recent years have seen the erosion of individual voluntarism and an attempt to adapt award bearing provision to systems identified training needs, initially at LEA, but now increasingly at school level. In this context much of the control over the selection of applicants for 'courses' has in effect been transferred from higher education to LEAs and schools. Even control over 'course design' and 'tutoring' has been eroded. Higher education is increasingly credentialed LEA and school-based training in a context where its control over the selection of entrants, the design of programmes and their staffing is considerably diminished.

All these trends in both initial and in-service teacher education can be described as a move towards greater collaboration between academics and practitioners, and even as an overcoming of the split between theory and practice in teacher-education. This is indeed the official line taken by most Education Departments and its representative body UCET. However, there is quite a bit of muttering about the dangers of 'falling academic standards' within this scenario. For some teacher educators at least these trends are viewed as compromises forced on Education Departments for the sake of survival in the social market.

In my view changes in teacher education at the level of higher education constitute an attempt to pour 'new wine into old bottles'. The basic organizational structures which supported the 'rational-autonomous' pattern of teacher education remain more or less intact; namely, the tripartite division between 'initial', 'in-service' and 'research'. The continued dissociation of the research process from the educational functions of Education Departments reflects the idea that the context of knowledge-generation is quite separate from the context of knowledge-application. And the distinction between initial and in-service education reflects the idea that a mastery of a body of theoretical knowledge is a necessary prior foundation for professional practice. This does not deny the necessity of opportunities during initial training to apply such knowledge, since the concept of mastery can be extended to cover the ability to demonstrate that one can use theory to inform practical judgments.

Although it can rightly be argued that the New Right's attack is founded upon certain myths about the state of teacher education, I believe there remains a strong element of truth in this attack. Although somewhat eroded by the ideology of the social market the principle of rationalism and the professional image of the teacher as a rational-autonomous individual substantially continue to underpin the organization, management and resourcing of teacher education in higher education. What we have achieved to date, and are attempting to defend, is an incoherent mixture of the old and new wine in bottles manufactured for the former.

The Hargreaves Proposals

In his Hockerill Education Foundation Lecture (1990) David Hargreaves challenges Education Departments in HE to move beyond a reactive defensiveness and piecemeal accommodation of the New Right's ideas. He calls for a national development plan for initial teacher training which sets out 'a vision for teacher education as a whole set within the broader context of the forces which have shaped recent reforms, in this country and elsewhere, and of the emerging problems which need to be solved over the next few years'.

Hargreaves' paper represents an attempt to sketch out such a vision in the light of emerging international trends in the field of education. Although he tends to represent his proposals for a holistic and radical restructuring of teacher education as non-party political I will attempt to show that it is certainly not non-ideological. His selection of salient international trends is, I will argue, coloured by a considerable amount of ideological bias. What Hargreaves does in his paper is to demonstrate far more ably than the New Right group associated with the Conservative Party what the implications of the social market ideology are for restructuring teacher education. They are the most radical and internally coherent proposals articulated to date. And Hargreaves is very perceptive in avoiding aligning himself with the present Government in making them, for the ideology of the social market increasingly appeals to all major parties as a basis for public policy in contemporary democracies.

Hargreaves identifies the following international trends as the broad context for an analysis of educational change in the UK.

(i) The demand for more education for more people generated by the need to compete successfully in the worlds' markets.

(ii) Increased Government intervention in education, but in a form which transcends the old bipolar categories of centralized and decentralized systems. Mirroring changes in large companies responsibility for educational delivery is devolved to small units, while a small central core determines broad policy and holds the former accountable for operating according to its requirements.

(iii) A marked change in professional–client relations away from the idea of the autonomous expert whose expertise rests on a body of infallible and certain knowledge and whom clients are expected to defer to without question. The trend is towards professionals becoming the providers of services to people conceived as consumers who have rights (of complaint), freedom of choice, and access to information in the form of performance indicators as a basis for rational choice.

(iv) The emergence of *quality* as the key concept for regulating activities in our social institutions.

(v) The emergence of *under resourcing* as a key problem in funding educational expansion.

Hargreaves proceeds to analyze the UK educational reforms in the light of these broad trends. In particular he focuses on Local Management of Schools (LMS), the professional development of teachers, and the growth of educational technology (ET) and information technology (IT) in schools. Schools under LMS are becoming self-managing institutions and increasingly independent from control by local education authorities. This means that the nature and quality of professional development for teachers becomes the responsibility of each individual school, rather than of the individual teacher or the LEA.

Under LMS professional development becomes closely tied to school development or improvement plans, which through the mechanism of a newly-established teacher appraisal system, result in personal action plans for each individual teacher. Professional development needs are thus determined by school development needs. Schools become 'the focus and often the base for professional development activities'. They need to acquire highly skilled senior staff to identify training needs and plan how they are best met. In this context teacher educators in higher education and LEA advisers are seen as people whose resources can be bought and who are held accountable to schools — their consumers — for the quality of training provision. Hargreaves argues that under LMS schools will become more sophisticated centres of professional development expertise and thereby more able to take responsibility for initial teacher training; buying in the services of higher education where appropriate. Of especial importance for him is the opportunity this transference of responsibility will afford for establishing greater continuity and progression of professional development between the initial training phase and the early years of teaching (induction).

Hargreaves sees the development of IT skills in schools not simply in terms of a need to make education more relevant to the world of work but as a tool for learning National Curriculum content more effectively and efficiently. IT is an 'essential means for raising educational standards; and most teachers have yet to realize this'. Under the National Curriculum teachers are required to teach more content and they will therefore have to teach more effectively and efficiently than they have done in the past.

IT becomes essential for many reasons, according to Hargreaves. Firstly it provides easy and rapid access to knowledge. Secondly, it enables differentiation in teaching and learning to meet the highly varied needs of pupils. It can be used to pace learning according to the individual's 'level, style and speed'. Thirdly, IT can be used in many different places other than schools. Hargreaves argues that more and more pupils will be using IT at home as a natural part of their working lives. 'Pupils too can become telecommuters — which will give the notion of homework a quite new meaning'. Finally, IT will free teachers from 'narrowly conceived didactic roles . . . to become tutors, supervisors and counsellors in support of independent pupil learning'.

Hargreaves sees IT as a way of handling the 'under-resourcing problem', by enabling 'the quality and quantity of output' to be improved 'without an equivalent increase in the cost of the input'. Teachers are having to work harder. But by learning to use IT they can begin to 'work smarter' in raising educational standards. Such a teaching revolution he argues will be 'driven' by three crises:

> — of role overload. In schools specific learning and academic functions have been displaced by social and welfare functions. This displacement can no longer be sustained at a time of increasing accountability for higher educational standards. IT will 'enable schools to accept the necessary standards'. IT will 'enable schools to accept the necessary narrower definition of the specific tasks of the school and to jettison functions which must be more widely shared in society'.

— of underachieving pupils. IT and ET will enable more pupils to learn because it allows for greater flexibility in approaches to learning than traditional didactic methods.

— of teacher supply. IT and ET will enable us to manage with fewer teachers, and to develop a new conception of the teaching profession and the way it is restructured and organized.

The final part of Hargreaves' paper contains some pretty radical proposals for restructuring the teaching profession and its training requirements in the light of the trends he has discerned and his analysis of the UK reforms in their light. In many respects they reflect ideas put forward by Charles Handy in *The Age of Unreason* (1989). In articulating what he calls the 'Shamrock Organization' Handy argues that the slimmed down flexible and responsive organizations of the future will consist of a core group of professionals who are responsible for ensuring that the major functions of the organization are effectively and efficiently carried out. This group will have something like a traditional career within the organization. Their major tasks will be concerned with planning and monitoring.

This 'core' group of professionals will contract in skilled personnel on a temporary part-time basis to carry out some of the functions of the organization. Those skilled individuals will be basically self-employed and will contract out their services to a variety of organizations over time. For them the idea of a career will be a redundant notion. Instead they will accumulate evidence of their activities and experience in the form of a 'portfolio'. A third group of individuals will undertake unskilled or semi-skilled tasks which are necessary if the functions of the organization are to be effectively carried out. They will also be on temporary contracts: their number and tasks varying according to the needs of the organization at any point in time.

Hargreaves' proposals for a differentiated structure within the teaching profession closely parallel Handy's three-pronged organization. Three professional sectors are envisaged by Hargreaves:

1 Career teachers

These are teachers who spend ten or more years in school teaching and are likely to become numerically less. Entrance into this sector would be governed by a first degree qualification of a conventional kind but not the BEd.

Hargreaves is not clear about his reasons for rejecting the BEd, but his general proposals for training career teachers suggest one. The PGCE, he argues, tries to do too much too soon in professional development terms. And presumably he feels that the BEd would be even worse in this respect. His basic argument is that the full range of skills necessary for high quality teaching cannot be packed into an initial training period because they take several years to develop through practical experience which is well planned and continuously supported.

What Hargreaves proposes is to effectively change the balance of training resources away from initial training towards induction. Initial training is shortened to a period of three–four months duration in which the trainee is expected to attain a basic level of competence necessary 'to assure everyone that the new teacher can be left in charge of a class without supervision'. Hargreaves acknowledges that there are problems with securing agreement about the constituents of this basic competence but does not elaborate them.

The basic qualification 'would then be followed by a five year period of continuing professional development under the supervision of senior career teachers ('mentor(s)'), leading to an *advanced* second level qualification'.

Some teachers, having completed the *advanced* level qualification would take a third level one in *professional development*. These teachers would be responsible for the *basic* and *advanced* levels of training, for coordinating professional development activities in their schools, and for establishing links between school improvement plans and such activities.

Such a training programme could be viewed as a preparation for the 'core group' of professionals within Handy's 'Shamrock organization'.

2 Assistant teachers

This is the group who provide the skilled professionals with technical aid and other forms of help and support which do not call for the high levels of professional skills possessed by the career teacher. They are needed to free teachers up to spend their time on those core tasks which only the skilled professional can perform.

Such a group appears to correspond to Handy's semi or unskilled pool of contract labour within the 'Shamrock organization'.

3 Associate Teachers

Most of the members in this group would contract into teaching on a short term or part-time basis. Many would be seconded for periods from business and industry or operate on a part-time basis while retaining their main employment base. Others would be self-employed and home-based individuals contracting their services part-time to schools. Through such arrangements schools would be able to utilize people with high levels of knowledge and skill from different sectors of society. They closely correspond with Handy's group of highly skilled individuals who contract into the organization on a temporary and often part-time basis.

Hargreaves argues that the short basic qualification for career teachers should be taken by individuals in this group or alternatively they should demonstrate that they already possess the skills specified for this qualification.

These radical proposals for restructuring the teaching profession require, according to Hargreaves, fundamental changes to the present pattern of teacher education, which will be 'painful and difficult'. He sees them as having many advantages over the Licensed Teacher Scheme, 'which does not challenge the structure of the profession or the pattern of teacher education in any radical way'. The proposals incorporate the idea behind the Licensed Teacher Scheme but extend it in ways which achieve a more coherent vision of the future of the teaching profession. I would agree. Hargreaves is far more imaginative than the New Right 'intellectuals' in spelling out the radical possibilities suggested by the social market metaphor for the organization of the teaching profession in the future.

Higher education-based teacher educators may feel betrayed by Hargreaves, the maverick 'insider', outdoing the New Right in pushing its ideas in even more radical directions; in ways that make it difficult for them to sustain their defence of the present structures.

In my view Hargreaves is right to challenge the present structures. They are grounded in a platonic rationalism which can no longer be sustained as a basis for teacher education. The process must be fundamentally reconstructed, and I see Hargreaves proposals as an invitation to do this. But we do not have to reconstruct the structures in the ideological form of the social market. And this is precisely what Hargreaves does.

Let me try to spell out the key assumptions which underpin his proposals:

(i)   Governments have a role in socially engineering the educational system through the construction of national policies.

(ii)   Educational policies should specify production targets which are measured by standards specifications called 'performance indicators'.

(iii)   The educational system can be specified as a set of production functions, and educational processes as a production technology.

(iv)   The school is the basic unit of production within the educational system.

(v)   The relationship between schools and society is basically one of *producers* and *consumers*. As consumers of education parents have rights of choice and complaint.

(vi)   The identification of professional training needs should be based on planning to improve the school as an efficient and effective production unit.

(vii)   Professional development should be school focussed and controlled by senior staff who possess training expertise.

(viii)   The contribution of teacher educators in higher education is conceived as services commissioned and controlled by training experts in schools.

(ix)   Standards of professional learning are best described as skills (competencies) which enhance the production functions of schools.

(x)   It should be possible to agree on a set of minimal or basic teaching skills — defined as the competence to be left in charge of a class without supervision.

(xi)   An efficient and effective production technology in schools, which maximizes the use of IT and ET, will imply a reduction in the need for large numbers of highly skilled career professionals and an increase in the numbers of (a) part-time and temporary associate teachers who have demonstrated a 'basic competence' to teach; and (b) teaching support staff.

(xii)   An efficient and effective school implies minimal skill levels for effective functioning in face-to-face transactions with learners but higher skill levels for effective functioning as technologists (systems designers, developers, evaluators and appraisers). In other words transforming schools into production systems involves making learning less person-dependent and more system-dependent.

The 'core' of career teachers within schools appear to be viewed by Hargreaves as technologists responsible for the planning, development and quality control strategies which enhance the efficient and effective functioning of schools as production units. Associate teachers on the other hand appear to be viewed as skilled operatives responsible for product-delivery at the 'chalk face'.

These assumptions, if correctly inferred from Hargreaves paper, are permeated by market metaphors. If Educational Departments in the higher education sector were to embrace Hargreaves' radical proposals for reconstructing teacher education and the assumptions which frame them, one might ask what distinctive professional services they might render. And the answer surely must be two-fold. Firstly, they will develop forms of applied research aimed at generating the kind of knowledge which enables schools to improve the efficiency and effectiveness of their production technologies. Such research will focus on the conditions under which productivity is optimized in classrooms and schools (for example, school effectiveness and teacher effectiveness research). Secondly, some will have a consulting role in designing and developing technological systems for establishing such conditions in the light of research. This will include the design and development of training systems. It is likely that the number of Education Departments in higher education will be drastically reduced. Market forces will ensure that educational 'knowledge production' and the development of 'new applications' of that knowledge will be restricted to only a few higher education institutions.

References

HANDY, C. (1989) *The Age of Unreason*, London, Business Books Ltd.
HARGREAVES, D. (1990) *The Future of Teacher Education*, Hockerill Education Lecture 1990, Hockerill Educational Foundation.

Chapter 3

Evaluation, Economics and Performance Indicators[1]

Nigel Norris

Every society keeps the records most relevant for its major values.
(Lazarsfeld, 1959, p. 108)

What Are Performance Indicators?

Generally speaking performance indicators are time series data that reflect and record change across a number of significant dimensions relevant for judging the effectiveness and efficiency of a system in achieving its goals. This definition highlights two characteristics commonly associated with performance indicators.

First, information about the performance of an individual, organization or system is usually collected at regular intervals so as to provide data on change over time. A familiar example is the measurement of temperature and blood pressure of a patient as indicators of improvement to, or deterioration in, health.

Second, performance indicators are meant to reflect quality and output. They may be a direct measure of the quality or output of a service, for example, the number of patients successfully treated for malaria. Mostly, however, they are only indirect measures or indices of things which themselves are too difficult to measure — for instance, school ethos.

Central to the construction and use of performance indicators are decisions about organizational goals and what is of most importance and value. Performance indicators have become associated with the political imperative for more effective and efficient public services. The concern for effectiveness is manifest in the specification of objectives, the measurement of progress towards them and consideration of alternative courses of action to reach the same ends. A concern for efficiency usually reflects an interest in minimizing inputs to achieve the same level of output, or maximizing outputs with the same level of input; it is essentially an economic calculus.[2]

Why Has There Been a Growth of Interest in Performance Indicators?

Investment in economic calculation and visibility tends to increase during periods of financial restraint (Hopwood, 1984). In times of prolonged economic decline or threat there is a much greater emphasis on costs, financial information and on measures of input and output. More often than not an apparent concern for the effectiveness of public services such as education or health masks a more politically sensitive concern for efficiency. Efforts to improve the effectiveness or efficiency of a service are often presented as neutral and uncontroversial technical matters when they really represent certain political priorities as opposed to others (Metcalfe and Richards, 1984, p. 190).

For at least a decade there has been a considerable growth of interest in the construction and use of performance indicators in education. One reason for this trend is the widespread disappointment with the contribution of education to social and economic change. Another reason for this trend is undoubtedly political concerns about the economic costs and benefits of public services in general.

Performance indicators have become central to modern strategies for reforming the management of public services. As governments all over the world try to control the escalation of public expenditure, business and industrial values have come to the fore in the management of public services. In Britain during the 1980s the Government identified evaluation as one component in its strategy 'to control public expenditure, change the culture of the public sector and shift the boundaries and definition of public and private spheres of activity, (Henkel, 1991, p. 9). The measurement of performance against clear objectives is what lies at the heart of managerialism in education and other public services.

There is nothing new in the application of industrial and business values to education — similar tends were apparent in the late nineteenth and early twentieth centuries in both Britain and the USA (Urwick and Brech, 1957a and 1957b; Callahan, 1962; Haber, 1964). However, information technology and new measurement techniques permit more comprehensive and large scale forms of survey than was previously possible. It is now conceivable that all children in an education system could be regularly tested and the results used to indicate performance at teacher, class, school and local level. It is at least feasible, although not defensible, to compare one teacher with another or one school with another in terms of pupil outcomes. Given the availability of this kind of information, it is also possible to think of the education system as a market in which schools sell educational services to parents or local authorities who can judge the quality of service provided in terms of a common criterion of value — pupil test scores. It is a very short step from here to giving parents vouchers to buy an education for their children from the school of their choice and for schools to compete for business. It is in this way that public services can be treated like private enterprise and controlled by supply and demand. What performance indicators offer are the surrogates for information that would otherwise be available through the market.

Performance Indicators and Education

In the United States of America the National Assessment of Educational Progress was established in the 1960s to monitor change and provide data on the relationship between student performance and the resources that go into education (Norris, 1990). In Britain the Assessment of Performance Unit was set up in the 1970s to measure national trends in educational performance. More recently in Britain a national assessment system formed a major part of the 1988 Education Act heralding a centralized curriculum and a massive increase in the construction and use of testing.

These efforts at large-scale achievement testing to measure the national performance of education are, of course, very expensive. Since the information they provide is of little or no diagnostic use it is difficult to see how the costs of national testing could be justified. National testing, however, is not about improving education. National testing is about controlling teachers and creating the raw data for judgments about efficiency and effectiveness of schools so they can be held accountable to market forces and consumer choice. It is a testament to our times that the most likely effect of performance data is to give more to those that already have most; the survival of the richest.

The most commonly used performance indicators for education are student test results of one kind or another; public examinations, national or local tests, school or classroom-based tests. At first acquaintance the logic of this position is impeccable; the essence of education is changing the individual so if we want to judge the performance of the system or any part of it we should measure changes in the learner and aggregate the results. If overall test results are stable or going up then things are good, if they are going down then things are bad.

In most education systems it is the teachers who are seen as responsible for changes in test results. Thus teacher effectiveness as well as the performance of the system is judged in terms of teacher impact on the performance of pupils on tests. Concern about the impact of public services is not unreasonable, however this focus is often 'accompanied by a restricted interest in understanding the contingencies on which impact depends' (Cook and Campbell, 1979, p. 64).

The inadequacies of tests data for evaluating the effectiveness of teachers or schools have been known for some time. As the measurement theorist Gene Glass (1974) has noted 'nothing short of random assignment of pupils to teachers as an ironclad administrative necessity would ensure that the teachers were in a fair race to produce pupil gains' (p. 12). If this improbable aim were ever to be realized there would still be the problem of the instability of teacher actions over time. Generalizations about teacher or school performance may be very short lived. Even if pupil test data provided an adequate description of learning outcomes at a particular point in time and from situation to situation it would not necessarily provide a reliable basis for the prediction of future performance.

A major assumption in the construction and use of performance indicators is that educational qualities can be readily defined and measured (Gamble, 1990, p. 20). Not all the qualities or outcomes of education are equally well suited to operational definition and measurement. To take an extreme example there may be little problem at all in weighing the evidence of an educational programme designed to combat obesity (Nunnally, 1983, p. 236); yet even here it is by no means straightforward given the unintended outcomes that might be associated with the programme — anorexia, for example. By comparison, when we think about measuring the effects of educational processes that aim to enhance confidence, autonomy or problem solving it is clear that the measurement problems involved are considerable if not presently insurmountable.

Some Methodological and Political Problems in the Construction and Use of Performance Indicators

The Problem of Data Overload and Cost

As the number of performance indicators increase and the contextual variables that have to be taken into account also multiply there is a consequent need on the part of policy makers for aggregation, simplification and cost reduction. Once committed to performance indicators politicians and administrators challenged by experts on the grounds of oversimplification of the problems tend, paradoxically, to move towards even greater simplification. It is probable that if and when the sophistication of measurement and analysis begins to approximate an adequate representation of performance in context, the results will have to be discounted in favour of summary judgments because they are too difficult or too ambiguous to interpret.

Problems in Measuring Change

A common research strategy for measuring change is a pretest–post-test design yielding gain scores that are supposed to represent the effects of inputs over time. Thus if we want to determine teacher effectiveness we first establish a learning baseline for each child using a pretest before teaching has occurred, and then measure the impact of teaching by using a post-test after the children have been taught. The logic of these research designs is simple and compelling: measure the state of the system before an input and the state of the system after an input and the difference between the two represents the amount of change caused by the input.

In practice there are many problems associated with pretest–post-test designs in education. Here are some of the more obvious: (i) in addition to teaching many other things can happen to children between the first and second measurement and it is not possible to control for all the other factors that might be related to student test performance; (ii) the fact of taking the first test may influence performance on the second test; (iii) the composition of the group who take the test may change between the first measurement and the second; (iv) the tests may or may not measure what they are supposed to measure and may do so for some children and not for others; (v) the reliability of measurement can be corrupted by deliberately depressing pretest scores; (vi) the interaction between measurement and seasonal trends may mask or heighten real effects. Perhaps the most consequential and serious problem is that the way the tests are constructed greatly affects the scores, favouring some groups rather than others or some teachers rather than others.

The Problem of Corruption

Performance indicators tend to influence the way any system operates. The more a performance indicator is used for decision-making, the more it will be subject to corruption and the more likely it will be to distort the social processes it is intended to monitor (Campbell, 1976). These pressures either affect the reliability or integrity of the measure or they distort organizational goals. A few examples will suffice to illustrate the point.

- When the ratio of public examination success to examination failure is used as an indicator of school effectiveness there could be a tendency for the authorities to restrict the number of children entered for public examinations.
- If change in the frequency of serious crime is seen as a indicator of police effectiveness then serious crime is likely to be downgraded and recorded as something else; thus creating the image of a decline in serious crime. Conversely if the level of serious crime is used as an indicator of the resources needed for policing, there is likely to be a steady increase in the amount of serious crime recorded.
- If the effects of a specific educational programme or of teaching are to be measured in terms of the difference between pre and post-test scores then gain scores can be greatly improved by administering the pre-test in a way designed to make the scores as low as possible.
- Where teacher performance is judged in terms of pupil performance on attainment tests teachers will tend to protect themselves against the consequences of low scores and teach to the test. As Smith (1991) concludes in her study of the effects of external testing in elementary schools: 'testing programs substantially reduce the time available for instruction, narrow curriculum offerings and modes of instruction, and potentially reduce the capacities of teachers to teach content and to use methods and materials that are incompatible with standardized testing formats.'

The Problem of Standards Fixing

As performance indicators are used to provide feedback on performance they also become the standards against which performance is judged. Every increase in performance provides the potential for setting a new standard. This has two likely consequences: first, it can lead to an intensification of work which may have unintended consequences like increased levels of sickness or absenteeism; second, it often leads to tacit agreements not to exceed certain levels of performance in order to control the working environment.

Problems of Validity and Reliability

The most fundamental methodological issues raised by the construction and use of performance indicators are ones of reliability and validity. Reliability usually refers to the stability of the measures over time and the consistency of measurement across raters and sites. Questions of validity refer to the warrant or reasons we have for making inferences on the basis of performance indicators. In this respect it is important to determine whether an indicator measures what it claims to measure and if it is in fact a measure of performance or a measure of something related to performance or neither of these things.

Because of the time series nature of performance indicators and their political sensitivity, questions of validity require a consideration not only of what indicator data actually means, but also consideration of the consequences of using the indicator on the system itself. As we have noted the use of indicators can so distort organizational goals or the provision of reliable information about performance that they alter performance in unintended and undesirable ways. An instrument that is primarily intended to improve the effectiveness or efficiency of the system can easily have exactly the opposite effect.

It is often argued that performance indicators based on routine record keeping provide the most cost effective information available on the performance of a system. However, the effort involved in establishing the reliability, integrity and construct validity of particular measures may well outweigh their apparent and immediate utility. For example, if student scores on tests are used to compare the performance of teachers or schools then among other things the validity of inferences from this indicator will depend on: (i) the actual degree of standardization both of the tests and their administration; (ii) the rules for inclusions and exclusion of students in the assessment; (iii) the sampling procedures used in each setting; (iv) the similarities and differences in the characteristics of students in the different settings; (v) the extent to which the test is a representative sample of content covered across the settings. Collecting information about all these things greatly increases the costs of ensuring that the performance indicator can be used to make valid judgments.

Performance indicators in education are meant to provide simple and unambiguous measures of quality. They do not and they cannot. Because the aims and purposes of education are many and its values various it is not susceptible to simple forms of measurement. Performance indicators are highly reductionist. They disregard the social fabric of schools or other service environments. In so doing they tend to under-represent the quality of education and misrepresent it as well. If a measure under-represents the values of a process it is simple enough to remedy by systematically adjusting the scores. However, when measures are known to misrepresent a process then they should be abandoned in favour of other forms of evaluation.

Concluding Remarks

There has been a sharp divergence between the development of evaluation theory and the practice of evaluation on the part of Government. At a time when evaluators have come to acknowledge the complex and contingent nature of public programmes, the Government has pressed for simple and generalized methods of evaluation. As the evaluation community has moved from exclusive reliance on quantitative measures of impact towards more holistic accounts of programmes and policies, the Government has become more dependent on econometrics and value for money audits to calculate the effects and effectiveness of social programmes. The appeal to economics and the taken for granted values of economy, efficiency and effectiveness serve to reduce the influence of service professionals and subsume professional authority under managerial authority (Henkel, 1991, p. 15).

The image of the citizen as consumer is deeply rooted in our industrial societies. When public services like education, health and welfare are seen only in terms of production and consumption they are more easily subject to managerialism and dominated by the logic of individual economic choice. Under these circumstances the values of both equality and community are undermined.

Notes

1 This is a revised version of a paper presented to a symposium on Judging Quality in Education, 17th annual meeting of the British Educational Research Association, Nottingham, 28–31 August 1991.
2 This economic calculus is well described by Levitt and Joyce (1987) in their specification for how to improve the efficiency of public spending. 'If efficiency is to be improved we need to: (a) define and, if possible, quantify the intended outputs and their associated costs; (b) assess and if possible quantify the impact on output of a change in inputs after allowing for factors beyond the control of the management concerned; (c) establish whether input minimization or output maximization is the objective in particular services; (d) assess and if possible quantify the scope for improving technical efficiency; given the existing mix and volume of inputs, can output be increased or alternatively can total resources be reduced given output?; (e) assess and if possible quantify the scope for improving allocative efficiency; given existing output, can inputs be substituted for one another so as to reduce total costs?; (f) assess and if possible quantify the extent to which efficiency can be improved by bringing the outlying worst performers near to the average or the best,' (pp. 95–6).

References

CALLAHAN, R. (1962) *Education and the Cult of Efficiency*, Chicago, IL, University of Chicago Press.

CAMPBELL, D.T. (1976) *Assessing the Impact of Planned Social Change*, Evaluation Centre Occasional Paper no 8, Kalamazoo, MI, College of Education, Western Michigan, University.

COOK, T.D. and CAMPBELL, D.T. (1979) *Quasi-experimentation: Design and Analysis Issues for Field Settings*, Boston, MA, Houghton Mifflin.

GAMBLE, R. (1990) 'Performance indicators' in FITZ-GIBBON, C.T. (Ed.) *Performance Indicators*, BERA Dialogues No 2, Clevedon, PA, Multilingual Matters, pp. 19–25.

GLASS, G. (1974) 'Teacher effectiveness' in WALBERG, H. (Ed.) *Evaluating Educational Performance*, Berkeley, CA, McCutchan, pp. 11–32.

HABER, S. (1964) *Efficiency and Uplift: Scientific Management in the Progressive Era, 1890–1920*, Chicago, IL, University of Chicago Press.

HENKEL, M. (1991) *Government, Evaluation and Change*, London, Jessica Kingsley.

HOPWOOD, A. (1984) 'Accounting and the pursuit of efficiency' in HOPWOOD, A. and TOMKINS, C. (Eds) *Issues in Public Sector Accounting*, Deddington, Philip Alan, pp. 167–87.

LAZARSFIELD, P. (1959) 'Sociological reflections on business: Consumers and managers' in DAHL, R., HAIRE, M. and LAZARSFIELD, P. (Eds) *Social Science Research on Business: Product and Potential*, New York, Columbia University Press.

LEVITT, M. and JOYCE, M. (1987) *The Growth and Efficiency of Public Spending*, National Institute of Economic and Social Research Occasional Papers XLI, Cambridge, Cambridge University Press.

METCALFE, L. and RICHARDS, S. (1984) 'Raynerism and efficiency in government;' in HOPWOOD, A. and TOMKINS, C. (Eds) *Issues in Public Sector Accounting*, Deddington, Philip Alan, pp. 188–211.

Norris, N. (1990) *Understanding Educational Evaluation*, London, Kogan Page.

Nunnally, J. (1983) 'The study of change in evaluation research: Principles concerning measurement, experimental design and analysis' in Struening, E. and Brewer, M. (Eds) *Handbook of Evaluation Research*, London, Sage, pp. 231–72.

Smith, M.L. (1991) 'Put to the test: The effects of external testing on teachers', *Educational Researcher*, 20, 5, pp. 8–11.

Urwick, L. and Brech, E. (1957a) *The Making of Scientific Management Volume 1 Thirteen Pioneers*, London, Pitman.

Urwick, L. and Brech, E. (1957b) *The Making of Scientific Management Volume 2 Management in British Industry*, London, Pitman.

Chapter 4

One in a Million? The Individual at the Centre of Quality Control*

Saville Kushner

Prologue

When British Leyland produced the 'millionth' mini off the production line they issued a car sticker which said 'One In A Million'. I recall first seeing it and feeling a spontaneous revulsion. Using the aphorism in this way they were playing with the dual meaning — the uniqueness of the individual who is unlike a million others against the mere counting of each individual as one-millionth of the herd — flattering to deceive. It was a clever slogan but, in the end, abusive of our efforts to stand apart, an ostentatious flaunting of the power of the business community to play with individuality — a cynical caprice. I have since wondered about the slogan appearing on the front cover of records of achievement, personal profiles, appraisal reports and lists of school performance criteria.

One of the artifices of evaluation is to portray individuals but to invest them (and their lives) with meanings derived from the projects in which we observe them — like clothing dolls. We tend to interpret actions and reasons of teachers, curriculum developers, administrators and pupils as responses to the institutions and events which are the real focus of our enquiries. The increasing predilection for incorporating biographical accounts in evaluation does not necessarily advance our understanding of how innovations, for example, are extensions of the values and experiences of people. Rather, they tend too often to show people as extensions of innovations. What I argue here is that we ought to invert the conventional relationship in our reports between people and projects. Instead of drawing a boundary around a project experience and reading individual lives within the context of the project, we need, just a little more often, to provide life experiences as contexts within which to understand educational projects.

What this allows, of course, is a perspective that rarely emerges in our reports — the occasional irrelevance of projects to people. The fundamental bias built into evaluation is that the very act of looking exclusively at a project affords that project with more significance than it may actually warrant. This may be no

* Paper presented at the 1991 annual meeting of the British Educational Research Association held at Nottingham Polytechnic at a symposium entitled 'Judging Quality in Education'.

accident — the less significant the project the less significant the evaluation. It is in our interests to assert the prominence of a project however marginal to the lives of its participants.

I have sometimes taken this to extremes — only within the cosy protection of a three-year evaluation, I should say. On the evaluation I am thinking of and which I shall extract from in a moment, there was a point at which I wanted to document the impact of an innovatory course in a music conservatoire on its students some time after they had left it. Given that the students I spoke to knew roughly what I was interested in (I virtually lived with them for three years) I decided not to ask them the question — i.e. what impact the course had had. Instead I just spoke to them about their studies, their clothes, their families, their futures. Occasionally a student would refer to the innovation and only sometimes it would be a significant reference. A singer who had played a prominent role in the early project experience couldn't remember what the project had been about eighteen months later — her current pursuit of a music career focussed her mind on wholly different (actually, more technical) concerns; a flautist remembered the innovation only too well since the course was bound up with personal issues to do with her and her music and which had endured. These discrepant accounts of the impact of the innovation were understandable only in the context of these two people's life experiences.

This was at the forefront of my mind towards the close of that evaluation as I, perforce, became preoccupied with how to summarize the achievements of this innovatory project. Thinking aloud, as it were, I wrote this following chapter (for my final report) which I reproduce in full. It is in retrospect — in fact, following the use of this piece in an MA seminar — that it gained significance in this discourse about quality indicators in education. I will draw the link between evaluation and quality control at the close of this chapter.

Data

(MPCS = Music Performance and Communication Skills, an innovatory course for music training developed at the Guildhall School of Music and Drama and which has since achieved some prominence.)

> Peter Renshaw (Director of MPCS) received a letter from a prominent arts administrator responding to a proposal for a seminar which was to look at accountability in the arts. The letter ended, 'we consider that the seminar should be concerned, not only with "providing a starting point for deriving guiding principles etc." but should also seek to determine the units in which the benefits of art to education and indeed to the wider community can be expressed'.
>
> Susie and Caroline were sitting in a restaurant reflecting on their experience of working in the hospice. For Caroline, there were issues that were springing to mind all the time. It had changed her, somehow. Susie says that she probably wouldn't think about it were she not being asked. 'It wasn't something that you did on your own, so it's not something you can think about on your own', she says. But she had, at the time, been deeply disturbed by the experience. Susie had sat in a rehearsal of their

quartet, recalled Caroline, crying and unable to play. So was it worth doing? Was it a 'good' experience? 'How can you say it was a success or a failure', protests Caroline, 'when that sort of thing took place?'. She raises her hands from the table in a gesture of insistence. 'She couldn't play!'

There are criteria against which to measure the performance and impact of MPCS — and, certainly, MPCS can offer a guide to more general practice in the arts. Perhaps the crudest and most direct are simple statistical calculations. For example, the total cost of MPCS (excluding hidden institutional subsidies) was £80,587 and the course reached approximately 120 students (forty each year). That is roughly £650 per student, (all of whom had already paid their college fees). Formal contact time was one morning per week with an additional half-day, say, for site visits. There were, generally, at least two tutors with the course at any one time.

By such indicators, and measuring MPCS simply as an optional course in the college, the level of resourcing was lavish and set high standards for judging outcomes. What sort of outcomes? A rough estimate would show approximately one-third of all MPCS students as using some approaches learned on the course in their jobs and careers — Claire creating a music therapy career for herself; Sara, still teaching at Wormwood Scrubs after two years, still inspired by MPCS; the Jagdish Mistry Quartet resident at the University of York doing MPCS-style workshops with students; Barbara, returning to Frankfurt and introducing MPCS-type workshops to the Junge Deutsche Philharmonie; various students on the ILEA music teacher 'panel' and teaching through workshops as well as through conventional approaches; Hilary, playing with a London-based orchestra and finding herself being asked to run children's workshops at the community centre where they rehearse; and Fiona, teaching for the Pre-School Music Association greatly relieved to have MPCS experience to draw from. There are more ex-students of the course who say that their musical lives continue to bear the imprint of MPCS through a continuing allegiance to its philosophy and principles.

But outcomes spread more broadly than this. MPCS represents a body of experience at innovation that is now available for other institutions to learn from — perhaps, but not necessarily, to try their own version. This is already being done at the Welsh College of Music and Drama (see the case study attached to this report) and at the University of Toronto. Within the Guildhall, that body of experience has been drawn from to make changes to the general musicianship programme and to develop a unique (fifteen student) postgraduate course. Elsewhere, Peter Renshaw has disseminated his philosophy and some of the more successful aspects of MPCS such that there is a wide constituency in education and the performing arts who admit to some influence from MPCS-type approaches.

But from here on, there are no objective guides. The reader has to make his and her own judgments about whether or not these outcomes justify the resourcing. There will be varying opinions — some may be coloured by a general political principle such as, for example, that MPCS stands as a worthy example of a free-standing entrepreneurial arts programme in an enterprise economy. Alternatively, opinions may be coloured by a feeling that MPCS is a good example of the tenet, 'to those that have, more shall be given' — that a private, elite institution does not merit such large investments of social funding. Those whose experience of conservatoire training was painful may tend to approve of such efforts being made to improve it; those who are loyal to conventional practices may see MPCS as an expensive 'gloss'. (Leaving aside external visits, the Jazz option at the Guildhall School achieves performance and improvisation training with no special funds.) The cost-benefit approach, ultimately, rests upon private judgments.

Another route in search of criteria by which to judge the performance and impact of MPCS might be to look at the Aims and Objectives of the innovation as they were originally laid down and to assess how far it met or meandered from its stated intentions. This is, indeed, a popular and conventional approach to take in evaluating projects of this kind. But there are problems here too.

The Second Interim Evaluation Report of MPCS took a detailed look at the periodic restatements of aims and objectives by Peter Renshaw. The occasions for rewriting intentions were applications for additional funds, but each time offered an opportunity for Peter to make a fresh assessment of what was reasonable to hold as an ambition. 'In the end', wrote one well-known curriculum developer, (Shipman, 1974) 'it was what worked that survived'. It would, for example, be foolish, in the face of an opportunity to reshape and redirect, to doggedly stick to an objective that has proved by experience to be either unrealistic, expensive, controversial or, as it turns out, undesirable. Equally, for course, there is an element of gamesmanship involved — impression management — where Peter would couch project intentions with emphases designed to appeal to particular sponsors. 'One's using different strategies all the time', he explained.

We could look at one example of such a change. In the original project proposal, Objective (d) was written as:

To demonstrate the therapeutic value of music.

This was taken out in the first redraft some six months later. The reason was two-fold. Firstly, Peter had recognized that though MPCS might have a therapeutic value (for clients, but also for musicians) it was important to focus on the fact that the innovation was primarily concerned with artistic and educational principles. It was proving too easy to limit MPCS as music therapy (the Guildhall School already had a postgraduate course in MT). Secondly, there had, in the opening months of the project, been a near territorial clash with a professional association of music therapists, and it was felt to be fair and judicious to maintain the boundary.

There were other, significant changes made in succeeding redrafts as MPCS developed a more experience-based view of what it might and could do. There was an emerging educational theory of using a combination of action and reflection to encourage students to examine themselves and, by doing so, to discover and develop their creative repertoire. There were even moments when Peter thrust the project into the heart of the political milieu by redrafting project objectives. The following objective was published during the time when the Department of Education and Science was thought to be toying with the notion of cutting back conservatoire funding to create 'centres of excellence'.

Within the context of an institution which sets out to foster excellence in its performing musicians, actors and composers, to provide a wide range of experiences which facilitate a responsiveness to changing artistic, educational and social needs within the community.

Such redefinitions represent a process within which can be charted the changing relationships of MPCS with its educational and political contexts. Each change embodies some aspect of learning that has taken place — either out of interactions with students which reveal weaknesses or new ideas; or out of Peter's developing skills in exploiting the political opportunities he constantly faces in his extensive travels around the arts communities.

But more problematic, if we are looking to aims and objectives as sources for making judgments about this project, is the fact that successive redrafts become more descriptions of what the project does, than expressions of hope or intent. Nor is this evidence of a project that vacillates or fudges on its opportunities (there is plenty of evidence to show that MPCS sought rather than shrank from adventures). Rather, it is evidence of a project that is responsive to its environs and realistic about its potential — cautious, perhaps, in focussing on 'what worked'. But whatever the case, it is clear that aims and objectives are unstable criteria — albeit useful in revealing a project's adaptability.

There are other sources for judgments we might make of the worth or the success of MPCS. We could look at client responses — and such there are. Headteachers, prisoners, pupils, mentally handicapped adults, hospice residents and staff, youth club leaders, professional musicians, other Guildhall tutors — all these, and others, have commented on MPCS. For the most part institutional responses were congratulatory — often with suggested adjustments to programmes and to ways of working. But these responses often are unreliable indicators. MPCS comes with no charge to institutions increasingly starved of luxuries for care and containment.

Individual responses within these institutions were more complex. Young girls in a school who took part in a performance of Roald Dahl's *The Enormous Crocodile* for MPCS but who were accustomed to drama sessions which took their everyday lives as material — drug abuse, domestic conflict — were happy to go along with the exercise though aware that they felt 'childish'. The band at the City Literary Institute made up of adults with learning difficulties who expressed in a song their frustration at the inability of MPCS students to properly meet them:

Where I live   There are many ways people think
is a very long way   there are many ways people talk
from where you live   some say this
and I don't suppose you   some say that
ever come my way . . .   and there are gaps between.

In the hospice, where we have already seen the project evoke controversy, responses from residents were mixed. The two women who wrote the poems that were put to music were clearly grateful for the experience. But other responses were more complex as confusions in the minds of residents spilled over into interactions. One man, in a state of anxiety, said that he found the performance of improvised music unsettling and 'cacophonous'.

At the Lewisham Academy, some of the youth MPCS worked with were pleased with their exposure to more disciplined musicians and there were moments when techniques were swapped between a conservatoire cellist and a jazz-rock bass player, for example. Some black youth at the Academy were encouraged to see that there were black students at the Guildhall. But, again, responses were uneven.

There was scepticism (shared by MPCS students) at the quality of musical interactions and at the often anodyne treatment of social issues in the performances MPCS generated.

But the file of client responses that Peter Renshaw has is largely one of positive and encouraging responses, asking for more frequent visits and for more of the same. It is clear that positive responses indicate a real contribution, but such are, once more, not reliable critical indicators.

There is adequate evidence among researchers that, in spite of the confidence of the Assessment of Performance Unit tests for artistic development are unsophisticated and limited in what they can apprehend (see, for example, Braskamp and Brown, 1975).

So where are we? We have looked at different kinds of data which we might use to judge the worth of MPCS and we have seen flaws in all of them. Indicators do not just jump out. There are other data sources which have not been included — perhaps the most obvious being students assessments. Grade the students and judge the value of the course in terms of measured increments to student learnings. But here, too, similar problems occur. Peter Renshaw has, in fact, been asked to grade students, and encounters no difficulty in doing so — As here, Cs there. But this has been controversial among students who see the whole thrust of MPCS as confounding rather than confirming differences between them. And Peter readily admits that whatever grades satisfy examiners bear little relation to the educational process on the course.

Of course, problems can be ironed out — the data can be 'laundered' by focussing on positive aspects. When Peter Renshaw was asked, by one of his sponsors, whether MPCS had encountered any failures, he redefined the word 'failure' into 'challenge', a less incriminating word in a world which is increasingly intolerant of dissent or failure. What makes judging the worth of this innovatory project difficult is that it has encountered failures in a number of ways — but that, by virtue of being a project that is reflective, these failures have often generated the most productive learnings. The search for 'units in which benefits of art to education' might be expressed does not have to be fruitless, but it will always have to stand the test of validity that Caroline posed at the opening of this section.

This is not a 'fudged' position. In the end we have always to return to the student data. What that says is that MPCS was, above all, an educational project. The best that can be hoped for in an educational project is good educational interactions, and the very difficulties we encounter in measuring the impact of the project are suggestive that there are at least good educational opportunities there. And there is ample evidence in the hesitations and the contradiction in which students talk of their capitalising on those opportunities.

Let us take a final look at this issue — what follows is an extract from a conversation with a student who was trying to express precisely how MPCS had an impact on him on his violin playing.

> Charles is quiet, intense, and intense in his love for music and in his ambitions to play professionally. He plays in the Jagdish Mistry String Quartet. On school visits on MPCS he felt a little uncomfortable — 'there was a big contradiction between what was in my mind as to what I should be doing in terms of a musical career'. Which is to say that he felt he ought to be 'at home practising my Paganini'.

Were the two activities (school workshops and Paganini) separate — or did one feed the other?

'Oh, yeah, sure they did. I mean, I think more Peter's course fed the other — I'm not sure practising the violin fed what we were doing there.'

How?

'Oh — well — it freed me up a lot — my playing. Less hyper-critical, perhaps. I was able to accept just to play something which doesn't have to be absolutely note-perfect — although that is an aim as well . . .'

So did MPCS make a difference?

'I think so. I mean, it's not absolutely dramatic, outstanding, amazing, you know. But it's the changing — it's probably something that's still changing in me as well. I mean, freeing up. I'm not a very free person in myself — I do get very self-conscious.'

He can't think of any part of the course that wreaked spontaneous change in him — just the principle which he saw at the heart of the course that music was a medium for relating to people (as opposed to performing 'at' them).

'It was always that that idea was in the air — and it's something which sort of sinks in and becomes part of you.'

Now we see the problem in its full force. The 'unit of benefit' — the basic unit of measurement of success and impact — is the individual. This innovation, by virtue of making such intimate and desirable promises to individuals like Charles, and by coopting them as the 'innovation principals', becomes internalized by them. Here, again, is a transfer of stake-holding and of meaning in the project which takes it from the realm of sponsors and administrators and which lifts it out of the language and discourse of aims and objectives and relocates it in the real experience of individuals. 'It becomes part of you', says Charles. The measurement of impact becomes the measurement of personal growth (which is why personal biography plays such a prominent role in this evaluation) — but against what standard? And what difference does it make to the measurement when Charles goes on to say that these changes in him were part of a normal process of maturation, that they would probably have happened anyway — but that they were precipitated by MPCS?

There is, fortunately, a solution to this dilemma — that the reader has to arrive at their own judgment. When the evaluation first emerged on the conservatoire scene, a common question raised was, 'how can anyone evaluate an artistic experience?' The response was that, it principle at least, this was simple. The fact is that everyone makes their own private evaluations of artistic (and educational) experiences — even as crudely as 'I didn't like that'. The task of an evaluation is to help articulate those private evaluations and then to make them public in such a way as to allow people 'beyond the frame', as it were, to make their own judgments. The data in this report is the raw material of judgments any reader might make.

This does not, of course, avoid the problem implicit in the plea of the arts administrator which opened this section. He lives in a political world — as do performing arts groups — and in that political world artists are currently being asked to defend their activities in the engineering language of 'units of benefit', 'aims and objectives', 'skills development', and other categories which speak more of industrial and managerial aspirations than of artistic enterprise. The challenge represented by MPCS is to somehow find a match between the need to hold such innovations to public account, but to do so in such a way as to avoid doing violence to the richness of the experience.

Conjecture

There, then, was my dilemma and it was neatly sidestepped at the end. In truth I had no easy answer for the arts administrator — in fact, I would probably have argued that leaving him with the problem and no solution was educational and the best — the only — service I could offer him. I was reluctant to have transferred to me the intractability of his problem in discovering measures of 'benefit' — reluctant, that is, to have the evaluation contaminated by the crudities of simplistic quality control aims. I am one of those who feel (strongly) that the educational research community should be far more reflective about promising tractability in respect of assessment and appraisal than we currently are. We ought, for example, to be as critical in our reflections on quality control as we are in our reflections on evaluation practice — quality control is merely a form of in-house evaluation and should be played by the same rules. In fact, a large body of evaluation theory would argue that there is a tension between *quality* and *control*. Quality, you might argue, is a feature of professional practice that is nurtured by freedom and discretion but compromised by restraint and standardization.

Let me close by saying why I believe this to be so. It has something to do with competing logics of performance assessment and personal portrayal in educational research.

I have heard a number of times people saying that one of the interesting things about naturalistic evaluation of appraisal or student profiling or some forms of quality control is the parallel between the process of observation and the substantive act being observed. When we, as evaluators, interview a teacher about appraisal of her performance that teacher is undergoing a similar experience to her appraisal interview, and this raises special issues to do with replication, saturation and ethics. I am one of the people who has voiced that viewpoint but I now believe it to be wrong. I do think both (appraisal for quality control and evaluation of it, for example) are interpretive acts, but that the logic of interpretation differ for each.

For quality control purposes as commonly experienced (most immediately through appraisal and, for us researchers, such events as 'research selectivity exercises') performance appraisal is an attempt to interpret the effectiveness of system performance. There is an assumed link between the performance of individuals and that of the system and that the way to measure the latter is by measuring the former. This is reductionist and, for good measure, functionalist. As evaluators we, too, are concerned to interpret innovatory systems by theorizing about and interpreting individual experience, but our assumptions are — well, I would like them to be — different. For us, individual professionals and the organizations they work in are essentially in tension. Individual aspirations (as professionals we all know this) are generally vitiated by institutional and political contexts; institutional processes — particularly innovations — are subject to reinterpretation and distortion by those responsible for discharging them. Granted, both the performance appraiser and the evaluator are concerned with improving the delivery of professional services, but the reasons they have for conducting interviews, for example, and the use they make of the data may well be at odds. The former tend to be concerned with control and predictability; evaluators with speculation and understanding. Quality control too easily looks to the individual as the source of organizational failures; evaluation looks to organization as the source for individual failures. These are, by now, well rehearsed arguments in the discourse about performance indicators.

This is an argument about the empirical experience of quality control. It is not inevitable — only highly likely — that quality control in education will end up turning teachers and administrators into artificers (with the complicity of the educational research community). The probability is increased where reliance is placed on performance indicators which represent the apotheosis of functionalism and the nadir of evaluation. The alternative approach to quality control is one which focusses on the individual and requires system managers to become more concerned with speculation than control — more concerned to analyze and understand the organization than to engineer it. It is one which asks that arts administrator to pause for a while to reflect on why Caroline couldn't play her music. In that case the distance between quality control and evaluation does, indeed, fade away (though there remain important questions about independence and political relations to do with in-house evaluation). The search, then, is for quality as an alternative to control.

Even so, even where, for example, performance indicators are substituted by qualitative measures — perhaps even centred on individual experience — issues will collapse down to role and political relationships. Indicators of whatever kind are instruments for generating data and they work on behalf of managers who have lost (or never had) contact with the programmes they manage. This is how quality control functions as in-house evaluation. The important questions are about what use is made of data — how data is interpreted by those managers — what political relationship between manager and professional is implied by the generation and use of data. Think of the situation we live in as educational researchers. The assumption that you can gauge the quality of my research centre by measuring my publications output would be laughable were it not so catastrophic in its impact. Like many other researchers I am dismayed at my lack of control over the quality control/evaluation criteria; suspicious and uncomprehending about its use; angry at the absence of feedback, negotiation or dialogue.

As a research community we help to establish the conditions under which individuals can account for themselves and their work in much the same way as those people of limited imagination dreamt up research selectivity exercises. We legitimize and test out mechanisms designed for the job. By doing so we give currency to policies which are, in educational terms, sensible or silly. In this particular area of educational enquiry I do not regard our community as marginal or lacking in impact as is frequently alleged. Whether current developments in schooling — National Curriculum, school improvement measures, appraisal of teachers and pupils — help or hinder the struggle for individuality and autonomy has at least something to do with what educational researchers are prepared to go along with. We are increasingly defined by a service economy. Sustaining the insupportable fiction that there are such things as an *exemplary practice* or an *effective school* or an *attainment target* that means the same thing to different pupils in different places may be good and useful 'service' but it has at least questionable educational validity. They satisfy the simplicity criterion for indicators but not the complexity criterion for representing individual experience.

Refutation

Thus far I have argued that the ethical necessity of putting individuals at the centre of evaluative enquiry should transfer across the case of institutional and professional quality control — that quality control is a form of in-house evaluation and should be played by the same rules, as I put it. Performance indicators as an increasingly popular form of quality control militate directly against the interests of individuals in that their logical provenance is in holding people to account for the failure of programmes, whereas the proper (ethical) concern of evaluation should be to hold institutional arrangements to account for their failure to support individual professionals. The thrust of the argument supports the notion of some approach to quality indicators as an alternative and that these should feature individuals — their needs and experience — as a central evaluative device.

There is a good argument for refuting that, and it needs to be made here.

In my estimation it is unlikely that we will live to see — in the education system — a quality control process that both documents and is sensitive to the needs and experience of its individual actors. There are too many implications for power and control associated with that — too many risks for institutional managers and politicians. One clear example is the case of staff appraisal. As an instrument for quality control it can serve both of those competing logics — blaming the individual and allowing the individual to express their needs.

The educational/liberal interpretation of staff appraisal is that it is — its pedigree in radical right attacks on the educational professions notwithstanding — an essential element in the development of both the professional and the profession. In reality, it is hard to imagine institutions (now I am thinking of my own siege-ridden university) responding to the predictable welter of demands for training, retraining, resources and policy changes that are forthcoming from appraisal interviews. Staff appraisal (goes the cynical argument) was always an artifice for distracting demands for more resources, and though its operation might well backfire and serve to give greater voice to those demands, there is no reason to think that the institutional/political response will be sympathetic. It would be more realistic to think of the process being redefined or tightened up or, simply, marginalized into a bureaucratic ritual. In respect of research selectivity exercises we are virtually there — all of us desperately elbowing our way up the queue for resources and shuffling down the queue for punishment.

Even so, staff appraisal and similar instruments in the struggle to reform our professions — as with proposed quality indicators — do and will generate data on individuals. The more 'qualitative', as it were, the instrument, the more personalized the data. Where there are only restricted opportunities to negotiate the brief and the criteria for generating this personal data, in evaluation terms the process is unethical. This is before we begin to think about what controls exist regarding the use and potential misuse of personal data — and some might think that it is just as well not to think of that.

By contrast (goes this refuting argument) performance indicators focus not on the individual so much as what that individual is *perceived* to be doing — i.e. they focus on aspects of performance. The already emerging folklore about performance indicators — highlighted by Norris in this collection of papers as one of their fundamental weaknesses — is the degree to which they can be suborned and subverted by those under scrutiny. Professionals and professions can, and regularly do, hide behind performance indicators by altering those perceptions. In some sense, the more familiar we are with them the more competent we become at manipulating them. A (less than ideal) instrument, you might think, for self-protection. And why not. The scenario, then, is one of professionals as groups of outlaws protesting that they are 'goin' straight guv' while actively being recidivists in their increasingly clandestine practices.

This, indeed, is virtually status quo. One (just one) of the reasons, for example, that the police service senior ranks went along with an otherwise intrusive and threatening review of probationer training (MacDonald *et al.*, 1987) was that Chief Officers had only limited access to what their constables were doing down on the beat. They received regular, too often deceptive, self-reports but no comprehensive data and they suffered considerable erosion of control as a result (cf. repeated failures to 'root out corruption' in the Metropolitan force). The review proposed by CARE promised — in respect of training — direct access and a quality control system for sustaining that access. We were only partially successful in introducing it. Performance indicators (currently virtually paralysing aspects of police operations) are more elaborate concoctions of the organizational poison they were originally suffering from.

Nonetheless, given changing contexts of accountability and political economy many professionals may feel more comfortable with the sandbagging option promised by performance indicators and too threatened by the uncertainty of personalized quality indicators to take them seriously. It may be that our role as a research and evaluation community (I include, here, those researchers who are implicated in the design and implementation of quality control measures) is to encourage and support institutional resistance to unethical evaluation practices flying under the flag of quality control. That is not an attractive message to all — few, indeed, would be in a position to act upon it. Offering services to teachers and parent groups, for example, to engage in more democratic forms of reflection on educational processes while perfunctorily ticking boxes to keep administrators and politicians happily ignorant is expensive in terms of resources and may even be a dangerous political game to be involved in.

The alternative, as we have seen over the past ten or fifteen years is an aggravation of an enduring truth about research and evaluation that its professional services are available to the highest bidder and that those who can afford them tend to be the over-enfranchised. Everyone is accountable these days all the way up to No. 10, as they say. We are all roughly equal in our need of evaluation services — but some are more equal than others in their capacity to call on it and pay for it. We generally have to oblige, so that as a community (I have used that term more often than my discomfort with it should allow) we are all complicit.

I have no idea what the resolution of this situation will be — other than the certain knowledge that it will be highly varied. I would dearly like to think that at long last a culture of resistance might emerge — perhaps sheltered by performance indicators and school effectiveness measures and the like. It will not be coordinated — it could not be — so that it might well find LMS and the demise of LEA control conducive. What is almost a certainty is that the combination of LMS/GMS, the demise of independent evaluation from the research community and the imposition of meaningless measures like pupil testing and school effectiveness indicators will divorce the culture of educational practice from the culture of educational politics. That may, of course, bring schools closer to parents and communities . . . but that may be part of the master-plan, too — to abandon those schools which no longer feature in the fantasies of the rich and powerful and which have been squeezed dry of their resources. But whatever the case, whichever of these two analyses suits you — the argument about the individual at the centre of quality control or its refutation — we need to be able to make a decision and defend it. On balance I appear to have persuaded myself of the refutation.

References

BRASKAMP, L. and BROWN, R. (1975) 'Accountability for the arts' in STAKE, R.E. (Ed.) *Evaluating the Arts in Education: A Responsive Approach*, Ohio, Charles Merrill Pubs.

MACDONALD, B., ARGENT, J. and ELLIOTT, J. (1987) *Police Probationer Training: The Final Report of the Stage II Review*, London. HMSO.

SHIPMAN, M. (1974) *Inside a Curriculum Project*, London, Methuen.

Chapter 5

Are Performance Indicators Educational Quality Indicators?

John Elliott

Introduction

The idea of 'performance indicators' did not emerge from within the professional culture of teachers. It is essentially a construction of 'outsiders' rather than of 'insiders': a device for establishing a technology of surveillance and control over the performance of schools and the teachers who work in them. The justification for the quest to identify 'performance indicators' is that they provide valid and reliable data on which to base judgments about the educational quality of school and teacher performance. If this is so, then why did not the teaching profession think of the idea long ago? Surely, it cannot simply be because teachers have shown a blatant disregard for considerations of quality. The fact that they have in the past adopted an 'autonomous expert' view of their professionalism which does not require them to open their practices to public questioning and scrutiny does not warrant the conclusion that they lack any concern for improving the quality of their work.

Indeed, the largely teacher-initiated curriculum reform movement of the 60s and early 70s was motivated by a desire amongst many teachers to improve the quality of curriculum provision for the vast majority of the nations children. I have argued elsewhere that it was from this movement that 'action-research' and 'self-evaluation' emerged as forms of reflective practice within the teaching profession (see Elliott, 1991, chapter 1) with the intention of improving the quality of teaching in schools. Over twenty years ago many teachers embarked on the project of trans-forming their professional culture from an unreflective 'craft culture' into one which emphasized reflective judgments as a basis for improving the quality of teaching and learning. They even began to provide 'outsiders', such as pupils, parents, governors and employers, with evidence about their practice and engage them in a dialogue about its quality (see Elliott *et al.*, 1982). Such dialogue was increasingly viewed as a significant aspect of internal self-monitoring: an important contribution to improving the quality of professional judgments and decisions.

The self-development of a reflective professional culture within the teaching profession was further evidenced throughout the late 70s and 80s by the consid-erable amount of school-based curriculum development and evaluation which took place coordinated and supported by LEAs and influenced by the curriculum framework generated by HMI in *A View of the Curriculum* (1980). This activity had virtually established something like a National Curriculum in schools. Moreover, more and more schools had begun to involve parents and employers in active dialogue about the shape and form of curriculum provision.

Yet all these developments appear to have been ignored by the Government in formulating and implementing the Educational Reform Act. Indeed at the political level there has been strong pressure on Secretaries of State for Education and Science to avoid showing any signs of widespread consultation with the teaching profession, in case they became contaminated with the educational values and theories teachers were believed to endorse, and which were perceived to underpin such self-initiated activities as school-based curriculum development, self-evaluation and action-research. Such activities, and the values and theories which informed them, were politically perceived, with some perceptiveness, as '60s talk' and in danger of ideologically contaminating the reforms of the late 80s and early 90s.

Of course, now that the ERA is in something like a mess at the implementation phase this 'contamination' fear is expressing itself in a different form. The right wing of the Conservative Party is explaining 'the mess' in terms of contaminating effects introduced by the academic educationalists on the National Curriculum working parties. After all as the educators of teachers they are the people responsible for introducing the contaminating ideas to the profession, and therefore must take the blame: thereby removing it from the Government and the ideology they have employed to shape educational policy through the ERA.

The Right Wing's explanation for our National Curriculum 'mess' contains a tacit denigration of the teaching profession. I have argued that the emergence of a reflective professional culture in schools was an aspect of teachers' initiated curriculum change. The values and ideas which underpin such changes were not simply foisted on the profession by academic teacher educators. They were embedded in the innovatory educational practices of teachers. What the teacher educators did was to articulate the internal logic of those practices, by explicating the values and beliefs embedded in them. Of course, many were able to do this because of their previous experience as teachers participating in school-based innovations.

In the rest of this chapter I shall argue that the current debate about performance indicators is not simply a technical one. Underlying the technical debate is an issue about how *educational quality* is to be understood. The concern to improve the quality of educational action which underpins the teachers' initiated development of a reflective professional culture rests on a radically different conception of educational quality to the one which underpins the Government-initiated reforms. I shall argue that this conception, and the idea of performance indicators as measures of quality, are embedded in the particular political ideology which has driven these reforms. It is not that teachers were tacitly using the idea as a basis for developing their reflective practices in schools, but using a different terminology. Nor, I believe, will the development of a sophisticated technology for 'measuring quality' persuade teachers to integrate the idea of performance indicators into their reflective professional culture. I will argue that the idea of 'performance indicators' constitutes a threat to such a culture. But it also constitutes a challenge to stimulate its development and growth. I will provide an example of one creative response to this challenge by a group of Italian teachers. They have identified what they call *quality indicators* as a basis for developing a curriculum for environmental education and as an alternative to the idea of performance indicators.

Performance Indicators and the Ideology of the Social Market

Norris (1991) provides us with a comprehensive account of the technical issues involved in identifying valid and reliable performance indicators which he defines as:

> time series data that reflect and record change across a number of signifi-
> cant dimensions relevant for judging the effectiveness and efficiency of a
> system in achieving its goals

He cites Gamble (1990) in pointing out 'that a major assumption in the construction and use of performance indicators is that educational qualities can be readily
defined and measured'. In other words performance indicators are sets of data
which can be numerically represented and the numbers statistically aggregated.
Such measures of quality can be either direct or indirect. A direct measure will
measure the central effects or outcomes of performance, but as Norris claims many
'educational performance indicators' are indirect measures: surrogates for effects
which are not susceptible to quantification in themselves. Indirect measures are
'indices of things which themselves are too difficult to measure'. He cites as an
example the view that 'pupil satisfaction with a school might be judged by looking
at truancy rates'.

I am not going to rehearse Norris' account of the technical issues surrounding
the identification and use of performance indicators as a basis for judging quality
in education. I would, however, point out a discrepancy between Norris' broad
conclusion that the technical research literature renders the quest for valid and
reliable indicators an extremely problematic one and Jack Straw's claim in the
Labour Party Policy document *Raising the Standard: Labour's Plans for an Education Standards Commission* (1991) that there is 'reasonable agreement among
educational researchers about the most appropriate measures of the relative performance of schools'. He argues that the 'technology is now available for the
development of valid measures of educational progress which take account of
social class, previous attainment, family and ethnic background'. Contrast this with
Norris's conclusion that 'when measures are known to misrepresent a process then
they should be abandoned in favour of other forms of evaluation'.

If Norris is right then the ex-Shadow Minister of State has been misinformed
about the current state of the art in educational research circles. But such misinformation may be politically expedient for reasons I shall now explain. The quest
for performance indicators as Norris points out, can be unambiguously located in
the political ideology of 'the social market': the view that public services like
education are essentially systems of production and consumption. This 'social
market' ideology is framed by certain basic assumptions which have been transferred from the economic to the social/cultural sphere of human activity. In the
context of education these assumptions imply:

(i) that educational goals should be treated as 'product-specifications' or
     'production-targets';
(ii) that 'production targets' in education should refer to learning outcomes,
     which must therefore be specified and standardized in advance of the
     educational process;

(iii)   that educational processes should be viewed as 'production techno-
        logies' for bringing about certain end-states in pupils. The relationship
        between processes and outcomes is conceived as a causal one, in which
        pupils are relatively passive recipients of 'treatments' designed to pro-
        duce certain effects on them;

(iv)   that the quality of an educational process lies in its instrumental value
        as a production function. The key values for judging the quality of a
        process are 'effectiveness' and 'efficiency';

(v)   that evidence of the quality of an educational process should consist of
        data which is relevant to judging its 'effectiveness' and 'efficiency'. Such
        data constitute 'performance indicators';

(vi)   that the rights and responsibilities of parents, employers, and other social
        groups with an interest in education should be defined as those of
        consumers of the products of education rather than as those of active
        participants in education;

(vii)   that schools should be viewed as units of production whose perform-
        ance is regulated by the mechanism of consumer choice based on infor-
        mation about their relative 'effectiveness' and 'efficiency'.

The 'social market' perspective generates a whole new language for talking about
education: 'targets' rather than 'aims and goals'; 'programmes' and 'delivery systems' rather than 'the curriculum'; 'functions' rather than 'roles and responsibilities'; 'efficiency' and 'effectiveness' rather than 'educational values'; 'performance
indicators' rather than 'evidence'; 'quality control' rather than 'evaluation'; and
'consumer choice' rather than 'parents as partners'. What should be clear is that the
idea of performance indicators has its meaning and significance only in the terms
of this 'social market' discourse and the assumptions which frame it. This implies
that the idea of performance indicators presupposes a particular conception of
'quality' in a school's performance; namely, the latter's instrumentality as an efficient and effective production unit. On this view quality has little to do with values
as ends of education. Considerations of educational values are ideologically screened
out from the realm of ends, which are redefined as products, and value-questions
in education are reduced to questions about the instrumental effectiveness and
efficiency of means conceived as production processes. In order to do this the
ideology has to separate means from ends. From its perspective considerations of
the quality of the performance in educational systems are framed by purely instrumental values. There is little room in the 'social market' ideology for educational
theorizing.

    As Norris suggests there is considerable symbolic significance in a 'social
market' view of education for politicians in Western democracies concerned about
'the economic costs and benefits of public services in general'. The 'social market'
ideology provides the basis for an economic calculus which will meet the political
imperative for efficiency in the used and distribution of public resources. Norris
claims that a concern for efficiency 'usually reflects an interest in minimizing inputs
to achieve the same level of output, or maximizing outputs with the same level of
input'. In fact one might conclude that 'cutting costs' rather than 'concern for
quality is the primary value underpinning the political imperative'.

    The Labour Party knew that it was vulnerable in the lead-up to the General
Election of 1992 to the Government's claim that it would increase public spending

on education. It had to demonstrate a commitment to efficiency to stand a chance of becoming the next Government. Hence, the 'social market' ideology prompted by the Conservative Government was perceived as something which had to be politically accommodated in the opposition's educational policies.

The idea of performance indicators had not an unproblematic accommodation for Jack Straw, although he defined the problem as one of degree of technical sophistication. He attacked the Right Wing of the Conservative Party for its unsophisticated reliance on crude measures of exam results as performance indicators and argued that valid measures of educational progress need to take account of the effects of school policies and processes in the context of differences in 'social class, previous attainment, family and ethnic background'. Although Straw apparently believed that a sophisticated technology for validly measuring the quality of school performance actually existed, he did acknowledge that there was a problem about 'using this technology to present this information in a useful form'. This problem was construed as a technical matter and not one of the technology encountering the limits of its ideological utility at the political level. Norris argues that 'paradoxically when the sophistication of measurement and analysis begins to approximate to an adequate representation of performance in context, the results have to be discounted in favour of summary judgments because they are too difficult or too ambiguous to interpret'.

There is an inevitable conflict, I would claim, between increasing sophistication in the measurement of performance and a political ideology which can only use simplified and decontextualized data about performance if it is to provide a basis for 'consumer choice'. No consumer is going to be grateful for being given lots of sophisticated information which is high in ambiguity and difficult to interpret. Consumers have a right to information which will tell them what 'the best buy' is in fairly unambiguous terms. If data about educational quality cannot yield such information then perhaps there is a problem about casting parents and other sectors of the public in the role of consumers, and indeed about the whole enterprise of construing education as a production system.

The problem the Labour Party faced in accommodating the 'production-consumption' view of education as a public service is how to square it with its traditional social values of 'equality' and 'justice'. This problem made it rather more receptive than the Government to the technical discussion surrounding the quest for a sophisticated set of performance indicators. But will this receptivity have its limits? The cynical reply is that the political imperative to demonstrate a concern for 'efficiency' will in the final analysis override a concern for valid representation. The likely casualities will be the traditional socialist values. However, there is just a chance, that given certain conditions, the Labour Party will realize that 'the social market' view of education fundamentally contradicts its traditional social values. If this happens then the alternative idea of quality indicators proposed in this chapter may carry some appeal.

In the end it is not the technical critique of the validity and reliability of performance indicators which break up the cross-party collusion in commodifying education. What may ultimately convince the Labour Party to relinquish its commitment to performance indicators is more research into the social effects of an educational system driven by the 'social market' ideology. Such research might profitably test Norris' hypothesis 'that the most likely effect of performance data is to give more to those that already have most; the survival of the richest'.

As researchers we should be wary of investing our efforts in the quest for performance indicators to provide politicians and policy-makers with spurious legitimacy for their ideological constructions of education. And I say this in the awareness that our survival as researchers increasingly appears to depend on our collusion in the ideological fantasies of policy-makers. At least we should be aware of what we are doing: of the ideological nature of the ideas which shape the direction of our research, and ask ourselves whether these are the best ways of representing a concern for educational quality.

Educational Values, Quality Indicators, and the Reflective Practice of Education

I will now outline an alternative method for informing judgments about the educational quality of schooling. I want to argue that the quality of a school's or teacher's performance is constituted by its consistency with *educational values* that constitute the ends of education. These values are not instrumental values like 'effectiveness' and 'efficiency' but conceptualizations of the human potentials which an educational process aims to foster and develop in pupils, for example, potentials for understanding the meaning and significance of certain kinds of events and situations; for critical, reflective and imaginative thinking; for appreciating human values; for intelligent and wise action in complex and unpredictable human situations. As ends of education such potentials are not 'products' in the sense that they are causally determined by educational processes. *Educational processes* establish *enabling* rather than *causal* conditions. As such their outcomes are unpredictable. Enabling conditions give pupils access to the resources they need to develop their potentials. They provide opportunities and support for self-development. Whether these opportunities are grasped and the support accepted is not something educators can control. What they can control is the extent to which they establish educative processes in classrooms and schools, and one can judge the extent to which processes are educative quite independently from assessing their outcomes.

This does not imply that the development of human potentials should not be assessed. Pupils development needs to be monitored and recorded as a basis for continuing judgments and decisions about their learning needs. All my argument implies is that the assessment of pupils progress is a different activity to that of evaluating the quality of the processes which aim to foster it. Let me explain.

Peters (1966) claimed, more than twenty-five years ago, that when we talk about *educational aims* we are referring to educational values (qualities of mind). And he argued that such values are appropriately analyzed, not into outcomes extrinsic to processes, but into *principles of procedure* which provide criteria for what is to count as a worthwhile educational process. In other words educational values as statements of ends imply criteria for making judgments about appropriate means, processes, and strategies. These are very different criteria to the instrumental criteria of 'effectiveness' and 'efficiency' which govern judgments about means in the 'production-consumption' model of education.

For example HMI, in their review of secondary schooling over ten years ago (see *Aspects of Secondary Education,* 1980a), argued that they found little evidence of teaching for understanding, as opposed to teaching for pure memory learning, in secondary schools. And their evidence for this was a lack of any genuine discussion taking place in the lessons they observed. Tacitly they were assuming that the educational value of understanding implies a classroom process in which discussion is a significant teaching method. They did not have to assess the level of pupils understanding to establish whether or not teachers were 'teaching for understanding'. What they did was to look for methods of teaching which were consistent with this aim. 'Discussion' provided them with a criterion or principle for judging the consistency/inconsistency between educational processes and what they believed to be a worthwhile educational aim.

I would argue that the analysis of educational values into procedural principles furnishes us with criteria for selecting evidence which is indicative of the *educational quality* of a performance. The performance of schools and teachers intrinsically manifests educational quality if the performance satisfies appropriate quality criteria (procedural principles).

Stenhouse drew on Peters' ideas in his design of the Humanities Curriculum Project (see Stenhouse, 1975), which he described as an example of a 'process model' of curriculum design and development, and contrasted it with the 'objectives model' — the production-consumption model in its infancy — that was beginning to emerge in the UK during the late 60s and early 70s, and which he felt to be anti-educational.

The Schools Council-funded Humanities Curriculum Project (1967–72) provides us with an early example of a clearly articulated educational ethic in the form of procedural principles. Stenhouse analyzed the project's aim of 'developing an understanding of human acts, social situations, and the controversial issues they raise' into a set of procedural principles to guide teaching performance. These included such principles as:

— discussion rather than instruction should be the core activity in the classroom;
— teachers should protect divergence in discussion;
— teachers should avoid using their authority position to promote their own views by adopting a role of procedural neutrality.

Teachers were invited to develop their classroom practice in the light of such principles, and asked to collect evidence from observations, recordings, and pupil interviews about the extent to which they were manifested in their practices. Thus the procedural principles provided criteria for collecting evidence about the quality of classroom performance.

It was in the context of teacher involvement in the Humanities Project, with its 'process model' of design, that the teachers-as-researchers movement was born in the UK. For such principles do not prescribe concrete forms of behaviour but the qualities which any form of behaviour ought to manifest. It was left to teachers to judge the extent to which their conduct actually manifested the qualities specified by the procedural principles. For example, they were asked to identify on the basis of recordings of lessons the kinds of questions which protected or failed to protect divergence in discussion. On the basis of this kind of research teachers were helped to formulate diagnostic hypotheses about which concrete elements of performance matched, or failed to match, the procedural principles.

Such hypotheses identified what we might in the present climate of educational discourse appropriately call quality indicators. They refer to concrete elements in a situation which evidence suggests conform or fail to conform to certain quality criteria.

The teachers in the Humanities Project were asked to treat the elements they identified as hypotheses because the extent to which they constitute or fail to constitute manifestations of quality may vary from situation to situation. For example, teachers who respond to pupils contribution in discussions with comments like 'that's interesting' or 'good point' in many circumstances inhibit the free expression of views while in other circumstances they appear not to. The term 'hypothesis' constituted an invitation to other teachers to explore the extent to which the significance attributed to a particular act or process could be generalized to their own situations. By sharing hypotheses and exploring them in the light of evidence about their own performance, teachers in the Humanities Project did in fact develop a considerable number of general hypotheses i.e. they identified concrete elements of performance which were significient for quality across a range and variety of situations. In this way, through collaborative action-research, what we might appropriately call quality indicators were identified and a measure of agreement reached about many of them. However, even generalizable elements retained the status of 'hypotheses' to emphasize their limits and provisional status; in the sense that they may not apply in circumstances which were not investigated or in future circumstances. Following my involvement in the Humanities Project I have coordinated two funded action-research projects — The Ford Teaching Project (1972–74) and in the early 80s the Teacher-Pupil Interaction and the Quality of Learning Project (see Elliott, 1991, chapter 2) — both of which involved teachers collaboratively developing general hypotheses about elements of performance which are indicative of the quality of their teaching. All these action-research projects were fundamentally concerned with a quest for quality indicators.

In Italy a group of teachers associated with the OECD 'School Initiatives and Environment Project' (ENSI) have recently been working with Michela Mayer at the European Centre for Education at CEDE to define a set of quality indicators as a basis for action-research in the field of environmental education (see Mayer, 1991).

The OECD project is a rare example of cross-national curriculum development and currently involves schools in nineteen countries across the world. It was originally proposed by the Austrian Ministry of Education and designed by Peter Posch at the University of Klagenfurt. Posch, whose work over the years in Austrian curriculum development owes much to the seminal influence of Stenhouse, used the 'process model' as a basis for the project's design. His idea was to get OECD member countries, many operating with long-established highly centralized curriculum frameworks, to endorse school-based initiatives in the area of environmental education but within an overall framework of educational aims and the procedural principles they implied. Two basic aims were specified:

(i) to help students develop an understanding of the complex relationships between human beings and their environment through interdisciplinary learning and inquiry;

(ii) to foster a learning process which requires students to develop 'dynamic' rather than 'passive' qualities, for example, 'exercising initiative', 'accepting responsibility' and 'taking action' to resolve real environmental problems within their locality.

Four guiding principles were derived from these aims:

— that students should experience the environment as a sphere of personal experience, i.e. by identifying problems and issues wthin their local environment;

— that students should examine the environment as a subject for interdisciplinary learning and research;

— that students should have opportunities to shape the environment as a sphere of socially important action;

— that students should accept the environment as a challenge for initiative, independence and responsible action.

Another feature of the project's design is that teachers are expected to undertake action-research into the extent to which these aims and principles are being realized and to report it in the form of case studies for wider discussion.

The DES has shown itself to be very reluctant to fully endorse and support participation by schools in England and Wales. The author was present at a DES meeting to discuss the project, and actually witnessed an official explaining that the project was perceived as incompatible with the requirements of the National Curriculum. In my view this shows a great deal of perceptiveness on the part of the DES, for whereas the National Curriculum Framework is underpinned by a 'production-consumption' model of education the ENSI project is underpinned by what I shall, following Peters, call an 'ethical model' i.e. a view of education which is framed by value-concepts and a set of principles that together constitute an educational ethic.

It was within the general perspective of the design features of the ENSI project that Mayer worked with her group of Italian teachers to identify quality indicators that could be used not only as a basis for recognizing quality in the context of the project, but more generally in relation to other school-based initiatives in environmental education.

Mayer clearly saw the quest for quality indicators as a way of reconciling greater freedom for schools and teachers to initiate curriculum change in the light of educational values and the need for quality assurance. She and her group were intent on articulating an alternative basis for quality assurance to performance indicators. Mayer writes that 'for us quality indicators are rarely statistics, more often they present observable features or behaviours, which can be interpreted as signs of the consistency between the EE project and the model and the value system . . .'. She argues that quality indicators can only be identified in the light of teachers' educational values and their reflections about their experience of attempting to realize them in the educational process. They are 'clues, traces, signs' that their values are being realized in action. This Italian project bears a strong resemblance to Peters' view of education as an ethical activity and Stenhouse's 'process model' of curriculum development as exemplified by the Humanities Project. Yet to my knowledge neither Mayer nor her group of teachers were familiar with this earlier work in England.

Mayer reports that the Italian teachers had little difficulty in agreeing about the general aims of environmental education but discovered considerable divergence of view about strategies and processes. So they embarked on a process of reflecting together about the different strategies they used in terms of their consistency with the agreed aims. From this process they reflexively identified a number of process values, and principles for evaluating the consistency of their strategies with agreed educational aims. In the light of such quality criteria they embarked on a quest for quality indicators and identified three sets. The first set is concerned with the *relevance and concreteness* of the curriculum to local environmental concerns. 'The indicators identified for this dimension refer to aspects of school involvement in local issues. They were identified as:

— *field work*, 'considered not only as an active way to gather data, but also as an important educational tool to broaden perception abilities, to develop an overall vision, and to establish a feeling of belonging';
— *school territory relationship*, 'where not only is the school brought into the environment, but also the environment into the school'. The school should operate as an active partner with the community to improve the environment;
— *acknowledging the complexity* of environmental problems, with respect to the uncertain state of much 'knowledge' and the importance of different points of view within the community.

The second group of indicators describes aspects of *school innovation*:

— the *transversality* of content, methods, and actions. This refers to the creation of connections between 'different disciplines, . . . different teachers, their methods, their value systems and their behaviours';
— *structure and organizational* changes that manifest environmental education values, such as flexible time scheduling; the development of forms of assessment which enable the development of dynamic qualities to be recorded; the amount of collaborative work undertaken by pupils; the development of a system for rewarding the energy and commitment of innovating teachers.
— *joint research* by teachers and pupils which informs action in relation to local environmental problems while acknowledging that there are limits on the extent to which their consequences are foreseeable.

The third group of indicators describes the direction or *path of change* realized in the educational process:

— *change* in pupils and teachers' conceptions, attitudes, behaviour and values in relation to the educational process used;
— the *flexibility* of teachers' programming as an index of their receptiveness to pupils needs and unanticipated events;
— the importance attributed to *respecting* individual differences between pupils with respect to their values, attitudes and beliefs in relation to environmental issues;
— the extent to which provision is made for the development of dynamic qualities such as decision-making abilities, sense of responsibility, independent judgment and action.

The categorization of the quality indicators into three sets reflects the three significant dimensions implicit in the aims and principles of the OECD project; namely, *intervention* in the local environment and *collaboration* with the local community, *organizational change* in the school, and *pedagogical change*. As such the work of this Italian group in its quest for quality indicators represents a sophisticated piece of action-research. It provides to my knowledge one of the most thorough attempts yet to articulate, in the context of a process model of the curriculum, comprehensive and wide ranging sets of quality indicators.

In the final section of this chapter I want to examine the question of whether quality indicators of the kind I have described can provide a credible basis for quality assurance and public accountability about the performance of schools.

Quality Indicators and Public Accountability

Norris argues that the national assessment system which emerged as a major part of the 1988 Education Act yields information that is diagnostically useless with respect to improving educational performance. National testing is not about improving education he asserts but about 'controlling teachers and creating the raw data for judgments about efficiency and effectiveness of schools so they can be held accountable to market forces and consumer choice'. The assumption underlying his argument is that this form of ideologically driven control and accountability has little to do with educational improvement. I would agree, and if this is so then one can claim that all performance indicators, not simply test results, are of dubious diagnostic utility for improving education.

What is striking about the kinds of quality indicators I have described is that they yield information which is clearly diagnostic of strengths and weaknesses in the quality of educational provision. It is information teachers can use to reflectively improve the quality of their performance in schools and classrooms. But some will argue that such information is contaminated by the value-biases of teachers: by their controversial educational theories. It is consequently useless information for the purposes of public accountability. Accountability requires objective data as a basis for judgments of educational quality.

'Performance indicators' appear to achieve the status of 'objective data' because they are constructed from an ideological perspective which attempts to eliminate considerations of values as conceptions of the ends of education from the public debate about educational quality. From this perspective the public debate about educational quality is largely reduced to a consideration of the instrumental effectiveness and efficiency of schools as production units. From the 'social market' perspective there is little point in publicly debating the intrinsic quality of ends conceived as products. The quality of products largely resides in their market value as commodities which large numbers of individual consumers want as outcomes of schooling.

There is a sense then in which we can say that performance indicators although objective measures in one sense are also biased measures, inasmuch as they imply a set of ideological assumptions about the nature of education. Indeed the 'social market' perspective on education from which they are constructed constitutes in itself a theory of education. Performance indicators are as theoretically biased as quality indicators. What is really at stake, as the Right Wing of the

Conservative Party makes abundantly clear, is 'which theories of education are going to regulate educational performance in the future?' And this appears not to be a topic for widespread public discussion. The question is preempted through the formulation of state educational policy.

Quality indicators can never be fixed bench-marks. This is partly because of their context-bound character and partly because of their relationship to values. Teachers' understandings of educational values are biographically shaped by their professional and life experiences and vary accordingly. An individual's under-standing of his/her own values also grows with experience, and an increased capacity for self-reflection. Value-concepts are ever receding standards. There are always new meanings and interpretations of them to be grasped, and therefore fresh implications for action to be discovered. Values, including educational val-ues, are never perfectly realized in any particular form of action, in the sense that one can never be completely certain that one's conduct is perfectly consistent with one's values.

It follows that quality indicators as 'traces' or 'signs' of consistency between means and ends can never become fixed bench-marks for evaluating performance. One must expect, even amongst teachers, some diversity of view concerning what sorts of things are indicative of educational quality. And one must expect indi-viduals over time to change their views on what the relevant indicators are.

Given this open-endedness about how values as standards of educational quality are to be interpreted, and therefore what are to count as indications of their consistency with practice, and given the context bound character of such indica-tions, some may conclude that the quest to identify quality indicators as a basis for an alternative system of quality assurance and public accountability is a pretty futile one. I would disagree.

The usefulness of a particular set of quality indicators is that they provide evidence for establishing a form of reflective discourse between teachers and their public in which ends and means are joint objects of reflection in particular circum-stances. This stands in stark contrast to 'performance indicators' which provide evidence only for a consideration of means. It is precisely because quality indica-tors are paradoxically problematic and contestable as relevant evidence that they provide a focus for a reflective discourse about the nature of educational values. In other words they legitimate and support a type of discourse between profes-sionals and citizenry which is not possible of the basis of 'performance indicators'. But in reflective discourse of this kind a consideration of the ends of education cannot be separated from a consideration of means. If evidence about educational means stimulates a discussion about educational ends, then the latter in turn in-fluences people's understanding of what constitutes appropriate means. In other words, the discussion of ends, stimulated by the problematic status of evidence held to be indicative of the quality of the means employed, in turn throws new light on what constitutes relevant evidence for judging the quality of means. In this kind of reflective discourse people's understanding of both educational ends and the means which are consistent with them change and develop interactively.

The problematic and provisional status of quality indicators in no way implies that they cannot support judgments of quality and thereby cannot make provision for quality assurance. But they do this via a mediating reflective discourse which respects divergent of view while offering the opportunity for participants to reach new levels of agreement. For example, evidence presented by a group of teachers to parents as indicative of the quality of their work may help the latter to appreciate values which previously carried little meaning or significance for them. Also the parents may suggest to the teachers that a type of evidence be gathered which reflects their values but had not previously been considered to be relevant by the teachers. In discussing this evidence together the teachers may come to appreciate its significance for educational quality for the first time.

Shared understandings of educational ends, and of the processes and strategies which are consistent with them, can evolve through a reflective discourse between professional teachers and their 'public audiences' on the basis of problematic and contestable evidence of quality. This kind of reflective discussion can provide the public with an assurance of quality even when their judgments of quality rest on provisional and limited evidence and are therefore open to constant revision. Quality assurance in education cannot rest on fixed and certain benchmarks. But it can rest on mutual understanding achieved through a reflective discourse about evidence of performance. This evidence will largely consist of 'ethnographic' and 'qualitative' data about performance in particular contexts and be represented in the form of case reports and records for purposes of public discussion. The discussion will operate largely at the level of local accountability, for example, between the staff of a school and local parents, employers etc. The evidential basis for such discussions can be either generated by teachers' own action-research to improve the quality of their practices or by an independent evaluator using a 'democratic evaluation' methodology (see MacDonald, 1974).

The use of quality indicators in accountability contexts which take the form of a reflective discourse between teachers and their local audiences will not satisfy policy-makers committed to a 'social market' perspective on education. But it does provide us with a basis for dissolving the apparent dichotomy between different kinds of evidence; namely, between evidence which can be used diagnostically to improve the quality of educational performance and evidence which can be used for purposes of public accountability. The dichotomy is in fact created by a 'production-consumption' model of education.

Quality indicators, used in the way I have outlined, satisfy the purposes of both improvement and public accountability. In doing so they place members of the public in a different role to that of the individual consumer within the 'social market' perspective. Through their participation in a reflective educational discourse citizens become active partners with teachers in the tasks of clarifying educational ends, evaluating the consistency of processes and strategies with these ends, and diagnosing what needs to be done to effect improvements in the quality of processes. Parents, employers and other sectors of the local community adopt an 'insider's' perspective on education as opposed to the 'outsider' perspective of the consumer of education who is detached from an active role in improving its quality. The 'social market' construct of the citizen as an educational consumer is essentially a device for legitimating an external surveillance and control technology over the activities of teachers.

Those educators who wish to preserve liberal humanist values as ends of education, in the face of changes driven by the 'social market' philosophy, will need to develop strategies for creatively resisting such changes. Creative resistance avoids a purely oppositional stance. The validity of the concerns which underpin certain policies and strategies is acknowledged, but an alternative way of responding to them is developed.

The use of performance indicators is a response to public concern about the quality of schooling. I have proposed an alternative response to that legitimate concern. It is not enough to simply raise objections to the idea of performance indicators. Such objections can easily be ignored in the absence of any alternative response to quality assurance concerns. These concerns must be addressed. The idea of quality indicators challenges people to reflect constructively about an alternative form of quality assurance which can operate outside the ideological framework of 'the social market'. It is therefore a more powerful and challenging response than simply opposing the use of performance indicators.

The idea of quality indicators as an alternative to performance indicators can provide the basis for a constructive debate about alternative forms of quality assurance and the possibility of a degree of ideological disenchantment with a 'production-consumption' model of education. The involvement of both teachers and parents in school-based action-research, enabling them to develop shared understandings of quality indicators as a basis for judging and improving the quality of schooling, would constitute a significant counter-innovation to the current direction of change. Such a counter-innovation will not constitute a reactionary revival of ill thought out and undisciplined interpretations of liberal-humanist values in the field of education. It will embody a new intellectual and practical rigour, evolved in response to the ideological challenge of the 'social market' philosophy. The clarification and use of quality indicators provide the foundations of such rigour.

References

ELLIOTT, J. (1991) *Action Research for Educational Change*, Milton Keynes, Open University Press, chapters 1 and 2.

ELLIOTT, J. *et al.* (1982) *School Accountability*, Grant McIntyre (currently distributed by Basil Blackwell, Oxford).

GAMBLE, R. (1990) 'Performance Indicators', in FITZ-GIBBON, C.T. (Ed.) *Performance Indicators*, Clevedon, Philadelphia, Multilingual Matters, (Bera Dialogues No 2), pp. 19–25.

HER MAJESTY'S INSPECTORATE (1980a) *Aspects of Secondary Education*, London, Department of Education and Science.

HER MAJESTY'S INSPECTORATE (1980b) *A View of Curriculum Matters for Discussion*, Series 11, London, HMSO.

MACDONALD, B. (1974) 'Evaluation and the control of education' in TAWNEY, D. (Ed.) *Curriculum Evaluation Today: Trends and Implications*, London, Macmillan.

MAYER, M. (1991) 'Environmental education in Italy: Proposals for an evaluation strategy', paper prepared for OECD 'Environment and School Initiatives' Project. (available from author at CEDE, European Centre of Education. Villa Falconieri, 00044 Frascati, Rome, Italy).

NORRIS, N. (1991) 'Evaluation, economics and performance indicators', paper originally presented at the annual meeting of the British Educational Research Association, Nottingham, August.

PETERS, R.S. (1966) *Ethics and Education*, London, Allen and Unwin.

STENHOUSE, L. (1975) *An Introduction to Curriculum Research and Development*, Milton Keynes, Open University Press, chapter 7.

STRAW, J. (1991) *Raising the Standard: Labour's Plans for an Education Standards Commission*, June, The Labour Party, 150 Walworth Road, London, SE17 1JT.

Chapter 6

Professional Education and the Idea of a Practical Educational Science

John Elliott

The Practical Science Paradigm

Changes in teacher education over the past three decades cannot simply be described in terms of the collapse of the rationalist tradition and the emergence of a behaviourist social market orientation. A third perspective on the relationship between theory and practice has emerged and provided a basis for the design of teacher education programmes in higher education within the UK. This perspective has been variously described in such terms as 'teachers as researchers', 'educational action research', 'action inquiry' and 'reflective practitioners'. I have argued elsewhere (Elliott, 1991) that this perspective did not simply emerge from academia, but constituted an articulation of a professional culture which emerged amongst teachers engaged in school initiated curriculum reform during the 60s and 70s. The academics who spearheaded the articulation of this perspective (such as Stenhouse, 1975) had themselves been actively involved in supporting such reform, either directly as school teachers or indirectly as external change agents producing curriculum materials to support development in schools. This association stimulated them to launch into an internal critique of the rationalist assumptions which governed views of the theory-practice relationship that obtained within the academic cultures of higher education and which proved unworkable in the context of school-based curriculum change.

The 'teachers as researchers' perspective became the basis for a proliferation in the 70s and 80s of part-time award-bearing advanced courses for serving teachers at Diploma and Masters levels in many higher education institutions within the UK. During the 80s the attempt to incorporate more school-based experience in initial training, in response to criticisms of theory-based courses, resulted in an emerging internal critique of rationalism within this sector, and consequent attempts to incorporate the 'teachers as researchers' perspective. The attempt was further stimulated by the publication of Schon's *The Reflective Practitioner* (1983).

Although the 'teachers as researchers' perspective now informs an international movement in the field of teacher education it has received virtually no recognition amongst the UK policy makers. In other countries such as Spain and Austria it has become increasingly recognized as a basis for educational change. The curriculum reform policies of the Spanish Government explicitly acknowledge the importance of grounding educational change in systematic inquiries conducted by practitioners. The Austrian Government has recently commissioned a group of teacher researchers to undertake action research into the best use of 'project time' within its National Curriculum.

It is indeed ironic that there has been virtually no dialogue between the external and internal critics of the traditional pattern of teacher education, because they both agree on what is wrong with it; namely, that its theory driven character is inadequate as a basis for competent professional practice. What they disagree about is their view of what constitutes 'competent professional practice'. Some may feel that the differences between the 'social market' and 'teacher as researchers' perspectives are so radical that there is little point in dialogue: only in confrontation and opposition. I would disagree and claim that dialogue resulting in a degree of mutual understanding, tolerance, and accommodation of the different perspectives at stake is possible. The argument in defence of this claim may become more apparent as I proceed.

The reasons for using the terms 'practical science' to characterize this third perspective on teacher education is to locate the emergence of the image of the 'teacher as a researcher' in the broader context of changes in the occupational cultures of the public service professions more generally. The new occupational images which are emerging from within these professions, as opposed to being imposed from above, have a number of features in common which I have summarized previously (see Elliott, 1990) but will elaborate further here. Together they define a general view of professional practice which can justifiably be called a 'practical science'. Its key features are as follows:

(i) Professional practice in advanced modern societies needs to be responsive to unstable states of discontinuous and fragmentary, as opposed to incremental and evolutionary, social change. Such change is now large scale and wide sweeping in its scope.

In this context human needs become increasingly complex, various, and open to redefinition, and individuals and communities want more control over defining what is good for them in their particular circumstances and how their needs are to be met.

(ii) The practical situations public service professionals confront in relation to their 'clients' are increasingly experienced as problematic inasmuch as their particularity, complexity, and fluidity makes them difficult to predict, laden with value issues and dilemmas, impossible to stereotype, and resistant to clear cut and fixed solutions.

(iii) Intelligent professional practice involves the exercise of practical wisdom; that is, the ability to discern an appropriate response to a situation in the face of uncertainty and doubt.

(iv) Wise professional judgments and decisions rest on the quality of the situational understandings they manifest.

Situational understanding involves discriminating and then synthesizing the practically significant elements of a situation into a unified and coherent picture of the whole.

(v) Situational understandings are conditioned by a practical interest in realizing professional values in a situation.

There are no value-free understandings of the concrete and complex practical situations which confront professional practitioners. Value-concepts are constitutive of the ends of social practices for example, the conceptions of the human potentials to be developed through education, or of the physical/mental well-being to be fostered in medical practice, or of the social order which it is the task of the police to maintain and enforce.

They guide the selection of practically significant elements in situations and shape the forms in which they are synthesized into meaningful holistic pictures.

(vi) Professional knowledge consists of repertoires of experienced cases which are stored in a practitioner's long term memory and represent his or her stock of 'situational understandings'.

As Schon has argued, experienced professionals do not recall and apply sets of abstract/theoretical propositions when confronted with a decision about how to respond in a practical situation. Rather they intuitively or reflectively compare and contrast the present situation with cases experienced in their past, and in so doing develop a picture of its significant features.

(vii) Professional judgments and decisions are ethical and not simply technical in character.

In evaluating the decisions of service professionals considerations of technical effectiveness are not enough. The most fundamental consideration is the extent to which decisions are ethically consistent with the realization of those values which define the ends of the professional practice concerned. A psychiatrist may cure a patient of depression through electrotherapy but there is the further question of whether such treatment enhances or diminishes that patient's mental health. A teacher may be technically very effective in getting pupils to process information in a form which enables them to recall it for the purpose of examinations.

But there is a further question of whether the techniques employed are consistent with the development of certain human potentials, for example, of their powers to think critically and imaginatively about the information. Finally, the police may employ highly successfully crime detection techniques which nevertheless pose the question of whether they are ethically consistent with the preservation and protection of public order.

The value-concepts which define the ends of a professional practice do not refer to concrete and tangible states of affairs and events, but to the qualities they may or may not manifest. The extent to which they do or not is a matter of inference from, and interpretation of, evidence. Attempts to reduce professional practice to a production technology are now frequently accompanied by the citation of performance indicators to measure its technical efficiency and effectiveness. It is simply assumed that statistical measures of certain tangible and concrete states and events are measures, albeit indirect ones, of quality. A performance indicators approach to education might evaluate teachers' practices on the basis of exam results. In the field of medicine it might measure cure rates as an indicator of medical competence, and when it comes to police competence crime detection figures become a major performance indicator.

However, the use of such statistical indicators pre-empts any further consideration of the ethical consistency of practices with the concepts of value that define their ends. Such considerations can only occur in situ in the light of all the complex factors involved. The reduction of value concepts to a set of measurable correlates is a key feature of behaviourist psychology. Although now somewhat discredited in the academic domain it continues to linger in the political domain as an ideological device for eliminating value issues from the domains of professional practice and thereby subordinating them to political forms of control.

Value concepts are notoriously vague and ambiguous with respect to their meanings. People may differ considerably in their interpretations of the same concepts, and the meanings they attribute to them often change with age and experience. One cannot define values in terms of fixed standards of interpretation. Given this instability of meaning practitioners' understanding of the interrelationships between value concepts will also vary and change over time. For example, some politicians clearly see the concept of 'equality' to be incompatible with that of 'freedom' as a basis for policy making. They believe one simply has to choose between these conflicting values. However, others, while acknowledging a conflict between incompatible values, feel their commitment to both values obliges them to seek a course of action that accommodates each. They are prepared to tolerate the ambiguities and dilemmas practical situations present them with. Still others may experience no incompatibility between the meanings they ascribe to different values. They feel under no pressure to choose between their values when confronted with a decision to act, nor experience any ambiguity or dilemma in making such a decision.

Inasmuch as situational understandings and the practical decisions which flow from them are conditioned by practitioner's concepts of value, we must conclude that neither rest on stable, sure, or certain foundations. People will differ in their understandings of the same practical situations and therefore draw different implications for decision making from them. Moreover, any individual's understanding of his/her situation may change over time. Nothing is clear cut, certain, beyond question and to be taken for granted.

> (viii) Systematic reflection by practitioners in their practical situations plays a central role in improving professional judgments and decisions.

Within the 'practical science' model of professionalism, systematic inquiry becomes an integral feature of professional practice. However, it involves a distinctive form of reflection, which can be contrasted with both the means-ends reasoning involved in justifying technical decisions and reasoning a course of action from a particular set of theoretical principles or rules.

The form of reflection which supports wise and intelligent decisions in particular, complex, and fluid practical situations can be characterized in terms of three major dimensions.

Firstly, it is a form of reflection which is highly **personal** in the sense that a practitioner views him or herself as part of the situation (s)he wants to understand. In reflecting about the situation (s)he does not dissociate it from his or her own agency and influence. The form of reflection involved is **reflexive**.

Secondly, there is a problematic dimension opened up by this reflexive stance. The practitioner calls into question his/her own actions and responses within the situation, in the light of evidence which suggests they are more inconsistent with professional values than (s)he originally assumed. This in turn opens up a third **critical** dimension, in which the practitioner reflects about the taken-for-granted beliefs and assumptions which underpin his/her practical interpretations of professional values and their origins in his/her life experiences and history. (S)he begins to reconstruct his/her constructs of value and discovers that this opens up new understandings of the situation and new possibilities for intelligent action within it.

One implication of this account of reflection from a 'practical science' perspective is that situational understanding is not developed in dissociation from decision making. The practitioner does not simply suspend making judgments and decisions until (s)he has understood the situation. Reflexive inquiry occurs both within the practice and during off-practice periods. In reflecting in action the practitioner is observing the situation as (s)he participates in it. (S)he is gathering evidence, analyzing it and synthesizing his/her insights in a form which inform his/her subsequent decisions. These in turn change the situation in ways which reveal previously hidden dimensions of the situation that are significant for practice. The development of situational understanding is not an independent process to practical decision making. The latter generates practical hypotheses which test the practitioners' understanding of the situation at that point and reveals new aspects which extend and modify that understanding. In the context of a 'practical science' reflection not only informs decision making but decision making informs reflection and is an integral component of an inquiry which aims to develop situational understanding.

Within the 'practical science' paradigm of reflective inquiry there is no dissociation of means from ends as there is in technical reasoning, where the means alone become the focus of reflection with the ends remaining as fixed targets to aim at. In the 'practical science' paradigm reflection about means (the problematic dimension) and reflection about beliefs and assumptions which frame conceptions of ends (the critical dimension) are inseparable and interactive.

Nor within the 'practical science' paradigm are there any indubitable theoretical principles in which to ground reflection. The practitioner becomes aware through this personal, reflexive, and self-critical form of reflection that the meanings (s)he ascribes to practical situations are personally constructed. This need not mean that the outcomes of reflection, situational understandings and practical decisions, are purely subjective and that the practitioner can make no claims with respect to their validity. (S)he can attempt to demonstrate on the basis of evidence that his/her understanding of a situation provides a more unified and coherent interpretation of that evidence than other interpretations, and opens up more promising and fruitful possibilities for acting in ways which are consistent with professional values. To deny that one can ever break out of one's personal constructions of meaning to check them against a reality which exists independently of human consciousness is not to deny the possibility that people can come to agree that some interpretations of experience, however provisional and capable of improvement, make better sense than others.

The aim of reflection from a 'practical science' perspective is to enable practitioners to improve the quality of their decisions by developing situational understandings which make the best sense of the available evidence. The 'practical science' paradigm of reflection does not ignore the contribution of theoretical analysis to the development of situational understanding. Theories may illuminate particular aspects of practical problems and the insights they provide can then be synthesized into an understanding of the whole situation. In practical reflection, as Schwab (1970) pointed out, theories are selected and utilized eclectically in terms of their perceived relevance for discerning and discriminating the practically significant features of the situation. Their selection and use is subordinated to the practitioner's quest to understand the problematics of their practice in a situation as a totality. According to Schwab a theory always abstracts a particular aspect of a situation and thereby dissociates it from the whole. It provides only a limited and partial insight which needs to be reintegrated into an understanding of the whole. Theories are useful tools of analysis. But they are dangerous when they are used to simplify and reduce the complexities of practical problems in order to derive clear cut and certain solutions.

    (ix)   In reflecting in and about their practical situations professionals need to gather perceptions of problems, issues, and solutions from experienced peers and clients and involve them in discussions of differing interpretations of the situation.

From a 'practical science' perspective the process of developing and validating understanding is discursive and unified. Emerging analytic insights and interpretations of a situation are continuously informed and tested through dialogue with fellow professionals and clients (in the case of teachers with pupils and their parents), whose own perceptions and interpretations can illuminate aspects which have been ignored, and challenge the taken-for-granted assumptions which shape the practitioner's interpretations and decisions. This form of reflective discourse enables practitioners to develop a more coherent and unified interpretation of their situation than could be achieved solely through a process of solitary reflection. And in doing so it offers the possibility of a growing consensus in understanding between the practitioner and his/her clients and professional peers. Both collaborate with him/her in a process of discursive reflection which values divergence while at the same time enabling participants to achieve a measure of shared understanding.

    The 'practical science' model of professionalism is a far cry from the rationalist model of the infallible, rational, and autonomous expert which the 'social market' advocates spend a great deal of energy attacking. It views professionals as career-long learners who improve their practices collaboratively through a process of discursive reflection with each other and their clients. The latter are not placed in the role of passive consumers of services, who influence the quality of their delivery by the withdrawal of custom or the right to complain to a higher authority. Rather clients are from a 'practical science' perspective on professional practice, active partners in the process of improving and shaping the quality of the services they receive. It is through active participation in dialogue rather than 'passive choice' and 'consumer rights' that they come to exercise more control over defining what is good for them and how their needs are to be met. From this perspective professional practitioners exercise accountability to their clients but not in the form constructed from the 'social market' perspective.

Constructing a Practical Science Model of Teacher Education

Let me now explore the implications of a 'practical science' model of professional practice for a process of professional education in general and for teacher education in particular. I want to examine three implications. Firstly, for developing continuity and coherence in professional learning, secondly for curriculum design, and thirdly for the role of schools of education in higher education institutions.

The Dreyfus Stage Model

Dreyfus (1981) has developed an empirically-based model of the development of situational understanding with respect to practical decision-making in the field of business management. His argument for placing situational understanding at the centre of the business managers expertise can be equally applied to other professionals such as teachers. He writes:

> Only rarely can problems and opportunities in the business world be objectively recognized and defined. Those that can are generally technological problems, or problems calling for an operating manager's logical deduction of the cause of some undesired event. This sort of problem solving, the subject of many training programs . . . is not what concerns us here. Nor are we concerned with certain fairly objectively defined problems such as petroleum blending, insofar as these problems concern only clearly defined physical constraints and an objectively specified cost criterion. Objectively defined problems are clearly within the proper domain of systematic analysis. We are interested instead in unstructured problematic situations. For all of these unstructured, problematic situations, both major and minor, no objectively defined set of facts and factors completely characterizes the problem setting, permissible actions and the goal of the activity. While in each of the above activities certain objective facts and events are clearly relevant, many others may be seen as either crucial or as insignificant depending upon the decision maker's interpretation of the situation. Yet other events may critically affect a manager's behaviour without his conscious awareness even of their presence. Such is the nature of unstructured situations, and it is these situations, not the rare objectively structured ones, that pervade the business world.
>
> Understanding through interpretation is an essential activity of policy makers.

It is not too difficult to identify the kinds of objectively defined problems teachers have to handle, for example, how to set up an experiment in the science lab, use accounts, place orders for text books, use sophisticated reprographic equipment etc. In addition to these technical and administrative problems there are also objectively defined problems related to a teacher's subject knowledge, such as his/her lack of knowledge about the subject matter (s)he is expected to teach.

Solutions to all these problems can be learned quite independently of the educational situations in which they may arise. They may constitute elements in such situations but no one will describe a teacher who can only solve these kinds of problems as a good educator (even a teacher who clearly knows his or her subject). This is because they do not intrinsically possess any educational significance. The latter is a matter of situated interpretation. Educational problems can be described as unstructured situations because intelligent responses in them cannot be predefined. They rest upon interpretative judgments made *in situ*.

Dreyfus argues that situational understanding (interpretation) involves the exercise of four mental capacities:

Component recognition i.e. discerning various aspects of a situation
Components may consist of either objectively or subjectively defined attributes. For example, a teacher may recognize that a pupil is unable to begin a learning task because (s)he is ill or unable to read the instructions on the blackboard. This is a very different type of recognition to the recognition that a pupil's failure to proceed is due to 'laziness', 'sheer bloody mindedness', 'lack of interest in the task', or even 'collusion with a disaffected minority to sabotage the lesson'.

Attributes like 'feeling ill' or 'unable to read instructions' are not dependent upon the particular context of the lesson. If the pupil were removed (s)he would still 'feel ill' or be 'unable to read instructions'. However, attributions like 'laziness' or 'lack of interest' are very situationally dependent. Removed to another classroom situation the pupil may prove to be 'hard working' or 'full of interest'.

The ability to recognize situation dependent, as opposed to nonsituation dependent, components, according to Dreyfus, rests on experience. On this account a teacher's ability to recognize situation-dependent components in a particular classroom situation will depend upon the extent of his/her experience of life in classrooms.

According to Dreyfus component recognition can be either an analytical or intuitive process, depending on the amount of experience a person has of the type of situation involved. The inexperienced person will need to consciously observe what is going on and from the evidence collected explicitly infer patterns. Later, (s)he will be able to process and interpret evidence more intuitively on the basis of similar cases experienced in the past.

Salience recognition i.e. discriminating those situational components which
need to be taken into account in pursuing a particular course of action (goal)
Discerning non-situational and situational attributes is one thing, but discriminating which of these are significant for the course of action one decides to undertake is quite another. A teacher may ignore the 'bloody mindedness' of a reluctant learner because his/her chosen course of action, for example, to concentrate only on her well motivated pupils, renders this attribute insignificant for his/her. Or (s)he may ignore the knowledge that during a discussion a pupil lacks an understanding of certain facts (a non-situational attribute) because this aspect is not immediately relevant to his/her goal of helping that pupil to participate fully in classroom discussion.

Discriminating salient components presupposes that the practitioner has consciously or unconsciously a course of action in mind. Relatively inexperienced practitioners will choose a course of action on the basis of reflection about the various components of a situation. Many experienced practitioners will choose a course of action intuitively on the basis of an unselfconscious appreciation of a situation.

*Whole situation recognition i.e. the ability to synthesize all the salient
components of a situation into an understanding of the total situation*
Dreyfus identifies two forms of whole-situation recognition which he calls analytical and holistic. When the synthesis is derived from conscious reflection about the relationships between salient components then whole-situation recognition takes on an analytic form. However, for those with a great deal of experience the synthesis may be based on an intuitive appreciation of relationships between salient components. Dreyfus calls the latter 'holistic synthesis'. However, in my view an analytic synthesis might also be described as holistic. So in the discussion which follows I shall refer to this form of whole situation recognition as 'intuitive'.

Decision making i.e. deciding on an appropriate response
It is one thing for a person to recognize all the practically significant aspects of a situation in the light of a chosen course of action, and quite another to decide upon the concrete action strategies for implementing that course of action. For Dreyfus, decisions about specific strategies can either be rationally derived from a consideration of alternatives or simply emerge as an obvious implication of a certain intuitive understanding of a situation.

Dreyfus uses this analysis to depict a five-stage model of the development of a capacity for situational understanding (see table 6.1 below).

Table 6.1

		Component recognition	Salience recognition	Whole-situation recognition	Decision making
1	Novice	non-situational	none	analytic	rational
2	Advanced beginners	situational	none	analytic	rational
3	Competent	situational	present	analytic	rational
4	Proficient	situational	present	intuitive	rational
5	Expert	situational	present	intuitive	intuitive

There are some critical questions we might ask concerning whether the development of a capacity for situational understanding must proceed in the invariant sequence depicted. Let us take a few examples. Is there any reason in principle why the ability to discern non-situational components of situations must be developed prior to the ability to discern situation-dependent components? Cannot the two be developed together? In which case the distinction between the novice and advanced beginner stages is incorrectly characterized. The novice is simply someone who has little ability to recognize situation dependent components because they lack experience of certain kinds of situations. They may or may not possess the foundation knowledge necessary to recognize non-situational components.

Again, we may ask whether the ability to discern situation-dependent components must be achieved before the learner acquires any ability to discriminate the significance of components for concrete decisions? Cannot the development of these abilities again proceed interactively? If so then one cannot differentiate the advanced beginner from the competent stage simply in terms of the absence of an ability for salience recognition.

Finally, one can ask whether an ability for analytic whole-situation recognition must develop prior to an ability for intuitively synthesizing parts into wholes? If the answer is no then there is a problem about discriminating the competent from the proficient in the way Dreyfus does.

In my view the value of Dreyfus' work is twofold. Firstly, he provides us with a basic framework for conceptualizing the constitutive cognitive abilities of situational understanding; in terms of the distinctions between:

— non-situational and situational component recognition;
— component and salience recognition;
— analytic and intuitive forms of whole-situation recognition;
— rational and intuitive decision making.

Secondly, he acknowledges that the development of these cognitive abilities, with the exception of non-situational component recognition, depends upon the amount of experience the practitioner has acquired of these situations. This latter insight may indeed have certain implications for professional development, in suggesting that:

(a) the learner need not acquire all the relevant specialist knowledge neces-
     sary for recognizing non-situational components in the context of
     experience;
(b) the amount of experience necessary for being able to recognize situation-
     dependent components fully is probably less than that required for being
     able to discriminate their salience for concrete decisions fully.
(c) the validity of a practitioner's intuitive understandings of whole situa-
     tions is likely to be enhanced if they draw on a personal repertoire
     (stored in memory) of cases which have been analytically processed;
(d) the wisdom of a practitioner's intuitive decisions in the present probably
     depends upon the extent to which (s)he has in the past rationally delib-
     erated about alternative courses of action.

I would regard the above as hypothetical implications which are open to challenge in the light of further evidence, and not as metaphysical principles of experiential learning. They do, however, give a surface plausibility to much of the Dreyfus model of continuity and progression in the development of a capacity for situational understanding. We can say that they constitute reasons for emphasizing particular kinds of learning needs at different times during the experiential learning process; such that:

— the need to acquire specialist foundation knowledge should not negate
   an emphasis at the novice stage with learning to recognize situation-
   dependent aspects on the basis of experience. The more this specialist
   knowledge and skill has been acquired prior to experience the better;
— once the learner has demonstrated the ability to recognize both situational
   and non-situational components in the context of experience, and achieved
   advanced beginner status, the emphasis should be placed on the ability to
   discriminate those components which are salient for decision making in
   particular cases (the competent level);
— once the learner has demonstrated the ability to discriminate salient components analytically (s)he can be allowed to rely more on intuition as a

basis for whole-situation recognition, and support for learning should now focus down on helping the learner to make better decisions in the light of his/her situational understanding.

Four Phases of Experiential Professional Learning

From the Dreyfus model we can derive four phases of experiential learning with respect to the development of a capacity for situational understanding. These are:

1 The Advanced Beginner Phase — from Novice to Advanced Beginner

Here learners need to develop an ability to discern, on the basis of observation and analysis, a wide range of aspects both situational and non-situational — which are potentially relevant to intelligent action.

It is at this phase that access to theoretical concepts and ideas may prove to be particularly useful as tools of analysis inasmuch as they illuminate aspects of situations which would remain hidden without them. They do this by suggesting questions to be asked and types of data to be gathered.

One way of summarizing the learning needs at this phase is to describe it as an 'observational research' or 'reconnaisance' phase.

2 The Competent Phase — from Advanced Beginner to Competent

Here the learning emphasis shifts to choosing a course of action (or goal) and discriminating all those aspects of a situation which have to be taken into account in reaching a decision about how to implement that course of action. The relationships between these salient components needs then to be analyzed to provide a picture of the problem and opportunity structure which defines the situation as a whole.

At this phase learners will have had sufficient experience of cases to be able to formulate a course of action for themselves. According to Dreyfus, at the advanced beginner stage learners are largely dependent on guidelines established by higher authorities. These suggest courses of action which take into account a range of aspects that learners should be capable of recognizing in the situations they handle. Such guidelines protect learners against choosing quite inappropriate courses of action, but they cannot help them choose the best in the circumstances.

Learning-needs at the competent phase can be summarized as the need to develop diagnostic abilities i.e. abilities to analytically discriminate and synthesize those components which define a situation in terms of its problematics and possibilities for action. This is why *situational understanding is practical* in character.

3 The Proficiency Phase — from Competent to Proficient

At this phase learners will have had so much experience of a variety and range of cases that they are now in a position on the basis of intuition to discern potentially relevant aspects of situations, to discriminate in the light of their goals which are salient, and to synthesize saliences into a view of the situation as a whole. The main learning needs at this phase are focussed on the decision-making process itself: on the need to formulate alternative action-strategies, deliberate about their relative advantages and disadvantages, and evaluate their impact.

This phase might be summarized as the need to develop the ability to self-evaluate actions and decisions.

4 The Expert Phase — from Proficiency to Expertise

At this phase the extent and range of experience accumulated by the learner is so vast that learners begin to make even intelligent decisions on the basis of intuition rather than conscious deliberation in the light of evaluation data gathered around past decisions. The 'reflective space' between interpreting a situation and deciding what to do in it gradually disappears as learners progress through this phase.

Progress here depends partly upon the amount of situational decision-making learners have to undertake. If having achieved the proficient stage they have reduced opportunities for decision making then they are less likely to progress to expert.

Also, progress at any stage will depend upon the frequency with which novel and unfamiliar situations are encountered, as increasingly happens in organizations and institutions which have to respond to discontinuous and fragmentary social change. In this respect practitioners may discover that competence, proficiency, or expertise acquired from past experience is of only limited use and that in order to handle a situation they may have to regress to a previous stage. Professional development may not be a straightforward matter of incremental progress but involve periods of unlearning and relearning.

In the future it may be more difficult for professional practitioners, including teachers, to achieve expertise. Professional development is increasingly a 'career long' process, and the pace of social change makes coherent and continuous structures of support for it crucial.

The developmental phases I have derived from the Dreyfus model appear to be very consistent with the 'practical science' perspective on professional practice I outlined earlier. Since Dreyfus says little about the relationship between the development of a capacity for situational understanding and values, I will attempt to clarify what I see to be the relationship between his model and professional values.

Value issues emerge at phase two with the increasing ability to formulate courses of action or goals in a situation. A goal can be viewed as a focus for action. Which focus a practitioner chooses will be shaped by values. The teacher who chooses to focus her efforts on her well motivated pupils expresses different values from a teacher who chooses to focus on improving the motivation of reluctant learners. Therefore, the action-strategies they employ to achieve their specific goals raise issues about the nature of educational values and whose strategies are most consistent with them.

From the Dreyfus stage model of the development of a capacity for situational understanding I have derived four developmental phases which emphasize particular types of learning-needs. I would suggest that they could be used as a basis for conceptualizing a coherent teacher education curriculum which caters for progression and continuity of learning throughout teachers' professional lives.

In my view these developmental phases make sense if one looks at teacher professionalism from what I have characterized as a practical science perspective. They illuminate images of professionalism which are already floating around in the system, such as 'teachers as researchers', 'reflective practitioners', 'self-evaluating teachers' and 'educational action-research'. Each of these images is suggestive of certain phases rather than others. 'Teachers as researchers' appears to be a particularly appropriate term to describe the aims of professional education at phase 1.

At phase 2 Schon's 'reflective practitioner' image is particularly appropriate inasmuch as it focuses on the importance of reflecting about the problematics of practical situations. The image of the 'self-evaluating' teacher highlights the decision making aspects of practice and is especially significant for phase 3. 'Action-research' on the other hand is an image which covers both the diagnostic and the evaluatory forms of reflection that are emphasized at phases 2 and 3 respectively.

A Practical Science Curriculum for Teacher Education

The developmental phases outlined above suggest a pattern of continuing experience-based teacher education which consists of:

(i) A basic curriculum that provides student teachers with an opportunity to achieve the status of advanced beginners and emphasizes the analytic study of cases in the light of relevant theory.

(ii) A curriculum for beginning teachers which helps them to achieve the competent level, emphasizing diagnostic reflection to enable them to clarify the problematics and possibilities of teaching in their classrooms.

(iii) A curriculum for experienced teachers progressing towards proficiency which emphasizes support for deliberative decision making and self-evaluation.

Each element in this pattern is not intended to be discrete with respect to the learning experiences provided. Beginning teachers will need to continue to analyze situations in the light of relevant theory, and given support with decision making. Experienced teachers will also need to be given support for reflecting about new and unfamiliar situations which past experience has not equipped them to handle. The focus of each of the elements outlined should be treated simply as a matter of emphasis.

At this point I want to extend the conceptual framework for a teacher education curriculum by linking the constituitive cognitive abilities of situational understanding, outlined by Dreyfus, with a generic competency model developed from research into the nature of good professional practice by McBer and Company (see Klemp, 1977; Spencer, 1979).

The McBer model of professional competence can be contrasted with the more behaviourist models which identify competence as an ability to produce certain pre-specified behavioural responses to situations. The latter are usually generated from tasks/functions analyses, that attempt to identify those behaviours that are necessary to the effective performance of certain key tasks and functions. Such an analysis is largely concerned with the objectively definable performance requirements of structured situations. It assumes that competence primarily consists of technical skills.

The McBer model mainly focusses on those abilities which are manifested by good performances in the kinds of unstructured practical situations service professionals frequently have to respond in. Such abilities cannot be defined in terms of pre-specifiable behavioural responses or outcomes, and cannot be derived from a tasks/functions analysis of the job. Rather they consist of personal qualities which performers bring to the job and which differentiate the superior from the average. Klemp (1977) summarized a variety of job competence analyses carried out by McBer & Company from 1972–77, and identified a number of key abilities that generalized across a diversity of occupations involving problem-solving and decision-making in complex, unstructured situations. The general model he described contains three clusters of abilities which can be linked to the cognitive, interpersonal, and motivational dimensions of performance.

The cognitive abilities Klemp identified are as follows:

— Discerning thematic consistencies in diverse information and communicating them.

This ability is very similar to Dreyfus' concept of situational component recognition.

— Understanding the controversial issues at stake in conflicts between people, and the different perspectives the conflicting parties hold.

Again this can be linked to Dreyfus' concept of salience recognition, since people may disagree about the practical significance of a particular aspect of a situation because their discriminations are conditioned by different value perspectives.

— Learning from reflection on experience by observing and analyzing one's own behaviour in the context of other people's in a situation.

This ability can be linked to Dreyfus' concept of rational decision making. In reflecting on the extent to which possible or actual decisions are ethically consistent with the values (s)he espouses the practitioner assesses their rationality.

Klemp goes on to describe the key interpersonal abilities of good practitioners as:

— accurate empathy, which involves recognizing the thoughts and feelings of peers and clients in a form which enables them to feel understood;
— promoting feelings of efficacy in others. This ability has three aspects: positive regard for others, providing them with active support, and controlling feelings of hostility and anger which if unleashed would make others feel powerless and ineffective.

The third cluster of abilities are linked to achievement and power motivation or the need to exert influence in pursuit of organizational goals.

Achievement Motivation:

— Risk taking: to take moderate risks in pursuit of new and original solutions.

— Goal setting: to set time-phased, realistic goals.
— Eliciting feedback: to seek information for use as feedback on one's own performance.

Power Motivation:

— Networking: the ability to learn interpersonal influence networks and use them to do the job.
— Goal-sharing: the ability to influence others by sharing a superordinate goal.
— Micropolitical awareness: the ability to identify work-group coalitions with regard to both their level in the hierarchy and their orientations to the goals of the organization.

Klemp claims that underpinning achievement and power motivation and their constitutive abilities is a fundamental perspective which he calls **cognitive initiative**. It refers to practitioners who see themselves as capable of changing a situation for the better rather than as the helpless victims of events.

I have already suggested similarities between the cognitive abilities outlined in the McBer model and those indentified by Dreyfus. But it is not only the cognitive dimension of the model which can be linked to the capacity for situational understanding. There is also a relationship between this capacity and the other two dimensions.

Situational understanding and the decisions derived from it are grounded in an awareness of the self as an active agent in the situations to be understood, and therefore as one who is capable of influencing the lives of others. This awareness (cognitive initiative) generates ethical obligations with respect to the care and concern for others the practitioner exercises in his/her conduct in the situation. In order to exercise such care and concern (s)he needs to be able to understand other people's thoughts and feelings in the situation (empathy).

In other words the interpersonal and motivational abilities cited in the McBer model are presupposed by a capacity for situational understanding and wise decision-making.

This all suggests that we could develop a broad competency-based teacher education curriculum to support intelligent practice in unstructured, complex and fluid educational situations. It would radically differ in its conception of teaching competence to the behaviorist conception embedded in the 'social market' perspective and the model currently promoted by the National Council for Vocational Qualifications (NCVQ). Inasmuch as this curriculum would aim to develop those abilities which are related to a capacity for situational understanding, the conception of competence which underpins it is highly consistent with the 'practical science' perspective.

More work needs to be done on the relationship between the different development phases implied by the Dreyfus model and the development of interpersonal and motivational abilities. The cognitive abilities cited by Dreyfus cannot be developed independently of the interpersonal abilities cited in the McBer research. Component, salience and whole-situation recognition depend on the quality of the data the learner is able to elicit through his/her interpersonal transactions with other participants in the situation. The interpersonal abilities are therefore very

important at the advanced beginner and competent phases of professional development. I also think that the motivational abilities would particularly need to be
emphasized at the proficient phase because of their obvious relevance to decision-
making processes.

In developing a coherent experience-based teacher education curriculum from
a practical science perspective it is worth considering different forms of learning.
The development of a capacity for situational understanding does not have to
exclusively rely on direct experience. People can also have indirect experiences of
case situations through using case studies, participating in role plays or constructing observational studies of particular situations. Situational components and their
significance for decision-making can be explored by all these means. Similarly,
they can be developed through case studies constructed by the learners themselves,
operating in an observer, rather than a practitioner, role.

The reflective study of vicariously or observationally experienced situations can
foster the interpersonal as well as the cognitive abilities associated with situational
understanding. Observational experience would take the form of participant observation, in which observers communicate and interact with participants to elicit
their perceptions and interpretations of situations. In doing so they would need to
develop the ability to empathize with participants in the kinds of situations they
are being trained to practice in. Even the study of vicariously experienced cases
provides opportunities for the development of relevant interpersonal abilities. The
context of such studies consists of a practical discourse, where those involved
explore each other's perceptions and interpretations of the situations depicted
in the case evidence. This again calls for empathetic communications between
individuals.

Observational and vicarious experiences of cases have a particularly important role in the development of situational understanding at the advanced beginner
phase of teacher education as I shall argue in a moment. However, this should not
diminish their significance at later phases. Their curriculum significance lies in their
capacity to extend the repertoire of cases, which constitute a teacher's 'stock of
professional knowledge', beyond the range of every day, direct experience. The
usefulness of such an extension lies in the way it enhances the practitioner's
capacity to handle discontinuous change. By extending the repertoire of cases in
the memory store beyond those encountered directly through every day practical
experience, the practitioner is able to select from a greater range in trying to make
sense of new and unfamiliar circumstances.

The type of case studies produced either for or by practitioners would vary
according to the developmental phase they are at. Those produced for the advanced beginner and competent phases will need to be of forms which support
a detailed analysis of situational components and their significance for decision-
making respectively. They will need to be rich in primary source data. On the
other hand at the proficiency phase a primary use of case studies will be that of
developing the ability to evaluate action-strategies. Also at this phase certain kinds
of case studies can help practitioners to intuitively synthesize parts into wholes.
They will portray situations in terms of metaphors which vividly capture their
holistic meanings and provide people with intuitive access to them.

The significance of observational and vicarious experiences of cases at the
advanced beginner phase lies in their value at accelerating the range of experienced and reflectively processed cases stored in the memory at the beginning of

teachers' professional careers. This is especially significant given the problem of occupational socialization which presents itself in the context of initial training programmes that involve an early immersion into a direct experience of teaching in schools (see MacDonald, 1984; Munro, 1989; Elliott, 1990).

Our present government espouses a contradictory policy in endorsing a Licensed Teacher Scheme that depends almost entirely on school-based on-the-job learning and at the same time casting doubts on the quality of teaching in schools. Munro's detailed study of initial training courses with substantial school-based experience components in New Zealand, clearly established the rapidity of student teacher socialization into undesirable practices from the standpoint of quality in pupils' learning . In doing so he was testing the generalizability of MacDonald's claim that school-based experience in the UK constituted a rapid induction into obsolete practices which the higher education training base was subsequently powerless to resist. MacDonald provocatively argued that initial teacher training should be largely research rather than practice-based i.e. grounded in detailed observational studies. Only on the basis of a certain kind of research-based initial teacher education curriculum would teachers be equipped to resist subsequent pressures to conform to the negative aspects of the occupational culture. Hargreaves' solution to the problem is to locate basic training for teachers only in the good schools, but this raises the question of whether these are in sufficient supply to cater for the demand.

An experiential teacher education curriculum should enable novices to progress to the status of advanced beginners who are reflectively analytical about practice in classrooms and schools. In my view this requires a very gradual immersion into direct experience which is collaboratively supported by both qualified on-the-job trainers in schools and higher education staff in schools of education. The curriculum could take a modular form, interspersing direct experience in schools under the guidance of their training staff, with observational research assignments and the discursive analysis, in groups, of case studies. Such case studies could be constructed on the basis of research carried out by academic staff in collaboration with teachers undertaking their own action or evaluation research, as part of their professional development at phases 2 and 3 of the learning continuum. This implies a process where educational research in schools is a collaborative enterprise that involves teachers and supports the reflective development of their practices, while at the same time generating resources for an experiential learning curriculum at the basic training phase.

How then could one sequence learning experiences at the basic phase of 'novice-advanced beginner'? Here are some suggestions for discussion.

Module 1 would largely consist of an observational research phase based on a series of assignments designed in the higher education context and supervised jointly by academics and school staff (the latter having qualified to at least the level of competent in a continuing programme of professional education within a 'practical science' paradigm). In module 1 student teachers would meet frequently and regularly to share their experiences and insights and to give each other mutual support. In the supervisions and fieldwork seminars tutors would have opportunities to introduce theoretical ideas in terms of their relevance to questions and issues which are raised concerning the interpretation of the data students collect. The module would conclude with a systematic and rigorous debriefing of the whole experience. Out of this debriefing an agenda of general educational issues could be developed as a basis for selecting learning experiences for module 2.

Module 2 would consist of a case study based core curriculum in the higher education context, which enabled student teachers to explore in a protected environment a number of complex and dilemma-ridden situations that have an important bearing on some of the critical educational issues they will face in classrooms and schools. Tutors would have a responsibility for providing students with access to theoretical ideas that could be of relevance in analyzing case data. Case data would be explored through a variety of activities such as group discussion, role play and simulation, library-based reading. Within module 1 students would also have an opportunity to undertake reading projects in which they review research and theory in terms of its relevance to the issues posed in the case studies.

Module 3 could consist of a period of direct classroom experience under the collaborative supervision of school training staff and higher education tutors. During it student teachers would be required to undertake, in the context of supervisory and seminar support, case study assignments into aspects of the practical situations they encounter. As in module 1 the experience would be systematically and rigorously debriefed, and utilize the research assignments as important resources for this end.

Module 4 would take place back in the higher education context and focus again on an educational issues agenda using case studies. However, this time the focus would be less on teaching situations and more on practical situations that arise in the school context and educational system more generally, and that have implications for the quality of teaching and learning. Again tutors would be responsible for helping students to use theory as analytic tools.

In *module 5* students would return to the school-context for a final period of direct experience. They would be required to undertake a case study research assignment, but one which focussed on the interface between their own teaching and the organizational and occupational culture in the school. The module would conclude with another rigorous debrief of the experience using the research assignments again as important resources.

I am not going to succumb to the temptation of dogmatically stipulating a time period for the above scenario. As a curriculum it might be feasible in the context of a year. It would not be feasible if combined with any requirement to learn specialist subject knowledge. In this respect I would tend to agree with both the present Government and Hargreaves and argue that the possession of such knowledge should be a prerequisite of acceptance into a professional training programme. However, given the longer time-span of the BEd, it should be possible to accommodate both.

Rudduck (1991) has interestingly suggested that more time within the PGCE year could be made available for an expanded 'educational issues' curriculum if responsibility for subject methods were devolved to the schools. The problem with this suggestion is that subject methods cannot easily be divorced from the broader educational issues. In my view it should be possible to reconceptualize the subject methods aspect of initial teacher education in a form which can be accommodated within the kind of structure I have outlined. I do not see why tutors in higher education should see their methods classes as somehow divorced from the broad educational context of teachers' work. Such a divorce implies a reduction of methods to techniques. If teaching methods are simply techniques then there is no reason why they need to be taught in a professional school of education. Tutors who agree with this view of methods are putting a nail in their own coffins. If teaching is simply a technology of knowledge transmission then the best place to acquire these techniques is the place where the technology operates. There is no reason why, on a broader interpretation of 'subject methods', they cannot be reflected about, used, and evaluated throughout the modular structure I have outlined. It seems to me that the professional development process I have depicted implies a continuing focus on the problematics of 'methods' in teaching situations. The problem really is to get the majority of academics in education departments within higher education institutions to see themselves as more than subject specialists: to be able to locate their specialist knowledge in a broader context of educational concerns. And it is to this issue that I now turn in concluding this chapter. It is the issue of what the distinctive role of higher education is in relation to teacher education.

The Role of Schools of Education in Teacher Education

It is the traditional task of institutions of higher education to support and nourish reflective inquiry. The forms of inquiry which have emerged have tended in the past to become increasingly specialized and dissociated from the problems of practice as these are experienced in everyday life. Yet academics have at the same time claimed that the knowledge they generate has a higher status in terms of its capacity to represent truth than the 'knowledge' encapsulated in the practical cultures of everyday life. The implication of this claim is that practice ought to be derived from the application of the theoretical knowledge generated by academic cultures rather than the vernacular cultures of everyday life.

However, academic cultures are in a process of transformation. Their internal critiques have produced new self-understandings of the nature of reflective inquiry: the provisionality of the knowledge generated; the inability of its forms to ultimately dissociate themselves from human values, interests and concerns; the need for more interdisciplinary investigations in areas of social concern.

Low status vocational education sectors, concerned with rationalist and technological applications of high status professional knowledge, have in this context an opportunity, with a little vision, to emancipate themselves from the bottom of the academic hierarchy. Sectors concerned with the education of professionals in particular have an opportunity to redefine the role of the *professional school* in higher education. In my view it would be a mistake to define this role in terms of developing and inducting students into social technologies for delivering public services. The preferable alternative, which makes better sense of the complexities of human needs and circumstances in the contemporary world, is to redefine the role in terms of the practical science perspective.

Let me finally conclude by stating some of the implications of this perspective for the role of schools of education in higher education. Firstly, their primary teaching role should be to foster those constitutive abilities of a form of inquiry which aims to generate practical understanding as a basis for intelligent decision-making in educational situations. This role need not be confined to the development of teachers in 'schools'. A professional school of education could be concerned with the vocational educational and training practices of all professional groups, for example, the education of doctors, nurses, social workers, police officers, lawyers, managers, etc.

Secondly, the primary research role of schools of education is to collaborate with educational practitioners in reflecting about the range and variety of practical situations they encounter as educators. This would entail helping them to collect case evidence and involving them in the theoretical analysis of that evidence. It would also entail the collaborative production of case studies and cross-case comparisons that represent dialogues about, and understandings of, educational situations, problems, and issues. The primary focus of such research would be on understanding whole situations — particularly those which are experienced as difficult, problematic and novel — and drawing comparisons between them. Its main aim would be to develop and maintain the stock of professional knowledge; the case repertoire educators can draw on as a basis for wise judgments and decisions in the complex and unstructured situations they handle. Such outcomes would themselves constitute a major part of the teaching resources within schools education.

Much of this collaborative research activity however could not be divorced from the teaching role. The research would itself be a constitutive dimension of the professional development programme within the school. From a practical science perspective the academic staff would teach through their research and research through their teaching. The division of labour between research and teaching in a professional school would be dissolved, as would the division of labour between academic researchers and teachers in 'schools'.

None of this negates the value of more specialized forms of inquiry within schools of education. The comparative study of cases would identify frequently recurring practical problem areas which need to be broken down into their components for more specialized investigation before they can be better understood.

A school of education operating from a practical science perspective would give an important role to specialized investigations in the fields of educational philosophy, psychology, sociology, linguistics etc. The difference would lie in their relationship to the broad form of practical inquiry. Rather than becoming dissociated from practice in the process of knowledge production, which then later has to be connected up through a separate process of application, the specialized forms of inquiry would take the questions they addressed from the problems and issues experienced by practitioners. The latter would be invited by specialists to participate in a continuing dialogue about the 'pragmatic validity' of their emerging theories.

Finally, the academic staff of a school of education will themselves need to have developed to a high level those cognitive, interpersonal and motivational abilities which are constitutive of a capacity for situational understanding. They will need to achieve at least the level of competent in some other teaching context prior to entry. Without this degree of development they could neither satisfy the requirements of a teacher educator or of an educational researcher in a practical science orientated school of education. To develop even further as educators of educators and educational researchers they will themselves have to view their own pedagogic practices as a field for self-evaluation and reflective decision-making.

There would be a lot of merit in rotating many staff between schools of education as I have depicted them and the educational institutions they support, such as 'schools'. These rotating teacher/researchers should not be on terms of secondment or temporary contracts to one type of institution. Rather the organizational boundaries between schools of education and their associated educational institutions should be more permeable to permit shared long-term appointments. In this way the gulf between the academic culture and the professional cultures of teachers can be bridged, as it must be if a practical science paradigm of educational practice is to shape the future of teacher education. The possibility that it might is something I remain optimistic about.

It is naive to assume that government alone has the power to shape academic and practical cultures within society. Social change in democracies is usually in practice, if not in intention, a matter of negotiated compromises and trade-offs. What have educationalists in higher education got to trade off against 'the social market' model with Government? Certainly not a long discredited rationalism which Government reforms are rightly trying to destabilise. Hopefully, the image of the professional as a practical scientist may increasingly hold sway as a shared future vision of how one might improve the quality of education in our increasingly complex and rapidly changing society.

References

DREYFUS, S.E. (1981) 'Formal models vs. human situational understanding: Inherent limitations on the modelling of business expertise', mimeo, Schloss Laxenburg, Austria International Institute for Applied Systems Analysis.

ELLIOTT, J. (1991) 'A model of professionalism and its implications for teacher education', in *British Educational Research Journal*, 17, 4.

ELLIOTT, J. (1991) *Action Research for Educational Change*, Milton Keynes, Open University Press, chapters 1, 2 and 8.

KLEMP, G.O. (1977) *Three Factors of Success in the World of Work: Implications for Curriculum in Higher Education*, Boston, MA, McBer & Co.

MacDONALD, B. (1984) 'Teacher education and curriculum reform: Some English errors', mimeo, Norwich, CARE, University of East Anglia, address to Spanish Teacher Trainers, Málaga.

MUNRO, R. (1989) 'A case study of school-based innovation in secondary teacher education', unpublished PhD thesis, University of Auckland, New Zealand.

RUDDUCK, J. (1991) 'Redefining the contributions of higher education institutions and schools to the task of initial teacher education', presented to the Teacher Education Symposium at the annual meeting of the British Educational Research Association, Nottingham, August, mimeo, School of Education, University of Sheffield.

SCHON, D. (1983) *The Reflective Practitioner*, London, Temple Smith.

SCHWAB, J.J. (1970) *The Practical: A Language for Curriculum*, Washington, DC, National Education Association, Centre for the Study of Instruction.

SPENCER, L.M. (1979) *Identifying, Measuring and Training Soft Skill Competencies which predict performance in Professional, Managerial, and Human Service Jobs*, Boston, MA, McBer & Co.

STENHOUSE, L. (1975) *An Introduction to Curriculum Research and Development* London, Heinemann, chapter 10.

Chapter 7

A Common-sense Model of the Professional Development of Teachers

David H. Hargreaves

It is a pleasure to respond to John Elliott's contribution on models of coherence and continuity in teacher education, since I am firmly convinced that the creation of such a model is the single most important challenge for policy and practice in teacher education. To put, furthermore, such a model into practice would be a major contribution to the task of improving the quality of teachers. Ideally I would (i) respond in detail to Elliott's critique of my Hockerill lecture; (ii) offer a critique of Elliott's analysis of the three models; and then (iii) make some suggestions of my own about a model of professional development. Given the severe constraints of time and space, (iii) is probably more important than (i) or (ii) and so I shall condense (i) and (ii) to provide a useful background to (iii).

Part of the problem with Elliott's three models and their differing philosophical foundations is that two of them are somewhat distorted caricatures, whilst the third (that espoused by Elliott himself, of course) is described in richer terms and then advocated with evident enthusiasm. The first model I shall neglect, since few adhere to this rationalist position in pure form. The second model needs examination, since Elliott assigns me and writers on the New Right to this camp. Elsewhere I have drawn attention to important differences between my position and that of the New Right, (Hargreaves, 1990, pp. 5–11), so will not reiterate that point. Elliott's general account of the Hockerill lecture is fair. It accurately records my assumption that certain international trends are affecting the structure of the profession and professional development and are in many countries, under governments of both the left and the right, providing a new common-sense or taken for granted context in which revised models of the profession and its development will emerge. He does not, however, directly attack the ideas or proposals. Instead, he infers a set of assumptions, ones presumably deeper than my explicit contextual framework, which allegedly underpin my model. He seeks to show that the assumptions he infers are close to the principle that he claims underlies the social market model, that of behaviourism. (He does this against the known fact that my work is in the field of symbolic interactionism and phenomenology, the arch-enemies of behaviourism!) If readers can be persuaded to reject the principle of behaviourism, then by Elliott's argument they must also reject the social market model in general and the proposals of my Hockerill lecture in particular.

Central to Elliott's critique, then, are his inferences about the assumptions underlying my proposals. If this inferential work can be shown to be faulty, then his argument collapses. It would be tedious, I think, to analyze all the assumptions Elliott infers from my proposals, so let me take a small selection of them and comment briefly to indicate the type of distortion involved. This is not to defend my proposals; far more important, is to show that they and their underlying philosophy are far more compatible with Elliott's third model, that of practical science, than he seems to (want to) allow. By distorting the assumptions underlying the proposals, and by describing them in a language and style which renders them unattractive, he makes it harder for any reader to recognize, at both the intellectual and affective levels, commonalities between our two approaches to professional development. It is always worth noting differences between models and approaches, but I see little purpose in exaggerating such differences to the point where it masks what different models share, actually or potentially. Yet these are the growth points by which better models of professional development can be created.

Three examples of Elliott's inferred assumptions:

(i) The school is the basic unit of production within the educational system

I am not at all sure what Elliott means by the notion of 'basic unit of production' but it, like much of the language of his imputed assumptions, has an aura of the industrial and commercial, the instrumental and utilitarian. My actual assumption, however, is simply that there is a trend for the school system, both in the United Kingdom and elsewhere, to become more **school-centred**, as schools assume financial and other responsibilities with a sharp weakening in the powers of local education authorities (or middle tiers of governance), and as initial and in-service training become more school-based.

(ii) The identification of professional training needs should be based on planning to improve the school as an efficient and effective production unit

I shall ignore the emotive description of the school as a 'production unit', but challenge Elliott's remarkable inference that the professional training needs of the individual teacher are now to be subservient to making the school more efficient and effective. My argument, by contrast, was that in an era when schools construct institutional development plans and adopt systems of staff appraisal, institutional and personal action plans will become inextricably linked in a way that contributes both to the school as a whole and to the individual teacher. My argument is about increasing teachers' rights to professional development and an improvement in policy and planning for professional development.

(iii) Standards of professional learning are best described as skills (competencies) which enhance the production functions of schools

Note once again the highly emotive use of 'production functions' to describe the activities of schools. I do mention the 'basic competence' of a teacher and very much in a common-sense way of referring to the new teacher's capacity to be left in charge of a class without supervision. I do not discuss 'competencies' or how 'standards of professional learning' are best described. I do say, on this matter, that 'there is no adequate agreement about the knowledge, skills and understanding that a teacher ... should have'. Like most who work in the field of professional development, I have an ambivalent attitude towards the term 'competence'. It is indeed an appropriate term in any sphere where training leads to a licence to practise (for example, medicine), and, like most parents, believe the incompetent should be excluded from practice as much in education as in medicine. But professional learning I always think of as a complex amalgam of — to use my words from the Hockerill lecture — 'knowledge, skill and understanding'.

Why should Elliott be so keen to attribute to me a belief that 'competencies' to enhance the 'production functions' of schools are the 'best' way of describing 'standards of professional learning'? It allows him, of course, to locate my proposals within the principle of behaviourism which underpins his social market model. Only by distorting inferences about my assumptions can Elliott make my work fit into this behaviouristic approach to 'competencies' and its concern, in his terms, with 'the pre-specification and standardization of job-functional skills' and 'behavioural outputs'.

That the assumptions Elliott attributes to me are neither mine nor ones inherent in my ideas can perhaps be made more persuasively through my own analysis of how one might approach a developmental model of professional development in a way that emphasizes coherence and continuity. Elliott fully acknowledges that we are both wholly committed to the value of such a model; I now show that our approaches to this task are similar and complementary.

There is an old saw that twenty years' experience as a teacher may be nothing more than one year's experience repeated twenty times. For most teachers, however, professional development is a much more complicated trajectory of aspiration and achievement. Undoubtedly one useful way of describing this trajectory is as a movement from novice to expert. This process of teacher education and informal professional socialization (in both training institutions and schools) is describable as a mixture of concerns with *competence*, defined as the knowledge, skills and understanding to manage classrooms and promote student learning successfully, combined with *values* which shape the assumptions and principles that influence how knowledge and skill are transformed into wise and intelligent action.

Models of professional development for teachers are of two kinds: first, a *descriptive* model which reports, on the basis of empirical findings, the forms and processes of professional development as they in fact occur; and secondly a *prescriptive* model which states how professional development ought to be. The two are closely related since a prescriptive model implies changes to the descriptive model and a descriptive model provides some of the constraints on the practicality of the prescriptive model. Those concerned with the initial training of teachers (ITT) have often seen themselves counteracting natural processes of professional socialization, insulating new teachers from bad professional practice and inducting them into better values and practices. Current developments towards school-based models of ITT threaten this approach, since it is practising teachers who are now to play the major role. But school-based ITT potentially generates new models, both descriptive and prescriptive, since the way is opened to a more explicit definition of professional development at the three interconnected stages of ITT, induction and continuing professional development (see Alexander, Rose and Woodhead (1992) especially chapter ix).

In ITT there is a profound concern to give trainees an appropriate set of values as well the knowledge, skill and understanding (competence) for successful classroom practice. It is the combination which is essential to the creation of the 'reflective practitioner'. Trainees, however, are often impatient with the values component of their ITT, especially where these are transmitted through 'theory' or the study of educational foundations. Trainees have a predominant concern: to learn (at least) how to survive in a real classroom and (at best) to manage a classroom successfully. At this stage in their professional development they often find it hard to understand how values aid this process. This is in part why for so many trainees the teaching practice is seen as the most relevant and useful part of their ITT.

Teachers, I believe, have two dominant concerns, which I shall treat as *sectors* that are part of every teacher's professional knowledge and professional development. The first sector concerns their performance as a teacher, and the second that of the performance of pupils. Each sector contains several analytically distinct *segments*. These are:

Teacher performance sector (with five segments)

(i)   Class management: the teacher's authority, and ability to control and organize the classroom.
(ii) Pedagogy: the content and methods of a lesson, involving selection, presentation, sequence and pace.
(iii) Continuity and coherence: the link between lessons to make up a course or scheme of work; links between subjects; links between year groups.
(iv) School structures and cultures: the structure of the whole curriculum and how it is allocated between groups; staff cultures and styles of working.
(v)   The school in the context of the education system: the different types of school and their interrelationships and relations with other aspects of the education system as a whole.

Pupil performance sector (with five segments)

(i)   Pupil behaviour and conformity: acceptance of teacher authority and manageability.
(ii) Pupils' abilities and motivation: their differentiation along these dimensions.
(iii) Pupil progression: the form and extent of pupil learning and achievement.
(iv) The social context of pupils: their family background, race, gender and social class; family and community environment; pupil cultures.
(v)   The wider social, economic and political environment: the ways in which pupils are shaped by these.

These two sectors might be seen as plates, each consisting of concentric circles of the segments, lying on top of one another. Segments (i) are at the centre of each plate and segments (v) at the outer rim. Each segment is closely linked with the segment of the same number in the other sector. For example, the first segment in the teacher performance sector (class management) is closely related to the first segment (behaviour and conformity) in the pupil performance sector. The trainee has variable knowledge of both sectors and their segments, according to their previous experience and interests. Through ITT, the trainee acquires an *intellectual* grasp of their content and relationships. The trainee's experienced problem, however, is a *practical* one, of what will actually work, as opposed to what is desirable, in classrooms. The knowledge in greatest demand by the trainee is that needed to get by. Moreover, the trainee quickly grasps that in classrooms the teacher makes many decisions and does so quickly, with little time for deliberation in most cases. Even where the trainee has considerable knowledge of the sectors, there is a lack of both time and skill to deploy the knowledge in practice. The most relevant and deployable knowledge, skill and understanding are those in the first and second segments which lie at the centre of the concentric circles that make up each sector. The trainee has a reduced interest in the outer segments except insofar as they help speedy and more effective decision-making for problems arising in relation to the first two segments.

Much trainee talk with supervisors and mentors at this stage consists of questions in the form 'What do I do when . . .' whereby a general or context-independent solution is sought on the basis of a specific and situation-dependent problem. This is often decried by teacher trainers (who find it difficult to supply a context-independent answer, as shown by replies which begin 'Well, it depends on . . .') as merely 'tips for teachers' when the trainee is desperately searching for those *recipes* that the experienced teachers appear to employ quickly and effectively through their tacit understanding of situations.

It is a mistake to take too lofty a view of recipe knowledge, not least since the work of Schutz has shown that it is in the nature of common-sense knowledge (CSK, for short) that it consists of recipes, that is, 'typical means for bringing about typical ends in typical situations' (Schutz, 1963). Indeed, the stock of knowledge that allows us to negotiate our everyday lives consists of a vast number of such recipes. Early childhood learning is in part the acquisition of such recipes. And so, I suggest, professional development and socialization consist of what I want to call *professional common-sense knowledge* (PCSK for short) and its recipes. It is through PCSK that a teacher is able in educational settings to typify ends, means, situations, people, motives and construct solutions to problems. For PCSK contains recipes which allow the teacher to construct both 'a scheme of interpretation' to understand events-within-situations and a 'precept for action' (Schutz, 1971) with which to respond. For Schutz, the acquisition of (P)CSK is essential to becoming a competent member of any social group, that is, someone who does not find the social group's ways of working troublesome. Once acquired, CSK tends to be treated as unquestioned and unquestionable.

Put in these terms, the trainee teacher is trying to acquire PCSK to become, and be accepted as, a competent member of the teacher social group, whilst the teacher trainer is worried that the trainee will pick up an undesirable PCSK and will then indeed treat it as unquestioned and unquestionable. ITT has a tension at its heart: it has to help the trainee to acquire PCSK but a particular kind of approved PCSK and one that is potentially open to questioning and revision. Recipe knowledge is difficult to teach and is most easily picked up through imitation and practice, which helps to explain the popularity of teaching practice, where there is extensive trial and error learning.

I suggest that it is after trainee teachers have acquired the PCSK in the first two segments of both sectors that they achieve a level of professional confidence which makes them more ready to progress to the remaining three segments (and no doubt to other sectors not described here) as part of their professional growth.

The tragedy of some traditional ITT is that these outer three segments are taught, in the form of theory or educational studies, *before* the PCSK of the first two segments has been acquired.

I conclude with some questions and suggestions.

(i) Is there not a considerable amount of common ground between the ideas I have propounded, briefly and in outline form, and Elliott's account of the 'practical science' model, his emphasis on situational understandings and his use of the Dreyfus stage model?

(ii) Are not both my ideas and Elliott's clearly opposed to any crude model of professional practice as consisting of nothing more than being able to display mastery of a list of behavioural competences?

(iii) Is it not possible that trainers (as experts usually) are deeply concerned with values rather than just competence and seek to induct trainees into values (including ethical issues) at too early a stage, before the trainee has acquired basic competence in the Schutzian sense, whereas the trainee (as novice) is searching for, and needs to acquire, basic PCSK before being ready to interrogate and refine values to question this PCSK? Is Elliott right to insist upon observational research assignments and discursive analysis for the new trainee with only very gradual immersion into direct experience? Would it be better to let many trainees acquire their basic PCSK, under known good teachers as supportive mentors, before expecting them to research, discuss and deliberate in a highly sophisticated way? Would not this allow trainees to build the confidence to progress to the outer segments, where reflection and research are more likely to pay dividends since they are no longer in competition with the trainees' deep urge to acquire basic competence in the Schutzian sense?

(iv) Elliott speaks of two levels of problems for teachers, the simple, objectively defined (such as how to place orders for text-books) and unstructured situations for which intelligent responses cannot be predefined. There is perhaps a category which falls between these, namely the recipe knowledge of PCSK which can adequately handle many somewhat unstructured situations but which is sometimes tested to its limits or is challenged by emergent values and so requires reflection for a highly intelligent response to be made.

(v) Is it not in the nature of professional development that the transition from one segment to another requires a *revision* of the PCSK in earlier segments in the light of the new segment? Is it not precisely such reframing of PCSK through deliberation that is the mark of the reflective practitioner? Is progression in professional development not so much a simple sequence of stages from novice through to expert, but rather a more complicated process by which there is progression *within* as well as *between* segments? That is, even within the first segments of the two sectors, the trainee starts as a novice, makes progress towards the advanced beginner or competent stages, and then enters further segments but at the novice stage *for that segment.* True expertise within the first segments arises only when the teacher (now well beyond the trainee stage) is at least in the competent or proficient stages of the final segments.

It is precisely such a model that can take account of Elliott's important point that progression requires elements of unlearning and relearning.

(vi) Elliott's model is strong in prescribing the *processes* for professional development, but these apparently are apposite at all stages irrespective of *content*. It is astonishing that Elliott should side-step the issue of content, which has been a focus of debate for over ten years. He provides *continuity* through process, but is far too vague on *progression*, which demands attention to content. My model, if the notion of sectors and segments has a firm empirical base, offers a way forward on progression by content. A coherent model of professional development embraces both continuity and progression and matches process to content. Elliott's practical science model falls short of this ideal.

References

ALEXANDER, R., ROSE, J. and WOODHEAD, C. (1992) *Curriculum Organisation and Classroom Practice in Primary Schools: A Discussion Paper*, Department of Education and Science, London.

HARGREAVES, D.H. (1990) 'Another radical approach to the reform of initial teacher training', Westminster Studies in Education, 13, pp. 5–11.

SCHUTZ, A. (1963) 'Common-sense and scientific interpretation of human action' in NATANSON, M. (Ed.) *Philosophy of the Social Sciences: A Reader*, New York, Random House.

SCHUTZ, A. (1971) 'The stranger: an essay in social psychology' in COSIN, B.R. *et al.* (Eds) *School and Society*, London, Routledge and Kegan Paul.

Part 2

School-based Teacher Education:
Four Studies of Innovation

Chapter 8

A Case Study of School-based Training Systems in New Zealand Secondary Schools

R.G. Munro

Introduction

Concern about the nature of teaching practice in secondary teacher training and the relationship between institutional and school contributions to that training have been recurring themes in the recent New Zealand literature of training. In 1979 the Department of Education's Review of Teacher Training sought 'To encourage cooperation between all parties involved' in a search for closer 'coordination between colleges and schools'. As a result, in 1981, several school-based training innovations were established at the Secondary Teachers College, Auckland, and two, a mathematics/science programme (two terms in a school) and a history/ social studies programme (weekly practice in schools), became the subjects of this present study in 1982.

The focus of the study was on identifying those influences which most affected the dispositions and behaviour of the trainees during the period of training. The methodology was primarily that of ethnography and owed much to the tradition of descriptive case-study at the Centre for Applied Research in Education (CARE) (Stenhouse, 1975 and 1980) at the University of East Anglia.

In the early sections of the study, an outline of the history and training methods of northern hemisphere and New Zealand teacher training provided a background to the national and institutional context in which the programmes operated. Three trainees in each of the programmes were case-studied in depth and followed up in the schools some four years after completing training. On the basis of the evidence in their case-reports, dominant influences were identified and inferences drawn about the manner in which each influence contributed to the outcomes of training. Finally, the functioning of each of the two programmes as training systems was estimated and compared with that of systems in the northern hemisphere. The conclusions summarized in this chapter suggest some caution in embarking on extensive school-based teacher training.

The Structure of Training

In relation to the main research question of the study:

> Of the range of influences on trainees, what most influences their dispositions and behaviour during the period of training?

Those influences which emerge as most potent in the analyses are rarely given appropriate emphasis, either in reports and reviews of training or in training institutions themselves. In particular, the influence of personal biography, preoccupation with control and instrumental skill, and those influences which have arisen as a result of the **existing structure** of secondary training — trainees' and associates' perceptions of status differences between college and school (c.f., Taylor, 1987, p. 117); confusion about the nature of 'theory' and its relation to practice; and the fragmentation of in-college inputs — have often been neglected. The traditional curriculum of secondary teacher training would seem to have ensured that trainers widely accept the existing structure within university, college and school and, to a large extent, assume its dominant influence in the 'making' of secondary teachers. Further, there is general acceptance that the present divisions in training — subject studies in the universities, subject methodologies and education in the colleges, and teaching practice in the schools, are appropriate. This structure, first endorsed in the USA in 1960, became known as the McNair/Institute Curriculum in the UK by the late 1960s, and in New Zealand was incorporated into the Campbell Report as early as 1951. The New Zealand *Review of Teacher Training* in 1979 confirmed this structure when citing, as a basis for its own critique of training, the OECD (1974) training goals which preserved the divisions between the 'academic' studies, 'methodology', 'professional studies' (education), and 'practice' components of training (pp. 23–4).

Although in all such statements of intent there are suggestions for partnership between training institutions and schools and for the integration and articulation of theory and practice, it appears to be generally assumed that the separation of the component parts of training is appropriate and that their individual and combined relevance is assured. The following discussion of the influences identified in this study offers some commentary on this assumption.

The Influences at Work in the School-based Programmes

Personal biography, until recently a relatively neglected independent variable in research into training, has been shown in this study to provide useful evidence with which to explain aspects of trainees' disposition and classroom behaviour. Much of the case-report evidence suggests that trainees' intentions, teaching styles and their response to issues in schooling are strongly influenced by what they bring with them into training. To ignore this influence, is to ignore the fact that by the time secondary trainees enter training they have experienced a minimum of sixteen years of primary, secondary and tertiary schooling. As a consequence they have extensive knowledge about the work of teachers and, in particular, about the ways in which teachers, in their own past, have gone about establishing relationships with them in classrooms. Trainees' comments on associates and tutors are therefore informed by their past experiences and possess an authority which derives from their long apprenticeship as observers and recipients of schooling (Lortie, 1975).

Nonetheless, what is typically absent from this biography is experience of what it is to actually fulfil the role of a teacher, and what it is like to be responsible for the behaviour of thirty or more adolescents. However, notwithstanding trainees' unfamiliarity with the teaching role itself, their ability to readily (and sometimes graphically) anticipate the detailed consequences of failure is an insight which is possibly unique to teacher trainees as beginners in a profession. It is perhaps predictable, therefore, that a significant outcome of trainees' socialization in the classroom should be a *preoccupation with control* which has been identified in this study.

This powerful socializing influence, which can overwhelm the trainees' capacity to reflect rationally on their classroom experiences, was clearly evidenced in the case-reports. However the findings also suggest that, despite trainees' inevitable preoccupation with control, the college inputs on the issue are often ineffective in overcoming this source of stress in trainees. The issue of control is touched on in all training courses, but it is not central and few systematic attempts appear to be made to identify the teacher's sources of power in the classroom or to suggest ways of exercising them. There is a sense, suggested by some evidence, that teachers and trainers may tend to rationalize their own control dilemmas (or remembrances of them) and avoid discussion about control for fear they might themselves be thought to be inadequate in the classroom or, alternatively, in the hope that it will be assumed that they have no difficulties when managing classes. Within teaching and training, discussion about control could well be an example of what Van Maanen (1979b), has called a 'taboo-violating activity' and, as such, something to be avoided.

Although the influence of personal biography appeared to have a significant impact on the behaviour of all trainees, socialization in the programmes through *the impact of the college inputs*, together with that of attempts to make these inputs relevant to trainees in the schools, affected trainees more unevenly. In turn, such impacts appeared to have varying effects on the intensity of trainees' preoccupation with control and the extent to which this preoccupation persisted during the year. Of the two programmes, that in *mathematics/science* appeared least able to provide trainees with a ready capacity to analyze or cope with the effects of pupil-disruption or with the skills to deal with organizational routines. In contrast, the relative effectiveness of the *history/social studies* programme seemed to arise through the trainees' acceptance of skill- and resource-based routines which appeared to lessen the likelihood of pupil-disruption and, as a consequence, diminished the intensity of their preoccupation with control.

In the *history/social studies* programme, the effectiveness of the tutor's routines appeared to be reinforced by a *partnership between the tutor and the associates* and by the consequent endorsement by associates of the arrangements adopted during the periods of weekly teaching practice. For the *mathematics/science* programme, the absence of a close partnership between the tutor and the associates resulted in an apparent lack of useful college inputs during the long period in the schools. Because of this, trainees tended to model their teaching on that of their associates and on remembrances of their own schooling.

There was evidence too, that the tutor/associate partnership in the *history/social studies* programme did tend to encourage the trainees to attach greater credibility to other college inputs. For example, although both groups of trainees appeared to reject much of what they thought of as 'theory' in education, criticism by the *history/social studies* trainees was more muted. Thus, as a result of the influence of coherent and effective inputs in both college and school, and in a context of partnership between tutor and associates, the *history/social studies* programme appeared to overcome, at least in part, the college/school 'institutional rack' identified by Lacey and Lamont (1975).

The relative absence of *reflective action* among the trainees, however, appeared to be less a function of structural deficiencies in training than to simple neglect. Examples of such action were noted, but there was little evidence that these were reinforced by either the tutors or the associates in the programmes. Indeed, most trainer inputs appeared limited to the application of known techniques to given ends. As a result, this study concluded that what reflective action was noted was unlikely to be a function of supportive training inputs but of personal biography. A recent New Zealand study of primary teacher training (Ramsay and Battersby, 1988, p. 20) in calling for trainees to '. . . be encouraged to become self-reflective and self-analytical about their teaching performance', does appear to accept the need for greater support for trainees in attempting such action. By recommending a 'mentorial team' of tutors, teachers and curriculum specialists to design individualized programmes in collaboration with the trainees, it appears, not only to take into account variations in what trainees bring to training (biography), but also the need for collaborative support from trainers. However, the study does not acknowledge the possible extent of 'unlearning' required of both trainees and trainers (Zeichner and Liston, 1987, p. 42) and also fails to note the impediment to reflective action of the trainees' likely preoccupation with the rigours of initial survival in the classroom.

Despite differences in the response of the two groups of trainees to college inputs, they shared common ground in their perceptions of the influence of *status differences between college and school* and in their perceptions of their own status in the two venues: During training, all except one trainee appeared to regard the status and credibility of schools as greater than that of the college and, by the time of the follow-up interviews, the dissenting trainee, too, had joined that consensus. In making this case, trainees appeared to approve their work in the schools as 'practical' and 'real' and to denigrate that in the college as 'theoretical' and remote from reality. In this, the trainees' position was consistent with that observed in other systems. As well, and despite some doubts about the way some associates treated them, trainees perceived that in the schools they were accepted as mature adults who were very nearly 'real teachers', whereas at times in the college they felt demeaned by a tendency to treat them as 'pupils' who still had *everything* to learn about teaching. This sense of status loss in the college was accentuated by the often fierce desire of all but one of the trainees (during training) to see themselves as self-socialized and thus fully 'owning' all aspects of their own development as teachers.

The acceptance of their status in the schools, however, appeared to inhibit trainees' efforts to take a reflective view of teaching. Three trainees, in particular, displayed some propensity for reflective action but appeared reluctant to commit themselves fully to it. They were aware that to act in a reflective manner was often inconsistent with what was regarded as professionally acceptable in the schools and that to persist could lead to some diminution of status in the eyes of their associates. The extent to which both teachers and trainees may be subject to pervasive imperatives which limit their independence and could ultimately determine their goals and behaviour, is a matter which suggests alternative influences beyond those identified in this study.

Despite attention to the influence of personal biography on aspects of trainees' behaviour, the other influences identified in this study have been very much 'within-training' phenomena and no attempt has been made to relate them to the external social and political forces which are claimed by Giroux (1983) and Popkewitz (1987) to affect teaching and teacher training. Giroux (1983) in seeing schools as influenced by a 'hidden curriculum' which results in '. . . classroom relations that embody specific messages which legitimize . . . particular views of work, authority (and) social rules' (p. 263) suggests another way of viewing the kinds of pre-occupations experienced by trainees in this study. Specifically, in arguing that '. . . classroom relations are influenced by: . . . forms of social organization (hierarchical or democratic); and forms of personal interaction (interaction based on individual competitiveness or interaction based on collective sharing)', Giroux identifies choices which were encountered by trainees in this study.

All except one of the trainees commented extensively on their difficulties in reconciling hierarchical and democratic procedures in the classroom and, by the time of their follow-up interviews these trainees indicated, in varying degrees, that they had tended to accept an hierarchical emphasis in their relationships with pupils in the interests of survival. As well, again with the exception of one trainee, all sought opportunities for 'collective sharing' with their pupils while admitting to difficulties in attaining this goal in a context that was, in general, antithetic to it. However, the extent to which trainees' behaviour here can be seen in Giroux's terms as 'oppositional' and therefore constituting 'resistance' to accepted practice, is minimal (*ibid*). Although trainees' attempts at democratic management and 'collective sharing' were genuine, at no time did they appear to consciously promote such action as a general alternative to the 'typical' expository secondary lesson.

Thus, in positing that 'dominant school ideologies' emphasize hierarchy and individual competitiveness, Giroux provides an alternative basis for interpreting trainees' preoccupations with control and instrumental skill and their relative absence of reflectivity. However, the impact of such '. . . issues of power and social determination' (*ibid*, p. 291) on schooling and teacher training were not adequately addressed in the study. Neither the data sources nor the methodology allowed for the kind of in-depth sociopolitical information that would be necessary.

Nonetheless, in exploring the influences on trainees it has become clear that the impact of the larger social and political context could well provide for more cogent explanations of trainees' actions than those that have been given. In seeking explanations of trainees' dispositions and behaviour in their personal biographies and in their socialization in the programmes, the study has been able to suggest *immediate* influences and the context in which they operate. The extent to which these influences are a function of forces acting in a wider context can only be a matter of tentative extrapolation.

The Programmes in Relation to Established Systems

The findings of the study provide a basis for commentary upon other teacher training initiatives. Three systems of training were surveyed — competency-based teacher education, theory/practice models and apprenticeship forms of training. The latter, while not widely practised at the time of the study, were nevertheless represented, to an extent, in the teaching practice requirements of all systems.

Competency-Based Teacher Education (CBTE)

The study's findings on the *history/social studies* programme provided some comment on *CBTE*. Although the programme was never characterized by its author as derivative from overseas competency-based models, there were nevertheless features which matched those adopted by such systems in the USA in the 1970s and briefly experimented with in New Zealand. In particular, the programme was organized in terms of discrete stated skills and resources, trainees were held accountable for their performance by being assessed against performance criteria and, to an extent, pupils' work was used to estimate the trainees' effectiveness as teachers.

The findings suggest that where such a programme is organized in terms of specific skills and resources, it does provide trainees with routines around which to organize and present their lessons. Further, that where the sequencing of the skill- and resource-components becomes a matter of habit (and despite the trainees' objections both during and after training), they appeared to offer a security to the trainees and, thus, a way to avoid some of the stress over control experienced by the *mathematics/science* trainees.

There is little sense in which the *history/social studies* programme can be regarded as a full developed 'system' in the manner in which Houston and Howsam (1972) conceived of a comprehensive *CBTE* training package. But, at a more pedestrian level, it did appear to satisfy the trainees' need for a mechanism which could ensure their routine effectiveness in most classes. At the same time, it was also clear that while responding to the tutor's 'insistence' on carrying through the details of the programme, there was, in practice, little opportunity for trainees to attempt anything other than the forms of expository teaching required of them.

The Theory/Practice Model

Because in both programmes in-college 'theory' was expected to be applied in the field, both conformed, at least in part, to the theory/practice model of training. However, whereas in the *mathematics/science* programme such in-college 'theory' was derived solely from the professional education course taken by the tutor (most methodological inputs being the responsibility of the associates during the extended practice), the *history/social studies* trainees experienced two quite separate inputs, one from their education course and another from their tutor.

In the *mathematics/science* programme, although 'given' propositional knowledge and self-constructed theory were suggested as inputs in the original proposal, in the event, the theoretical constructs dealt with were implied rather than explicit and there was no evidence that the notions were consciously applied in practice. In the *history/social studies* programme the education inputs, although endorsed more positively than by the *mathematics/science* trainees, nevertheless also appeared to have little impact on them. In contrast, the tutor's inputs, rather than being seen as 'theory', were generally interpreted as 'practical' selections from a repertoire of conventional and self-evident skills. In terms of the *CBTE* goal of integrating theory and practice which was espoused by the tutor, this last trainee-perception would suggest that for the *history/social studies* trainees the tutor's programme had realized this goal through the trainees accepting a match between in-college inputs and experience in the schools.

For all trainees, however, there was an overriding tendency to uncritically categorize and reject many in-college inputs as 'theoretical'. At the same time, there were few indicators that trainees had any clear idea of what they meant by the term. Indeed, in relation to the different forms of educational theory, there was little evidence that trainees had noted or explored at any depth any aspects of theory, 'given' or otherwise. As a consequence, and in relation to what has already been noted of trainees' sense of status difference between college and school, Taylor's (1978) comment that the theory/practice issue in training '. . . turns into one of institutional relationships, or alleged status differences that separate those who teach from those who teach about teaching' appears to be illustrated in the context of this study.

Thus, like teachers, trainees do not appear to claim to 'own' theories and their theories-in-use can only be deduced from their practice. (Munro, 1981). Denis Lawton (1973) in the introduction to his book *Social Change, Educational Theory and Curriculum Planning*, in acknowledging this situation calls for a shift in the position taken by teachers:

> . . . all teachers are involved in decisions of a theoretical nature: if they decide to teach mathematics but to forbid playing cards in class, they are basing their decision on some kind of theory of what is worthwhile; if they decide a book is too difficult for a certain class or pupil, they are making use of psychological theories about intelligence, or ability, or stages of development. This book is an appeal for teachers to become more aware of the theoretical substructure of their own practical teaching activities and to be more systematic in its use. (pp. 7–8)

In relation to the findings of this study, the extent to which such an appeal is likely to be heeded will depend more on the credibility of those making it than on the intrinsic merits of the appeal itself. If such an appeal were to be made by teachers themselves, or by a close partnership of tutors and associates such as suggested for the 'mentorial teams' proposed by Ramsay and Battersby, the chances of some response could be enhanced. In the meantime, it would appear that the issue at the heart of the theory/practice model, that of articulating and integrating theory and practice, remains unresolved.

The call for the articulation and integration of theory and practice in training may, however, in itself be an inappropriate goal. Popper (1963) would suggest that it is much more important to *test* theory than to accept it as a given and attempt to integrate it with practice. Of the many approaches to theory in training, the processes associated with the notion of the 'teacher as researcher' come closest to satisfying Popper's position. In this present study, however, there was little evidence that such processes were either promoted by the tutors or noted by the trainees.

Forms of Apprenticeship

Whenever trainees are on teaching practice there is always the possibility that in modelling their teaching on that of their associates they will conform to an apprenticeship mode of training. In the *mathematics/science* programme there was strong evidence that this did in fact occur. The three trainees appeared strongly influenced by associates during their extended practice and admitted, in varying degrees, that they tried to imitate the techniques which were modelled. In contrast, in the *history/social studies* programme, it would appear that on weekly teaching practice the influence of the associates was qualified by the agreement with the tutor to proceed with his skill- and resource-based routines. Indeed, so effective was the programme in ensuring that trainees met its requirements, that even where they were under the direct influence of associates in their normal block teaching practices they tended to structure most lessons in terms of the tutor's requirements. Thus, because of the power of the tutor's technology, the extent to which these trainees became apprenticed to associate teachers was minimal. This finding is consistent with the claim that where an institution exercises control over the kinds of experiences trainees have in schools, it can more effectively counter the criticism that a school-based component is a form of apprenticeship (Hirst, 1980). At the same time, it must be admitted that the carefully structured experiences of the *history/social studies* trainees at the college could themselves be regarded as a form of *institutional apprenticeship*.

Nonetheless, only the *mathematics/science* programme provided unequivocal evidence of the effects of *school-based apprenticeship* on trainees. Because of the extended nature of the practice and the infrequent visits of the tutor and other college personnel, (in contrast to the history-tutor's visits to *all* weekly teaching practices), these trainees appeared to become dependent on their associates for much of their training. As a result, two of the trainees in the programme identified closely with the schools and, in the end, saw themselves already as 'real' teachers and expressed impatience with the strictures laid upon them by the college. The third trainee perceived a lack of associate support and, through a sense of failure, felt 'let down' by the experience. Thus, apprenticeship experience in schools for these trainees appeared to have an uneven impact. But irrespective of whether this was for better or for worse, the associates' influence was undoubted.

Future Trends in Secondary Teacher Training

The moves to introduce a new school-based emphasis in training in the United Kingdom have been associated with the recent review by the *Council for the Accreditation of Teacher Education (CATE)* of all institutions offering training. An announcement by the British Government at the time this review was nearing completion noted that 'A proposal to make new teachers serve a form of apprenticeship in schools . . . is regarded as vital for the Government's sweeping education reforms' (Castle, 1988, p. 5). In outlining the new provision Castle notes that:

> Instead of graduate entrants going to college or university education departments, ministers want them to be based in schools, thereby gaining a solid grounding in classroom techniques. Approved universities or colleges would give theoretical instruction on a block release basis. (*ibid*)

Later in the article Castle details the Government's reasons for the move (eventually drafted into legislation (Graham, 1989, p. 1)):

> Ministers clearly aim to switch the emphasis away from academic study of subjects such as child development, multicultural education and special needs, towards experience at the 'blackboard and chalk face'. They believe that 1960s educational theory has lived on in many teacher-training colleges and is given prominence over academic excellence. (Castle, 1988, p. 5)

Thus, in England and Wales, a return to student-teacher apprenticeships after a century of institutional training is apparently justified in terms of the irrelevance of '1960s educational theory'. Without rehearsing here the possible economic reasons for such a move, it is important to this study to assess the significance of the stated reasons which call into question the relevance of theory taught in universities and training institutions. It is also important to attempt to explain the reported public *and* teacher disaffection with existing training which has apparently encouraged the British Government to propose the present reforms.

The evidence of this study does point to considerable ambivalence abut the applicability of *something* which commentators have chosen to call *theory*. Neither in the literature of training nor in reports on its condition, has the nature or scope of such 'theory' been clearly and unequivocally defined. Most often definition is avoided, but where it is attempted it can vary from such aphorisms as 'Theory is good practice made conscious' to the tenets of particular schools of thought such as behavior-analysis (Glynn, 1975), to extensive listings of principles derived from all social sciences (Alexander, 1984). In the past two decades the emergence of 'propositional', 'self-constructed' and 'applied' theories, for example, did little to clarify the issue of what 'theory' is appropriate to what purpose in training. It is not surprising, therefore, that whenever educational 'theory' is cited in regard to training it is not only vulnerable to the ignorant and malicious, but also to those who recognize that it has yet to attain the disciplined authority of having a tested and agreed structure of explanatory concepts.

The publication of the findings of the 1984 *DES* research project on school-based training — *Initial Teacher Training and the Role of the School* (Furlong *et al.*, 1988) — has added to an already extensive list of attempts to resolve the theory/practice issue in training. Under the title 'The Enigma of Theory v Practice', Tomlinson (1989) summarized the findings and noted that the research team distinguishes the following '. . . four levels or forms of teacher training'.

- Level 1 — direct practice: in the classroom;
- Level 2 — indirect practice: practical training in classes and workshops within the training institution;
- Level 3 — practical principles: critical study of the principles of practice and their use;
- Level 4 — disciplinary theory: critical study of practice in the light of theory and research. (p. 236)

The schedule avoids the orthodox training labels, but nevertheless appears to preserve the familar components of: — teaching practice, methodology and education — while adding an extra component of 'indirect practice'. With an increased school-based emphasis in the proposed model, it is argued '. . . that professional practice is best understood and developed through "reflection-in-action" rather than as "application of theory"' (ibid). Although associate teachers are given full responsibility for Level 1 training, institutional trainers retain control of the other three levels with the proviso that, at Level 3, they '. . . must work with students in school'.

However, the recommendations that are most pertinent to this study address the issues of reflective action and mediation of theory. On reflective action (referred to as 'critical reflection'), the report emphasizes the role of teachers:

> . . . to develop a critical approach in students, they need to be introduced to analysis of the professional practice of the teachers they work with in school. This means that the teachers themselves need to be able to undertake and share such critical reflection. (as quoted by Tomlinson, 1989, p. 237)

In order to fulfil this latter goal, the report calls for '. . . considerable in-service training' for teachers before they attempt this role and '. . . extra resources to provide the extra time required for training student teachers' (ibid, p. 236). Such training, resources and time could provide the knowledge and the incentive for teachers to enter into the promotion of 'critical reflection' in themselves and their student-teachers, but the evidence of this present study would suggest that this process will be neither easy nor certain of achievement.

On 'disciplinary theory' in Level 4, the report appears to anticipate the doubters and to ask them to accept its value as an act of faith:

> Level four work can, generally, only be undertaken by trainers. It is essential. If decision-makers ignore these truths and try to get school-based training on the cheap, a great opportunity to improve professional practice in both schools and training institutions will have been missed. (as quoted by Tomlinson, 1989, p. 237)

'Disciplinary theory' is seen here as not only 'essential' but also as consisting of 'truths' which will 'improve professional practice'. This spirited defense of the contribution to training of the educational disciplines, together with the recommendations suggesting an increased collaboration between training institutions and schools, appears to have been substantially ignored by the 'decision-makers'. Nonetheless, the fact that in future the Government will ensure that 'theoretical instruction' will be given to trainees at approved universities and colleges on 'block release' from a two-year apprenticeship in schools (Castle, 1988, p. 5), suggests that, despite its strong reservations about the usefulness of certain kinds of theory, it is still prepared to endorse such instruction.

Notwithstanding these moves to forms of apprenticeship in England and Wales, there remain many well publicized critics of any move to reduce the autonomy of teachers or trainees by emphasizing the importance of a school-based setting (Elliott, 1985; Stake, 1985). One of these, Professor Barry Macdonald of the Centre for Applied Research in Education (CARE) at the University of East Anglia, has published a comprehensive critique of the status of school-based training.

He views young teachers as having great potential as curriculum innovators, sees '. . . apprenticeship as induction into obsolete practice' and school-based training as closing '. . . yet another door to teacher-led development' (Macdonald, 1984, p. 4). He is equally doubtful about the value of traditional models of training which induct trainees '. . . into ideal models of pedagogy that have little resilience when exposed prematurely to the operational culture' (*ibid*, p. 8), and which force new teachers to adopt defensive patterns of behaviour. (cf Lortie 1975). The situation described by Macdonald is well illustrated in this present study by the frustrations trainees experienced when attempting to adopt interactive teaching styles during training.

Macdonald's own view is that a dramatic 'radicalization of the training process is necessary if young teachers are to realize their full potential and thus contribute to improved practices in schools:

> What would such radicalization look like? In my view the answer to this is sharply opposed to the apprenticeship concept of the trainees. We should think, rather, of the trainee as a student of schooling, a critical and reflective observer and theorist of its contemporary conditions, practices and beliefs. I believe initial training should emphasise investigation of local communities, study of children in non-school settings, case studies of schools and their practice. We should train students in investigating and reporting curriculum issues embedded in realities of contemporary schooling . . . I further believe that in time such a trend would lead to the integration of pre-service, in-service and school development activities into a unified system. And within such a system the isolation of academic theorising would break down as the roles of trainee, trainer and researcher become merged in a shared focus. (Macdonald, 1984, p. 7)

Macdonald's vision here moves reflective action from its present position as a difficult-to-attain yet desirable extra, to central prominence in the training curriculum. In doing so, he bypasses the influences most likely to frustrate it — premature and extensive socialization in schools and the modelling of associates — and, instead provides the trainees and teachers with the non-threatening settings likely to encourage and reinforce them in becoming 'critical and reflective' observers and theorists of schooling. As well, he places the theory likely to arise from reflective action in a new perspective that allows for trainee and teacher 'ownership' and endorses its value as derivative from practice.

However, in terms of the findings of this study, perhaps the most significant feature of the model is to be found in its potential for resolving the issues associated with status — both between institution and school and in the minds of the trainees. If, as is suggested, '. . . the roles of trainee, trainer and researcher become merged in a shared focus', the present debilitating distinctions between those who teach and those who teach about teaching could become blurred in a collaborative partnership which is no longer threatened by the existing and destructive distinctions between 'theory-based' and 'practice-based' contributions to training. For the trainees too, the issue of status is effectively dealt with by making them full contributing members of the training team.

The contrasts between the Macdonald model and those presently proposed by the British Government and by the report on *Initial Teacher Training and the*

Role of the School can be readily interpreted in relation to the influences identified in this study. As well, the noted impact of such influences provides a basis for critiquing these latter proposals.

The apprenticeship proposals of the British Government and the subsequent experimentation with 'articled' teachers, shift the major responsibility for training to the schools. In these circumstances the socializing influences of school class-rooms and of teacher-modelling become dominant. The findings of this study suggest that if this were to occur, the trainees' preoccupation with an urgent, immediate and continuing need for control and instrumental skill in the classroom is likely to lead to imitative and unreflective responses which will reinforce existing practice. Indeed, in the absence of any opportunity or incentive to stand back from their experiences, the trainees are the more likely to experience an accentuated form of the stress noted both during and after training by the *mathematics/science* trainees. As well, the separation of the practical training in schools from the 'theo-retical instruction' in 'block release' courses in university or college would appear to ensure that such instruction is likely to continue to be seen as irrelevant to practice. In this study, only where trainees were able quickly to relate in-college 'theory' to their school experiences was there any likelihood that they would attach value to it.

The proposals in the recent report to the DES (Furlong *et al.*, 1988) are also likely, through their increased emphasis on school-based activity and on an in-creased authority for associates as trainers and assessors, to place trainees in con-ditions near to those of an apprenticeship. As a consequence, they are likely to be heir to the same conservative influences outlined above. In addition, the continued isolation of 'disciplinary theory' as a solely institutional responsibility, is likely to have the same consequences for its relevance as those noted for theory taught in the 'block release' courses. Indeed, neither of the proposals promise any release from the influences presently at work. Both would appear to perpetuate the status divide between institution and school, the separation of theory from practice, and the effects of unreflective practices in the schools.

The future of secondary teacher training in New Zealand would therefore appear to depend on choice between the United Kingdom trends to apprentice-ship, the recommendations for collaborative 'mentorial' training in the most recent New Zealand report (Ramsay and Battersby, 1988) or continuation of existing provisions. The implications for schooling of each of the choices would appear to be relatively clear cut — forms of apprenticeship training are likely to maintain the status quo; collaborative (and costly) alternatives *may* promote reflective action by teachers, while existing provisions are likely to leave open the present ambivalent possibilities. However, notwithstanding consideration of costs, the choice is likely to be a matter of what outcomes of schooling are to be most valued in the future.

It has been been accepted throughout this study that improvement in school-ing is, in part, dependent on the development of reflective action in teachers and the consequent establishment of classroom conditions which promote independent thought in students. Such goals are part of a tradition which was articulated by Dewey (1909) when he called for 'reflective thinking' (p. 13) in teachers and students and argued that the 'aim of education' is attained when the '. . . mind is able to manage itself independently without external tutelage' (*ibid*, p. 63). Since that time similar goals for teaching and learning have been widely espoused. Most recently in New Zealand, such goals did appear to be substantially endorsed by the twenty thousand submissions to the *Curriculum Review* (1987). Here, teachers were sought who would: '. . . be able to reflect critically on what they are doing and how they are doing it' (Department of Education, 1987, p. 16), and who would 'enable' learning by empowering students:

> . . . to take increased responsibility for their own learning; and be in-volved with the teacher in setting their own goals, organising their own studies and activities, and evaluating their own learning achievements. (*ibid*, p. 11)

However, alternative goals appeared preferred in a Heylen Opinion Poll (1987) at that time. Most respondents saw improvement in schooling as consisting in the promotion of the basic goals of literacy, numeracy and vocational preparation in a 'well disciplined' environment. This latter, appeared to be consistent with the notions of hierarchy and individual competitiveness noted by Giroux.

Despite the apparent ambivalence in public perceptions of educational goals, this study has suggested that, in general, demands for 'well disciplined' conditions appear already to exist in our schools and secondary teachers are typically social-ized to promote them. If, therefore, an increased emphasis on school-based sec-ondary teacher training were to be promoted with the consequent endorsement of existing practice, some public expectations would be likely to be satisfied, but attempts to move teaching and training in a direction of greater intellectual openness would continue to be frustrated.

Although there is, as yet, no public demand for apprenticeship training for secondary teachers in New Zealand (although it is thought the present Minister of Education Dr Lockwood Smith entertains such a notion), the tenor of recent reforms in educational administration (*Tomorrow's Schools*, 1988 and *Learning for Life*, 1989) suggest that, in future, such training could prove an attractive alternative to the present institution-controlled provision. With the call for greater accountability of schools and teachers to the community through the recent establishment of Boards of Trustees, (and through the use of performance criteria for assessing teachers and institutions which are reminiscent of *CBTE*), the control of training promises to be an issue which could increasingly claim public attention. Recent information from the *DES* in the United Kingdom states that:

> Under the new arrangements (for qualified teacher status) . . . the local education authorities and some school governing bodies . . . will be re-sponsible for applying for a license to teach for the candidate, for provid-ing such training, either on or off the job, as is considered necessary and for recommending after a 2 year period that qualified teacher status be granted to the candidate. (Graham, 1989, p. 1)

In these circumstances the substantial control of training provisions has passed from the training institutions to the employers of teachers. Given, that the New Zealand Boards of Trustees have now comparable powers to their United King-dom counterparts in the employment of teachers, the resolution of training issues in the future is unlikely to be decided solely in terms of professional argument about the relative merits of different forms of training, but will be influenced by the demands of the new local administrators who are now accountable, to an increased degree, for the quality of schooling.

References

ALEXANDER, R.J. (1984) 'Innovation and continuity in the initial teacher education curriculum' in ALEXANDER, R.J. (Ed.) *Change in Teacher Education: Context and Provision since Robbins*, London, Holt, Rinehart and Winston.

BATES, R.J. (1976) 'The organisational framework' in CODD, J.A. and HERMANSSON, G.L. (Eds) *Directions in New Zealand Secondary Education*, Auckland, Hodder and Stoughton Ltd.

CASTLE, S. (1988) 'Apprenticeship plan for teachers in school', *The Sunday Telegraph*, 7 December.

DEPARTMENT OF EDUCATION (NZ) (1951) *Recruitment and Education and Training of Teachers*, (the Campbell Report), Wellington, Government Printer.

DEPARTMENT OF EDUCATION (NZ) (1979) *Review of Teacher Training*, Wellington, Government Printer.

DEPARTMENT OF EDUCATION (NZ) (1987) *The Curriculum Review*, Wellington, Government Printer.

DEPARTMENT OF EDUCATION AND SCIENCE (UK) (1984) *Initial Teacher Training: Approval of Courses*, (Circular No. 3/84) London, HMSO.

DEWEY, J. (1909) *How We Think*, Boston, Heath & Co.

ELLIOTT, J. (1985) 'Educational action-research' in NISBET, J. and NISBET, S. (Eds) *Research Policy and Practice*, (World Year Book of Education)

FURLONG, V.J. *et al.* (1988) *Initial Teacher Training and the Role of the School*, Buckingham, Open University Press.

GIROUX, H.A. (1980) 'Teacher education and the ideology of social control', *Journal of Education*, 162.

GIROUX, H.A. (1983) 'Theories of reproduction and resistance in the new sociology of education: A critical analysis', *Harvard Education Review*, 53, 3, August.

GLYNN, T. (1975) *Behaviour Modification*. Wellington. NZ Educational Institute.

GRAHAM, L (1989) Department of Education and Science, Correspondence, 28 June.

HEYLEN RESEARCH CENTRE (1987) Heylan Opinion Pollon Education, Ackland.

HIRST, P.H. (1980) 'The PGCE course and the training of specialist teachers for secondary schools', *British Journal of Teacher Education*, 6, 1, January.

HOUSTON, W.R. and HOWSAM, B. (Eds) (1972) *Competency-Based Teacher Education*, Chicago, IL, Science Research Associates Inc.

LACEY, C. and LAMONT, W. (1975) Partnership with Schools: An Experiment in Teacher Education, Falmer University of Sussex, Education Area Occasional Paper 5.

LANGE, Rt. HON. D. (1988) *Tomorrow's Schools: The Reform of Educational Administration in New Zealand*, Wellington, Government Printer, Wellington, August.

LANGE, Rt. HON. D. and GOFF, HON. P. (1989) *Learning for Life: Education and Training Beyond the Age of Fifteen*, Wellington, Government Printer, February.

LAWTON, D. (1973) *Social Change, Educational Theory and Curriculum Planning*, London, University of London Press Ltd.,

LORTIE, D.C. (1975) *School Teacher: A Sociological Study*, Chicago, IL, University of Chicago Press.

MACDONALD, B. (1984) 'Teacher education and curriculum reform: Some English errors', Address to Spanish Teacher Trainers, Valencia.

MUNRO, R.G. (1981) 'Report on school-based teacher training trials 1981', Auckland, Secondary Teachers College, November.

OECD (1974) New Patterns of Teacher Education, Paris OECD.

POPKEWITZ, T.S. (1987) 'Ideology and social formation in teacher education' in POPKEWITZ, T.S. (Ed.) *Critical Studies in Teacher Education: Its Folklore, Theory and Practice*, Lewes, Falmer Press.

POPPER, K.R. (1963) *Conjectures and Refutations*, London, Routledge and Kegan Paul.

RAMSAY, P. and BATTERSBY, D. (1988) *A Study of In-School Training for Division A Student Teachers*, Occasional Paper, Education Department, Massey University, Palmerston North and Education Department, University of Waikato, Hamilton.

STAKE, R.E. (1985) 'Case study', in NISBET, J. and NISBET, S. (Eds) *Research Policy and Practice* (World Year Book of Education).

STENHOUSE, L. (1975) *An Introduction to Curriculum Research and Development*, London Heinemann.

STENHOUSE, L. (1980) 'The study of samples and the study of cases', *British Educational Research Journal*, 6, 1.

TAYLOR, W. (1978) 'Problems of "theory" and "practice" in TAYLOR, W. (Ed.) *Research and Reform in Teacher Education*, Windsor, NFER Publishing Company Ltd.

TAYLOR, W. (1985) 'The future for teacher education' in HOPKINS, D. and REID, K. (Eds) *Rethinking Teacher Education*, London Croom Helm.

TOMLINSON, J. (1989) 'The enigma of theory v practice', *Education*, 10 March.

UNIVERSITY OF SUSSEX (1985) 'PGCE course document', Brighton.

VAN MAANEN, J. (1979a) 'The fact and fiction in organisational ethnography', *Administrative Science Quarterly*, 24, December.

VAN MAANEN, J. (1979b) 'The territory is not the map' in 'Reclaiming Qualitative Methods for Organisational Research: A Preface', *Administrative Science Quarterly*, 24, December.

ZEICHNER, K.M. and LISTON, D.P. (1987) 'Teaching student teachers to reflect', *Harvard Educational Review*, 57, 1, Feburary.

Chapter 9

Capital T Teaching

Les Tickle

During the 1980s the development of 'reflective practice' became a widely adopted aim in both initial teacher education and INSET. The slogan 'reflection' was widespread, used, as slogans are, to denote, in the catchy way of the watchword, a realm of meanings and attachments to complex ideas which often remained implicit and unexamined. It has been suggested that its popularity was established in part because it can be regarded as a generic conception which can be employed readily, if differently, 'by teacher educators of every ideological persuasion' (Zeichner and Tabachnick, 1991, page 2). Among that population certainly some of those who proselytized in the faith of action research, including myself, came to use reflective practice either as a substitute for, or interchangeably with, that other 'generic term' (see Elliott, 1991; Somekh, 1990; Tickle, 1987; Winter, 1989). However, its use was also part of a concerted extension of more elaborate and self-critical explorations of the complexities behind the slogan (see Tabachnick and Zeichner, 1991). The chapter which follows represents a part of my own attempt to reflect on the pursuit of the reflective practitioner. The work derives from a research and development project which focussed on the professional education of new entrants to teaching in one local education authority in England and Wales. This part is based on a case study of five new teachers who participated as a group in a research project through a full academic year, and six individuals who were part of a pilot induction project which I designed, and with whom I worked as a tutor throughout their first year of teaching. The context of the research, and the reason for doing it, was an initiative in the local education authority which aimed to improve provision for new teachers, and the introduction of the BPhil (Teaching) degree at the University of East Anglia, for teachers who had completed their first year of teaching. Both of these were conceived in terms of devising an induction curriculum for new entrants to teaching which would bring about a 'continuum' of professional development from initial training, through induction, into in-service teacher education. The aims of that curriculum in this case were centred on the notion of developing reflective practice and the assumptions of research-based teaching, or action research. The research itself derived from the problem that reflective practice and action research had been developed and tested with student teachers and experienced teachers, but not so far as I could detect with teachers in their first and immediately subsequent years. Despite extensive research on provision for beginning teachers there was a need to elucidate and understand the nature of their thinking and learning. It was my view, after extensive consideration of research literature on teacher thinking and learning, action research, and beginning teachers, that the induction period would reveal important characteristics of teachers' educational experiences, highlighted by what is commonly a period of frenetic activity and learning. The illumination of those characteristics was intended to help to develop practice and theory for the induction programmes.

My outlook in establishing the pilot project and the BPhil (Teaching) degree, as well as being prejudiced by my attachment to research-based teaching and action research as a mode of professional development (see Tickle, 1987), was specifically and substantially influenced by the perspectives of Schon (1971, 1983 and 1987). Schon argued that the relationship between practice and research in the professions centres on reflection-in and reflection-on-action. His theory is based on the idea that when a person reflects in- or on-action s/he becomes a researcher in a specific and particular practical situation. Because situations are complex and uncertain, and always unique because of the combination of variables which come together, practice problems are difficult to identify. They are also difficult to act upon since judgment and action need to be taken to fit the particular characteristics of each case — 'selectively managing complex and extensive information'. He points out that the purpose of the action in an activity like teaching is to change the situation from what it is to a desired state, so that once action has been taken further management of the situation is required to judge the effects of action and assess the newly-created situation. According to Schon this constant activity of appreciation, action, reappreciation, further action, leads to the development of a repertoire of experiences of unique cases, which are then available to draw upon in unfamiliar situations. That repertoire, he claims, is used in the recombination of elements of those other experiences, rather than as 'recipe knowledge', so that each new situation is dealt with through reflection, further enriching the repertoire of practice and enabling the quality of judgments made in practical situations to be improved. In this view the process of reflection in the construction of professional practice involves experiment and enquiry which is different from methods of controlled experiment, because the practitioner attempts to make an hypothesis come true, in situations where s/he does not have control of all the factors involved. Unstable situations and relatively unpredictable outcomes both pertain. This seemed to me to be not only a plausible view of professional practice, but an attractive model of practice to encourage among new teachers, since it was my view that the quality of teaching and learning depends substantially on the quality of teachers' judgments and actions, based on sound assessments of situations, events, and people. I regarded the pursuit of quality in professional action in terms of the development of the application of professional judgment in practice; the quality of such judgment being based on the capacity to perceive problems, elicit information, analyze and synthesize evidence, determine appropriate action, and monitor its consequences and effects.

In embarking on the induction project I held the view, and still do, that the first year of teaching is a period when practical experience is built perhaps more rapidly and more critically than at any other stage in a teacher's career, because of the frenetic activity and learning which is required in meeting the full demands of teaching for the first time. I believed, and still do, that this is when the problematic nature of teaching is confronted in its most acute form, opening up the potential for educational experiences for new teachers to be developed constructively, especially by acknowledging teaching as perpetually problematic. I adopted the view that new teachers represent a particular example of Schon's reflective practitioner, albeit at a novice stage, because there is only a very limited repertoire of experiences to draw upon in unfamiliar situations. Most situations are unfamiliar, at least initially. Because of the nature of teacher induction new teachers face those situations alone, and they must 'self-make' that repertoire of experiences through trial and error judgments.

For this reason I was also cautious about the application of Schon's view to new teachers (as well as to teachers in general). There was another reason to be cautious. Some aspects of teaching may be different from law, medicine, engineering and other professions which he considered. In teaching the concept of 'case' could mean each child at each point of intervention by a teacher, each group or class at each encounter, each event in corridor or playground, in circumstances where 'overlap' of cases is unavoidable, and where interpretation, inference, and response in behaviour is inevitable. In such circumstances it may be impossible to judge the effects or potential effects of action and to assess newly-created situations. Volatility of circumstances and human responses makes appreciation, action, reappreciation, further action, among numerous 'cases', which have to be handled at the same time and immediately, a chancy business. The selection of information may be rapid and impressionistic, the likelihood of missed information or misinformation considerable, and the potential for misjudgement enormous. But this suggested that the pursuit of the development of the application of professional judgment in practice might be all the more necessary in a complex practice such as teaching, undertaken in difficult material and social contexts.

In ideal terms, then, Schon's view suggested to me that the problem faced by new entrants in attempting to become effective teachers was that first and foremost they needed to become effective researchers, capable of enquiry from which problems can be framed adequately; capable of constructing hypotheses as a basis for 'experiment'; capable of taking appropriate action to effect change; and capable of monitoring changes. This, however, reflects an image of clinical, controlled cases. It also has overtones of 'models' of action research in which carefully selected cases or foci are subjected to a cyclical process of research and action (Elliott, 1991). In more practical terms I could recognize that, for example, information about the cause of a child's emotional state, the events of a previous lesson with another teacher, the micropolitics of peer groups in a class, and so on, may be the essential, yet inaccessible, information upon which acts by the teacher depend for their quality. Here I was faced with a tension. There were my aspirations to develop induction according to the principles of research-based teaching, within which I saw Schon's thesis as an elaboration of the research-action relationship, with potential for enhancing the quality of teaching. There was also my recognition of the need to research the nature of reflective thought and action among new teachers, working in what I thought of as complex and fragile informational and decision-making worlds. It is to aspects of the research into those worlds that I wish to turn my attention in this chapter.

As I have said, I believed it was reasonable to suppose, and the evidence from the teachers confirmed the supposition, that the first year involves extensive reflection. The five teachers in the research group, from first, middle and high schools, met every two or three weeks throughout the year (sixteen meetings in all) to discuss their experiences of beginning teaching. Matters for discussion were mainly decided among the teachers, sometimes by agreeing a structured agenda, sometimes in unstructured discourse. My interest was in hearing how they learned from, or within, their experience. They knew that within the project's aim to elucidate the educational experiences of new teachers I had particularly set out to explore the nature and potential of reflective practice in that education. Discussions were audio-taped and transcripts given to each teacher at latest by the next meeting, so that modification and elaboration of the discussion became a constant part of the research process. The pilot project teachers provided the opportunity to observe their practice in social and material contexts, and to work with them towards the central aim of the project: the development of reflective, classroom practice. The aim of the project and my role as 'neutral' (i.e. non-assessing) support tutor from outside the schools were discussed with the teachers from the start. It was agreed that I should take a research stance towards my role, as well as towards the development of their teaching and the circumstances in which they worked. The research methods I adopted with these teachers can best be described as 'observant-conversational'. Classroom visits and observations, interviews and discussions, telephone conversations, and notes of my own thoughts about their practice and mine, each contributed to data which was copied and given to each individual to whom it related. This journalistic processing of information helped to build a portrait of each teacher *in situ*, while acknowledging that I was part of the situation.

In their discussions the teachers recognized very clearly the principle and demonstrated the practice of reflection-in- and -on-action (so far as I had interpreted it): that they were 'constantly turning over situations' in their minds. It was clear that those situations were practical, problem-posing ones of considerable variety. Many could be categorized within a range of professional problem areas: understanding one's responses to being a teacher, and to specific episodes in teaching; knowing (or not knowing) subject matter; knowing different facets of pupils' learning needs; establishing personal and academic relationships with children; developing teaching strategies; managing space and resources; adjusting to school policies and the expectations of colleagues; and so on. Such classifications of teachers' knowledge (see Elbaz, 1983; Wilson *et al.*, 1987) — self, subject matter, students, school curriculum, and strategies for instruction — were accompanied by a host of other events and matters for consideration which were not so readily or simply classified: how to relate to parents; the social behaviour of colleagues; the conduct of headteachers; matters of salary and conditions of employment; and so on. It was teaching strategies, however, that provided the predominant focus of attention. Amidst this plethora of considerations the teachers were largely left to 'discern problems, consider alternative solutions, make a selection, and after acting assess the outcome' (Lortie, 1975). They confirmed the view that that occurs hundreds of times daily, (Jackson, 1968) leaving teachers to work things out as best they can without the personal and professional support which new teachers might need.

Such lonesome decisions and the assessment of their effects might well be expected to affect and be affected by personal qualities and predispositions such as confidence, perceptiveness, energy, insight, commitment, perseverance, will, the capacity to analyze situations, and so on. The experience of these teachers showed how such qualities were invoked and affected as they trod the road of status passage from student to novice and towards what they called 'Capital T

Teaching'. The process of learning by experience, which they saw as 'going through it', or 'being on the road', was elaborated in detail. It entailed 'playing it by ear' and 'playing the hunch' as situations were assessed, judgments made and action taken, often without adequate information or time to pursue each event in detail. There were immediate, on-the-spot judgments which raised questions for the teachers about how to gauge a situation before acting, so as to know how to act appropriately for the circumstance: treating different children's social behaviour differently, in what might appear to be similar situations, in order to achieve the best results from action for each particular child; judging the language appropriate for explaining concepts for different children; determining whether children were working to capacity, were over-stretched, or were giving full attention to their tasks, and how to respond. These and myriad examples of on-the-spot judgments were compounded by the complexity of decisions and information processing about the longer-term effects of actions. Decision-making was characterized by the teachers as 'mental gymnastics' within aspirations to develop what was 'best' in social and professional relationships with pupils and effective instruction. The uncertainty and unpredictability of situations, coupled with instability and inaccessibility of information amounted on occasions and especially in the early part of the year to a confrontation with situational anarchy. Even so, on-the-spot judgments applied in trial and error experience led to further reflective evaluation on the events which ensued. The aspiration to achieve 'Capital T' status, it seemed, might be realized by monitoring judgments, actions and outcomes, in the constant 'turning things over in the mind'. These evaluations of role performance were persistently spurred by a sense of 'minding' about the outcome of judgments and the quality of decisions. The question 'did I do the right thing in that situation' characterized the deliberative nature of the teachers' enquiries into their own actions, while portraying the sense of uncertainty *en route* to 'Capital T' status.

Gauging constraints in arranging priorities for the use of time and resources, and in determining what actions to take with children, formed part of making both on-the-spot and evaluative judgments. How much time was available to listen to children's explanations of social behaviour? How much time could be given to explaining concepts to particular children? What resources might be acquired for a topic? How long could one afford to spend on preparing individual worksheets? Each of these and so many other examples amounted to evidence of tactical decision-making in the face of competing demands, which needed the teachers as managers of their circumstances to engage in reflective problem-solving. Judging the appropriateness of planning decisions previously taken was another kind of reflection, which occurred immediately the consequences of the plan were manifest, or after the event when it could be combined with reflections on adjustments made in the execution of the plan. In discussing their own practice with colleagues it was necessary to judge how much to reveal of the rationale (or uncertainty and vagueness) in their thinking, or whether or not to expose their practice, let alone their emotions, to the scrutiny of others. In particular, thoughts about perceived gaps in competence and confidence were constant, often attached to reflections about how deficiencies could be rectified.

Most of the foci of reflection in and upon action, or reflectiveness about oneself, were part of a process of determining future action, either directly in classroom practice or in relation to one's own learning. Using the experience of events as perceived in reflection, the construction of potential action was carried out in that constant, mental, turning things over. As one teacher put it in the earlier part of the year, 'every single aspect of the day goes through my mind' (see Tickle, 1989). Throughout these reflective explorations of academic and professional matters, and the plethora of detail relating to 'technical' and 'clinical' competences i.e. respectively, day-to-day practical skills and teaching technique and judgments based on practical reasoning and problem solving which underlay actions (Zimpher and Howey, 1987) explorations of their own emotions were equally prominent. The emotional explorations were directly related to being 'half-way there' as learner teachers, and to 'going through it' as they acquired what they saw as the necessary experience to emerge from novicehood. The experiences of the emotions were as volatile and unpredictable as the experiences of gaining, using and reviewing technical and clinical competences, and were described and discussed exploratively among the teachers in a similar way (see Tickle, 1991). It seemed that having 'lived' the emotions, perceived what events or circumstances triggered particular emotional responses, and appreciated the relationship between these, the teachers' reflective analysis of 'technical' and 'clinical' teaching competences was accompanied by a corresponding analysis of the emotional self in the teaching context. That analysis seemed to enable most of them to establish greater understanding of this aspect of themselves as teachers, and to manage events related to it, providing another step towards 'Capital T' status, in respect of being a teacher, in addition to acting competently. In terms of reflective practice the teachers' accounts certainly provided evidence of their thoughtful deliberations on the detailed tasks of teaching; on particular incidents and actions; specific teaching strategies; longer-term reviews of, and prospects for, schemes of work with students; their own feelings at particular moments; and their image of themselves in relation to the job of teaching, for example. These show something of the range of phenomena which came in for reflective attention. That such attention was intensely focussed and perceptive I had no doubt. But could their reflective practices be regarded as research? Were they adopting a research stance to their practice? Or was there some other driving force, purpose, and interest behind their deliberations? Certainly they didn't follow the procedures of 'models' of action research, with which Schon's reflective practice has been equated (Elliott, 1991, p. 50), in the form which uses the 'action-plan' approach and a range of quantitative and/or qualitative research methods. Their thinking seemed nearer to Schon's view of reflective practice in which research *is* an activity undertaken by practitioners, conducted on the spot, triggered by practical problems, and immediately linked to action in the cycle of situational appreciation. Experiment and enquiry appeared to be conducted in the instability and unpredictability of practice situations.

Thus far that interpretation of Schon's view and the teachers' experience appeared to fit neatly. He had defined different kinds of experimenting in practice. These included 'exploratory experimenting', a kind of probing, playful, trial and error activity which I equated with the teachers' 'playing it by ear'; 'move-testing experiment', in which action is taken with the intention of producing change, equating with 'playing the hunch'; and 'hypothesis testing', which involves discriminating between competing possibilities and seeking confirmation or disconfirmation that they are correct, which I equated with the teachers' 'monitoring'. But was there a problem in this apparent neat fit?. Had I adopted, so far, a partial impression of Schon's thesis, and been seduced by it? It might be necessary to resist any seduction and review my impression. That seemed especially necessary when, as the year progressed, the teachers reported increasingly how they judged 'what worked', or amended practices by way of fine-tuning towards skilful performance judged by the 'what works' criterion. They also identified elements of their practice which they came to take for granted, or which became routinized. In relation to these elements the 'model' of appreciation of a situation, action, reappreciation of the newly-created situation, and further action eventually accumulating in an enriched repertoire of practical experience appeared idealistic and fluid. The teachers' experience of reflection as they described it was not the focussed, selective, systematic enquiry implied by this model, and those of action research, by way of which understanding of selected elements of practice might be developed, and further research questions raised and pursued through action. Rather it was conducted in recognition of the pace of events of classroom life, the need to handle so much evidence at once, elicited by pragmatic methods, and geared towards the provision of practical solutions. These were problems of teaching being encountered extensively during the first year, in which there was not space for the niceties of contracting research procedures, recording data by a variety of means, adopting 'triangulation' procedures and checking inferences in interpretations. In this informational anarchy there was, unsurprisingly I would suggest, a search for order. Attempts to deproblematize teaching, to 'know' that life can be secure in 'proven' actions, seemed to be a major impetus underlying much of the teachers' reflective thinking. Given their view of teaching as a practical activity, learned from the experience of doing it, that search for security was initially mostly about minor, but myriad, administrative tasks, organizational arrangements, managerial proficiency, teaching techniques, and pedagogical strategies. These aspects of practice were what I had previously called the prerequisites of professional credibility (Tickle, 1987). They were what these teachers saw as the first medals of 'Capital T' teaching. So the question which arose for me was whether they were to fall in among the many teachers who are said to be

> locked into a view of themselves as technical experts, find nothing in world of practice to occasion reflection. They have become too skilful at techniques of selective in-attention, junk categories, and situational control, techniques which they use to preserve the constancy of their knowledge-in-practice. For them uncertainty is a threat; its admission is a sign of weakness. (Schon, 1983, p. 68)

Some interesting paradoxes, therefore, were suggested by the data. The teachers acknowledged their search for 'situational control'. They acknowledged that as they proceeded through the year they engaged in 'selective inattention'. How else could they manage the pace of events and demands of the tasks before them? Being skilled implied being skilful at techniques of selective inattention, in the sense of coming to act quickly, intuitively, and without conscious thought in the multitude of situations faced. In some circumstances attention was regained when evidence emerged of misjudgment, occasioning reflection on the actions they had taken, might have taken, or would in future take, and why. Shifts of this kind, between unconscious action and conscious reflection, were indicated throughout the discussions. On the other hand there was still a good deal which remained problematic. So while there was not yet a 'constancy of their knowledge-in-practice' *to* preserve there was an apparent search for it, as a substantial intention in want-ing proven, practical proficiency in classroom management and instruction. In other respects, however, individual teachers willingly engaged in 'uncertain' and risky practices in the search for 'the best' teaching strategies. In relation to these activities the main constancy was that of a search for new ideas, for sound judg-ments about implementation of teaching plans, for reflection in the events, and for evidence of success after them. In some respects then there was evidence of the teachers locking themselves in to technical expertise, in the search for security and identity as 'expert'. Yet there were also continuous challenges to the barricades of inattention — 'surprising' evidence which drew them back from complacency; decisions to break out deliberately from 'boring' and routine teaching; the choice of new and risky strategies to achieve particular aims; and perpetual conditions in the circumstances of teaching which affected the realization of their aims. The paradox here is that an assessment that particular strategies 'worked' might lead to lack of reflection in future, and further deproblematization of teaching. There were indications that this was likely, as the notion of making 'adjustments' to practice was seen as a refining process, rather than to sustain reflection. Was this not the search for 'recipe-knowledge'? Schon himself disparaged such knowledge. Yet if these teachers' experimenting was purposeful action aimed at achieving a desired state, the process of 'assessing' the experimentation was potentially at least a process of deproblematizing teaching. The selective management of complex information allowed for such deproblematization — or so, seductively, it may have seemed in the teachers' search for security. But the further element of the paradox was that such deproblematization was hardly possible, given their lack of access to information, its undependability, and the unpredictability of situations. At best they seemed only able to engage in semi-appreciation of situations, to act largely speculatively but in good faith that they knew enough to make adequate judgments, and to measure the effects of judgments as best they could. When information was unmanageable and uncontrollable the constancy of unpredictability pertained. But even in discussing those events there was a sense that the turbulence created was unwelcome. The search for the predictable was engaged. Security was both an interest and an illusion.

It was this which constituted the main tension in my view of these teachers' reflective thinking. I could not doubt that the teachers were being reflective. In-deed I believed that I had revealed substantial data on the substance and modes of their reflection, as an illustration of Schon's view of reflective practice at a key stage of professional development. But I was also witnessing an emergent non-reflective practice as the teachers became embedded in 'Capital T' teaching, judged by their 'experience' of what 'worked'. Aspects of their teaching appeared to become subject to habituation and 'craft-culture' teaching techniques, consigned to the realm of technical competence without reflection, by virtue of the demands for attention to other, selected matters. Yet Schon explicitly argues that his notion of reflective practice would potentially overcome the tendency towards 'selective inattention' and habituated practice. On the evidence from these teachers, for that to occur would need attention to be maintained on multiple educational problems across a broad front. It would also need a corresponding depth of attention, in order to gain the appreciation of situations required for effective, or at least well informed, action.

It was at this point that a closer scrutiny of both the teachers' reflections and my appreciation of Schon's theory seemed to be necessary. Schon made his own appeal for both 'breadth' and 'depth' of reflection, and the use of 'rigour' in its practice. In doing so he implied that the subject of reflection ought to be more than the technical acts and clinical judgments of practice, though he is vague about what the other matters might be.

> The dilemma of rigour or relevance may be dissolved if we can develop an epistemology of practice which places technical problem solving within a broader context of reflective enquiry, shows how reflection in action may be rigorous in its own right, and links the art of practice in uncertainty and uniqueness to the scientist's art of research. We may thereby increase the legitimacy of reflection in action and encourage its broader, deeper and more rigorous use. (Schon, 1983)

His critique of the rational/experimental model of research as inappropriate to application in social practice was supported by an elaboration of an alternative mode of knowing — existentialism. In this view the inherent uncertainty of experience from which knowledge derives means that the generation and testing of knowing in the 'here-and-now' is not only necessary, but provides its validity. However, he argued that there are certain preconditions which are essential to the formation of existential knowledge: the maintenance of continuity over the learning process; recognition of the open-endedness of all situations; the subjecting of models derived from experience to testing, modification, explosion, or abandonment; a willingness of learners to make leaps in problem-solving; and ability of learners to synthesize theory and formulate new models while in the situation (Schon, 1971, p. 235). The worlds described by the new teachers illustrated and exemplified, in my view, how such a mode of research-based practice as that described by Schon existed in the potential of their deliberations but was in part displaced by the search for 'proven' practical strategies believed to be the medals of 'Capital T' teaching. What appears to have been manifest among these new teachers was certainly a felt need to achieve mastery of practice. They were not yet in a position to initiate change, to innovate, in their own work since it was not yet tried and tested. There was an intention to engage in new practices in their classrooms in a spirit of exploration. But the crucial question is whether the direction of their learning was to be towards existential knowing and an epistemology of practice sustained by that exploration of problematics, and, indeed, the further problematization of teaching, or whether it would be towards what in my view would be an illusory propositional or craft knowledge of teaching?

There was also another dimension which emerged in my quest to understand these teachers' educational experiences in learning teaching. Even though the felt need of the teachers was a paradoxical one which at the same time included risk-taking and the search for security of experience of what 'worked', their deliberations did appear to be held mainly within the realm of technical problem solving (or what Zimpher and Howey called 'technical' and 'clinical' competences, described earlier). Indeed, it may be that the initial apparent 'fit' between their reflections and Schon's view of reflective practice was evident because he was, like they were, concerned mainly with such technical problem-solving, rather than with deliberations about the ends to which practice was directed — namely the achievement of educational aims and the realization of the values which underlay them (Elliott,

1989). Perhaps this was something of an injustice to Schon? What did he imply when he wrote of the 'broader, deeper and more rigorous use of reflection in action'? Zimpher and Howey's (1987) conception of 'personal competence' opened up a view on that question which took me where the teachers took me, though by a different route, into understanding the nature of their reflectiveness on aspects of 'self'.

Personal competence might be seen to include such qualities as those mentioned earlier, and others such as self-esteem, willingness to take responsibility, initiative-taking, open-mindedness and willingness to learn. It might also be seen to include that other major focus of attention in the teachers' experiences and deliberations — the emotions and related aspects in the adjustments of self-knowledge in becoming a teacher. Most of the teachers reported that the more stable and secure teaching became as the year progressed, the more noticeable was the impact of each 'sticky patch' or 'bad week'. These tended to be times when 'basic things' such as classroom technique or relationships with pupils were deemed unsatisfactory in the teachers' own terms. Competence in such basic management skills and interrelationships was the earlier priority. The gaining of this competence and associated confidence meant that different exacting demands were made of themselves by the teachers. By this stage they expected to 'do the right thing in that situation', so that when they discovered that they had not, or when other factors outside their control became dominant, the emotional balance was tipped towards turbulence. Equally, when unanticipated events led unpredictably to a heightened sense of gratification, emotional 'highs' were reported. Furthermore, that competence and confidence provided the basis for different trends in the emotional experiences of the teachers, at least where classroom events were concerned. As 'basic things' were mastered, day-to-day tasks were routinized, and classroom management established, so the emotional responses to these matters stabilized, though with some sustained fluidity as I have just described. The sense of greater control and the use of 'experience' as a tool of management in new situations led in turn to greater degrees of self-conscious management of the emotions; to increased personal competence. This opened the way for testing new ideas in teaching. After half a year or so most of the teachers reported that new ventures were initiated and risks deliberately taken in order to test potential improvements in the quality of teaching and learning. Those developments aimed at achieving the 'redefinition' of teaching through carefully devised strategies (Zeichner and Tabachnick, 1985) were consciously undertaken in the knowledge that they would also test the emotions. They could potentially enhance confidence or undermine it in the short term.

This aspect of self-knowledge appeared to be linked not only to the search for what was 'best' in instructional strategies, but also to the aims and values which lay, albeit sometimes hidden and implicitly, beneath those strategies. It was not merely recognition and celebration of sound practical judgments which brought gratification, or acknowledged misjudgment which brought anguish. Among other aims, for example, Lesley was overtly concerned with 'active' learning strategies tailored to the needs of every individual 9-year-old in her class, implemented in ways which would ensure maximum motivation, participation and achievement. One of Anna's concerns was a determination to ensure that standards of mathematical performance by each of her secondary school examination groups were maximized. Mike aimed to teach a particular 'true' form of design and technology, based on multi-media, design/problem solving approaches. Richard's concern to effect 'freer' primary practice in a 'formal' middle school; Kathy's intention to maintain attention levels by 'reading' the responses of reception class pupils and frequently varying the activities they engaged in; Sue's devising of historical activities to convey concepts in an 'empathetic' way; and Dave's variations in explanations of scientific concepts in order to 'reach' all his secondary pupils, provided other examples. Within the data, however, such examples served mainly to show that the articulation of aims and values was more implicit in discussions, rather than conscious articulation or elaboration of them. The level of such discussion related to pedagogical knowledge (Shulman, 1986) in the sense that it emerged within 'ways of teaching' concerns. There was little evidence of reflection *about* aims. Where it did occur for some more noticeably was in the face of difficulties. Richard came to reconsider his beliefs about 'good primary practice' in the face of his circumstances and pressure from teachers to be more 'traditional'. Anna responded to a challenge of mathematically low-achieving fifth form boys with extensive soul-searching, and sought examples of 'good practice' to model from. It seemed she had to formulate her aims for the low achievers. Mike had to compromise his commitments in the face of specialist craft teaching of woodwork and metalwork in his department. He proposed to change the department or move to another school if he could not implement his ideas. Diane had difficulty formulating her aims for the reception class which she taught, and gave a great deal of thought to seeking a rationale for what she did in the classroom. It was into understanding this realm of the teachers' deliberations that I was led further by Elliott (1989) in my own attempt to elaborate on the teacher's personal competences:

> the aim of action research is to generate *practical wisdom* defined as a holistic appreciation of a complex practical activity which enables a person to understand or articulate the problems s/he confronts in realizing the aims and values of the activity and to propose appropriate solutions. (p. 84)

By now the significance of incorporating 'values clarification' (Zimpher and Howey, 1987) as a focus of attention for reflection became much more significant than when I embarked on the project. Incorporating understanding of the educational aims and values on which practice depends, and not just reflecting in and on action itself, provided a more complex matter for my role. There were examples, then, where reflection went some way beyond practical problem solving to incorporate educational aims and values and potentially put the teachers *en route* towards values clarification.

As I have suggested, however, the teachers did not articulate or reflect upon the aims and values of their work to any noticeable extent. They were largely implicit, and revealed through implication and inference in discussions about practice. Their reflectiveness was pursued mainly within the realm of practical propositions. The elements of aims and values, of educational theory, were not, it seemed, a matter for extensive deliberation, especially where they were not challenged by circumstance. There is an interesting problem here, in an area of teacher thinking and teacher knowledge which I had not derived from Schon's work, and which I came to see as a crucial deficiency in my conception of the induction projects. The importance of this realm of 'competence' for the education of teachers and for the qualitative improvement of the education of pupils is suggested by Salmon (1988), in a way which rests easily alongside the preconditions of Schon's existential knowledge and Elliott's practical wisdom. She points out that teachers' personal constructs of understanding are crucial to the kind of education on offer to pupils. The implication is that knowledge of self as an element of professional knowledge needs to be more substantially part of the agenda of learning teaching. The relationship of self to theories of teaching would also follow in that agenda:

> Education, in this psychology, is the systematic interface between personal construct systems. This view of formal learning puts as much emphasis on teachers' personal meanings as on those of learners. Here a Kellyan approach stands apart from most educational psychology, which while generally focussing on distinctive ways in which individual pupils see things, tends to lump teachers together. The knowledge they represent, the meanings they offer are, it is implied, essentially standard. Underlying this definition of teachers, in terms of a standardised curriculum, are certain absolute assumptions about knowledge itself. If we believe that history, science or maths embody particular ultimate truths about the world, then we can see all teachers of these subjects as representing essentially the same sort of expertise. But we cannot take this view if knowledge is provisional. Learning, from this perspective, is not a matter of acquiring what Kelly dubs 'nuggets of truth', a treasure house of human certainties. In learning, we cannot ever achieve final answers; rather we find new questions, we discover other possibilities which we might try out. Knowledge is ultimately governed by constructive alternativism; everything can always be reconstructed. (Salmon, 1988, p. 22)

This is the constructionist, 'worldmaking' view of the reality with which the practitioner deals, according to Schon (1983, p. 35). But there is a further layer here which needed to be considered in terms of new teachers' education. Although the teachers did not extensively articulate their aims and values it did appear that their practice in the main was in pursuit of realizing aims held with conviction. Now the generation of 'practical wisdom' as 'appreciation of a complex practical activity' could fit Schon's ideas. That that appreciation should 'enable a person to understand or articulate the problems s/he confronts in realizing the aims and values of the activity' however goes some way beyond Schon's reflective practice as I had understood it. Even this view by Elliott assumes that these teachers might have formulated aims and values to realize. In one sense of course they must have, since their very presence in teaching and their actions within it are driven by values and intentions. But how far were those aims and values formulated? The examples I have cited suggest that I hardly come close to uncovering the nature and extent of these teachers' personal constructs. The examples were only signals, indicators in some cases in relation to specific problematics, of the teachers examining their educational aims. Sometimes this was in a sense of frustration at not being able to implement their ideas in practice; sometimes it was in a sense of exploration for ideas; and sometimes with a sense of gratification at having achieved 'what works for me', a celebration of translating aims into practice. But perhaps more important was the indication that this aspect of practice, what might be seen as the power house and driving force of the activity of teaching itself, was a part of reality which was also open to 'constructive alternativism', or else to consolidation and deproblematization. The teachers' trial and error experimenting could be seen, as my initial interpretation of reflective practice would have it, as the construction of practice by way of attempting to make an hypothesis come true. This could tend towards demonstrating the truth of 'what works for me' — which was described as the central criterion in judging the result of such experimenting. However, in this other layer of the construction of self, the layer of values and educational aims, a different view of reflection might be needed. One was offered by Elliott:

> an alternative account of the practitioner's experimenting (is that it is) not so much to make an hypothesis come true but to actualise an ideal. The hypothesis is not about what is the case (truth) but about how to realize value in action (or in other words how to define oneself in terms of one's own values). And central here to hypothesis raising and testing is reflexivity — the self folding back on itself to reconstruct itself through action. Changing the self rather than actions is what action research is all about — or at least one form of action research. The point about unstable situations is that they destabilize selves and require their continuous reconstruction. Action is simply the material condition of this reconstructive enterprise which is basically and fundamentally a reflexive and not simply reflective one. (Elliott, 1991b — notes to the author)

In this Elliott elaborates his distinction between different kinds of practical reflection: that which is associated with realizing technical objectives in the curriculum, and consists of technical reasoning about how to achieve pre-specified ends; and that which is associated with process values and consists of ethical and philosophical considerations in the judgments made in trying to realize values (Elliott, 1991, p. 51). The location of the latter kind of reflection seems equivalent to the realm of personal competence whose essence is about generating self-awareness, values clarification, and self-growth. It would provide a means of examining and developing theoretical frameworks underlying teaching. The emphasis which the teachers placed on the conduct of their performance illustrates a relationship in their concerns between technical problem solving and personal philosophies. It now seems that what I set out to do as designer and tutor of the pilot induction project, following a particular emphasis derived from the ideas of Schon, emphasized the former, encouraging the focus on classroom practice and a search largely for improvement in technical problem solving. The development of personal competence, engaging the teachers in this additional layer of reflection, would provide a different conception of professional development and the education of new teachers.

These dimensions of the process of learning teaching, of professional development, were not only crucial to the way the induction project was, and might have been conceived. They also helped to explicate what was going on in the manifestations of thought and practice which I witnessed among the teachers. Was I witnessing, and attempting to encourage a process of self-construction of tried and tested techniques and strategies for teaching? Or was I witnessing and encouraging a reconstruction of the self, in terms of the values and personal qualities of the teacher (i.e. in terms of their education)? If the former, then the processes of reflection and practice towards becoming 'capital T Teachers' were about manifesting in practice a self which was brought to the situation. Being *en route* had a fixed destination in view and the development of a repertoire of practice represented strategies for reaching it. That view provides a distinctive interpretation of the criterion 'what works for me', which was a characteristic and powerful selection mechanism when the teachers judged their actions and the advice and ideas of others. Where the 'me' was determined the task seemed to be to match strategies and outcomes to it. The strategies themselves became a by-product of values and aims. Such a view goes a long way towards explaining why these teachers' focus of attention was on the technical and clinical competences of teaching. The important business was to see success in realizing aims, not to (re)construct the aims.

If on the other hand I was also witnessing and encouraging the reconstruction of the self then the reflexive process would have been directed towards maintaining instability, enabling the teachers to develop their ideas within the destabilizing situations in which they worked. That process was evident in some cases in respect of specific situations, where the important business was 'soul-searching', in attempts to define or clarify educational aims. It also went even deeper in some cases. Sue's perpetual crisis about 'is this what life's come to?'; Dave's crisis of personal confidence in the face of colleagues who 'don't understand me'; Anna's constantly being 'put down' by her headteacher; and Debbie's emergent sense of isolation and self-doubt were just some examples of the ontological dimension of these teachers' concerns, which were even deeper and more complex than educational aims and teaching strategies. These kinds of destabilization seemed to result in reflexiveness during instances of pain and destructiveness, rather than constructive development. Learning how to handle the emotions in relation to problem-solving strategies illustrates the potential of reflexivity for 'handling' these wider orientations of self as a teacher. In respect of both teaching strategies and aims/values, the capacity to manage instability in a way which maintains the problematic nature of self, of education, and of teaching, provides a key element for the development of reflexivity. For it seems that in many respects the teachers illustrated a tendency, or desire, to exit that mode of thinking in favour of termination of the learning process, closure of situations, firming up of models from experience, a desire to find trustworthy solutions, and a failure to address theory in favour of pragmatic responses to contexts. They aspired to some degree to enter what they denoted in various ways as the culture of 'capital T Teaching', seduced perhaps by a mirage of certainty in understanding 'what works' as a repertoire of technical and clinical competences. That aspiration may have diverted them from the uncertainty involved in examining their own beliefs, personal philosophies and emotional selves which lay at the heart of their educational enterprise. In talking of becoming 'capital T Teachers' they did seem to imply a possible escape from such reflexive practice as would be required for 'holistic appreciation' of teaching. The formal assessment of their teaching, based on the less complex technical and clinical skills, encouraged that endeavour to live by simple criteria. It may be that the holistic nature of teaching and the extent of 'problematics' was too great to handle at one time through rigorous research. The elusiveness of data was manifest; its inaccessibility evident. The means of interpreting data 'on the spot' itself required deliberation and sophisticated judgment. Methods of recording it as evidence for later analysis or even recall was time-consuming and subject to its own technical difficulties. The development of understanding without opportunities to scrutinize ideas or to engage in discourse was limited. Yet it is the development of these capacities which would constitute becoming effective researchers, and which would provide the basis, in my own terms, for becoming effective teachers. This would constitute a remodel-ling of their conception of 'capital T Teaching'. Yet to expect the teachers to have the ability to maintain control over the apparent anarchy of situations is a heavy demand to make. To expect them to engage in testing, exploding, or abandoning models derived from experience when they are only in the process of constructing them seems like iconoclasm gone mad. To go beyond that and ask them to deconstruct the personal values on which that experience must necessarily be built might be even worse. Yet the development of these capacities as part of personal competence, as emancipatory in the sense of extending personal understanding, can be seen as essential to the education of new entrants to teaching.

References

ELBAZ, F. (1983) *Teacher Thinking: A Study of Practical Knowledge*, London, Croom Helm.

ELLIOTT, J. (1989) 'Educational theory and the professional learning of teachers: An overview', *Cambridge Journal of Education*, 19, 1, pp. 81–101.

ELLIOTT, J. (1991) *Action Research for Educational Change*, Milton Keynes, Open University Press.

ELLIOTT, J. (1991b) notes to the author, School of Education, University of East Anglia, June.

JACKSON, P. (1968) *Life in Classrooms*, Eastbourne, Holt, Rinehart and Winston.

LORTIE, D. (1975) *Schoolteacher*, Chicago, IL, University of Chicago Press.

SALMON, P. (1988) *Psychology for Teachers: An Alternative Approach*, London, Hutchinson.

SCHON, D. (1971) *Beyond the Stable State*, San Francisco, CA. Jossey Bass.

SCHON, D. (1983) *The Reflective Practitioner*, New York, Basic Books.

SCHON, D. (1987) *Educating the Reflective Practitioner*, London, Jossey Bass.

SHULMAN, L.S. (1986) 'Those who understand: Knowledge growth in teaching', *Educational Researcher*, 15, 4, pp. 4–14.

SOMEKH, B. (1990) Some thoughts on action research, Mimeo, University of East Anglia.

TABACHNICK, B.R. and ZEICHNER, K. (1991) 'Introduction', in ZEICHNER, K. and TABACHNICK, B.R. (Eds) Issues and Practices in Inquiry-oriented Teacher Education, Lewes, Falmer Press.

TICKLE, L. (1987) *Learning Teaching, Teaching Teaching: A Study of Partnership in Teacher Education*. Lewes, Falmer Press.

TICKLE, L. (1989) 'On Probation: Preparation for professionalism', *Cambridge Journal of Education*, 19, 3, pp. 277–85.

TICKLE, L. (1991) 'New teachers and the emotions of learning teaching' *Cambridge Journal of Education*, 21, 3.

WILSON, S.H., SHULMAN, L.S. and RICHERT, A.E. (1987) '150 different ways of knowing: Representations of knowledge in teaching' in CALDERHEAD, J. (Ed.) *Exploring Teachers' Thinking*, London, Cassell.

WINTER, R. (1989) *Learning from Experience: Principles and Practice in Action Research*, London, Falmer Press.

ZEICHNER, K.M. and TABACHNICK, B.R. (1985) 'The development of teacher perspectives: Social strategies and institutional control in the socialization of beginning teach-ers', *Journal of Education for Teaching*, 11, 1, pp. 1–25.

ZEICHNER, K.M. and TABACHNICK, B.R. (Eds) (1991) *Issues and Practices in Inquiry-oriented Teacher Education*, Lewes, Falmer Press.

ZIMPHER, N. and HOWEY, K. (1987) 'Adapting supervisory practices to different orientations of teacher competence', *Journal of Curriculum and Supervision*, 2, 2, pp. 101–27.

Chapter 10

The Development of Teachers' Thinking and Practice: Does Choice Lead to Empowerment?

Christopher Day

The research is based upon a commissioned evaluation of a pilot project for the devolution of in-service financial resources to seven primary schools in an English Local Education Authority. It reports on the experiences of the teachers in those schools and discusses the implications of a government imposed financial devolution for the empowerment of individual teachers. The research results suggest that without supportive negotiated intervention from outside the individual system, in-service professional development is likely to remain at planning at the level of action (Handal, 1990); and that, whilst there may be some improvement in practice and teachers' understanding of practice, this does not constitute 'empowerment'.

Introduction

In May 1988 the University of Nottingham was contracted by Derbyshire County Council Education Department to carry out an independent evaluation of the devolved LEA Training Grants Scheme (LEATGS) funding pilot project. The project began in September 1987 with seven secondary schools participating. From September 1988 these seven schools were joined by eight primary schools and colleges of further education. The evaluation was concerned with the INSET experiences of teachers in the eight primary schools during the 1988/89 school year. The chapter reports these experiences within a political context of devolved funding which is claimed to empower those who are at the 'chalk face' of teaching. By cutting out the 'middle people' (for example, higher education, LEA officers, etc.) and thus providing the 'consumers' with the power to choose how to spend their money, albeit within priority areas identified by the Government, it is assumed that there will be better 'value for money'. A report on the first year of the scheme issued by HMI claimed success for the combined centralized-decentralized strategies in terms of teacher empowerment:

> there was substantial evidence that through devolved budgets, linked to
> an agreed institutional staff development plan, there was emerging a strong
> sense of ownership of the INSET by teachers and a view that the training

was far more relevant because it was directly related to issues associated with them and their school or college. This sense of 'ownership' and 'relevance' was strong and was resulting in teachers assuming increased responsibility for their own personal and professional development which in turn was releasing considerable energy and professionalism in many of the schools visited . . .' (3.24) (HMI, 1989)

The educational, economic, legislative and political contexts of the schools in which the research took place are detailed elsewhere (Day, 1991a). The focus of this chapter is on the problematic contribution of the new system of devolved funding for in-service to teacher development. INSET is defined here as, 'those education and training activities engaged in by primary and secondary school teachers and heads, following their initial professional certification, and intended mainly or exclusively to improve their professional knowledge, skills and attitudes in order that they can educate children more effectively' (Bolam, 1982).

The Design of the Project Evaluation

The pilot project was evaluated internally, by the schools themselves individually and collectively by the headteachers, and externally through the contracting by the LEA of the University of Nottingham. The University's role was to collect data from the accumulated documents and perceptions of the value of the scheme from the participants themselves. This was achieved through confidential in-depth tape recorded interviews with the headteachers and staff of all the schools. In effect, the headteachers were interviewed in December 1988 and again, with one exception, in March 1989. Staff in all but one school were interviewed in March 1989. The underlying rationale for using this form of data collection was that it is in the interview that the act of measurement (of worth, effect, effectiveness) comes to life. Despite its potential problems of bias (on the part of the interviewer) and reactivity (on the part of the interviewee), the interview is an interactional situation which is able to combine the complexities of factual and emotional responses in a richness of communicated understandings which cannot be found in other technical rational means of data collection.

It is important, very quickly in evaluation which is restricted by time and money, to establish trust and confidentiality with respondents who have a number of different perspectives, motivations and prejudices; and it is necessary to value and be seen to value what the respondent brings to the interview as much as the agenda carried by the evaluator/interviewer. The purpose in work of this kind is to encourage each interviewee to share freely and openly his/her own perceptions and in doing so, to try to delay until after the interview any attempt to interpret or judge. Essentially, the interviewer is the learner (of the interviewee's opinions, thoughts and feelings) so that if the interactional situation of the interview is conceived in terms of status or power and authority, it is the interviewer who is the 'underdog' during the interview process. Whilst it will be the interviewer who will initiate the questions, it will be the interviewee who determines the nature and quality of the response. To summarize, 'each form of the interview represents a 'tentatively' formulated plan of action the investigator may employ . . . . Reality 'out there' is present only to the extent that it is so defined' (Denzin, 1973).

In this sense:

> The interview is an understanding between the two parties that, in return for allowing the interviewer to direct their communication, the informant is assured that he (sic) will not meet with denial, contradiction, competition, or other harrassment. (Benney and Hughes, 1956)

The type of interview often used with each respondent may be described as 'non-schedule standardized' or 'focussed' (Merton and Kendall, 1946) in which certain types of information are desired from all respondents but, 'the particular phrasing of questions and their order is redefined to fit the characteristics of each respondent. This form of the interview requires that each interviewer be highly trained in the meaning of the desired information and in the skills of phrasing questions for each person interviewed' (Denzin, 1973).

The Project in Action

On 1 February 1988 a letter was sent by Derbyshire's County Adviser for Primary Education to eight schools calling a meeting to set up the primary school pilot scheme. The meeting involved two primary phase advisers, two area staff development coordinators and the heads of the schools which were to become the pilot group. The schools had been selected for a number of reasons: (i) they were geographically close enough to meet; (ii) they were from two of the four administrative areas in the county; (iii) they were at different stages of development; and (iv) they included urban and rural, infant, primary and junior, and were clustered around a particular geographical area. They all received an allocation of UK £150 per teacher with a minimum protected baseline of UK £450. The allocation of money was described by the LEA as 'a sum of money over which the school has more control, and so opportunities for choice and negotiation are increased' (Primary Schools LEATGS Pilot: The Formulation of a School/College Staff Development Programme 1988–9, Derbyshire LEA).

The summary findings were presented in a report to the LEA (Day, 1989). They appeared to have much in common with those of Her Majesty's Inspectors Report of the first year of the scheme (HMI, 1989). Certainly, schools had welcomed the opportunity to have a budget to spend on their own INSET, related to their own identified needs. Teachers had used a wider range of INSET provision than previously and had become more discriminating. Schools had a strong sense of ownership of the INSET and of its relevance. They had assumed increased responsibility and accountability for their own professional and curriculum developments. Problems of administration and management, tensions between individual institutional needs, match between institutional, LEA and DES priorities, and inadequate financial provision remained; and although there were clearly identifiable changes of perception, knowledge of, and attitude to, INSET by headteachers and teachers, there was as yet no overwhelming evidence that classroom practice was being affected significantly nor that 'professionalism' had increased. Teachers had for the most part increased their content and pedagogical knowledge without re-examining the situational assumptions or moral and ethical contexts for their work. Additionally, it was agreed that 'there can be no simple causal links between training and changes in teaching and learning as there are so many other factors playing a part in the process' (HMI, 1989 para 2.16).

Discussion

For the purposes of this chapter the data will be discussed under three themes:

(i) effects of the project on teacher development: self perceptions;
(ii) school culture: conditions for teacher empowerment;
(iii) reflection and empowerment.

Effects of the Project on Teacher Development: Self-perceptions

Between 70 and 95 per cent of the grant in all schools was spent on providing supply cover for teachers to be released from their classrooms to engage in a variety of in-service activities, for example, sharing a day's course with other schools; visiting other schools to look at aspects of good practice; time out with a colleague to put together a syllabus/write up policies; visiting colleagues in other classrooms in their own schools; exchanges of materials between schools; in-school training days.

It was interesting, though not surprising in the first year of the scheme, to note that less emphasis was placed on attendance at courses held outside school. A variety of reasons were given for this. Some, 'didn't really feel that there were many courses which were particularly useful . . .'. There was a perceived shortage of courses which focussed upon the needs of infant teachers, and some courses needed to address a narrower target audience. Responses to the quality of courses varied. Some were perceived as being too practical:

> When we go on these courses a lot of it is up to us . . . We have to do the work. . . .

In others there was too much theory and not enough practice:

> Some of the courses that are run are not as practically relevant to us as we'd like them to be. There's a lot of theory, whereas what we're mainly concerned about is getting in there and doing it at ground level.

> Some of the courses tend to be overbalanced by the theory of it and not heavily committed enough to the practical application in school, which for the classroom teacher is the priority.

Other teachers credited courses which they had attended as renewing their thinking:

> The course I went on was most worthwhile. It was over five Mondays. . . . We had two days looking at the National Curriculum, and coming up with ideas that he gave us, instead of trying to pick our brains to see what we did . . . I've tried a lot of the ideas out with the class . . . and that course renewed my thinking . . .

and being a great aid to self-development:

> For me it's been a great self development to be able to participate in the science course. It broadened my horizons . . . and opened up vistas for me as an Infant teacher that I would never have thought possible . . . You're learning different things by meeting other colleagues, by observing what other people are doing . . . Whilst you're learning anything, what ever it is, if it's contributing towards school, you're developing your skills as a teacher, you're learning different things.

One teacher did, however, speculate as to the value of a continuing emphasis on 'lighthouse' school experiences:

> Eventually one will have visited all the schools in your area appropriate to your needs, so where will you progress from there?

The most widely appreciated benefits of the scheme to the school as an organization were the opportunities to work outside the classroom on matters related to it during the school day:

> . . . It's given us breathing space for examining our responsibility posts. Before everything you have to try and do and cram in at the same time as everything else . . . This has given us the opportunity to stand back, reflect, think things out — some things you cannot do while you're still teaching a class of children and cannot be done out of hours if its something that involves seeing what's happening in each class at a time . . .

Almost all teachers spoke of the value of being able to engage in school-centred work. They related numerous examples of their achievements during the school day working either alone or with a colleague, sometimes off-site and sometimes on-site but outside their classrooms:

> . . . I think that's very good that you can actually work in school without the children . . . for instance, when we organized our own books, because there's never time. However long you stay after school, an hour isn't long enough. You need a full morning session.

This theme of time to stand back, plan and reflect, was a thread which ran through every interview. Teachers appreciated being able — some for the first time in their teaching careers — to work alone or collaboratively with colleagues on tasks which they had chosen and which they considered to be direct practical relevance to their school and classroom:

Many teachers spoke of the value of being able to work unimpeded by the normal stresses and strains of classroom life:

> I was allowed to go home for the day. Therefore, I could put everything out and there were no interruptions . . . and I really got a lot done . . . If I was having to do it at nights in my own time, then I wouldn't have got it (the syllabus) done. If I'm given time to do a specific job, then I can concentrate on it . . .

Headteachers, like their teachers, appreciated that the scheme had enabled them to review their curriculum and to act upon the review in a more concentrated period of time than would previously have been possible:

> The opportunity to sit down and discuss subjects in depth, which has really brought us together as a complete thinking unit, where previously we've not really had this opportunity. Staff meetings at school don't give the length of time that we've had on the full or half days, and we never really felt as if we'd gone far enough before we had to call a stop to it . . . It's made us think again about what we're doing and our aims and objectives. Sometimes we can lose sight of those. The use of our own funding has given us the opportunity to spend time on certain elements of the curriculum *in a shorter period of time* than otherwise we'd be able to. Therefore, we feel we're at the beginning of making improvements to the curriculum which really have been sadly in need of attention for some years.

A major issue related to the development of teachers' thinking which arises from these experiences, is directed at those who manage in-service in school, and this concerns *balance* and the associated danger of *parochialism*:

> Whilst we have benefited from being together as a staff . . . we do not wish to isolate ourselves from the rest of education, so it's important that we find a greater variety of activities.

The abiding problem of devolved finance will inhibit and possibly prevent support for teachers' attendance at longer courses outside school. Thus the pressure is likely to remain on many schools to encourage staff to engage in on-site activities which are self-generated and self-serviced and thus implicitly disempower teachers from moving to deeper levels of reflection. Those who are, like one teacher interviewed, 'looking for something more long term . . . more intensive . . .' may become increasingly frustrated. In the long term, this potential lack of investment in professional development as distinct from school curriculum development needs may prove to have a negative effect on the maintenance and enhancement of motivation, experience and knowledge among teachers in schools.

School Culture: Conditions for Teacher Empowerment

The conditions under which teachers learn are clearly vital, and the project provided an illustration in practice of what Purkey and Smith (1985) described as an 'inverted pyramid' approach to changing schools, for it recognized that whilst the LEA had legal responsibility for in-service work, for this to be effective, schools must be given 'strategic independence' (Finn, 1984) so that the inevitable tensions between systemwide uniformity and school-level autonomy might be reconciled, or at least become productive. Bruce Joyce (1989) reported that the contributing authors of the 1990 *Yearbook of the Association for Supervision and Curriculum Development* (of which he is editor), '. . . appear to have concluded that creating conditions where education personnel are growing productively and school improvement is an embedded feature of collegial life requires a major restructuring of the workplace':

> ... The challenge is to create an ethos that is almost an inversion of the one Lortie so accurately described in *Schoolteacher* (1975). That is, vertical and horizontal isolation and separation of roles will be replaced by integration and collaboration. (Joyce, 1989)

Almost all the in-service which occurred in the schools was related to their school development plan. Writing in an industrial context in the early 1980s, Ackoff (1981) makes a similar point about the interdependency implicit in any act of corporate planning, proposing three operating principles of interactive planning — participation, continuity, and coordination and integration:

> It is better to plan for oneself, no matter how badly, than to be planned for by others, no matter how well ... no parts of an organization can be planned for independently of any other unit at the same level ... planning done independently at any level of a system cannot be as effective as planning carried out interdependently at all levels.

The gains which may be achieved through interdependency have been well documented. Rosenholtz (1989) in America identified 'learning impoverished' and 'learning enriched' schools. The characteristics of 'learning enriched' schools were:

— Collaborative goals at the building level
— Minimum uncertainty
— Positive attitudes of teachers
— Principals supported teachers and removed barriers for them
— Principals fostered collaboration as opposed to competition

Characteristics of 'learning impoverished' schools were:

— No clear goals or shared values
— Teachers rarely talked to one another
— Teachers perceived the school to be routine
— Norms of self-reliance flourished, as did isolation

Headteachers used a variety of strategies to determine the kinds of learning which were to be promoted and the establishment of priorities within individual schemes. In general, staff were widely consulted about their own needs and those of the school, with the Head taking final decisions:

> We all put bids in ... stating what we thought our needs were, personal as well as school. Our bids were put into (headteacher) who then assessed the needs of the school against our needs and the money he'd got available to pay for it and it was sorted out from there on. He prioritised it. As a school we generally discuss things before we get to that stage, and so the others have agreed. So even though staff were not actively responsible for making the decision they put their oar in before the decision was actually

taken . . . The existing staff know each other very well, and so it's easier
to make decisions . . .

In schools represented by this statement there already existed *development cultures.*

No decisions are ever made without a team of three or four being involved in the decisions . . . and even then, it is most rare for a decision
to be taken without a follow-up going to the staff meeting . . .
We've got things down in writing perhaps that we didn't have before.
We always have been pretty good at communicating. We've had a good
background of working together in curriculum and spreading the responsibility from one or two people working together to seven or eight . . .

It is clear from these statements that opportunities for teacher development
had benefited from schools with a more 'democratic' ethos in which decisions
concerning school development were based upon active staff participation, and
where staff were treated, in the words of one teacher, 'as adults'. This feeling of
'having a say', of opinions being valued, and of the locus for need identification and decision-making having been moved closer to the source of action
(the school itself) was perhaps the most significant benefit reported across the
pilot schools:

If people feel that their opinion is valued, then they contribute more . . .
and then they started coming up with ideas . . . and then when we had a
staff meeting . . . we split up into teams (to work on review of maths) and
we bought supply in so that people could have time during the day,
which they thought was marvellous, that they were valued to the point
that you would provide cover to let them work on things . . .

. . . We've been able to have the things that we felt we needed . . . Its been
nice to feel that we could choose for ourselves . . .

In this sense, teachers perceived themselves to have a 'voice'. In schools where
there had been no tradition of collaboration there had been occasions when, 'one
or two of us feel we are being pushed out because our views aren't quite the same
as the younger people. We're not being asked, we're being told'. This kind of
statement served to reinforce the view expressed by a teacher in another school
that:

. . . I wonder, it we hadn't been in agreement, then it might not have been
as easy . . . We have regular meetings and we decide on the issues . . . It
could have been difficult. If you had a very dominant person who dis-
regarded everyone else . . .

There were examples of resentment among some staff:

It's been limited to a few . . . It seems that the hierarchy or the things that
are 'in', they're the one's who are going to get the time . . . There was
nothing in the bids for personal development.

Others indicated feelings of worthlessness:

> A lot of time is given to young teachers to go on courses ... but you get to the middle or towards to end of your teaching career and you think, 'Well, did I ought to go? Would it be better for other people?' You tend to go on courses now — which I feel we're going to be dictated — that deal with your area of the curriculum ... because of the money ... which is not always what you want ...

Others commented adversely on the apparent refocussing of in-service priorities from meeting individual to meeting institutional needs:

> ... It's giving you a very narrow view, whereas before this you were able to choose whichever course took your fancy ... I feel we're being pushed into one channel ... so I feel that it's going to be detrimental to your own development and what you're able to put over to the children ...

In schools with development cultures promoted by headteachers, however, the story was different:

> Part of our staff development policy is that money will be set aside for people to pursue things that they are interested in solely for themselves ... everybody agreed on that ... I think people feel quite strongly about that, and I agree with it. I always try to bear in mind the individual needs and what people want to do, because if we're doing our own staff development, with an emphasis on staff, that's what it should be about, but obviously we're having all these things coming at us and we've got to address those needs. So I'm feeling reluctantly that it's got to be those things first ... and then the personal if we can fit them in. I don't necessarily agree that's how it should be, but we're under these pressures.

The evidence from the teachers in this project suggests that they were generally sympathetic to these problems, and that they understood at this time that institutional needs must take precedence over personal needs. They also recognized, however, that, 'People's needs change from one year to the next', so that sensitive leadership is required in processes of prioritization.

'Where money is tight', one teacher commented, 'there's a danger that individual needs will be squeezed out'.

Some teachers were sceptical about the effect of this upon teacher and school autonomy:

> I feel sceptical about how much autonomy we'll have — with the National Curriculum and testing and assessment, and 'money' being the watchword at the moment, I can't see us having much freedom to choose ... I'm quite cynical.

Although external contexts may change, teachers will always feel the need to be valued during their professional lifetimes and this must always be remembered when considering the balance between identifying and meeting individual and institutional needs.

Yet headteachers were unanimous in acclaiming benefits in terms of change of attitude to professional development among their staff, and perhaps this was the most significant success of the year old scheme:

> I feel that the staff work cohesively together now in identifying the needs ... the fact that we have changed from thinking that in-service is all about courses so that it has been more school-focussed — that is a major change ... It's made us discuss things more. It's made us more aware ... We've had more time to look at the documents and do things ... The obvious answer would be from the results of the work with the children, but ... you also have to keep your staff happy. If your staff are happy and are interested in what they're doing, then that reflects upon the children ... So, look for a happy staffroom! It's part and parcel of how we see the school as a whole. I am trying to move people to a different approach in the classroom ... But it would have happened much more slowly ... But I've still got members of staff who prefer to work in their own way ...

> It is making a difference in school, because people are getting down to really talking about what is important, the way we must be going, really sorting ourselves out ... To some extent, because of the National Curriculum, it would have had to have happened, but it would have happened much more slowly ... I found it very difficult before 'directed time' came in to get people together on a regular basis. So directed time has helped. Then staff development money has been an extra bonus, a marvellous bonus really, because you can do that during the day, when people are fresh ... rather than at the end of the day when people are tired ...

High on everyone's agenda was the effect on practice, highlighted by a comment from a deputy head:

> Its very difficult to keep an overview of it and not get too obsessed with having the trappings of what's good but really it's not happening in the classroom. Having the wonderful documents ... but if there's nothing happening at the end of it all, then it's a complete waste of time. Really, it's 'How does this apply to us? What are we going to do in the classroom?' ... If we go out of school, if we don't bring it into school and if it doesn't do anything — whether it sparks off a discussion or whatever — then it's a total waste of money ... Now its got to be part of your staff development plan. That side of it I find sad, that you can't just go away and do something for your own benefit ... For me, whether something had worked or we'd got 'value for money' would be if I saw something change in the classroom for the children ... That's really what I'm after. If I could honestly say that I could walk in a classroom and see some practice that had been the product of the staff development ... The other thing is getting the staff to work together ... to talk ... all these are a process to try and get something better for the children, so ultimately that's how I would judge it.

Q Can you say that now?

A No ... I don't see it as years. It's an expanse of time ... Hopefully, people will move a little bit. You have to keep in your mind the overall picture ...

Most of the statements from heads and teachers associated the scheme with developments in classroom techniques and teacher collegiality — acceleration of developments which were already occurring, 'reinforcement' of current practice or trying out of new ideas gained from visiting other schools or attending courses rather than significant changes:

> ... most of the work we were doing before. It has, perhaps made us a little bit more conscious as far as science is concerned. We do a little bit more than we did before.

> I haven't changed anything that I'm already doing, in the classroom ...

> We're only just getting it into practice. We have put quite a lot of thought into it ... There must be concrete experience in what we do ... It's reinforced what I'm already doing ...

> It's not changed dramatically. But certainly I've seen lots of ideas which I've incorporated into my way of working.

In two instances, however, teachers did claim that there had been radical change in their practice and thinking about practice.

The first teacher had been motivated to, 'try things that I didn't do before ... It's made me do more practical things with children ...'

The second, who was 'trying to change' as a result of challenges to her thinking about practice was concerned that her own point of view might be ignored — a potential hazard for managers and a reminder of the need for moral as well as practical support over time for those in the process of changing:

> I've found it has challenged the way I have thought ... and I am in the process of trying to change ... Yes ... particularly on the maths and languages ... but I hope that people will listen to what I have to say ... but I'm a bit apprehensive — But I just have a feeling some things are being swept aside, that things we have done, and have done well in the past, are being questioned. I'm quite prepared to be questioned, but I hope that our points of view are going to be well listened to ...

Summary

In England, paradoxically, the in-service strategies and curriculum reforms pursued by national and local Government, have given added impetus to the breaking down of traditional school and teacher autonomy cultures and thus at least the potential for increased power of choice. However, power of choice over the management of finance for teacher development should not be confused with teacher empowerment. There is no causal link between schools' and teachers' increased power in the management of financial support for teacher development and the development of teacher thinking and the empowerment of teachers. This must relate to the nature of the learning processes themselves and to such factors as leadership and school culture which create conditions for teacher development, and individual teacher cultures.

Reflection and Teacher Empowerment

It was clear that most of the teachers interviewed perceived that they had gained significantly from involvement in a project in which INSET was:

> integrated with and part and parcel of concrete programme changes and problems experienced at the classroom and school level . . . intensive and ongoing . . . linked . . . to organizational development over time . . . (planned) at the school level . . . (Fullan, in Hopkins, 1986)

Additionally, though, many teachers had been their own developers. Some, as noted elsewhere, had, 'found their new role demanding both in terms of time as well as physical and emotional energy' (Kennedy and Patterson, 1986; Day, 1991). Within the context of school-based curriculum development doubts concerning the intellectual rigour of self-created learning opportunities have been expressed by Rudduck:

> I remain somewhat sceptical about the intellectual rigour and coherence of courses of study created by busy teachers in their own schools: creation must be disciplined by conscious articulation of the problematics of the relationship between materials and form . . . Major works of curriculum creation could be more safely left to others provided that we could rely on confident critique and adaptation from teachers. (Rudduck, 1987)

The broader issue of teacher learning does, then, concern its *quality*. A number of factors will affect this. For example the design of the in-service event or programme, the psychological, social and intellectual stage of the learner and his/her state of readiness to learn, and the nature of the learning process itself.

In 1978 Rubin claimed that, 'Any attempt to improve children's learning depends on some form of teacher growth . . .', and that, '. . . the best teachers must have periodic occasions for reflection, for readjusting their tactics to shifting social situations, and for utilizing new processes and procedures': and in 1988 Storr wrote that, 'as one engages in interactive professionalism it is essential that development and change are grounded in some inner reflection and processing. Otherwise we can too easily become alienated from our own deepest needs and feelings'.

Although the importance of reflecting on, in or about the action is acknowledged here and elsewhere (Zeichner *et al.*, 1987; Fullan and Hargreaves, 1991) there is still relatively little work concerned with the reconstruction of meaning and the notion of a 'reflective spectrum'. Reflection as a generic term and in practice needs to be 'unpacked' so that we may learn more about how the tacit may be made explicit, how and to what extent personal theories may be examined and, having been examined, how they may become public theories. In doing so we may learn more about the quality of professional learning. In the early 1970s Argyris and Schon (1974) developed the notion of single loop and double loop learning and stressed the need from time to time to move from the former in which planning, teaching and testing remains at the private, often tacit level, thus disempowering growth, to the latter, in which thinking, practice and discrepancies within and between the two are raised to an explicit, publicly accessible level. Since then, there have been several small-scale researches into ways in which teachers might be assisted, for example, journal keeping (Holly, 1989), stimulated recall through videotaping (Day, 1985), photographs, the use of metaphor (Munby and Russell, 1989) and image (Clandinin, 1989). Almost all require the use of mentors and clinical supervision through critical friendship or colleagueship of peers. This 'friend' requires not only technical abilities but also human relating/ interpersonal qualities and skills as well as time, energy and the practice of reflecting upon his/her own practice — not easy to find, except perhaps in higher education! If we are to take seriously Carr and Kemmis' (1983) notions of three levels of action research:

— technical (which aims to make educational practice more effective and to encourage teachers to participate in their own professional development);
— practical (in which groups decide the best ways to act within existing constraints);
— emancipatory (where the process of reflection leads to action based upon a critique of the social milieu).

then, we must continue to search out and develop ever more effective ways of promoting empowerment, enabling those who have been silenced to speak (Simon, 1987), and analyze more closely the 'reflective' processes which are so central to learning. We know already that, reflection in and on the action (Schon, 1983) is important, but then so is critical conversation (Carr and Kemmis, 1983) and the need to take note of the broader social context (Zeichner *et al.*, 1987). Unless we are able to promote work at each of these levels, unless we focus more upon the building of structural networks not only between individuals within institutions but between institutions themselves, then reflection for many teachers may remain at the private 'practical' level. We need also to tease out further links between reflection and 'better' teaching.

We do not know very much, for example, about how it is that teachers *make decisions* based upon reflection or how to judge the quality of the decisions in action, how to ensure that the reflective process really can lead to empowerment so that the micropolitical world of the classroom is seen within the social-political world of the school and the broader macropolitical world of society. And this is a world-wide debate (Oberg and McCutcheon, 1990). *We do not know how reflection leads to change.* Gunnar Handal is essentially pessimistic about teachers' opportunities to move beyond practical reflection. In research concerned with promoting the articulation of tacit knowledge through the counselling or 'critical friending' of practitioners (Handal, 1990), he identifies in Norway, as we have seen in England under the new system of devolved funding for in-service, a 'triple pressure' on schools and teachers to develop a more collective strategy of work through:

— the establishment of collective tasks;
— the provision of collective time to solve them;
— the ideological pressure on teachers to work together (often in 'contrived' collegiality).

Confronted with this task, he states that it is no longer sufficient to make curricular decisions on the basis of a largely implicitly personal practical theory of teaching. Teachers have to:

— formulate and develop their own personal practical theory;
— have the skills necessary to do this, and the skills to share them with others (here the work implicitly links to school culture research);
— have the fora and time to do so.

This has clearly not been achieved in the schools in the research reported here. In exploring how these may be achieved, he split the concept of 'reflective practice' into three hierarchical levels which may help us to think about reflection more analytically:

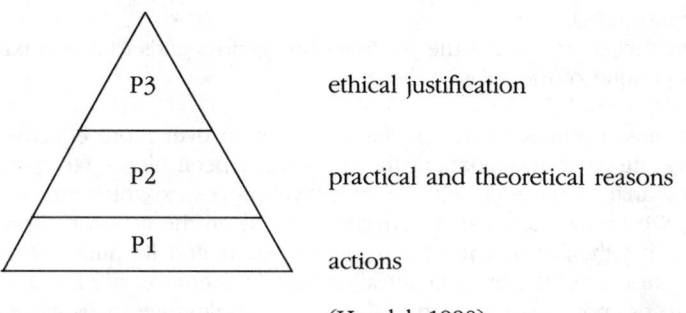

(Handal, 1990)

He found that teachers in Norway were used to talking about their work and deciding what to do, when to do it, and how to do it i.e. planning at the level of action, but rarely explicitly referring to reasons for this (P2) or the justification for the work itself (P3). These findings reflect those of the present study in England.

In finding this he was not making a critical moral judgment, but speculated that the reasons and justifications at levels P2 and P3 were not highly in demand in the 'busyness' culture of schools. Citing Carr and Kemmis' (1986, p. 186) action research planning cycle of planning — acting, observing and reflecting — he suggests, on the basis of his evidence, that the normal conditions for school-based action research may well be such that an incomplete 'self-reflective' spiral is encouraged. In most situations teachers spend most of their time planning and acting (constructing practice) at the P1 level and less on observation and reflection (deconstructing practice) at levels P2 and P3. The fundamental attitude of 'treating what counts as knowledge as problematic' (Carr and Kemmis, 1986), or studying critically one's own practice is not yet, he concludes, established. Change is mainly at the P1 level of action.

Three Levels of Reflection

In America, Zeichner and Liston (1987) pose three similar levels of reflection:

(i) Level One: Unproblematic technical proficiency at achieving pre-determined ends, 'the efficient and effective application of attaining ends which are accepted as given'. . . . where . . . . 'neither the ends nor the institutional contexts of classroom, school, community and society are treated as problematic'.

(ii) Level Two: Situational, theoretical, institutional assumptions and effects of teaching actions, goals and structures, where the problem is 'explicating and clarifying the assumptions and predispositions underlying practical affairs and assessing the educational consequences towards which an action leads'. Adler's (1991) summary is that Level Two reflection 'places teaching within its situational and institutional context'.

(iii) Level Three: Moral and ethical implications of pedagogy and of social structures ad concepts; whereby 'the teacher's 'critical reflection' incorporates moral and ethical criteria into a discourse about practical action. . . . Here the teaching (ends and means) and the surrounding contexts are viewed as problematic'.

In Australia John Smyth analyzes the learning cycle in a different but complementary way. He argues, with Day (1985), that in order to develop and sustain a critical form of teaching, teachers need to be concerned with four processes:

(i) describing . . . . (what do I do?)
(ii) informing . . . . (what does this description mean?)
(iii) confronting . . . (how did I come to be like this?)
(iv) reconstructing . . . (how might I do things differently?)
(Smyth, 1991)

Like Kemmis (1985) and Zeichner and Liston (1987) he subscribes to the notion that reflection is a form of political action. It:

(i) is not a purely 'internal' psychological process; it is action-oriented and historically embedded;
(ii) is not a purely individual process; like language, it is a social process;
(iii) serves political interests; it is a political process;
(iv) is shaped by ideology; in turn it shapes ideology;
(v) is a practice which expresses our power to reconstitute social life by the way we participate in communication, decision-making and social action.
(Kemmis 1985, p. 140, quoted in Smyth, 1991)

If, as may be inferred, reflection is a central part of Smyth's four (and Zeichner and Liston and Handal's three) stages in the learning cycle, then what will it involve? Certainly it will be more than feedback, for in reflecting upon action, the teacher as action researcher focusses, observes, selects, synthesizes and interprets. The quality of the data and thus the authenticity of information upon which confrontation will be based will be dependent not only upon the teacher's abilities and skills in these areas but also the way in which they are applied (systematically — unsystematically), the frequency, and the existing psychological as well as social contexts. It is likely that 'descriptive self-reflection' will operate at the planning level; and it is this level which predominates through the short-burst learning opportunities which are the hallmark of the new system of in-service funding in the UK. In order to move to levels of confrontation and ethical justification, reflection will need to be analytic and involve dialogue with others over time. Thus Schon's (1983) notion of the 'reflective practitioner' may itself be criticized for failing to deal with the importance of the discursive, dialogical dimension of learning which can only emerge from processes of confrontation and reconstruction. As Fay (1977) argues:

> what matters is not only the fact that people come to have particular self-understanding, and that this new self-understanding provides the basis for altering social arrangements, but also the manner in which they come to adopt this new 'guiding idea'. (Fay, 1977)

Figure 10.1 provides an indication at the meso level of factors which need to be considered in developing teachers' thinking and practice. National legislation and school culture will facilitate or constrain the provision of opportunities for development, but it is likely also that the effectiveness of the opportunities themselves — the levels at which teachers engage in reflection, for example, and their immediate and longer term impact upon thinking and practice — will be affected not only by their quality, but also the culture of the individual teacher. In a related piece of research with primary school teachers (Day, 1991b) a clear connection was found to exist between school cultures, teachers' own values, learning preferences and classroom practices, past life experiences and influences and between life and career stages and their perceived learning needs. Figure 10.2 indicates the factors which contribute to developing the learning culture (and so empowerment) of teachers. Both sets of factors must be taken into account in any consideration of or investigation into the development and thus empowerment of teachers' thinking and practice.

Empowerment implies the development of teachers who are able and willing to reflect upon and confront at all levels their thinking and practice and the contexts in which these occur, and to translate this into their practice; and the extent to which they are enabled to engage in this learning depends not only under the broader ideological, political, economic and educational contexts in which they work, but also the school cultures and their own biographies and stages of life and career development. For too long, policy makers and researchers have ignored the central moral and ethical roles that are fundamental to teachers' working lives.

The empowerment of teachers will not be achieved through reflection which results only in increased efficiency in achieving ends which are accepted as given, where, 'neither the ends nor the institutional contexts of classroom, school, community and society are treated as problematic' (Zeichner and Liston, 1987). Nor is it enough to move beyond that to placing teaching within its situational and institutional contexts (Adler, 1991; Tabachnick, 1991). Technical proficiency and situational knowledge (levels 1 and 2) on their own constitute a denial of the central moral role of the teacher. If we accept, with Elbaz (1991) that, 'moral

Figure 10.1: Factors affecting teachers' thinking and development

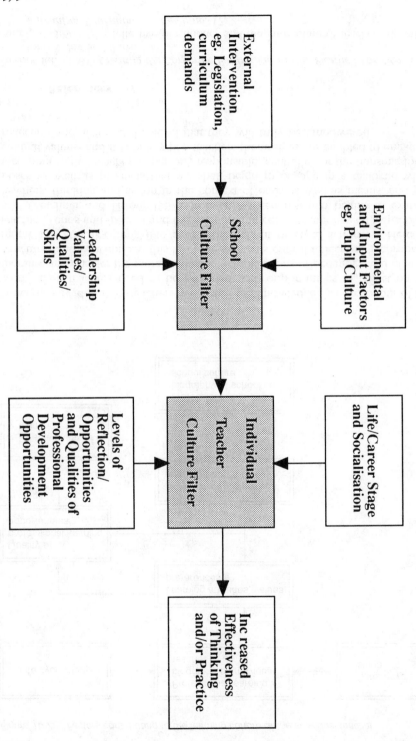

Figure 10.2:   *Factors contributing to the learning culture of the individual teacher*

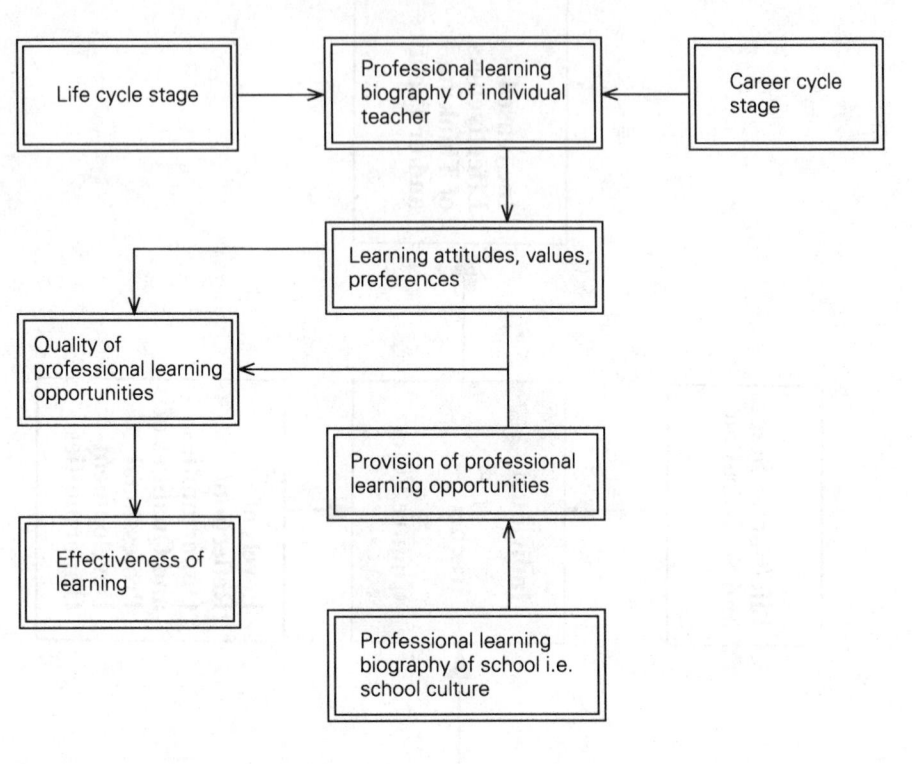

concern pervades all of teachers' work and the knowledge that grows out of that work', then teachers need to be provided with opportunities to reflect on that morality, to consider the moral and ethical implications of pedagogy and of social structures and concepts. At this level the teacher's critical reflection, 'incorporates moral and ethical criteria into a discourse about practical action ... Here the teaching (ends and means) and the surrounding contexts are viewed as problematic' (Zeichner and Liston, 1987). It is only when research begins to examine teachers' thinking and action in the context of ends as well as means, and purposes as well as products that we shall begin to engage in a dialogue which incorporates the 'teacher as person', responsible, centrally, for the transmission of cultural values; and it is only when teachers themselves are enabled to engage in reflection and action at this level that they will truly be empowered.

References

ACKOFF, R.L. (1981) *Creating the Corporate Future: Plan or be Planned For*, New York, John Wiley and Sons.
ADLER, S. (1991) 'The reflective practitioner and the curriculum of teacher education', *Journal of Education for Teaching*, 17, 2.

ARGYRIS, C. and SCHON, D.A. (1974) *Theory in Practice: Increasing Professional Effectiveness*, New York, Jossey-Bass.

BENNEY, M. and HUGHES, E.C. (1956) 'Of sociology and the interview editorial preface', *American Journal of Sociology*, 61, September.

BOLAM, R. (1982) *In Service Education and Training of Teachers: A Condition for Educational Change*, Paris OECD.

BROWN, G. (1989) 'The changing face of INSET: A view from a university Department of Education' in MCBRIDE, R. (Ed.) (1989) *The In-Service Training of Teachers: Some Issues and Perspectives*, Lewes, Falmer Press.

CARR, W. and KEMMIS, S. (1983) *Becoming Critical: Knowing Through Action Research*, Geelong, Deakin University.

CARR, W. and KEMMIS, S. (1986) *Becoming Critical: Education, Knowledge and Action Research*, Lewes, Falmer Press.

CLANDININ, D.J. (1989) 'Developing rhythm in teaching: The narrative study of a beginning teacher's personal practical knowledge of classrooms', *Curriculum Inquiry*, 19, pp. 121–41.

DAY, C. (1985) 'Professional learning and researcher intervention', *British Educational Research Journal*, 11, 2.

DAY, C. (1989) *LEATGS: Evaluation of a Pilot Project for the Devolution of INSET Resources to Primary Schools, 1988–9*, Mimeo, School of Education, University of Nottingham.

DAY, C. (1991a) 'Promoting teachers' professional development' in BELL, L. and DAY, C. (Eds) *Managing the Professional Development of Teachers*, Milton Keynes, Open University Press.

DAY, C. (1991b) *The Professional Learning of Teachers in Primary Schools and the Devolution of In-service Funding: A Research Report*, Derbyshire LEA.

DENZIN, N.K. (1973) *The Research Act*, Chicago, IL., Aldine Publishing Co.

ELBAZ, F. (1991) 'Hope, attentiveness and caring for difference: The moral voice in teaching', keynote address to Fifth Conference of the International Study Association on Teacher Thinking, University of Surrey, 23–27 September.

FAY, B. (1977) 'How people change themselves: The relationship between critical theory and its audience' in BALL, T. (Ed.) *Political Theory and Praxis*, Minneapolis, University of Minnesota Press.

FINN, C.E. (1984) 'Toward strategic independence: Nine commandments for enhancing school effectiveness', *Phi Delta Kappan*, February.

FULLAN, M. and HARGREAVES, A. (1991) *What's Worth Fighting For: Working Together for Your School*, OPSTF, 1260, Bay Street, Toronto, Ontario, Canada M5R 2B7.

HANDAL, G. (1990) 'Promoting the articulation of tacit knowledge through the counselling of practitioners', keynote paper at APC Conference, Amsterdam, 6–8 April.

HMI (1989) *The Implementation of the Local Education Authority Training Grants Scheme (LEATGS): Report on First Year of the Scheme 1987–88*, DES 136/89.

HOLLY, M.L. (1989) *Writing to Grow: Keeping a Personal-professional Journal*, Portsmouth, Heinemann Education Books.

HOPKINS, D. (1986) *In-Service Training and Educational Development*, London, Croom Helm.

JOYCE, B. (1989) 'Staff development as cultural change', paper presented at the International Conference of the Hong Kong Educational Research Association, November.

KEMMIS, S. (1985) 'Action research and the politics of reflection' in BOUD, D., KEOGH, D. and WALKER, D. (Eds) *Reflection: Turning Experience into Learning*, London, Kogan Page.

KENNEDY, K. and PATTERSON, C. (1986) 'Enterprise kids — Case study of a year 10 transition education course' in FRASER, B. (Ed.) *School Development Through Transition Education*, Perth, Western Australian Education Department.

KENNEDY, K. (1989) 'Policy and practice in school-based curriculum development', paper presented to the International Conference of the Hong Kong Educational Research Association, November.

MERTON, R.K. and KENDALL, P.L. (1946) 'The focussed interview', *American Journal of Sociology*, 51, May, pp. 541–57.

MUNBY, H. and RUSSELL, T. (1989) 'Metaphor in the study of teachers' professional knowledge' in OBERG, A. and McCUTCHEON, G. (Eds) (1990) special issue of *Theory into Practice*, 29, 3.

OBERG, A. and McCUTCHEON, G. (Eds) (1990) special Issue of *Theory into Practice*, 29, 3.

PURKEY, S.C. and SMITH, S.M. (1985) 'School reform: the district policy implications of the effective schools' literature', *The Elementary School Journal*, **85**.

ROSENHOLTZ, S.J. (1989) *Schools, Social Organization and the Building of a Technical Culture*, New York, Longman Inc.

RUBIN, L. (1978) *The In-Service Education of Teachers: Trends, Processes and Prescriptions*, Boston, MA, Allyn and Bacon.

RUDDUCK, J. (1987) 'Can school-based curriculum development be other than conservative?' in SABAR, N., RUDDUCK, J. and REID, W. (Eds) *Partnership and Autonomy in School-Based Curriculum Development*. Sheffield, University of Sheffield, Division of Education.

SCHON, D.A. (1983) *The Reflective Practitioner: How Professionals Think in Action*, New York, Basic Books Inc.

SIMON, R. (1987) 'Empowerment as a pedagogy of possibility', *Language Arts*, 64, 4, p. 374.

SMYTH, J. (1991) *Teachers as Collaborative Learners*, Birmingham, Open University Press.

STORR, A. (1988) *Solitude*, London, Flamingo Press.

TABACHNICK, B. (1991) *Issues and Practice in Inquiry Oriented Teacher Education*, Lewes, Falmer Press.

ZEICHNER, K. and LISTON, D. (1987) 'Teaching student teachers to reflect', *Harvard Education Review*, 57, February.

ZEICHNER, K.M., TABACHNICK, R. and DENSMORE, K. (1987) 'Individual, institutional and cultural influences in the development of teachers' craft knowledge' in CALDERHEAD, J. (Ed.) *Exploring Teachers' Thinking*, London, Cassell.

Chapter 11

Chronicles: Doing Action Research:
The Stories of Three Teachers

Richard Davies

This chapter contains the stories of three teachers who took part in a two-year action research project. The overall theme of the project was the development of more independent styles of learning supported by information technology.

A year after the project closed I was interested to see whether, according to the teachers themselves, its dimension of 'teacher research' had achieved any enduring effect on their perceptions of their professional practice.

Jane Eames

Jane began at S-High with a two-term contract to teach English and special needs. She has now been teaching at the school for seven years. It is an 11–18 comprehensive secondary school founded in September 1979. The catchment area is 'varied with intake from rural and urban districts'. The school is split-site and there are approximately 1250 pupils. As Jane observed in her submisson for her Certificate in Educational Research 'the school layout was important for the success of the project'.

In the first two weeks of the autumn term of 1988 she was approached by the school TVEI Coordinator and the Head of the Withdrawal Support System of the school and asked if she would be interested in working with computers. 'It was all' she said 'a bit hazy'. The project was mentioned. The Project Director came to the school for a meeting and 'we talked on into lunch'. Jane was still unsure. She felt she knew nothing about computers and 'didn't like them'. When the Director talked about the 'process' — in this instance, action research, and in particular collecting audio recorded data — Jane asked if she would 'analyze the pupil transcripts'. She felt disappointed when the Project Director said that she and not Jane, would undertake such work. She and a colleague, Sarah, also nominated to take part in the project, decided at this stage not to participate. However, for reasons she is not aware of 'the next thing I knew we were doing it'.

Sarah asked Jane to pick a class. She chose a group of twelve second years with writing difficulties 'I considered them a bright little bunch and some of them seemed too able for special needs'. They decided that the focus of the research would be to what extent laptop computers facilitated those with handwriting difficulties. 'My concern was with pupils who seemed to be confused by their own handwriting, unable to interpret what they had originally intended to put on paper, therefore unable to clarify the correct spelling'. She needed twelve laptops 'Each boy' she recorded 'was issued with a TOSHIBA 1000 LAPTOP portable computer weighing about 10 lbs with its bag'.

'There were all sorts of problems', she said later 'The computers didn't arrive and when they did the battery chargers wouldn't work'. She found the manuals 'hard to follow and the computers themselves were unreliable'. It was not until the summer term that 'we got under way'. Thus, although the project 'came into the school' in September it was not until May that systematic work with the group started 'with two out of five English lessons'. It was at this stage that she began to keep a research diary.

An extract from week one 'We introduced the computers. Went slowly and carefully through instructions for use. The students picked it up quite quickly . . . the boys were asked to print their name. They typed in their first thoughts on using the Toshiba and having learnt to save the text on the disc went ahead and printed it . . . the boys were asked to print their reactions . . . general excitement. An atmosphere of intense concentration. Some emotional reactions when frustrated, for example, Harry. Therefore his first reactions were coloured by his anger. He was keen but impatient. Harry: This computer is CRAP!

I am learning with this class so I feel to SOME extent I can sympathize . . .'

At around this time 'a funny thing happened', which was to have enduring consequences for the project in the school. The Project Officer designated to support the project in the LEA arrived with another Project Officer from a neighbouring authority in order to talk to Jane and Sarah about their progress. Before she left the visiting officer turned and said to Jane 'I suppose we'll see you at the weekend conference?' 'I didn't know anything about it but Sarah and Rob, the School Resources Coordinator, had been invited'. Jane 'put in a complaint as I was the one actually using the computers' and succeeded in taking Rob's place. As a result an important source of support within the school was alienated 'Rob ever after was rarely supportive'.

Jane went to the conference where, at first, she felt out of her depth 'I didn't know what I was doing. I came in through the backdoor, blindfolded'. The Project Director, however, 'was very understanding. She said that everyone was just a beginner'.

From the start of the project, Jane tried to establish liaisons throughout the school. She felt that the overall project theme of independent learning supported by micros, was best sustained as a whole school excercise. Such a philosophy and style of teaching/learning could be undermined if it was pursued in only one or two lessons a week. Unfortunately communication across the school proved logistically to be very difficult.

> I found the whole thing fell on me. Every lunchtime I would be waiting for the kids to come and print out their work. It was hell basically. I had no time, no time allotted. I was home every night, upstairs working. I had to bring the printer home with the kids' discs. It was the only way I could get it done — because the staff wanted work back straightaway. I was doing things much more slowly. It completely changed everything. I lost my social life.

It was, she said 'all very difficult'. But there was, nevertheless, some useful learning to be found in the experience 'It taught me a lot about organization. It made me more self assertive. I had to go up to people and say "I'm trying to do this thing and will you please be more cooperative" . . . It taught me a lot about staff and schooling. My school was not the right school physically, socially or educationally for the project'.

She gave an example of this resistance within the school in which one of the four house tutors 'complained that the kids had dumped their computers in his section of the building'. In essence she felt 'the staff didn't like it. They complained about the kids losing their work, the noise of the printers. The kids were taking much longer than usual to complete their work. The whole thing was so clumsy. There was only one printer which wouldn't always work. The group themselves coming from all their lessons that I had to deal with. The system of dinner with passes — whichever way you turned there was some admin, or someone's toes you trod on. It was murder'. In addition the poor keyboard skills of the group proved a serious handicap 'and they started to complain'. Furthermore her 'credibility as a teacher went. One pupil saw me as a stupid woman who couldn't cope, not Mrs Eames who knew everything but someone who couldn't manage a computer'. Problems of discipline followed 'I had to get ratty and enforce discipline which was another pressure'.

But she also discovered that the research dimension of the project brought some satisfactions 'I enjoyed it, collating the information and so on. Coming home and writing it all up I enjoyed. I would love to do some more but I would like it to be more organized'.

By Christmas of the second year neither the school nor the pupils in the group wanted to be involved any longer. The project, it seemed, had 'petered out'. Sarah had withdrawn 'disenchanted' with it. Jane became anxious that all she could write for the project was 'negative'. Again the Project Director calmed her fears telling her 'not to worry, just write it down'. At the next project conference Jane had the uncomfortable experience of overhearing other delegates talk about her writing and say ' "Oh, this is awful, It's so negative". I was hurt by that' she said 'I did my best to be honest'.

But then, in the second year 'funnily enough' with neither planning nor prompting by Jane 'because the computers were there' a parallel group of second years 'got started on their own initiative. And it was very productive. It was such a joy'. The project in its second year thus moved into a more positive phase. Jane talked of 'the Phoenix of the parallel group, who just began fiddling around with the laptops, and also by then I was more confident technically and could tell them what buttons to press'. She began, she said 'to feel more pride in the project'.

One aspect of this was her commitment to use the project as a means of doing (and obtaining) a research diploma, a Certificate in Educational Research (CER). She felt that it would be useful to get an additional qualification but she also 'found it exciting and the project personnel very supportive because I felt very vulnerable'. In particular she found the Project Director a considerable help 'She was decisive — lots of positive feedback. I really appreciated it'. She became very enthusiastic about doing the research and considered undertaking an MEd.

The reaction of the school, however, was not encouraging. When she was awarded her degree she 'got a pat on the back from the head but I never saw him again in connection with the project. No-one else congratulated me on getting my certificate'. When she asked for comments from staff as to the progress of the project she recalled one colleague saying 'That's a load of crap, Jane, you've been wasting your time'. As for action research another colleague commented 'It's just somebody wasting their time to get somebody else's qualification. It is not good for the school and you're just putting yourself out to get someone else's PhD. ' She was conscious that her colleagues were under considerable pressures of work. One English teacher indicated that he would have like to help 'but just couldn't stand the plugging in, the setting up, the needing to answer questions'. However one maths teacher was very supportive.

Looking back what was the value of action research to her professionally and personally?

> There was a lot of value. It widened my experience and gave me deeper insights — a greater knowledge of my colleagues and what makes things tick. It was psychologically useful . . . It made me reassess myself — I had to come to terms with myself. I had to go from being a qualified teacher who knew it all to someone plunged into a new situation in an environment I usually thought of as safe. I had to reorganize myself and change my thinking. And sometimes with a longing for a return to the familiar old ways. It was all very difficult but very challenging . . . It widened and deepened my understanding of the parameters of education — it was about introducing experience that would be educational for pupils and teachers alike . . . The project was heartening in that it seemed something was getting done. It was not static; it was a process evolving.

Although she was sceptical about doing the research at the outset she 'changed radically. It gave me hope — hope that people are still evaluating, looking at the process of education, seeking, working at it. Teachers' morale is so low, that this project gave me hope for the future.'

Daphne James

Now retired she taught at a school which had one computer but which by the end of the project had five. It was a middle school serving both a rural and a town catchment area with pupils aged between 8 and 12 years, a number of whom are bussed to school. There are altogether 400 pupils. The school is housed in modern buildings dating from 1971 to 1975 being divided into three 'houses'. Two houses contain large double classrooms with smaller adjoining quiet rooms and central library areas. The other house has specialist facilities for science, art, CDT, homecraft and French. The fourth year tend to be based in these areas. The computer is located in the homecraft room; 'I put the computer where the stoves were' Daphne reported.

She did not choose to become involved with the project. Instead she was 'chosen'. As Deputy Head she did not have a class herself but would support other teachers very occasionally taking a class. Therefore for the project her support was seen as essential. In its first year she was teaching B grade ('not the best grade') class of 11–12-year-olds four hours a week. The class numbered thirty-three. In the second year of the project she taught a parallel C grade group 'just above remedial'.

Only one other teacher at the time was 'doing anything with computers'. The curriculum area she decided to work in was maths. 'I'm not much good at technical things' she says and she found the program manual 'absolutely unintelligible — complete gibberish'.

She had one-hour sessions with the class. In that hour 'I had to arrange groups around the computer'. With such groups established she was left with the rest of 'a not very able class'. She found it very awkward 'Well my trouble was that I had thirty in that class, you see, and only about six or seven on the computer . . . and the others are clamouring for attention as well, so I'm sort of dashing backwards and forwards to see what they're doing'. There was some support in the first year of the project. A woman auxiliary would make visits to the school but, as far as Daphne was concerned, it was not a very satisfactory system, 'people who appeared and disappeared. Didn't know where they came from. Couldn't leave a class with them. The Project Officer was very good but was unable to appear every week and in fact hardly managed more than three visits a term.' There was no advisory support. Her colleague (also working in the project) knew most about computers 'but she was a full-time French teacher'. For the project she was asked to make observations of the pupils working with the computer. These pupils also had a book in which to write down their own thoughts. In the first year 'The pupils didn't do too badly at all'. For example they would write percentages on the computer and then explain to the rest of the class what they had done. Some, she pointed out, had computers at home which gave them useful experience.

'The whole point of the matter was that I couldn't leave the rest of the class. It is their education after all. You've got to do something valid and make sure they're doing it. I would be called over to help with the computer while trying to explain things to other pupils.' She found it 'all a bit wearing'.

The Project Officer was very good but 'I could have done with him there all the time'. Despite these drawbacks, the children seemed to enjoy working with the computer.

But in the second year of the project the brighter children 'became difficult — they'd spend minutes just changing colours'. They were also taken aback by being asked to write about what was happening in the classroom.

The research was 'interesting from a social point of view' said Daphne 'to see who took charge. Timid ones who insisted on doing their bit and being pleased — interesting to see them as individuals and how they placed themselves in a group'. She felt that through her observations she found out a lot about the children 'I would like to have observed them more'. Support remained the problem 'if there had been two of us in the classroom it would have made a tremendous difference'. At the beginning of the project she felt very 'diffident' about using a computer. She now feels less so 'but I never felt I mastered computers'. The Project Officer later recorded a somewhat more emphatic development. He wrote 'I was unable to get back into the school . . . for some weeks and was greeted on my arrival by the school cordinator with 'what have you done with Daphne? She's demanded to have a machine for every maths lesson.' (Davidon, 1990).

As a form of INSET in the area of IT she felt action research had been more effective than other approaches 'I had been to an after school lesson or two, but I still didn't seem to understand, I don't think you do understand until you actually use the thing and makes mistakes on it, do you. . . . You've got to do it like that, and the children are the same. They make mistakes and then they just go back and do it all over again . . . I think I gained confidence with the children.'

What impact did her involvement in an action research project have upon her teaching? 'I have taught so many years it is difficult to change — I was surprised I was the one chosen to be doing the project.'

The project happened in the last two years of her 30 years of teaching 'I thought about computers and their uses — if they were useful. And maybe I changed a little bit in the way I taught.' But she added 'the results you get and the conclusions you draw will be different in any classroom'. How did she change?

> I relaxed a little bit. I'm a bit old style teaching. I don't like to feel I don't know what's going on in every part of the classroom most of the time. It's very difficult with a large group of thirty or so kids — you have to keep a whole eye on everything. So I had to be very organized. I carefully planned the use of the computer, the whole layout — otherwise you were lost, a terrific noise here, tomfoolery there. Everything had to be very carefully planned beforehand but I was relaxed doing it . . . I think it was useful to have to look closely at how children learned, especially with a computer. It could be more useful than traditional methods and in the end I felt Yes. But I needed more skill and there is still not the perfect program and certainly not the perfect program book.

The Project Officer concluded in his report on the school 'It appears to me that (the project) offered this teacher a means of linking her vast experience with the innovation of the computer by removing the fear and technispeak that surrounds it. She was led into it via the involvement and excitement of the children, allowing them to hold the technical skills while she supplied the educational stimulation'.

Helen Jones

Helen worked in the same school as Daphne, 'Teachers are trained to know the answers. They're the ringmasters. It's all very overt. Initial training assumes you set up the classroom, with the children in the places you designate, in groups you designated and doing tasks you set up. It came as a shock when I discovered this. I almost packed up'.

How did she make this discovery for herself? 'Collecting data'. There was some irony in the timing of the project. Shortly before it started in the school, Helen and other members of staff had written a letter for parents and governors 'in which we talked about what a good group of teachers we were, how open'. They considered themselves as liberal 'in touch with childrens' needs, experiential learning in the true sense, got on very well with kids'. They felt that as far as the project was concerned they were a very good group to undertake research in more independent styles of learning — they were, they considered 'well on the way already'.

The project began in September. By Christmas her view of the nature of her teaching had begun to alter 'I hadn't realized how what we said in the letter was not the case'. It was through pupil diaries that she began to see her teaching differently. This was her primary source of data 'Although you go through all the business of confidentiality, it took some time for them to come out with what they felt. But they did'. It was at this stage that she made the discovery that the independent learning she thought she was promoting was not the case 'At some point I realized I was a ringmaster, the sort of person who couldn't let go. All I had done was try to be less overt — more covert e.g. by choosing software, organizing grouping, deciding outcomes. But my language had changed, it had become subtler "Don't you think if you do that it won't work out etc."'

She made the following discovery: 'The children only became more independent if the teacher did. The only way I could encourage more independent learning in the classroom was by letting go of the reins'. This proved an unhappy period for her professionally: 'At that stage I became very disillusioned. I felt a failure. I felt everything I had done in the past was wrong. There was little point in what I was doing. It was contrary to what I believed in but I couldn't find the method to let go'.

At this point she said, 'I would have done anything to get out of teaching'. However she persevered: '. . . pride doesn't let you give up. So you try to use what you've learnt'. By using the pupil diaries which developed in sophistication and bluntness over time she felt she was able get a picture of her class 'as it really was rather than how I thought it was'. She put it this way: 'you see an image in the mirror but you have to go behind that image to find the person. Collecting data is a way of getting behind the facade of the classroom.'

In Helen's view data-collection is 'essential for any teacher'. She started out she said with the presumption that 'it wouldn't tell me anything I didn't already know'.

The principal means of data collection, as we note above, was diary keeping, those of both pupils and teacher: 'There's no trouble fitting it into English and if you as a teacher value it then the kids value it'. There was the additional educational value, namely, 'if you want the kids to learn how to criticize constructively then you've got to give them the opportunity to do it privately'. This she achieved by negotiating a code of confidentiality with the pupils with included the principle that what they wrote was of equal importance to whatever Helen wrote. 'How often do kids read what the teacher writes and get a chance to dispute it?'. The code worked in the following way: Helen left her diary open on the desk for the pupils to read if they wanted to: 'at first they didn't'. They could offer to show her whatever part of their diary they wished. In the beginning, Helen said, they would write little more than 'I don't like so and so, or this or that'.

This changed over the course of the term. The pupils were allowed to write comments in Helen's diaries and slowly these became more illuminating. She highlighted those items in the pupils' diaries that she wanted to use for research purposes: 'I would give this back to them and if it was alright to use it they would just write "yes" or "no" in the next entry. There was no pressure.' If pupils had written something of interest 'in the widest sense I would ask them to talk to me. Nothing compulsory or vice versa. I would read the relevant parts of my diary to individuals. there were no secrets between me and what I had written about them.'

She subsequently found that this code of confidentiality had pastoral implications. The diaries had a structure of two basic sections: 'personal/academic — I didn't want them to write a diary that was about my research. They had to be able to write about things important to them from a school and personal point of view.'

Through the diaries one boy who had personal problems that he would not speak about began a 'correspondence' with Helen. He once wrote in his diary 'that he hated everyday and wished his parents wouldn't shout at each other.' Helen observed 'He wrote about things he would not have spoken about and I could respond in a way that would not have otherwise been possible.'

So in what way did her involvement in an action research based project affect her thinking and her professional practice?

Through action research — collecting and interpreting data — I moved from being in charge of individual work to supporting more group-based work. With action research you focus on yourself, focus on the children and focus on the environment. The more you look, the more you see, the more you change; round and round. Data collection — whatever data you're collecting, however you collect it — is a form of looking. If you don't collect data you're not looking. It's as simple as that. I changed the whole concept of what I thought teaching was, what I thought learning was through collecting data, I wasn't wrong before. I didn't think I was a bad teacher before. I just made it more difficult. Some people know instinctively how to change but the vast majority of us need help.

With action research you are going through the process the children go through and you understand why they feel so threatened when the teacher stops teaching. There is no success or failure, there is only development. You learn how to ask questions. You don't have to please anybody. The only thing you have to do is please yourself.

Data collection and reflection is also a way of looking at yourself, Helen argues 'looking at yourself is the only way to go ahead, to change. If you don't know who/what you are, you just go on reinforcing it. Change is a long and difficult process but it is also the most enlightening'.

What does she feel she learnt from her involvement in the project? 'There's no such thing as failure — there's success and less success. But even less success gives you a better idea of yourself, of how people learn, why they learn, and why you need to teach. After the project I knew more about myself as a teacher and a person. I don't like all I know — but you get more control over yourself and less control over others, You've got to have organized chaos.'

What does that mean for classroom management?

Children have to have facilities, know where to get them and have responsibilities to complete things. You've got to train kids to a realistic timetable. One thing I have learnt is that kids like a finished product. They like something to show that is tangible . . . I have learnt that children learn far more in groups than they would possibly on their own. You need to respond to when they need to learn on their own and when they need to learn as a group. By watching, listening, collecting data you can make conditions right for them.

If you're a teacher the thing you have to understand is the way in which children learn and provide the situation for that. We're always changing. Things are always new. It is not that you necessarily come up with a new methodology but you become aware of how you do the methdology.

Reference

DAVIDSON, R.L. (1990) unpublished PALM Project report, Norwich, Centre for Applied Research in Education, University of East Anglia.

Part 3

Researchers and Teachers:
Changing Roles and Relationships

Chapter 12

Through the Looking Glass:
The Use of Associative Methods
to Enhance Teacher Thinking

Michael Schratz

Then she began looking about, and noticed that what could be seen from the old room was quite common and uninteresting, but that all the rest was as different as possible. For instance, the pictures on the wall next the fire seemed to be all alive, and the very clock on the chimney-piece (you know you can only see the back of it in the Looking-glass) had got the face of a little old man, and grinned at her. (Lewis Carroll, *Through the Looking Glass*)

In Search of a New Perspective

Recent developments in educational research have shown a certain shift from so-called quantitative to more qualitative approaches in looking at what matters in pedagogical contexts (Lincoln and Guba, 1985; Clift, Houston and Pugach, 1990; Guba, 1990; Schratz, 1993a). Although the continuing dialogue has not yet come to an end (Buchmann and Floden, 1989) a certain paradigmatic change can be noticed in the research terminology: Teachers as educational technocrats, learners as recipients of teacher-proof curricula, learning machines as control mechanisms in classroom management represent terms which belong to educational terminology that enhanced both theory and practice of teaching in the sixties, but contributed little to the advancement of pedagogical practice at large.

Times have changed in the world of educational research: emancipatory movements have tried to do away with alienated forms of learning, school systems have been restructured, new technology has swept the educational market. Little, however, has really changed at the chalk face: In most classrooms teachers still dominate the scene, students have to behave in a drill-like way, discourse patterns reveal an unfolding series of initiation — reply — evaluation sequences (IRE) (Cazden, 1988; Edwards and Mercer, 1987; Mehan, 1979; Sinclair and Coulthard, 1975). Even modern computer software generates more drill and practice than anything that could be classified as tutorial (Longstreet, 1989).

Therefore it is not surprising that the authors of a recent analytical study entitled *Education for the Year 2000* (Klemm *et al.*, 1986) argue that school reform

— at least in German speaking countries — has fallen into a severe crisis facing the threat caused by the third technological revolution. Even after years and years of struggle for a change in school both teachers in the practical field and theorists still find learning in school as remote from reality, overly passive, insensitive, one-sided, rationalistic, dull, and abstract. They experience school as an alienated, bureaucratically over-organized and ritualized public institution. They condemn the misery of grading and characterize school as a closed system, a sorting machine and — in analogy to Goffman's asylums (1961) — even as a total institution.

There even seems to be a certain correlation between an inner crisis in the classroom and outer crises of economic and technological development in society (Dauber, 1988; Schratz, 1989), as can be derived by way of example from a statement by an 18-year-old girl graduating from a German *Gymnasium*, representing the view of a generation in our present-day society:

> We are not looking into a rosy future. None of us feels able to step out and take the world by storm. Juvenile exuberance, idealistic enthusiasm, storm and stress — these terms do not fit us. We are not like the post-war generation of students to which many of our parents and teachers belonged. We cannot be compared with the student generation of the 1968s either. We are not the ones who protest. There are even people who say we conform too much. We are celebrating our graduation on quite different premises. We have taken a hurdle, the first one, and we are proud of that. But our leaving certificate is as yet a useless piece of paper. There are aptitude tests and long waiting lists for all apprenticeships and other professional training courses, as well as there is a limit number for university entrance; unemployment threatens us — we will have to overtax ourselves again and again. We do not believe that we will be able to achieve anything we want to achieve. Indeed, we are doubtful about our future. (Jähnke, 1986, p. 44; my translation)

This German student's view compares with that of an American graduate's, quoted below, which seems to point towards a universal phenomenon of this time and society in an age of transition. However, theoretical 'voices' from the United States seem to look more optimistic: 'No matter how bad the reformers perceive the schools to be, they never consider them hopeless. In fact, reformers tend to think that there is no time more propitious for school reform than the present' (Cross, 1984, p. 167). This optimism is also noticeable in the following extract from a US student's graduation speech:

> We have before us the opportunity to make decisions that will affect the world for the next century. We are inheriting the problems of the world, and though we did not create them, we must be responsible for solving them. Our success, or failure, will be measured on a global scale. Therefore, although we will hug each other good-bye at the end of the ceremony, the bonds between us must not be severed. We must work together to maintain the spirit that has held us together. The individualistic 'me first' conventions that we have been taught have failed to solve the

problems that we face. Thus, we must refuse to live by these conventions, and, instead, begin to think in unselfish ways that require real vision. (Hairopoulous, 1989, p. 3)

If we want to meet this student's vision, we can no longer accept quick-fix, mechanistic solutions to the problems facing education today. Too many actions taken so far on either side of the Atlantic Ocean were determined by short-term policies. A great many of the measures came under the pressure of technological development and economic progress and were therefore absorbed by mere quantitative determination, as if the new generation of school leavers of this type were able to solve the problems of society today. The combination of the size and speed of development and the economic pressure of applying results immediately, which characterizes progress in many fields has also found entrance into educational planning and development as if one could logically argue and stringently develop changes in human relations. There have been tendencies in school development to achieve a standard of knowledge which is certain and universally accepted as that in mathematics and geometry. Such an orientation could easily lead to an acquisition of knowledge in which we learn more and more about less and less up to the point that we finally know everything about almost nothing (Guggenberger, 1987, p. 83).

Just the Latest Educators' Fad?

As a result, more recent findings in different areas of teaching reveal that educational reform cannot only be a matter of implementing new academic standards that project a negotiated knowledge-base into a curricular build-up with the assumption that it can be applied in any school situation. New approaches also require that we alter our more traditional ideas about the nature of knowledge itself and how it is acquired. Such new approaches can be found in the field of action research or reflective practitioner movements. 'Action research is simply a form of self-reflective enquiry undertaken by participants in social situations in order to improve the rationality and justice of their practices, their understanding of these practices, and the situations in which the practices are carried out' (Carr and Kemmis, 1986, p. 162). Action research concepts have mainly been employed in the context of classroom research (Altrichter and Posch, 1990; Gregory, 1988; Hustler, Cassidy and Cuff, 1986; McKernan, 1988; Oldroyd and Tiller, 1987), teacher training (Elliott, 1991; Goswami and Stillman, 1986) and higher education (Cross and Angelo, 1988; Schratz, 1990). Although Elliott (1989) optimistically states that action research 'is sweeping through faculties of education in universities across the world' (p. 2), I do not see this concept implemented in educational practices on a large scale yet.

Elliott seems to be right in so far as action research has had a considerable impact on the programme structure of almost all recent educational research symposia, and the first World Congress on Action Research took place. However, mainstream teaching to a large extent still lacks reflective practice as indicated in the previous paragraph. Vaughan (1990) justifiedly asks, 'Is reflective practice just the latest educators' fad or is it a potential cornerstone of efforts to unify the vast array of educational reform initiatives that will lead us into the twenty-first century?' (p. vii) When answering this question, we have to consider why after more than half a century since Dewey (1909/1933) started off the idea of reflective inquiry as an organizing theme for change, we are still entrapped in the continuing debate over qualitative inquiry in education (Eisner and Peshkin, 1990). At this point, I do not want to venture further into the ideological struggle for the promotion of reflective teaching, but rather deal with its underlying problem, which seems to be one of the transfer from theory to practice. In my experience, implementing new concepts of teacher thinking can put certain constraints on teachers, which can be best summarized in what a teacher expressed in the following way:

> Teaching which causes me to think of so many things at a time, some-times makes me sick. I'm somehow worried about this constant pressure of having to plan. I somehow get the feeling as if I constantly had to give myself up in order to deal with all aspects.

It is very often the complexity of the situation teachers find themselves in when they are asked to undergo a change. Changing teaching always means chang-ing one's 'practical theory' of teaching,

> which is subjectively the strongest determining factor in her educational practice. Counselling with teachers must consequently originate in each teacher's practical theory, seeking to foster its conscious articulation and aiming to elaborate it and make it susceptible to change. (Handal and Lauvås, 1987)

In conventional settings of teacher training it is rarely the case that the prac-tical theories of participating teachers can be consciously articulated. The reason for this is at least twofold:

(i) Teachers who have been socialized in a traditional way through their own schooling as pupils, through their training as students in higher education and through their thus aquired educational philosophy cannot turn their teaching style upside down from one day to the other. Even if somebody's practical theory of teaching is challenged in some sort or the other, it usually takes a long process of changing one's pedagogical habits which have proved to work fairly well according to one's own belief system.

(ii) The traditional set-up of pre- or in-service training often does not allow for a learning culture which promotes reflective teaching. Series of lec-tures on certain educational issues — even if they are practice-oriented — will hardly help in transforming the concept of teaching into a direc-tion which represents the value of learning as a way of thinking, reason-ing and understanding.

In order to create a suitable culture for the promotion of teacher thinking about their practical theories and their consequences on teaching practice we have to work on both the institutional and personal level. Different institutional approaches show how teacher thinking can be encouraged, among others, through

— enquiry-based learning concepts in initial teacher education (Altrichter, 1988);
— supervision in teaching practice (Handal and Lauvås, 1987);
— a reflective practicum in professional training (Schön, 1987);
— researching while teaching in higher education (Schratz, 1990)

on the macro level of educational change.

In this chapter, however, I want to concentrate on the micro level of initiating teacher thinking. Because of their openness to the teacher's own background, associative methods have proved most successful in achieving this aim. Therefore I want to present some of these practical methods, which can easily be adapted to various institutional settings in pre- and in-service training. In particular, these are:

(i)   The *magnifying glass* as a means of reflecting on teaching.
(ii) The *learning history* as a means of reflecting on becoming a member of the teaching tribe.
(iii) The *fantasy journey* as an immersion into the inner world of teaching.
(iv) The *teaching market* as a mirror of teachers' work.

(i) The Magnifying Glass: Reflection on Teaching in Action

In an interdisciplinary approach to improve faculty members' didactic competences in higher education at the University of Innsbruck (Austria), an action research type of programme proved most suitable to meet the participants' needs and interests. Its objectives were

— to take its starting point in the needs and interests of everybody involved, that is students and teachers irrespective of their disciplinary background;
— to give teaching the same status as is usually given a research interest;
— to aim at a longer involvement leaving enough space for reflective activities;
— to meet the participants at the very point at which they presently stand in their teaching;
— to include the students' reactions in the formative evaluation procedures;
— to make use of the participants' on-going teaching commitments and use them as a base for further reflections;
— to follow a cooperative design which is not subordinate to the usual practice of disciplinary thinking within a monadic, isolated approach;
— to strive for continuing self-evaluation practices which enable the individual to look at his or her teaching as an ongoing research activity.

After an introductory session individual projects were initiated, in which the participants undertook different approaches to action research by reflecting on their own teaching situation. As an on-going evaluative process between individual inquiry-based phases of lecturing and reflective plenary sessions the programme tried to offer deeper insights into the participants' own practical 'theories' of what they intend to accomplish in the classroom and how they want to achieve these goals (cf. Schratz, 1993b).

Most participants in this programme had not attended training seminars previously, since advancement and professionalization in teaching in higher education in Austria has always been neglected compared to the emphasis put on career development in laboratory work and scientific research. This neglect of teaching has led to observations similar to those which Sykes (1988) recently mentioned for the situation in the United States. For him professors

(i)   merely regurgitate the textbook;
(ii) rely on notes prepared when they were younger, more ambitious, and without tenure;
(iii) dwell on their own specialties without bothering to translate the material from the arcane jargon of their specialty;
(iv) turn their classes into rap sessions, a tactic that has the advantage of being both entertaining and educationally progressive;
(v)   fail to prepare at all and treat their classes to an off-the-top-of-the-head ramble; leaping from topic to topic in what they think are dazzling intellectual trapeze acts but which usually are confusing, frustrating muddles for the students. (p. 61)

Therefore it was necessary to discover more about the needs and interests of the participants wanting further incentives for the improvement of their teaching. The following quote from an interview gives an example of what one of the lecturers felt about her teaching:

What I'd like to know now is where I am with my own teaching. Can I say that I teach in a student-oriented, or in a traditional way? Or am I maybe somewhere in the middle? How can I find out more about my teaching?

Clearly, it may sometimes, perhaps usually, be impossible to answer this question in a satisfactory way. Moreover, this kind of labelling would not help any further in improving teaching competence at a higher education level. What is important, however, is getting beyond such labels to an understanding of how lecturers actually do teach, what they actually do in a classroom and their students do and how they react as a result.

How much do we know about the way students receive our lessons? Do they get the chance to find out about their teachers' processes of learning and thought? Is there room left for their own thoughts which are essential for their personal and social development? These questions are different from the usual ones. In traditional views teachers are mainly interested in the students' *products* such as exam results. The senate commission, however, sees human *processes* as an integral part of learner achievement. Moreover, it claims that the result becomes more sophisticated the more we rethink and reinterpret the processes involved in the phase of knowledge creation. If we want to bridge the gap between the products we expect from our students and the social processes leading towards those products, we have to find ways of developing new incentives through reflection in action (cf. Schön, 1983).

As teaching and learning are interrelated in the effectiveness of education, lecturers *and* learners have to be involved in this reflection on what is going on in class. Only then can we find out about the gap between what is taught and what is learnt in higher education. This reflection can be compared to a kind of research process, which has been defined 'as the study by classroom teachers of the impact of their teaching on the students in their classrooms. The basic premise of classroom research is that teachers should use their classrooms as laboratories to study the learning process as it applies to their particular disciplines; teachers should become skillful, systematic observers of how the students in their classrooms learn' (Cross, 1988, p. 3).

In order to get the participants used to this new way of looking at their teaching as a research process, we had to find a way that encouraged reflective processes from the very beginning. Since initial phases are often crucial for the outcome of an overall programme, it was necessary to allow enough time for finding into the new role of a teacher-researcher. Moreover, we had to find a way of avoiding lengthy discussions and the self-presentations university teachers are used to.

At the first meeting, after a short introductory phase, each participant received a sheet of paper containing an illustration of a full-page-sized magnifying glass. They were asked to express their own problems, fears or expectations concerning their teaching by drawing them onto the blank part of the lense of the magnifying glass. Some expressed themselves in a short text, as can be seen from the following examples.

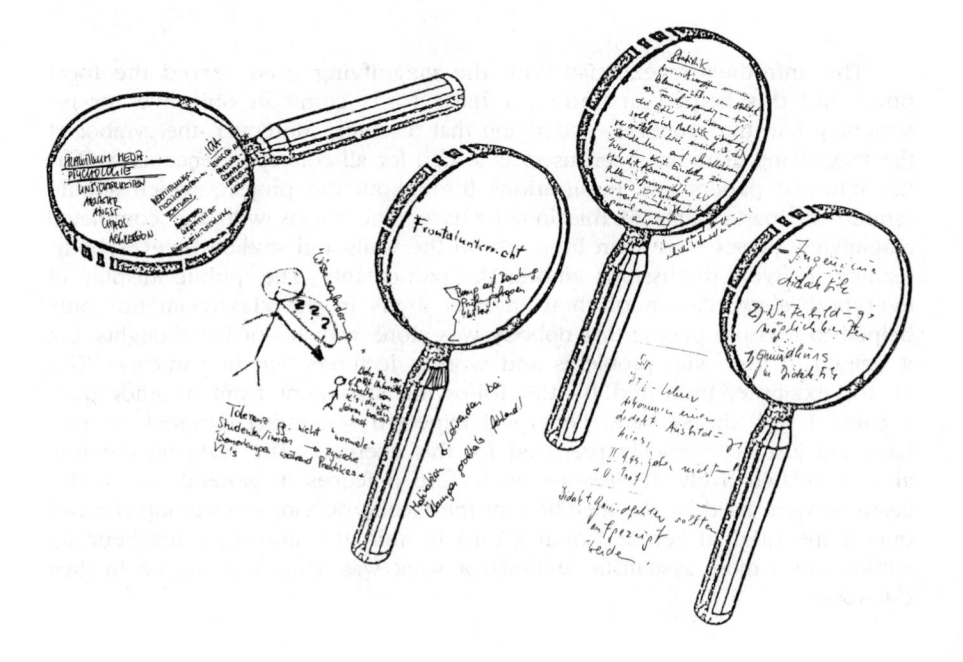

Other lecturers, freely associated by drawing pictures, which expressed particular problems of their 'artists', as can be seen from the following examples.

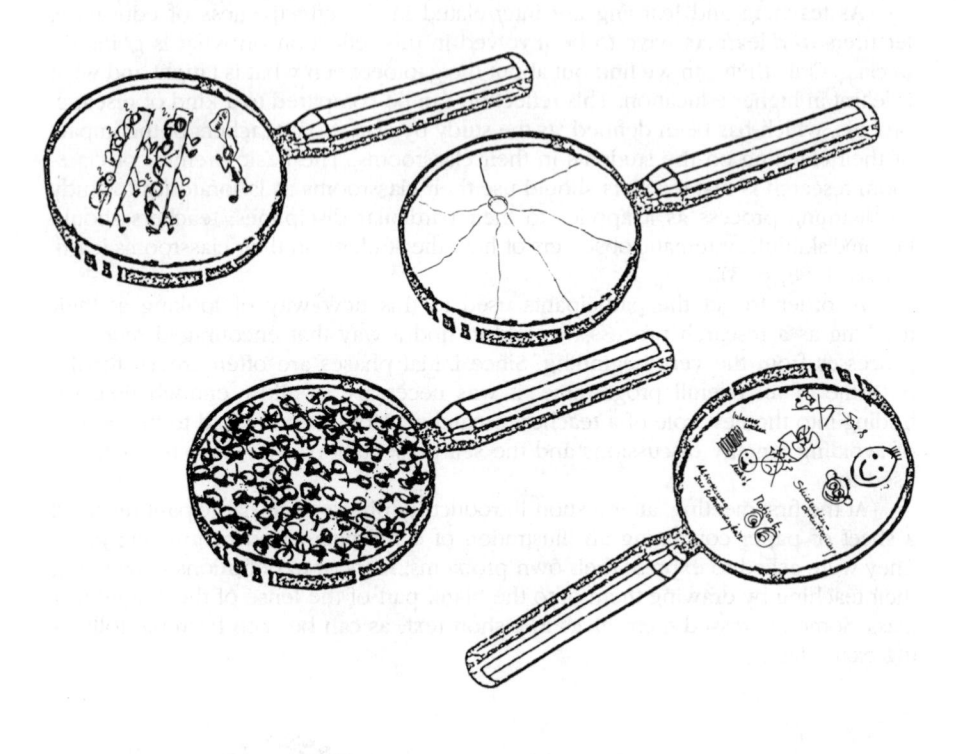

This introductory exercise with the magnifying glass served the focal point and this helped in finding a basis for a common objective for researching into the processes underlying that teaching. Moreover, the symbol of the magnifying glass has been used as a logo for all correspondence as well as the informal papers and publications throughout the project, which should remind the participants of this initial phase. The sheets with the completed magnifying glasses were then hung up on the walls and studied by everybody, leading to lively discussions among the participants. The 'public' display of everybody's expression of their interest areas in the classroom not only helped to reassure people that nobody was alone with his or her thoughts, but it helped to deal with problems and worries lecturers had in particular. This is, for example, indicated by the following statement from another participant: 'I feel uneasy here. Perhaps I expected something different, or perhaps I'm just not mentally prepared for this exercise.' The texts on the wall also stimulated lively discussions on lecture practices in general. These discussions were used by the members of the faculty development group (formed out of the original Senate Commission) to shift the university teachers' attention to a more systematic analysis of what was actually going on in their classrooms.

(ii)   The Learning History: Reflection on Becoming a Member of the Teaching Tribe

It is not until half-way through their discipline-oriented studies that teacher students (for the *Gymnasium*) have to go in for teaching practice in Austria. This puts a lot of strain on most trainee teachers since they are confronted with their actual professional perspective of working as teachers in a school for the first time. Therefore, for the students entering educational studies leading them into life in school is often seen as a factor of disruption in the course of their studies of the respective subject areas, as can be seen by the following statement of a student representing many others of a similar kind.

> It all started when I was right in the middle of my studies, which had began to become more and more interesting for me. I already began to doubt whether I really wanted to become a teacher, research work could perhaps be much more interesting. Perhaps I should change my course and go in for the research programme? However, since I've gone half-way through the teaching programme, I might as well finish it.
>
> Then there is the first meeting of the introductory phase. In a listless mood I go there and simply want to see what's going on there. The first thing I get is a timetable and my first shock. What? This is going to cover the whole week? (Tomorrow I actually wanted to study for an exam.) What will happen to my exam dates already fixed? Moreover, I notice that I have already missed the beginning, which doesn't bother me that much. Orientation phase doesn't mean a lot to me, anyway.

On the grounds of the findings in developmental psychology such periods of transition in a person's life are very often accompanied by identity crises caused by simultaneous contradictions, such as no longer being in a certain situation and not yet being in another one, identifying with the situation of no longer being the mere student and yet not being a fully qualified teacher or having gained a certain state of autonomy and yet not being independent (for example autonomically, socially, etc.). This constellation in life has appropriately been called 'psychosocial moratorium' by Erikson (1959) or 'phenomenon of transition' by Winnicot (1965).

The orientation phase has been introduced to make use of this transition in a positive way. In its curricular design it should enable the students to deal with their heterogeneous experiences at school and at university in a way that they get clearer about their — often hidden — motives. This aim can, of course, not be achieved in a lecture-driven form of conventional university teaching. Nadig and Erdheim (1984) tried to show how scientific experience is usually destroyed by the academic milieu. They argue that when we stick to academic routines emotional parts are suppressed into the sub-conscious, from where they destroy the liveliness of academic study and research in an uncontrolled and destructive way. Therefore it is necessary to aim at a learning culture that allows for the individual to deal with both their own learning history and the interactions with the other members of the group. This is why the number of students participating in one group is restricted to ten to twelve trainees.

When the students first get into one of the small groups at the beginning of the orientation phase, they are confronted with a different set-up of the seating arrangement, usually supported by some unobtrusive background music. This usually helps to overcome the threat students sometimes feel when confronted with something unfamiliar. Such a threat might easily match with the negative attitude towards the 'disturbance' of the teaching phase half-way through their studies, as indicated in the student's comment above. Moreover, it makes them sensitive towards a different quality of learning, which is usually intensified when the students are asked to pair off with a partner and 'just get to know each other'. For many of them it is the first time to find out more about one another, although they have spent two or more years together in the same study programme.

In the next phase, the students are asked to put down their *learning histories* from when they first went to school (or even earlier if they like) on a large sheet of poster paper (flip chart size). They should find their individual ways of expressing themselves using any medium they like. They get plenty of time for designing their posters, and again soft background music is tuned in to enhance their fantasy and creativity in the process of writing, drawing, sketching, etc. They are also encouraged to find a place inside or outside the seminar room where they feel comfortable working so as not to be disturbed by the others. They should get the feeling to work under no pressure at all, so it might help to tell them that it is not a competition for the best painter or poster designer or similar.

When everybody has finished the posters are spread across the floor (if there is not enough room available they are hung up on the walls), and everybody starts walking around trying to get an idea of the other group members' 'learning histories' laid out on the posters. In the first phase individual impressions are collected without referring to individual posters and either written up on a board or simply kept in mind by the teacher. There should neither be questions on nor criticism of what they see, nor should they interpret certain 'messages'. If the students are not familiar with this general form of feedback, the teacher can bring his or her views in helping the students in phrasing their comments, such as 'When I watch the posters on the floor it strikes me that . . .'

In the second phase the posters are dealt with individually. The producer of each poster first gives some background information on his/her 'work of art', giving a kind of tour d'horizon through the learning history as it appears on the poster. Then the other students are encouraged to ask questions according to the student's poster so as to gain further information on his/her learning background. If the students are more advanced and trained in paying attention to the representation system, they also try to listen to and watch *how* the student comments on his/her poster (pace, rhythm, breathing, tone of voice etc.). This extra information is used to give the respective student additional feedback afterwards. (It will not be used, however, to criticize him/her on the presentation.) All the information gained through the manifold learning histories will be used in the following phase to reflect on the personal motives and personality features in becoming a teacher.

The following three examples show how different students approach the same task, and each poster is unique in its own sense.

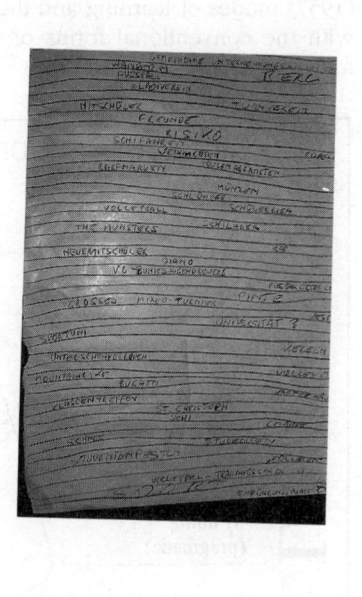

(iii) *The Fantasy Journey: Immersion into the Inner World of Teaching*

Teaching which causes me to think of so many things at a time, sometimes makes me sick. I'm somehow worried about this constant pressure of having to plan. I somehow get the feeling as if I constantly had to give myself up in order to deal with all aspects.

This teacher's statement goes back to an in-service training seminar where we discussed the implication of the individual teacher's personality for the teaching process. In the discussion referring to this statement lots of fellow teachers commented similarly that there was hardly enough room left to deal with the 'inner world of teaching' which is usually cut off from professional discussions. I have often experienced in in-service training courses running over a certain stretch of time that it is usually only outside the regular working hours that teachers openly discuss matters of this personal kind. However, when they start talking about these aspects, they often get more and more involved, and the conversation seems to get to the core of what affects the teaching/learning process in class.

Although this phenomenon is not really new, we have not done a lot in teacher training to overcome this misrelation between our intentions (such as introducing new educational measures) and how we achieve them. Abstract presentations of new curricula, for example, will do little in changing the teaching behaviour at the 'chalkfront'. Even observing other teachers implementing new strategies will not necessarily help in overcoming very personal problems in dealing with new teaching matter. This becomes obvious if we juxtapose Bruner's (1957) modes of learning and the segments in Dale's (1969) model of experience with the conventional forms of (in-service) teacher training, as depicted in the following figure.

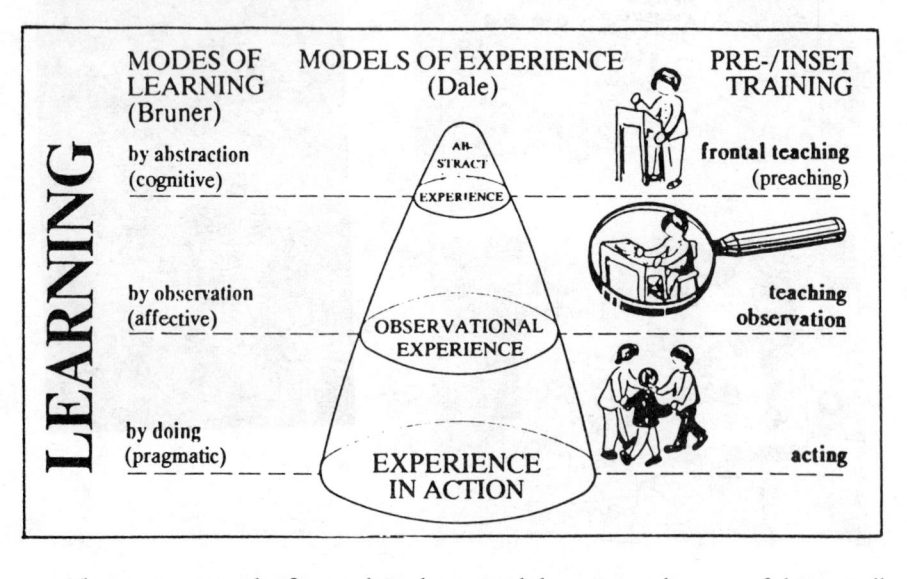

The segments in the figure show how much learning makes use of the overall potential in the human being. Through lectures we usually stimulate cognitive processes which enable teachers to get to know new forms of knowledge cognitively on an abstract level. Through observation of teaching in the actual classroom (or on audio-visual recordings like video-taped teaching sequences) more of the affective potential is reached since a greater part of the overall complexity of institutionalized instruction can be experienced. Therefore observations of this kind are often used to show that particular (alternative) approaches succeed in the real classroom situation.

And yet, a certain scepticism often remains after such 'polished', friction-free presentation of how good teaching could look like. This remaining of scepticism goes back to the original question of how much the individual teacher's personality becomes the main focus in the activity. An indication of this could be the balance of the share between content-related material and relationship-oriented methodology. In lecture-type presentations, for example, the contents share usually dominates and leaves little room for personal relationship, as depicted in the following figure.

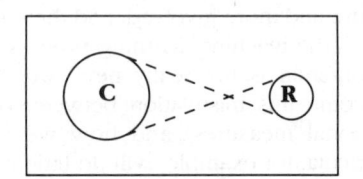

If the in-service training activities mainly aim at the personality of the individual teacher, he/she gets more affectively involved, which increases the relationship share and leaves less room for the contents matter. The figure could accordingly look somehow like the following graph.

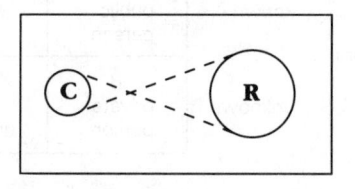

In running our in-service courses we have developed a sequence of phases which try to pay attention to the different modes of learning involving teachers on different levels so as to get a broad balance of contents-related input and personal involvement. The seminar structure usually runs along the following steps:

Phase 1: Elicitation of expectations and formulation of objectives
Phase 2: Immersion into the inner world of teaching
Phase 3: Evaluation of personal experience
Phase 4: Reflection on theory and practice
Phase 5: Knowledge transfer and 'cross-fertilization'
Phase 6: Simulation: Learning by doing
Phase 7: Content evaluation
Phase 8: Process evaluation

The description of the individual phases are described in detail elsewhere (Puchta and Schratz, 1984). Here I mainly discuss phases 2 and 3 because they are geared towards a particular form of reflecting on a teacher's personal approach to teaching and learning. After dealing extensively with the participants' fears and expectations and negotiating the objectives accordingly in phase 1, we use an approach which has its origin in gestalt pedagogy. The so-called *fantasy journey* begins with an introductory relaxation exercise. Usually with soft background music, the participants are unobtrusively guided on a fantasy journey through a (possible) situation where they try to deal with one of the objectives of the seminar. Although they are verbally paced, there should be enough room left for the individual's fantasy to go on its own journey.

In the following phase ('Evaluation of personal experience') the teachers exchange their fantasy journeys in small groups. The mirroring of the respective experiences in the fantasy phase helps the individual in finding out more about his or her present stand in a particular teaching situation. Moreover, the partners offer an outside perspective which often opens up new areas of awareness through commenting, questioning, interpreting etc. in the evaluative phase. This process can be best explained by means of the so-called 'Johari window' (explained in: Luft, 1971; Antons, 1973; Nagl, 1974). It is a simple graphic model which shows changes in the perception of oneself and others in the course of a group process.

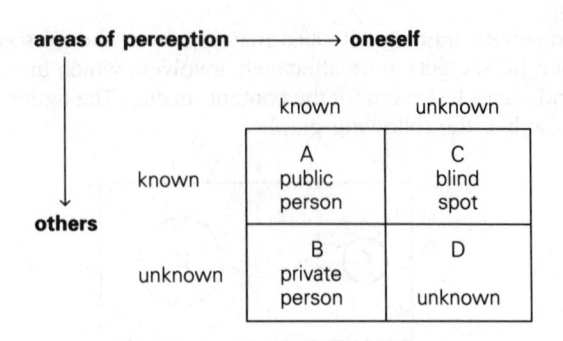

What it means to gain access to so far hidden areas of professional growth can be derived from what a participant commented after one of our intensive training worshops:

> As a result I'd like to learn to manage these tools even better, to explore further into my inner self and to gain from new groups how I can make myself understood and empower others in the same way as I do myself. Growth, awareness — discovering my infinite opportunities; showing others that these really exist: Solutions which are there for everybody only to be explored. Even to accept states of insecurity and mistakes as signals for 'rather not that way' . . .

(iv) The Teaching Market: Mirror of Teacher's Work

In the past few years national syllabuses and curricular materials have been re-organized towards a more communicative approach to teaching and learning in Austrian schools. This opening up of teaching strategies towards the everyday world of the learners, their needs and interests has also consequences for in-service activities in implementing new curricula. In order to comply with this claim, in-service training workshops and seminars have to be opened up towards the world of the teachers as a consequence. This move towards making one's own working territory more transparent to 'outsiders' is very new to many teachers because teaching itself has been a very private and sometimes even solitary activity to many of them. They often do not want to talk openly about the problems they encounter with certain pupils because it might be regarded as a failure on their part. As teacher trainers we have in a way contributed to this threatening attitude when we as 'experts' tried to convince them of what we understood by 'good' teaching. Whenever one phase of innovation in our educational system was hardly implemented we started a new one, often preaching as if it was the gospel of the new days' educational community.

It has only been recently, supported by action research projects and the new practitioner movements that a shift is taking place which renders the previous experience of the teacher more weight in in-service training activities. However, it is not that easy for a teacher attending a seminar to move over from a so far passive role to a more active one bringing his or her own experience into play.

We have developed a method which helps teachers to prepare themselves for such an opening process. To do so they are asked to look at their teaching beforehand and prepare a kind of 'portfolio' for the seminar, which also helps in making the introductory phase of the in-service activity a more communicative event.

Once the teachers have enrolled for the workshop, they get a letter of acceptance which is more than the traditionally formal letter of confirmation which is usually restricted to details concerning the when and where etc. It has to be sent out well in advance so as to give the participants the chance to do some classroom research beforehand. The following letter has been used in our context and can serve as a model for such an invitation for participation.

Dear seminar participant,

We are pleased that you will take part in our in-service seminar course and send you some more details about the training event. We would also like to invite you to participate actively in its preparation, which might help us in paying more attention to your experience in the classroom. We regard those just as important as our abstract theories.

We don't regard it as very helpful, however, if we just *talk* about your teaching experiences because a lot of the immediacy and vividness of the classroom work will get lost. Moreover, it usually takes a fair amount of time until an atmosphere can be achieved which allows to talk openly about experiences from everyday work. Therefore we as the planning team (people representing 'theory' and 'practice') propose to kick the seminar off with a *Teaching Market* that should help to gain a better understanding of each other and our work.

Every participant is asked to present 'teaching' in this market in his/her own way. This presentation could refer to highlights of one's teaching career as well as to difficulties one encountered when trying to teach a certain topic. Perhaps this letter could even stimulate you to try something out you have long been thinking about but never done. What is important is that the 'products' from the teaching/learning process are vivid documents that help in getting a good idea of what you actually did in class.

It would be best to put the documents on poster paper or similar for display, where there is also room for explanations etc. Do not simply give a lesson plan but add documents from its actualization in class (student responses, worksheets filled in by the students, copies from exercise books or similar) and add your personal observations (reactions by students, interactions in class etc.). Perhaps you find a lesson that worked very well (or not at all) once, which you want to try out again in a different class and collect materials for the poster presentation. Try to get as much feedback from the students as possible which will help you to present your experiences at the seminar.

We enclose one possible realization of such a presentation, which, of course, only serves as an example but not as a model to be imitated. Every experience asks for its own way of presentation. The more individually oriented your presentation is the more insight the other participants will gain from it.

We hope that this advance information will be sufficient to give you an idea of our intentions in planning this seminar. We are happy to give you further information if you need any, and we are looking forward to meeting you soon.

Yours sincerely

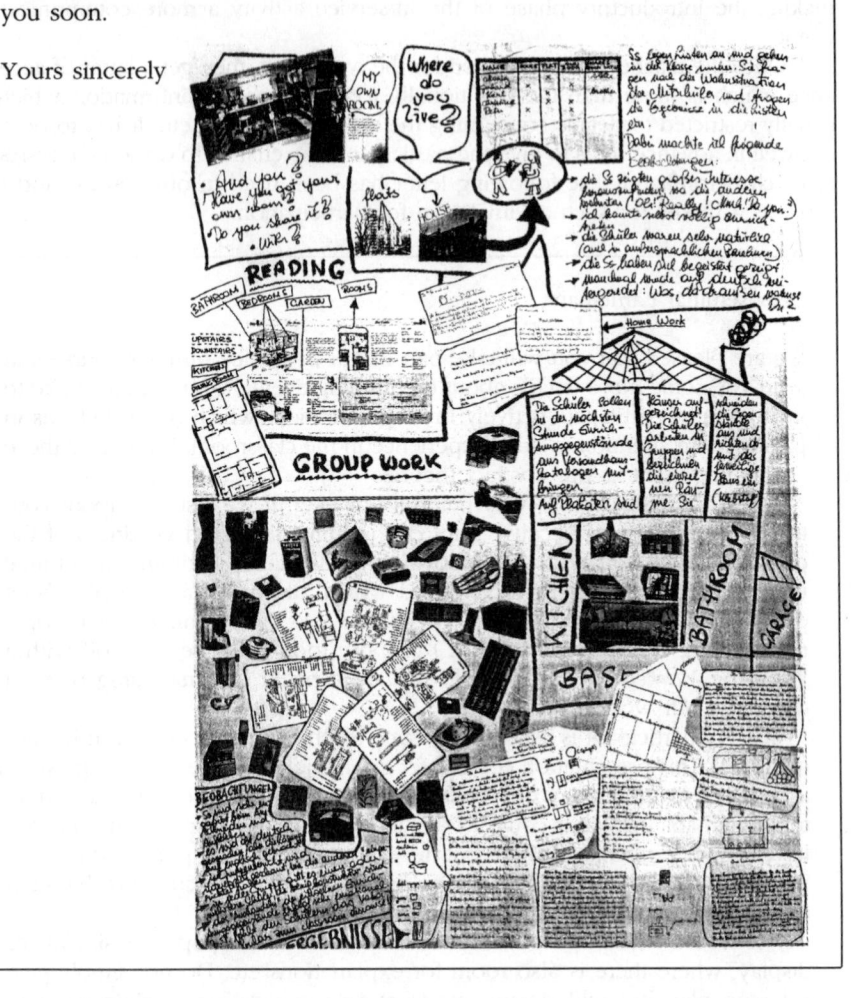

When the participants arrive at the seminar location (in our case usually early evening the previous day), they are asked to take their posters to the main seminar room and put it up on the wall on their own when they have finished with everything else (check-in, room allocation, meal etc.). In that room all the necessary material (glue, pencils, felt tips, markers, sellotape, bluetak and extra poster paper in case somebody has brought their materials loosely). In the morning or after the formal opening of the seminar (greetings, organizational business etc.) the participants are asked to walk around and look at the 'exhibits' from classroom work. Some sort of background music is turned on so as to give this situation an extra touch of a market scene.

In the next phase, everybody is asked to give feedback on the presented materials from the participants' classroom practice. This is first done in written form so as leave enough time to reflect on the individual exhibits. Everybody gets a pack of small cards (about index size), writes down his/her comments, questions or other kind of feedback and sticks it on the poster (s)he refers to. In the following phase, with the participants arranged in a circular seating order, every poster creator is encouraged to comment on the feedback, answer questions etc., thus providing further information from his or her experience. This phase is an important part for the planning of the further steps in the workshop because it allows 'practical theories' to develop in a trustful atmosphere. Since they form the basis for further work, the following activities should take this 'learning culture' as a powerful starting point for reflective learning and teaching. (Further information on the teaching market is given in Schratz, 1983, and Puchta and Schratz, 1984.)

References

ALTRICHTER, H. (1988) 'Enquiry-based learning in initial teacher education' in NIAS, J. and GROUNDWATER-SMITH, S. (Eds) *The Enquiring Teacher. Supporting and Sustaining Teacher Research*, Lewes, Falmer Press, pp. 121–34.

ALTRICHTER, H. and POSCH, P. (1990) *Lehrer erforschen ihren Unterricht. Eine Einführung in die Methoden der Aktionsforschung*, Bad Heilbrunn, Klinkhardt.

ANTONS, K. (1973) *Praxis der Gruppendynamik*, Göttingen, Verlag für Psychologie.

BRUNER, J.S. (1957) 'Going Beyond the Information Given', *Contemporary Approaches to Cognition*, Cambridge, MA., Harvard University Press, pp. 41–70.

BUCHMANN, M. and FLODEN, R.E. (1989) 'Research traditions, diversity and progress', *Review of Educational Research* 59, 2, pp. 241–8.

CARR, W. and KEMMIS, S. (1986) *Becoming Critical*, Lewes, Falmer Press.

CAZDEN, C.B. (1988) *Classroom Discourse: The Language of Teaching and Learning*, Portsmouth, NH, Heinemann.

CLIFT, R.T., HOUSTON, W.R. and PUGACH, M.C. (Eds) (1990) *Encouraging Reflective Practice in Education: An Analysis of Issues and Programs*, New York, Teachers College Press.

CROSS, K.P. (1984) 'The rising tide of school reform reports' *Phi Delta Kappan*, 11, pp. 167–72.

CROSS, K.P. (1988) 'In search of zippers', *Bulletin of the American Association for Higher Education*, 40, pp. 3–7.

CROSS, K.P. and ANGELO, T.A. (1988) *Classroom Assessment Techniques. A Handbook for Faculty*, Ann Arbor Michigan, NCRIPTAL.

DALE, E. (1969) *Audiovisual Methods in Teaching*, New York, Dryden Press.

DAUBER, H. (1988) Angst: Versuch über den Zusammenhang von äußerer Bedrohung und innerem Zusammenbruch' in SCHRATZ, M. (Ed.) *Geben Bildung, Ausbildung und Wissenschaft an der Lebenswelt vorbei?* Munich, Profil, pp. 120–33.

DEWEY, J. (1933) *How We Think: A Restatement of the Relation of Reflective Thinking to the Educative Process*, Boston, MA, Heath (original work published in 1909).

EDWARDS, D. and MERCER, N.M. (1987) *Common Knowledge: The Development of Understanding in the Classroom*, London, Methuen.

EISNER, E.W. and PESHKIN, A. (Eds) (1990) *Qualitative Inquiry in Education. The Continuing Debate*, New York, Teachers College Press.

ELLIOTT, J. (1989) 'Academics and action research: The training workshop as an exercise in ideological deconstruction', paper presented at the annual meeting of the American Educational Research Association, San Francisco.

ELLIOTT, J. (1991) Action Research for Educational Change, Milton Keynes, Open University Press.

ERIKSON, E.H. (1959) *Identity and the Life Cycle*, New York, Norton.

GOFFMAN, E. (1961) *Asylums*, New York, Doubleday Anchor.

GOSWAMI, P. and STILLMAN, P.R. (1986) *Reclaiming the Classroom. Teacher Research as an Agency for Change*, Portsmouth, NH, Boynton/Cook.

GREGORY, R. (1988) *Action Research in the Secondary School*, London, Routledge, Chapman and Hall.

GUBA, E.G. (1990) *The Paradigm Dialogue*, Newbury Park, CA, Sage.

GUGGENBERGER, B. (1987) *Das Menschenrecht auf Irrtum. Anleitung zur Unvollkommenheit*, München, Hanser.

HAIROPOULOS, E. (1989) 'So, what did you learn in school?', unpublished manuscript.

HANDAL, G. and LAUVÅS, P. (1987) *Promoting Reflective Teaching: Supervision in Practice*, Milton Keynes, SRHE and Open University Press.

HUSTLER, E., CASSIDY, A. and CUFF, E.C. (Eds) (1986) *Action Research in Classrooms and Schools*, London, Allen and Unwin.

JÄHNKE, B. (1986) Lektion für die Lehrer, *Zeit*, 22 August, p. 44.

KLEMM, K., ROLFF, H.-G. and TILLMANN, K.-J. (1986) *Bildung für das Jahr 2000. Bilanz der Reform, Zukunft der Schule*, Reinbek, Rowohlt.

LINCOLN, Y.S. and GUBA, E.G. (1985) *Naturalistic Inquiry*, Newbury Park, CA, Sage.

LONGSTREET, W.S. (1989) 'Human factors in educational computing: Toward software efficiency for education' in SCHNEIDER, U. and SCHRATZ, M. (Eds) *Permanent Education Between New Illiteracy and High-Power Technology*, New Orleans, LA, University of New Orleans, pp. 19–34.

LUFT, J. (1971) *Einführung in die Gruppendynamik*, Stuttgart Kiett.

MCKERNAN, J. (1988) 'Teachers as researchers: Paradigm and praxis', *Contemporary Education*, 59, pp. 154–8.

MEHAN, H. (1979) *Learning Lessons*, Cambridge, MA., Harvard University Press.

NADIG, M. and ERDHEIM, M. (1984) Die Zerstörung der wissenschaftlichen Erfahrung durch das akademische Milieu. Ethnopsychoanalytische Überlegungen zur Aggressivität in der Wissenschaft', in BECKER, H. *et al.* (Eds) *Der Spiegel des Fremden. Ethnopsychoanalytische Betrachtungen (Psychosozial 23)*, Reinbek, Rowohlt, pp. 11–27.

NAGL, L. (1974) 'T-Gruppe, Organisation, Institution' in HEINTEL, P. (Ed.) *Das ist Gruppendynamik. Eine Einführüng in Bedeutung, Funktion und Anwendbarkeit*, München, Heyne.

OLDROYD, T. and TILLER, T. (1987) 'Change from within: An account of school-based collaborative action research in an English secondary school', *Journal of Education for Teaching*, 13, pp. 13–27.

PUCHTA, H. and SCHRATZ, M. (1984) *Handelndes Lernen im Englischunterricht. Vol 3: Trainerbuch*, München, Hueber.

SCHÖN, D.A. (1983) *The Reflective Practitioner: How Professionals Think in Action*, New York, Basic Books.

SCHÖN, D.A. (1987) *Educating the Reflective Practitioner. Toward a New Design for Teaching and Learning in the Professions*, San Francisco, CA, Jossey-Bass.

SCHRATZ, M. (1983) 'Unterricht zum Herzeigen: Plakate als Mittler zur Gestaltung von Lehr-/Lernprozessen in der Fortbildung'. *arbeiten und lernen*, 5, 25, pp. 90–3.

SCHRATZ, M. (1989) 'The threat to the future: A challenge for pedagogy' in SCHNEIDER, U. and SCHRATZ, M. (Eds) *Permanent Education Between New Illiteracy and High-Power Technology*, New Orleans, LA, University of New Orleans, pp. 9–18.

SCHRATZ, M. (1990) 'Researching while teaching. A collaborative action research model to improve college teaching', *Journal on Excellence of College Teaching*, 1, pp. 98–108.

SCHRATZ, M. (1993a) *Qualitative Voices in Educational Research*, London, Falmer Press.
SCHRATZ, M. (1993b) 'Researching While Teaching: Promoting Reflective Professionality in Higher Education; *International Journal of Action Research*, 1, 1.
SINCLAIR, J. McH. and COULTHARD, R.M. (1975) *Towards an Analysis of Discourse: The English used by Teachers and Pupils*, London, Oxford University Press.
SYKES, Ch. J. (1988) *ProfScam. Professors and the Demise of Higher Education*, Washington, D.C., Regnery Gateway.
VAUGHAN, J.C. (1990) 'Foreword' in CLIFT, R.T., HOUSTON, W.R. and PUGACH, M.C. (Eds) *Encouraging Reflective Practice in Education: An Analysis of Issues and Programs*, New York, Teachers College Press.
WINNICOTT, D.W. (1965) *The Maturational Processes and the Facilitating Environment. Studies in the Theory of Emotional Development*, London, Hogarth.

Chapter 13

Academics and Action-Research: The Training Workshop as an Exercise in Ideological Deconstruction

John Elliott

Introduction

Talk of promoting teachers' based action-research in schools as a process of educating teachers to be reflective practitioners is sweeping through faculties of education in universities across the world. Academic teacher educators now debate something called action-research theory, and there is a growing literature which attempts to establish the epistemological and methodological foundations of action-research.

Some of this philosophical and methodological debate is grounded in the experience of actually attempting to facilitate the professional development of teachers through action-research. But there are some who engage with the theory and not with the practice of action-research. In my view this is bound to distort the way action-research is articulated to teachers because it contradicts the theory of the theory-practice relationship which underpins action-research; namely, that theory is generated from, and interactively with practice.

The academic action-research theorist may well argue that s/he is not focussing on the practical theories which are generated via participation in action-research. S/he is concerned with generating a meta-theory of the enterprise as a whole. This kind of distinction between *a posteriori* and *a priori* theorizing is in my view largely ideological, because it legitimates a theoretical hegemony between academics and teachers. It sanctions conceptual imperialism. The academic becomes the arbitrator as to whether teachers who may think they are engaged in action-research really are. In other words, teachers' self-understandings of their teaching as a form of action-research have to be placed against the meta-theoretical slide rule of the academics.

In a previous chapter I attempted to demonstrate that action-research did not emerge in the UK from the application of a meta-theory of the theory-practice relationship generated *a priori* by academic educational theorists. It emerged in schools as a dimension of teachers' initiated curriculum change and development.

What academics associated with the 'teachers-as-researchers' movement, such as Lawrence Stenhouse and I, did was to articulate the theory of the theory-practice relation embedded in the reflective practices of innovatory teachers in schools. This meta-theory, albeit unarticulated by teachers, was constituted by their practices. In other words, teachers generated a meta-theory of the theory practice relation through the development of a reflective practice of education; i.e., educational action-research. Such a practice constitutes a form of professional learning. Therefore a theory of action-research is a theory of learning.

One can view the question '*how can I facilitate learning?*' as quite separate to the question '*what is the nature of learning?*'. The answer to the first is a practical theory and it can only be discovered by reflectively trying to improve one's teaching strategies as the means of facilitating learning. The second question is about the nature of the ends of teaching; how one defines them conceptually. It constitutes a conceptual, rather than a practical, form of inquiry. If we view the two questions to entail quite separate forms of inquiry, then the first is a purely technical question about the most reflective methods for achieving desired learning outcomes.

Now action-research theorists do not in the main accept this separation. They tend to endorse the Aristotelian, and indeed Deweyan, view that practical inquiry implies reflection upon means and ends jointly. With respect to education this implies that teachers clarify and develop their conceptions of learning by reflecting about the teaching strategies they employ, and in developing such conceptions become aware in turn of new strategic possibilities. On this account teachers doing action-research are also engaged in what Aristotle called practical philosophy. Reflecting about practice and the ends of practice are simply two aspects of a unitary process.

If educational theorists subscribe to this account of reflective teaching, then to be consistent they should also argue that theorizing about the nature of action-research cannot be separated from reflecting about strategies for facilitating this kind of professional learning. In other words as a conceptualization of professional learning action-research theory should be developed in conjunction with attempts to develop strategies for facilitating action-research amongst teachers. This implies that the context for developing action-research theory is itself a form of second-order action-research.

In my view academics, who teach and write about action-research theory, should see themselves as under an obligation to undertake second-order action-research into their own teacher education practices. Submission to such a discipline is essential if academics are to avoid perpetrating ideas which misrepresent and distort action-research in order to legitimate the hegemony of academics in their relations to teachers.

In the rest of this chapter I want to illustrate how second-order action-research can help a theorist to clarify and deepen his/her understanding of action-research. The illustration I have selected is of a piece of action-research I conducted into my own teaching at an action-research training workshop sponsored by the Central University of Venezuela in Caracas. The membership of the workshop largely consisted of either teacher educators attached to the university or teachers and others undertaking postgraduate research in education. It was a good opportunity to explore the assumptions academic educationalists bring into an initial encounter with the idea of action-research. Indeed it was necessary for me as the facilitator

and a fellow academic to reflect about the extent to which I reinforced or challenged these assumptions through the way I structured and conducted the workshop.

Methodological Criteria

Contrary to customary practice when working overseas, there was no detailed
initial plan for the workshop. Plans inevitably have to be modified and adapted as
one goes along, but they have usually been produced for a number of reasons.
Firstly, I am accustomed to doing one-week workshops for about forty participants
with a team. Whenever possible I like to involve senior teachers who have first-
hand experience of action-research in their schools. They give credibility to the
exercise, especially when the participants are also school teachers. I have also
involved other researchers within CARE, who have been involved in facilitating
teacher-based action-research. Joint planning in this context is necessary because
it enables team members to explore each other's understanding, experience, and
skills, and to sort out the contribution of each to the total enterprise.

Secondly, our overseas workshops sometimes involve making very complex
arrangements concerning the use of technology (for example, video-recording and
play-back facilities), rooms, and even sites. With respect to the latter we have twice
held one-week workshops in Spanish schools to give participants a real experience
of facilitating teachers' action-research in classrooms. One has to plan such a
workshop in sufficient detail to negotiate acceptable periods for classroom observation, and interviews and meetings with the teachers in the school.

In the case of the Caracas workshop the pressure to plan was not great. A
CARE team would have been too costly for the Central University to host. I went
on my own. Also the schedule I had been given — four hours a day for four days
— suggested that there was going to be a time problem for the experiential learning
workshops we were accustomed to leading. The effort of organizing and utilizing
sophisticated technology for data collection would probably only exacerbate the
time problem. I decided to wait until I had more details about the context before
deciding how to handle the workshops. However, I did have some methodological
criteria in mind, distilled from past experience. These criteria can be described as
follows:

(i) Provide opportunities for participants to reflect upon and share their
     actual experiences of teaching and learning situations.
         Such experiences can be recalled, documented and analyzed in
     ways which develop participants capacities for reflective self-analysis,
     and their understanding of key aspects of action-research.
(ii) Structure the workshop to provide participants with the experience of
     developing strategies for facilitating action-research with teachers, and
     opportunities to reflect about that experience.

(i) and (ii) mark a distinction between first-order and second-order action-research.
The former refers to strategies of reflective teaching, and the latter to strategies for
facilitating reflective teaching in others, which in themselves can constitute a focus
for reflection.

(iii)   Establish an interactive relationship, between presentations of action-research theory/methodology and participants' reflections and discussions about their experience of practical activities in the workshop.

This interaction should consist of a number of cycles. In each cycle the presentation of ideas is followed by a practical exercise, where participants experience the ideas in a concrete form then reflect about them in the light of the experience. Such reflection in turn will generate more theoretical/methodological questions which become the focus for new theoretical input, and so on into the next cycle.

(iv)   Refrain from attempting to establish a comprehensive system of surveillance and control over the development of participants' understandings of action research and the role of the facilitator.

Such surveillance and control prevents participants developing a critical understanding of the ideas introduced by the workshop leader, and transforms him/her into an authority figure whose ideas are not contestable. It inhibits dialogue between leader and participants and negates the former's role as a facilitator of reflective practice.

Workshops for potential action researchers and facilitators need to give participants opportunities both to reflect independently — out of 'ear-shot' — about ideas introduced by the leader, and to exercise a measure of control over the development of an 'issues' agenda. In this context the role of the workshop leader is to respond to critical issues initiated by participants. S/he must possess the ability to remain *in control* over his/her performance within a dynamic and fluid discourse without stifling it by resorting to strategies for *taking control* over its direction.

The criteria or principles listed above have been abstracted from concrete strategies my colleagues and I at CARE have used in conducting training workshops. They are process criteria, tacitly embodied in our practices as trainers, and gradually made explicit in a piecemeal fashion as we reflected together in prior planning meetings, debriefings at the end of each day during the course of workshops, and summative appraisals at the end of them. In other words the principles governing our pedagogical practices in action-research training workshops were articulated in a context of second-order action-research where we deliberated about teaching strategies. They emerged as explicit principles interactively with practical experience and not in advance of, or in isolation from, it.

It is difficult to bring such principles to mind without also bringing to mind some of the concrete strategies in which they are embedded. Although I did not plan the Caracas workshop in detail in advance of my arrival, I did have certain strategies in mind. For example:

(i)   A strategy for implementing criterion (i) consists of placing participants in small groups and getting each to articulate and discuss in turn a practical problem they persistently experience in their teaching situation.

This strategy is usually linked with an exposition, at the start of the workshop, of the nature of action research as a process of both educational inquiry and professional learning.

(ii)   The major strategy I associate with criterion (ii), in a workshop context where participants are unable to return to their classrooms, or to work with another teacher in a school during part of the day, is to set up situations in which a number of volunteers teach their peers.

In an initial briefing conference participants are told that:

— this is a real and not a simulation exercise. Volunteer teachers should not pretend they are teaching children or students, and the other participants should not pretend to be children or students. The volunteers should teach something they are genuinely interested in, and would like to convey something of its interest to their peers.

— the volunteer teachers will have a period of time — 45 minutes to an hour — in which to plan their lessons. (Team teaching is not ruled out). They have access to certain teaching aids if they require them, e.g. OHPs. The lesson length will be 30–45 minutes.

— during the preparation period 'the class' of each teacher will plan a data collection exercise around the lesson. The key questions to be addressed are:

    (i)   what kinds of data would it be appropriate to collect?

    (ii) how do we collect and analyze this data? Who collects it? Using what techniques?

    (iii) how do we organize and assemble the presentation of data for the purpose of group analysis/discussion?

— time will be allowed for the collection of interview data before and after the lesson, for example, from the volunteer teacher(s) during the preparation period.

— the data gathering process should not be so intrusive that it prevents the teacher and majority of the class from fully engaging with the subject-matter of the lesson.

— the group analysis/discussion of data will take place the day following the lesson to give people in data collection roles time to process information and prepare its presentation to the group.

— the experience of the practical exercise as a whole, which normally consists of two three-hour sessions, will be debriefed in a subsequent session where the groups (classes) share their experience of the exercise and discuss emerging methodological issues and themes related to action-research. The practical exercise is usually linked with an exposition of a methodology for action research and the sorts of methods/techniques which can be employed in implementing it.

(iii)   The interactive relationship between presentations of action-research theory/methodology, practical experiences, and participants' reflections about those experiences had become associated in my mind with something like the following sequence of activities:

Lecture + discussion:
the nature of the action-research process

Small group exercise:
problem identification and articulation

Discussion of theoretical issues:
between leader(s) and participants

Lecture + discussion:
action-research methodology and methods

Group exercise:
data collection and analysis around a lesson

Discussion of methodological/theoretical issues

This sequence not only allows ideas presented in lecture form to be explored experientially but the discussion which follows the experiential component provides an opportunity for further reflection on those ideas in the light of experience. However, the experience of the Caracas workshop significantly modified my understanding of these relationships.

(iv) One strategy restricting the degree of control workshop leaders exert over participants' thinking, is to provide plenty of opportunities for learning in small groups which the leaders do not directly monitor. They can be invited into a group to respond to particular queries or questions, but then dismissed to allow the group to get on with the assigned task.

The value of this strategy has been clarified for me by having to operate with participants who speak a language I have no knowledge of. By providing considerable time for group work in the native language of participants, the temptation to establish overt and covert mechanisms of surveillance and control over their thinking is something I have become more aware of, and therefore able to resist. Well briefed English speakers amongst the participants can function very well as group leaders and mediate any necessary transactions with the 'outsiders' leading the workshop.

Techniques for Analyzing and Collecting Data about my Facilitation Strategies

In the Caracas workshop I attempted to establish a process of action-research into my own practice as its leader. This was partly because I was aware that a lot was at stake. The person who had secured money and funds to bring me to Venezuela needed the workshop to be a success. And from the standpoint of CARE we were hoping to establish a basis for future collaboration with educational researchers and teacher educators in the Central University. So we needed the workshop to be a success. I was also aware that I was largely ignorant of the academic and cultural context of the workshop, and therefore unable to anticipate participants' needs. This called for an even greater degree of responsive decision-making on a day-to-day basis than perhaps one would engage in when operating in contexts one is more knowledgeable about. Finally, I had been allocated less than half the time I normally used to carry out the training workshop. I was going to have to exercise not only considerable flexibility in my decision-making but also handle a great deal of complexity in managing within a short timescale a process which was consistent with the principles outlined earlier.

In establishing a second-order action-research process into my own teaching strategies within the workshop I also wished to demonstrate a point; namely, that facilitating action-research as a mode of professional learning and inquiry constituted in itself a reflective practice. I knew that many of the participants were academic educationalists interested in exploring action-research as an approach to teacher development. My own action-research was, in part, intended to demonstrate the value of undertaking second-order action-research into the strategies one employs to facilitate others' capacities for reflectively improving their professional practices.

At the beginning of the workshop I outlined the action-research procedures I intended to adopt; namely:

— I would, at the end of each day, reflect about events in the form of a diary. I suggested that the workshop participants do likewise.

I explained that I would not only describe events but also the ways I subjectively experienced them; how I felt about and interpreted them at the time. The diary would also contain retrospective and reflective commentaries on these feelings and interpretations.

I emphasized that this kind of reflective writing (see Holly, 1989) helped us to recall experience and explore its significance for identifying, clarifying, and resolving practical problems in teaching.

— My two interpreters were also asked to keep a daily diary and at the beginning of each day to interview workshop participants about their experience of the workshop. They would then present me with summary accounts of the interviews, and in addition could volunteer extracts from their own diaries.

In this way, my own record of experience could be constantly compared and contrasted with records elicited from participants, and with records produced by two 'observers'.

This multi-perspective approach illustrates one application of triangulation methods of data gathering. It is an application which grounds a procedure for assembling subjective data for release to others in a procedure that enables individuals to recall and reflect about their subjective experiences in a 'private space', before it is released, via such methods as interviews, into more 'public space'. Intrinsic to this procedure is placing individuals in a position to exercise a large measure of control over the release of subjective data and the ways it is represented to others.

I always make the point that diaries are confidential to their authors. What is disclosed from them should be under their control. Diaries can be drawn on in responding to interview questions or discussing one's practices with others. They can be released in whole or in part at their author's discretion. Reflective writing in private space protects the individual from tendencies which are activated in situations that require them to produce more public accounts of their experience. For example, there is a tendency for individuals to misrepresent and distort their experience in interviews in order to present it in a favourable light. The private context of diary writing allows individuals to reflect about their experience in a more detached, open, and honest manner. Reflective writing, in private, increases the capacity of individuals to engage in authentic self-disclosure in data gathering situations which are directed towards some form of wider release.

— At the beginning of each day I would read from the diary entries made on the previous day, and compare them with the accounts of both participants and interpreters/observers. I would then invite participants and observers to discuss the issues which emerged.

In this way I hoped to illustrate how a teacher can use multi-perspective data as a basis for developing critical self-understandings of their own practices, and for involving students and professional colleagues as partners in the deliberative process of action-research.

Theorizing about Action-research through Second-order Action-research

The following account draws on my diary entries, those of my translators, and data supplied to them by participants in daily interviews.

Day 1

At the beginning of the second day I read out an account of my thoughts and feelings, both prior to the previous day's sessions, and retrospectively. The following extracts are pertinent to the theory-practice issue which subsequently emerged:

> I didn't want to simply begin with a lecture on action-research. Of course, they will probably expect this. Shouldn't the visiting expert tell us what he/she knows? But 'telling' has to connect with experience and assist self-reflection. I don't know, as the Americans say, where these people are coming from . . . Young Mi (the host institution's organizer and one of my observers/translators) told me they were mainly teacher educators/researchers in universities, but a few teachers, and also some master's degree students in education.
>
> So I need a lot from the group before I can judge which inputs will be best coming from me. I have to practice what I preach . . . I must teach through action-research. We must gather data throughout the workshop. I don't know what problems I will encounter, but I guess the problem of my authority in relation to their learning will crop up as a theme. Also the problem of communicating a different paradigm of research to the one they are familiar with.

It is clear that I was entertaining a departure from my normal sequence; namely, starting after the preliminaries with a lecture on the nature of the action-research process. And I was entertaining beginning with a practical exercise to dramatically destabilize expectations I anticipated a largely academic group of individuals would have of the workshop; namely, that it would emphasize theory and engage them in theoretical discourse about action-research as opposed to the practical discourse about how to do it.

The sequence of activities I finally settled on for the first morning were included in the diary:

(i) Get them to define themselves as professionals to get an idea of the areas of practice they might wish to undertake action research into ... (½ hour)

(ii) In threes, each person to articulate a problem area or area of improvement in their practice (whether school teaching, university teaching, or research). The other two should only ask questions, or seek clarification, elaboration, or explanation. Each person should have ten minutes. Then after each individual has articulated an area of concern the three 'problems' should be discussed for a total of twenty minutes. Following this discussion each individual should produce a rearticulation of their 'problem' on a large sheet of paper which is then posted on the wall. All participants will be asked to tour the posters and review their contents.

(iii) General discussion in whole group.

(iv) JE to give a lecture on the action-research process.

Things didn't turn out as planned, as my retrospective account of day 1 records:

I started to brief them on the format for the morning, explaining why I would not be giving a lecture on action-research. But in 'briefing' and 'explaining' I found an opportunity to make some basic points about action-research. For example, I drew a distinction between: (a) first and second order action-research, when explaining why I needed to undertake action-research into my teaching strategies within the workshop; (b) theoretical and practical problems, when providing a rationale for the small group 'problem articulation' exercise; (c) 'educational research' and 'research on education' when elaborating on the reasons for the practical exercise.

I spoke for around forty-five minutes and didn't leave time for discussion. Young Mi reminded me that participants had not yet introduced themselves. I decided to incorporate opportunities for discussion into the period following the practical exercise. The introductions gave everyone an opportunity to speak, but they took a long time to complete.

Participants got into the exercise, after coffee, fairly quickly ... They appeared very committed to the task and did not want to be rushed along on my time schedule. I allowed them more time but kept up some pressure. They stayed on three-quarters of an hour beyond the official closing time (12.30 pm) to allow for discussion after the exercise.

I asked them whether the group work generated discrepant views of each of the problems raised. Evidently it did. I built a point about action-research methodology on this in terms of developing a comprehensive view of a problem area by entertaining alternative perspectives.

I then asked how many groups attempted to achieve a consensus of view about the nature of the problems explored. Some groups evidently did while others were content to tolerate divergence. At this point I posed a fundamental theoretical question about the truth of accounts of social situations, and contrasted the consensus theory of Habermas with the interpretative hermeneutics of Gadamer. I was explaining clearly, although very abstractly. Yet I hoped the abstract issues would be understood on the basis of participants' experience during the practical exercise. However, I gained the impression that some were 'lost'.

I was asked to clarity the difference between the views of Habermas and Gadamer on 'truth'. My long-winded 'repeat' indicated my anxiety whether I was 'getting through'. Some people seemed worried by my expressed preference for divergent and diverse 'understandings', leaving the final assessment of what constitutes a valid interpretation to personal judgment. I felt accused of being a 'relativist' and 'subjectivist'.

In response I did not deny truth existed, but argued that we only partially and incompletely grasp it. Also I suggested, but did not clearly articulate, that the path to truth lies not in simplifying complexity and diversity but in facing diversity and incorporating it into one's understanding.

. . . I could have made my points more clearly, but I was thinking some of this out 'on the spot' in response to unanticipated questions which tended to assume objectivity equals objectivism, and that if knowledge is provisional then 'anything goes'.

. . . I suggest that this part of the session made some feel 'destabilized': assumptions were challenged. However, I could have done a better job in clarifying my own position on the nature of understanding. I was worried about losing those who were not interested in these abstract issues. Did I?

. . . When explaining Habermas' consensus theory of truth I cited the idea of a hierarchy of credibility in groups which prevents free and open discourse. I asked if anyone had experienced this phenomemon in the practical exercise. Some people started to smile and laugh knowingly.

By the end of the day a whole set of theoretical themes surrounding the nature of action-research had been explicitly placed on the workshop's agenda. But I was worried about colluding with those who wanted to operate at a purely theoretical level on the assumption that a theoretical understanding of action-research does not have to be grounded in reflection upon one's practical experience of it. If I succumbed to this temptation I would only reinforce a theory of theory and practice which legitimates hegemonic relations between academics and teachers. I felt that my intuitive resistance to starting with a lecture had been well-founded. However, the fact that I gave a lecture did not constitute a total reversal in the plan. Theoretical distinctions and ideas were articulated in the context of briefing participants for a practical exercise in action-research, not in advance of the briefing or retrospective to it.

The form of my presentation — a response to a dilemma about whether to start with a theoretical input or a practical exercise — embodied a new understanding for me of the relationship between theoretical understanding and practice.

I always knew that teachers did not grasp theoretical conceptions of practices independently of implementing a form of practice which embodied them in concrete form. But I always felt that some prior presentation of theory was necessary as a broad orientation, however imperfectly they were grasped. Now I realize, since the Caracas workshop far more clearly than previously, that theory renders practices practically intelligible; i.e. in a way which enables people to participate in them confidently and competently. It is no good presenting the theory before the practice since one is likely to have little understanding of what is required to render it practically meaningful to others. And it is no good simply asking people to engage in a novel practice prior to theorizing about it, since they cannot competently proceed with a practical assignment without reflecting about the ideas which give it form. So the ideas must be elucidated in the context of a practical discourse with participants about how they are to proceed with practical tasks.

Theorizing about the nature and purpose of a practice is not a separate activity, albeit an interacting one, to reflecting about how to proceed competently with it. The latter must involve theorizings about the practical aims and principles which shape the practice. This understanding of the relation between the theory and practice of action-research was realized in the way I resolved my dilemma about how to begin the Caracas workshop. It has led to a considerable shift in my understanding of the third methodological principle governing the facilitator's role, as I outlined it earlier. Such an understanding is in my view less distorted by an ideological misrepresentation of the theory-practice relationship which functions to perpetuate the intellectual hegemony of professional educational theorists. This is why I became anxious after the practical exercise about being caught up in a process which dissociated the discussion of theoretical issues from reflection about the concrete experiences of participants. And my enriched understanding, realized in a concrete form of practice, also explains why at the end of my day I listed the following problems, as urgent matters to address in the days which followed:

(i) Developing participants self-reflection about their experiences as a context for understanding action-research methodology.
(ii) Structuring work of a large group, with different interests and experience, in a responsive rather than highly predetermined manner.
(iii) Securing continuity of learning experiences.
(iv) Building on ideas by continuously spiralling back on them in new learning contexts without becoming repetitive.

These concerns were reinforced by the contents of the observers'/translators' diaries. For example:

Obs 1: During the small group work, participants seemed pressurized for time and worried about what they were putting on paper. Whether it was any good. They want individual attention. I was wondering whether John would give enough time to follow through this exercise before Friday.

I was concerned about the time because it was running behind the schedule. I did not comment because I thought I must respect his style.

Obs 2: Time ran against us in this session. Important data based on participants' needs were not taken into consideration for reflection.

The (practical) task was performed by all participants. Some were anguished, others confused; some had questions to be answered.

The interview with a group of participants indicated that they perceived the first day as a very experiential process rather than one focussed on abstract theory. This perception surprised me. All is relative (perhaps to culture). Some appeared to approve of what they perceived to be an experiential learning exercise. Others were less happy.

> Yes, it made me think about myself. I realized that I had to go little by little to be a good professor.

> I do not disagree with the experiential strategy. But it will be very fruitful if we would take time to analyze critically the pros and cons of action-research for us in the following sessions. The activity is pretty and attractive, but it is important to discuss the problematic aspects of doing action-research in our context. Some authors criticize action-research because it is too pragmatic and only concerned with practical problems.

Day 2

I had intended to give a lecture on the logic and methodology of action-research. Old habits die hard. But I hadn't embarked on it for very long before questions came. I abandoned the straight lecture and went into a series of mini-lectures; each in response to a question from participants, but each was used to weave a pattern or framework of ideas concerning 'the logic' of action-research. I used the questions as 'hooks' on which to build the framework of ideas. The performance lasted for two hours, largely due to numerous 'action-research strategies' I told about classroom events in an attempt to contextualize the ideas, although I also linked the ideas to the practical exercise yesterday. The following diary extract illustrated something of this attempt to establish links between the experience of participants and the ideas I was elucidating:

> One piece of feedback I received via my observers/interviewers was that yesterday the trios didn't have time to reconstruct their 'problem-articulations', and had indeed tended to state ideas for action-research rather than explicate the problems they experienced in realizing them in practice.
> I attempted this morning to explain to the group that I had hoped the task would make them aware of the ideas (theories) which framed their articulations of problems and tacitly underpinned their practices. I then talked about the 'tacit theories' which underpin teaching strategies and how it was the task of action-research to explicate and test them. 'Tacit theories' were illustrated with two stories about teachers' definitions of the problem of handling reading materials in classrooms as a basis for discussion.

I attempted to extend the practical task of the previous day into 'what data do we need to collect to test these understandings of problems?' But given the difficulties they had experienced in problem articulation on day 1 they lacked the experiential foundation for the extended exercise. However, in spite of my dominance and the relative failure of the practical exercise I recorded in my diary:

> ... the atmosphere in the group was relaxed and humorous: as if many were now feeling they were grasping a framework which made the action-research process intelligible.

Some might argue that I had merely entertained. But I would argue that my mini-lectures were continuous with the initial strategy on the first day. They constituted the elucidation of ideas in portrayals of practical experience, both those of work-shop participants and those of teachers whose 'realities' they could readily identify with and generalize (naturalistically) to their own experience. One observer's diary for day 2 reinforced my own impressions of both the difficulties in the practical exercise and the influence of the mini-lectures in facilitating the development of a conceptual framework which rendered action-research a practically intelligible process:

> Two things I liked most about today's session were: John's diary and stories in order to make a point. All participants were concentrated, had shining eyes and laughed ... All the things including the stories produced a strong impact on the participants and me because they seemed more relevant than the theoretical concepts.
> ... I noticed some frustration from the participants not being able to figure out how to do the task in the small group ... The trouble they encountered was that the problems they stated yesterday were too vague, and needed to be modified as an initial idea to proceed further.

The other observer was more parsimonious in his interpretations:

> John lectured for a long period of time. He answered several questions.
> ... One group member attacked the way he developed yesterday's session. No group reaction.

Day 3

For the first time the 'time problem' began to vanish. The schedule of activities I had planned for that day the previous evening was implemented with only a few adjustments. It was as follows:

(i) Read my Day 2 diary. In the event I didn't invite discussion of it. One has to make choices. I was determined to maintain the schedule.

(ii) Lecture on methodology and techniques of action-research. In the event I did not go into specific techniques in detail but looked at the rationale for triangulation as a broad strategy, and developmental stages for gradually involving teachers in a process of data collection and analysis which culminates in triangulation. Again I 'peppered' the presentation with stories and examples.

(iii) Continuation of exercise in determining methods of data collection around practical problems identified in the trios. In this exercise I wanted participants to draw on illustrative accounts of data collection strategies introduced in the lecture.

(iv) Preparation in four 'classes' for practical exercise in data collection and analysis around a lesson.

(v) 'The lesson'.

(vi) Brief feedback.

In the event (iv) and (v) seemed to proceed so smoothly that I did not see much point at bringing them together at the end of the day. They knew how to proceed into the analysis on day 4. I was developing the view that the time problem disappeared when most of the workshop participants had integrated theory and practice within their understanding. There was no longer a great problem for the majority about how to proceed with making action-research intelligible. They anticipated developing theoretical insights by reflecting about their experience of the practical assignments.

However, this integration of theory with practice in the thinking of the majority didn't occur with a minority. In my diary I wrote:

I feel some people want more time to discuss theory with me. A few do not seem interested in the practical session . . . Others feel they already know the things we have covered so far. How can one overcome the problem of academics feeling they can teach teachers action-research without doing it themselves?

One of my observers also commented:

Some university staff members seem more interested with theoretical aspects of the workshop. The evidence shows them looking for books and other written material. They do not get involved in practical group work.

Day 4

I was amazed by the fact that the vast majority of participants arrived before 9.30 am (the official start to the day) and without any prompting settled into their groups to analyze and interpret the data they had collected around 'the lessons' of the previous day.

Some of the participants had earlier in the workshop expressed a concern to know about, and master the techniques for analyzing data. They assumed that there existed an established body of 'objective' techniques and that doing action-research simply involved applying them. I had argued that there is no orthodox corpus of techniques; they have to be selected, and even invented, in the light of emerging definitions of practical problems. Since such definitions are not bias free, the application of techniques cannot be prescribed on the basis of objectivist dogma.

No doubt part of the motivation of the participants on this day was a search for the 'holy grail' of technique. But they were also on the point of realizing that more important than techniques are the methodological insights they might develop through the group analysis exercise, i.e. development of an awareness of the principles which guide the quest for understanding.

I had briefed one of my interpreters to chair a period after coffee which was designed to enable participants to share the methodological problems and issues the data collection and analysis exercise had generated in their groups. This period was to proceed in a very rule governed way. Firstly, the members in each group were to be interviewed in turn by members of other groups. They were only allowed to respond to questions, and the 'interviewing groups' were only allowed to ask questions. During the interviews the chairperson should prevent any 'outbursts' of discussion from persisting. The idea was to get experiences articulated and publicly shared prior to any discussion. Each group was allocated about fifteen minutes of interview time. After the interviews the idea was that the whole group should identify some key issues and themes which had emerged from the data presented and discuss them.

Once this session had begun after the coffee break I used the other translator to 'clue me into' the topics which were emerging from the group interviews. I listed them as follows on the blackboard:

— Should data collection be negotiated with the teacher?
— Should one discover student as well as teacher expectations of lessons?
— The problem of unstructured interviewing is one of feeling confident.
— Discovering discrepancies in triangulation data. Does this betray a negative bias which is threatening for the teacher?
— The difficulty of observing in a non-judgmental manner.
— Should feelings as well as views be elicited in interviews?
— Individuals (students) experience things differently in the same situation.
— Who defines the observer's categories?
— Do *a priori* categories restrict observation?
— The problem of subjectivity in observation. Can one get agreement on categories?
— Problem of reflexivity; participating and observing at the same time.
— Teachers get anxious about observers' criteria/categories of judgment.
— The problems of role-playing children and teachers of children.
— Is action-research too complicated?
— Conflicts over leadership roles in groups.
— Power relations between teachers and students.

In the discussion that followed all the participants focussed in on a major theme which appeared to permeate many of the topics brought out in the interviews. This was the problem of how one handled subjective bias as an observer in an action research facilitating role. Does bias have to be set aside for the sake of objectivity or is it a condition of understanding practice in any educationally meaningful way? Are biases things which those involved in facilitating action-research must become detached from or are they 'tacit theories' which can be tested, modified and refined in the light of observational data looked at from the standpoint of different biases to one's own.

And so we returned to our original theme about the nature of our understanding of educational situations and how we verify it. But this time it was not treated in abstraction from reflection on the experience of a second-order action-research process. What the experience had demonstrated for many participants upon reflection was that there was a very real problem about developing one's understanding of practical problems by attempting to eliminate one's biases.

The data collection-analysis and the inter-group exercise which followed it, provided a context in which many participants were able to deconstruct their conception of objectivity. Such a conception pre-supposed a dichotomy between theoretical understanding and practical knowledge and thereby legitimated the intellectual hegemony of the academic researcher. In beginning to reconstruct their concept of objectivity by reflecting about their attempts to facilitate the reflective practice of teaching through research, participants had also begun to reconstruct their theory of the theory-practice relationship.

It was only at the end of the workshop after the inter-group exercise that participants realised that they had learned how to analyze data; not by applying certain techniques but through a group process which had enabled them to identify a range of theories for facilitators of action-research and to discover the fundamental problem which underpinned nearly all of them. The problem lay in their ideologically distorted self-understandings of their practices as educational researchers. The problem which they unearthed was a problem about their own professional identities.

I will conclude with a few extracts from the diary I produced on the final day, and from the diary of one of my observers:

JE: I was delighted. Deep down I had feared that the practical exercise on data collection/analysis would descend into chaos. But it didn't . . . The groups stayed with the task in a highly motivated manner until 11am (coffee) . . . I stopped worrying about time. The problem may not exist if one is confident that the students are using available time well . . . I lost the temptation to insert a theory session today because I felt the participants could easily tolerate its absence given their immersion in the practical exercise.

         The inter-group exercise worked superbly as a means of illustrating how experience can be shared and reflectively analysed. The credit must go to the participants and not the procedure. They generated and sustained a process of grounded theorizing: eliciting experiential themes from their questions and then in discussion weaving them holistically into a key theme concerning the role of the observer and 'the problem of bias'. When I commented on this process I think they suddenly understood that they had been competently analyzing data without realizing it. Perhaps their hunger to encounter theory in abstraction from practice may lessen now that they are able to develop their theoretical insights through reflective forms of practice.

Observer: I couldn't do any interviewing today. When I arrived in the classroom, almost all participants had arrived, and were working on the task . . .

When I checked each group they were all task centred. Participation was very high, and in some groups a confrontation of ideas prevailed and in only one group was the search for consensus leading their intentions.

. . . Participation was excellent during the inter-group exercise. I had a deep understanding of how theory can be constructed from data.

Reference

HOLLY, M.L. (1989) 'Teachers' reflective writing', *Cambridge Journal of Education*, 19, 1.
RUDDUCK, J. and HOPKINS, D. (Eds) (1985) *Research as a Basis for Teaching: readings from the work of Lawrence Stenhouse*, Oxford, Portsmouth NH (USA), Heinemann Educational Books.

Chapter 14

The Relationship Between 'Understanding' and 'Developing' Teachers' Thinking

John Elliott

Two Accounts of Professional Learning

I want to begin this chapter with two teachers' accounts of their learning over a period of two years when members of a part-time Masters course in Applied Educational Research at CARE. The course is based on a number of applied research assignments which members carry out in their own institutional settings, either into aspects of their own practice or into institutional practices in which they are implicated. The conduct of these assignments is regularly discussed with peers and tutors at weekly evening sessions.

Teacher A

Entering the world of research was for me like entering an oak panelled hall where I realized there was a door only because I could see the handle. I went over to the door and knocked. There was no response: so with very great difficulty I managed to push the heavy door open. The room that I entered had pictures on one side that were somewhat familiar to me. On the other side of the room there were mirrors which showed my reflection and at the same time reflected the pictures that I had first seen. This showed me that I was part of these pictures. The room was very bright in contrast to the hall and I felt an excitement about being there together with the challenge of trying to identify all that was happening in this room. There were some parts of the floor that were revolving round and round rather slowly, whilst there were other parts which were moving out into a long corridor and seemed to be inviting me to step on. There was also a number of doors in this room that had to be opened from time to time because they provided the clues and information with which to interpret the room. It was on closer examination of the room and the pictures that I realized that I needed to interpret and analyze what I was seeing and that this was difficult for me. I realized that my questioning had been on a superficial level and that it was not always the obvious that was the cause of what I was seeing but rather the result of what I had seen.

The teacher appears to be using an analogue to represent a change of consciousness during the course. In other words the analogue constitutes a study of her own thinking. It is a reflexive act. Let's then look at the major elements in this representation.

Firstly, the research represented by the oak-panelled hall gives access to a new realm of consciousness but only with difficulty. The door cannot be seen — only the handle — and it is heavy to push open. It is a realm which incapacitates normal responses to things because there is no fixed standpoint from which to view them: 'some parts of the floor were revolving round and round rather slowly'. There is the challenge to take risks and venture out into the unknown, to depart from the certainties of ordinary consciousness: other parts of the floor were 'moving out into a long corridor and seemed to be inviting me to step on'. The objects of ordinary consciousness are pictured in this realm: 'the room I entered had pictures on one side that were somewhat familiar to me'. But it is destabilized by a reflexive self-awareness: 'mirrors which showed my reflection and at the same time reflected the pictures that I had first seen'. She became aware of herself as an aspect of objects which in ordinary consciousness were depicted as external realities, and realized that their features were not the cause of her 'seeing' but rather the result of it. The objects which in ordinary consciousness appeared to be such obvious features of reality now appeared as constructs of that consciousness. New ways of interpreting experience are opened up through the achievement of a reflexive consciousness: 'There was also a number of doors in this room that had to be opened from time to time because they provided the clues and information with which to interpret the room.'

Teacher A discloses a change not so much in the specific contents of her thinking about her experiences but in the form of her thinking. Moreover, she does so in a particular context. She is writing for her course tutors about her professional learning. Later the text she has constructed will be subjected to a formal interview procedure which constitutes the 'examination' component of the course. Her performance in the interview will be taken into account along with the research assignments she has submitted in deciding whether she will pass the course. Her account of her thinking is therefore produced in an assessment context where she has to interpret her tutors' expectations of what would constitute an appropriate account of the way applied research contributes to professional learning.

Teacher B:

I went to see my dissertation supervisor and tried to listen to his interpretation of the transcription of my first interview on 'learning'. He told me to go back and interview the same person and go deeper — 'beyond the platitudes'. I sat there wondering what he meant. I thought I had something different. Something a little controversial.

I wanted to tell him about the really exciting one with the third years but he pulled me back. He had seen something in it I hadn't and it told him something about the person I had interviewed and something about ME.

So there it was. A different interpretation. A different perception of reality.

I went home and took my rough hand-written transcription and typed it onto a computer disk. As I did so I noticed something happened again. It kept changing. When I did it . . . the interview and taped it, it was something. When I listened to it it became something else. When I painstakingly copied it, playing and replaying the tape, fretting about the punctuation, it changed into something else again.

When I read some of the rough copy to my supervisor, I got confused because it had done it again. Changed. Finally at the keyboard it took yet another shape.

At this point I began to reflect on what could be happening. It had to be nonsense that an event, the interview, now a past personal MA event, could change and continue to after it is gone. I wondered if I was changing it. If I was introducing my own subtle bias like a sneaky worm wriggling in.

As a mere verbal record on tape, I was aware of its imperfection. There were little bits here and there inaudible. All the non-verbal data is stored in my memory. No, not all, only the bits I actually received . Okay — did I sneak any bits out or in? No, my transcription was as accurate as possible. The natural scientist still rules in some places. Perhaps I didn't hear things? No, I'm not worried about my auditory apparatus. Yet something bothers me in my methodology.

I noticed as I typed the plain bare words onto the screen, my mind was composing both from memory and from the words before me a different version. I was reading between the lines, listening to the metalanguage and mentally meshing it with my recall of the context, the nonverbal language and so on.

. . . My present methodological dilemma is interpretation of data. What sort of process turns the interview data into something with meaning?

. . . My concern had been first 'how did the data change' then secondly if I was changing it. Gradually I realized that even though both of these were relevant the real change that was taking place was me. I was changing. I had noticed I was learning. There was a 'process of processing' during the whole exercise.

Again we have an account of a change of consciousness, from a conviction about the meaning of the interview data via the destabilizing experience of ever-shifting meanings to a state of reflexive consciousness in which the teacher processes her own mental processes; examining the changes in the meaning of the data for her as a reflection of changes in herself.

Both the accounts of A and B refer to a destabilizing experience. The content of their thinking (meaning) no longer appears as obviously inherent in the data of experience and existing quite independently of the thinker as it does to ordinary consciousness. Rather, the meaning is viewed as the creation of the thinker who becomes interested in the process by which she creates meaning for herself.

Teacher B's account of her professional learning was produced in the same context as teacher A's. But she quite explicitly cites the critical role of a tutorial intervention in accomplishing the transition from ordinary to reflexive consciousness. It was the supervisor for the final major research assignment — the dissertation — who helped her to see a different interpretation of the data. This was not a matter of demonstrating that she had misunderstood the 'objective meaning' inherent in the data, but of showing her that the data indicated something about herself as well as about the thoughts of the interviewee. Although citing no specific examples teacher B also characterizes the world of research represented by her MA tutor as revealing things about the relationship between her pictures of reality and herself.

The research context of these accounts is that of insider research. Course members were required to research situations within their own educational institutions. But the course tutors did not simply assume that this was largely a matter of inducting insiders into methodologies of inquiry employed by outsider researchers. Insiders are practically related to the situations they study, and this has implications for the methodology of insider research. I do not want to characterize the methodological perspectives introduced by tutors on the course as action-research. There is a considerable amount of controversy about what methodologically distinguishes action-research from other forms of educational research. And the tutors responsible for the course will tend to disagree about the extent to which methodological perspectives they introduce can be appropriately regarded as integral features of action-research. What they would agree about is that the validity of these perspectives resides in the extent to which they help insiders to develop their understanding of how they are practically related to the situations they investigate. And it is this form of understanding which enables insiders to change the practical relationship between situation and self. In other words the aim of insider research as interpreted through the CARE MA is to foster *reflexive educational practice*. But this does not imply that the appropriate methodological perspectives cannot accommodate a significant role for outsider researchers as facilitators of reflexive practice. The important question for them, as for insiders, is the appropriateness of their methodological perspective for the development of a reflexive practical consciousness.

Dimensions of Reflective Consciousness

The idea of 'reflective practice', stimulated by the work of Schon (1983 and 1987), is now widely employed by educationalists as a new basis for teacher education which overcomes the problematics of the traditional rationalist paradigm (see Elliott, 1991) by integrating theory and practice. The idea has gained considerable currency in the field of initial teacher education, as the rationalist tradition has collapsed to the intrusion of the 'social market' ideology — of the New Right — into all areas of public education. The radical alternative to the commodification of professional learning in the form of tangible behavioural outcomes or 'competencies', and to the transformation of teacher education into a school based production-consumption system, appears to be that of reflective practice. In the field of in-service teacher education the ideas of 'teachers as researchers' and 'educational action-research' gained currency following the work of Stenhouse (1975) during the late 60s and early 70s in the field of school-based curriculum development. Action-research theorists, such as myself, have tended to assimilate Schon's idea of the reflective practitioner into their thinking; pinpointing, perhaps overhastily, its similarities rather than differences to the evolving action research tradition in the UK (see Elliott, 1985). We have now reached a state of affairs where people need to clarify

the concepts of reflection being employed in our discourse about 'reflective practitioners', 'teachers as researchers' and 'action-research' in teacher education.

Louden (1991), drawing on Habermas' theory of 'knowledge-constitutive interests', distinguishes four forms of reflection in terms of the different concerns or
interests which underpin them. These are the *technical, personal, problematic, and
critical*. This is a slight amendment of Habermas' tripartite distinction between
technical, practical and critical reasoning which were later employed by Carr and
Kemmis (1983 and 1986) to differentiate three types of action research. Louden
further sub-divides 'the practical' into the 'personal' and 'problematic'. The 'technical' derives from an interest in the prediction and control of events and involves
the application of means-ends rules, which are derived from 'some set of empirically
or theoretically derived standards'. Schon characterized this form of science-based
reasoning as technical rationality.

Louden describes reflection with a personal interest as connecting experience
with an understanding of one's own life. It involves creating narrative stories which
render one's thoughts, feelings and actions intelligible to oneself and others.

Reflection with an interest in problematics focusses on the resolution 'of the
problems of professional action'. It is concerned with changing situations from a
problematic to an improved state of affairs. According to Louden this is the interest
most fully represented in Schon's account of the 'reflective practitioner'. And one
might also argue that it is the interest most fully articulated in the development of
educational action-research theory within the UK.

Finally, the critical interest 'involves questioning taken-for-granted thoughts,
feelings, and actions'.

I have previously criticized Carr and Kemmis' use of Habermas' theory of
knowledge-constituitive interests to distinguish different types of action-research in
terms of the technical, practical, and emancipatory (see Elliott, 1987). This is because,
following Gadamer (1975), I cannot see why practical reflection, which is interested
in how to act consistently with the values embedded in our social traditions, need
not require us to think critically about values. As Gadamer argues, Habermas tends
to assume that social traditions are unchanging mechanisms of ideological suppression from which human beings need to be emancipated. For Gadamer social
traditions can be far more dynamic and changing, and inasmuch as they are it is
because the values they transmit are continuously reconstructed on the basis of
practical reflection. In other words practical reflection incorporates the critical as
an intrinsic dimension. According to Habermas the emancipatory interest incorporates the practical interest but also transcends it. From a Gadamerian point of view
the critical aspect of reflection does not serve an emancipatory interest in the sense
of emancipation from social tradition. Rather as an intrinsic feature of practical
reflection it serves an evolutionary interest.

Gadamer's position is reinforced by Dewey's account of practical inquiry.
Dewey argues that ends and means are in this context joint objects of reflection.
In reflecting about the means (actions) which are consistent with our ends (values)
we also come to question our conceptions of ends, and in modifying those
conceptions we become aware of new possibilities with respect to means.

In my work with teachers on various action-research projects I have always
found that when teachers reflect about the consistency of their actions with their
educational values they also begin to question the taken-for-granted beliefs and
assumptions which define those values for them. The extent to which they do this

may be limited but this does not constitute a tendency to reduce reflection to a merely practical form. Rather such limitations constitute a lack of depth in the quality of practical reflection itself. Habermas' theory of knowledge constitutive interests at best enables us to differentiate between two forms of reflection: 'the technical' and 'the practical'.

Louden's six forms of reflection are, in my view, based on a confused understanding of Habermas' notion of interests. I understand these to refer to contexts of human action, such as predicting and controlling their consequences, or ensuring their fidelity to the values one is committed to. The 'personal', 'problematic' and 'critical' are not interests of this kind. Such terms characterize dimensions of a form of reflection which is constituted by the practical interest of acting in ways which are consistent with human values. They do not differentiate distinct forms of reflection. But they do differentiate the practical from the technical. Technical reflection can be characterized as *non-problematic, impersonal,* and *non-critical.* It is non-problematic in the sense that, although it addresses a problem of controlling things to achieve a certain outcome, there is nothing problematic about how that outcome is best understood. Technical problems presuppose a clear and unambiguous impersonal standard for evaluating solutions. And this is precisely what 'practical' problems lack. One may experience values as ends to be in conflict when faced with a concrete practical situation, and one's conception of them as limited and open to revision. The problem of choosing means which realize our values lies in our ambiguous and limited conceptions of the action-implications of those values in the particular circumstances of everyday living.

The experience of a practical problem challenges us to question the framework of beliefs and assumptions we bring to the situation, and to personally reconstruct that framework.

From this analysis I am left with two forms of action-orientated reflection: that which serves a technical interest in controlling and predicting the material and social environment, and that which serves a practical interest in acting consistently with human values. Each form will possess rather different characteristics, which can be contrasted as follows:

Dimensions of Reflection

The Practical Interest	intrinsically problematic standards	the person as the source of standards	critical self-reflection
The Technical Interest	clear and unambiguous standards	impersonal means-ends rules as the source of standards	instrumental thinking

In the light of this analysis of the idea of reflection let me now return to the two teachers' accounts of their professional learning. The personal dimension, an emerging interest in their own subjectivity as the source of the meanings they find in the situations they research, is highlighted in both accounts. For both teachers reflection is *reflexive*. But in both accounts there is a sub-text which refers to the problematic and critical aspects of reflection.

In teacher A's account her 'pictures' of the world are challenged by research. She is aware there is new data to be gathered and fresh questions to be asked which will change her way of seeing things. And she experiences this going 'beyond' her existing understanding to be a difficult task. It involves questioning the assumption that her 'pictures' of things are faithful copies of the things themselves, and looking at them as personal constructions about which further questions could be asked. She sees her previous understandings of experience as superficial. Her 'commonsense' pictures of reality are opened to doubt and questioning. The critical dimension, according to this reading of the sub-text of teacher A's account, is intimately related to the personal. Does the emergence of a reflexive self depend upon the destabilization of taken-for-granted understandings of her professional world, or is it the prior condition of such destabilization?

The problematics of action in her professional world also appear in teacher A's account. There is no firm standpoint from which to fix the meaning of the objects in the room and what constitutes an appropriate response to them. Parts of the floor are revolving around, but at the same time there is the challenge to act in the face of uncertainty as represented by other parts of the floor moving out into a long corridor.

Teacher B is a chemist working with chef tutors in an FE college. She was concerned about the extent to which the research approach of the course was scientific. Her assumption was that in order to qualify as a science a form of inquiry must involve impartial and disinterested observation of objectively existing realities. This explains why the experience she recounts in the extract quoted at the beginning of this paper was destabilizing. Her taken-for-granted assumptions about the nature of science had been challenged. The extract cited mentions only the encounter with her supervisor. But in her full account she describes two previous incidents of her assumptions about objective reality being challenged and her resistance to them.

> I sat in the staff common room with a maths lecturer. He had been telling me that mathematics is the only truth. He banged on the wall saying that matter, my chemistry, atoms and molecules were not truth but just my perception of reality and that my perceptions were limited by my senses. He told me that I could only conceive of three dimensions because that was the limitations of my senses. He got metaphysical, apparently there are eleven dimensions . . . I got lost about the fourth or fifth. I put it in my field notebook and now pull it out again.
>
> I am Anglo-Catholic and I visited a Pentecostal church. When a member of the congregation 'spoke in tongues' I was borderline on alarm. The Pastor told me about it as a spiritual thing. I would not wish to insult him or his denomination but to me it was 'hysterical gobbledegook'.

Commenting on her experiences after the meeting with her supervisor she wrote:

> The MA course is bringing out a change in the way I study things. Before I was a chemist and there was a specific way that I had been trained. Before I had colours in chemical solutions, learned how to use an analytical balance and balanced my equations. Now I am part of what I study and because it is a social science I need to change.

> What changes are taking place, I am unsure ... Sometimes I am
> struggling to understand and at others I have an 'aha' experience. The fact
> that I notice these things may be my saving grace. Perhaps that is exactly
> the ability I am looking for and with that I will have reached that differ-
> ence between natural scientist and social scientist that's really worried
> me. Am I getting the hang of it? It's part of the methodology. I have to
> simultaneously observe and interpret myself.

These additional extracts from teacher B's account reveal the process by which she
came to critique her assumptions about the nature of science, although she still
clings to them when it comes to the natural sciences. As with teacher A this critical
dimension, the calling into question of basic assumptions, is intimately connected
with the personal dimension of reflexive thought.

Teacher B's account in full also contains a reference to the problematics of
social action and its connection with the critical and personal dimensions of reflection. She tends to feel an outsider to the 'chef culture' in her department, and finds
it difficult to see herself as an insider researcher with respect to it. She finds it
easier to fall back into an image of herself as the scientist who adopts a detached
observer stance towards the practices she researches. However, as she reflects
about her observational practice she begins to suspect that:

> I am more part of the culture than I realize. I must study myself in order
> to understand better. I have error and bias and I am part of the study.

She begins to see her practical relationship to her colleagues differently and tries
to involve them in a discussion about her data. The critical and personal aspects
of her reflection render her role as a detached observer problematic and initiate an
attempt to change her relationship with her colleagues through her research so
that she becomes more of an insider within their professional culture.

Validating Theories of Reflection

In the previous section I developed an account of practical reflection which I
believe constitutes an improvement on those provided by Carr and Kemmis, and
Louden. But what is the basis of this claim? As I wrote I began to ask myself
numerous questions about it. I became aware of possible ways in which it could
be criticized, and was tempted to hedge the account with 'a thousand qualifications'. In other words I had numerous doubts about it, and if I have produced it
in an assertive manner for the sake of communication, I also view the account as
a provisional one, and capable of further development and refinement.

In claiming that it constitutes an improvement on some other account of
reflection I am not assuming that it corresponds with some true nature of reflection
that exists quite independently of my thinking about it. In other words my account
of the meaning of reflection is not a description of some essence which inheres in
human mental activity independently of my interpretations of the data that activity
presents to my consciousness. There are alternative readings of teacher A and B's
accounts of their professional learning. No doubt Carr and Kemmis or Louden
would construct rather different accounts of that learning to mine. And there is no

way in which we can transcend the intentionalities of particular acts of consciousness to check out these alternative accounts from some archemedian standpoint.

On what basis then do I rest the claim that my account constitutes some kind of improvement on others'; for there is a sense in which I believe it to be more valid than theirs? Here I am going to draw on Madison's exposition (1990) of Husserl's analysis of the relationship between consciousness and its objects in the fourth part of *Ideas*. He draws attention to Husserl's distinction between the object as it appears to consciousness in specific acts of interpretation, the *noema*, and the object, *simpliciter*. The latter is the 'real object', the standard by which we judge the validity of the meanings we construct in specific acts of interpretation. But this standard is itself constructed by consciousness as an ideal which gives unity and cohesion to particular acts of interpretation. Madison explicates Husserl's position as follows:

> The relation between the noematic object and the object *simpliciter*, between consciousness and reality, is itself constituted by consciousness. Reality is nothing other than the ideal object of all possible conscious acts, and in this sense it is immanent to and indispensable from consciousness. It is the immanent teleological goal or ideal pole of all conscious acts.

Thus in evaluating the validity of the particular objects of consciousness against the real object — the object *simpliciter* — consciousness transcends itself but not in the objective sense of grasping a reality which exists independently of it.

> There is no conceivable place where the life of consciousness is broken through or could be broken through, and we might come upon a transcendency that possibly had any sense other than that of an intentional unity making its appearance in the subjectivity itself of consciousness. (Husserl quoted by Madison, 1990)

Let me now, in the light of this digression into the phenomenology of ideas, return to my account of practical reflection and my interpretations of teachers' accounts of their learning in the light of it. The content of my specific interpretations of teacher A and B's texts are meaning constructed by me through a 'conversation' with those texts. They are in Husserlian terminology the *noema*. The general theory of reflection I have outlined is the object *simpliciter*. It represents a unity and cohesion I have perceived in the data: qualities which could not be expressed adequately from my point of view by using Carr and Kemmis' or Louden's accounts of reflection.

In claiming that my general account of practical reflection constitutes an improvement on these other accounts I am claiming that it helps me to make better sense of certain kinds of data about teacher's thinking than they do. Whether it does for others I must leave them to judge. But the claim does imply that others can also come to perceive that it opens up new horizons of meaning and therefore the possibility of more fruitful and promising interpretations of data about the reflective consciousness of teachers.

Two further things need to be said about the relationship between the theory of reflection I have outlined and my interpretations of teacher A and B's texts.

The theory has not been developed independently of my specific interpretations of data about the professional learning and thinking of teachers. Before writing this chapter I had problems with the theories of teacher reflection emerging in the literature. They did not make sense of my experience as a teacher educator in trying to facilitate action-research amongst teachers as an approach to improving their educational practices. I had previously embarked on a critique of Carr and Kemmis' distinction, between practical and emancipatory forms of reflection, because the teachers I worked with appeared unable to reflect on their practice in more than a technical or instrumental form without engaging in a critique of the assumptions and beliefs embedded in them. I began to articulate the unity I perceived between 'the critical' and 'the practical' in the data I had access to through my work with teachers (see Elliott, 1987). However, I did not directly address the relationship between 'the personal' and the other dimensions of reflection until other teacher educators using action-research approaches, often women, began to highlight its significance and importance (for example, Dadds, 1991 and O'Hanlon, 1991). I had simply accepted the relationship between reflexive personal development and the development of professional practice through action-research as an obvious one. It was only in trying to interpret teacher A and B's texts that I began to articulate connections between 'the personal', 'practical problematics' and 'the critical' in the reflective process. I certainly came to the data with certain biases, with an emerging theory of reflection based on past experience, but this theory not only guided my interpretations of teacher A and B's texts but was in turn further shaped by them. The relationship between theory building and interpretation is an interactive one. Madison explicates this relationship nicely in his commentary on Husserl's concept of objectivity.

> The meaning of the text is no more identical with any given interpretation than the object *simpliciter* is reducible to any given *neoma* or intentional object. But the meaning of the text, like the object, is not, of course, something totally other than its various determinations, either.

As I read the implications of this for research into teacher reflection it suggests that the theory which gives meaning to the data about reflection is not simply the sum total of our specific interpretations of that data. We cannot derive theory from data through a straightforward process of induction. There is a sense in which theory is developed only through a succession of interpretative acts and not through some detached contemplation of universal essences which exist independently of our interpretative consciousness. Our specific acts of interpretation not only apply a theory of meaning but in turn contribute to its reconstruction in consciousness.

The theory of reflection sketched out in the previous section is not value-free. It is an account of a human potential which I am committed to realizing, in myself, and helping others to realize. I cannot therefore divorce the standards I employ in understanding my own and other people's mental processes from value-judgments about the extent to which they constitute worthwhile realizations of human potentials. I am aware, for example, that there is a form of non-reflexive reflection where a person does not call into question the standards of reasoning (s)he employs. But, given the ideal of reflection I have articulated in this chapter, such a form constitutes only a potential realization of human reflective potential. Reflection is a value-concept, and different theories of reflection manifest different views of human nature: of its worthwhile potentials. Our theories of reflection and our interpretations of data about it are conditioned by our values. There is therefore an important sense in which our research into the professional thinking of teachers cannot be divorced from a very practical interest; namely, in helping to develop their thinking. Must we therefore conclude that the activity of researching teacher thinking is an integral part of teacher education rather than a separate enterprise? It is to this question that I will now turn in the final section of this chapter.

The Double Hermeneutic in the Study of Teachers' Thinking

Research into teachers' thinking involves a double hermeneutic, in the sense that it constitutes interpreting teachers' interpretation of their professional world. Both researchers' and teachers' interpretative acts may involve both linguistic and non-linguistic forms of expression. The specific content of a researcher's interpretations of other people's interpretations will be framed by certain assumptions about the relationship between consciousness and its objects. These assumptions will determine the range and kinds of questions the researcher addresses, his or her view of what constitutes relevant evidence and appropriate methodologies for collecting and analyzing it, and the kinds of conclusions that are drawn from it.

Let me suggest a range of rather different assumptions which may frame research into teachers' thinking.

— It is the meaning-content of teacher's interpretative acts which is important to understand. The classification of this content will provide a description of the professional culture of teachers.

These assumptions 'screen out' any attention to the agency of individuals in the creation of meaning, or to their reflexive capacities. They also make no discrimination between intuitive and reflective interpretative acts.

— The interpretative acts of teachers are rationally based. Therefore it is important to gather data about their reasons and justifications for their interpretations of their professional world.

This assumption implies that teacher reflection is largely a matter of ascribing meaning on the basis of certain standards of reasoning and evidence. The major purpose of research based on this assumption will be to describe the standards of rationality employed. It will ignore the possibility that many interpretative acts are non-reflective, as well as the possibility of interpretations being reflexively, rather than simply reflectively constructed.

— The interpretative acts of teachers are personal constructions. This assumption implies that the standards teachers use as a basis for their interpretations do not exist independently of their consciousness.

Research based on this assumption will focus on the process by which teachers create meaning to make sense of their professional world. It will be open to reflexive accounts of this process, but not assume that all interpretative acts are reflexive in character. This constructivist perspective will also acknowledge intuitively grounded interpretations as personal constructions.

The constructivist perspective may express a subjectivist view of meaning but not necessarily so. It can acknowledge that 'societies' are the source of individuals' standards of judgment, without implying that they have no creative role in reconstructing them. It is also consistent with the view that not all interpretations of events and situations are equally valid; that some are more insightful than others. Research framed by a constructivist perspective need not necessarily imply a psychological subjectivism which negates the possibility of being able to justify the validity of interpretations through reflection (i.e. 'validity' understood in the terms outlined in the previous section).

I wish to suggest that different ways of understanding other people's interpretative acts, differentiated in terms of the kinds of assumptions outlined above, can be organized to represent levels of development. Kitchener and King have produced an empirically grounded account of the development of 'reflective intelligence' in individuals. Seven forms are listed in a hierarchical scheme of development. Each is demarcated by certain epistemic assumptions about the nature of knowledge. Corresponding assumptions about how the content of this knowledge (beliefs) are justified are also described.

The first three stages assume that knowledge is certain. It is either obvious to the senses or known indirectly through authorities. In areas of temporary uncertainty (experienced at stage 3), where it is either not obvious or mediated through authorities, then things can still be known through intuition.

At these levels justifications of belief are either non-existent or simply refer to authorities or intuition.

At levels 4–7 the uncertainty of knowledge is acknowledged in different forms. The course of uncertainty at level 4 is perceived to lie in deficiencies in the data one has access to. Justifications therefore provide only partial and often biased reasons for belief.

It is at levels 5–7 that the epistemic assumptions which frame the relevant forms of understanding give rise to justifications that can appropriately be described as forms of reflection.

Knowledge at level 5 is viewed as subjective and contextual, and reducible to subjective interpretations of the world. These subjectivist and relativist assumptions imply that beliefs are justified via rules which are relative to the culture of a particular social group. Competing interpretations will be justified in terms of quite different sets of rules. Individuals at level 5 find it difficult to choose between rival interpretations and resist doing so. When called upon to justify their own they can do so only in terms of the particular rules which obtain in their own social context.

At level 6 knowledge is viewed as a personal construction through a process of reflection upon evidence, drawn from a range of social contexts; for example, the interpretations of others operating in a different social context concerning a particular situation or event. Thus individuals can compare their own emerging constructs of a situation with the personal constructs of others.

Justifications at this level consist of individuals evaluating their personal solutions to controversial issues in terms of personal criteria.

The personal dimension of reflection, which I have characterized in terms of the concept of 'reflexivity', only emerges at Kitchener and King's level 6. At levels

4–5 reflection manifests no meta-awareness of knowledge as a personal construction of the self.

Finally, the epistemic assumption which governs the level 7 form of understanding is that knowledge is personally and reflexively constructed in a provisional and hypothetical manner which nevertheless implies that the preferred interpretation makes better sense of the evidence available than other possibilities. Interpretations at level 7 are justified 'probabilistically' in the light of generalizable rather than merely personal criteria. For example, a theory which claims to provide the greatest unity and coherence to the evidence.

I hope the reader will forgive me for suggesting that the justification for my interpretations of teacher A and B's accounts conform to this description of justificatory reasoning at level 7.

Let's now look at the three assumptions I outlined earlier in this section in the light of Kitchener and King's stage-model. I would argue that:

(i) Researchers who explicate teachers' thinking purely in terms of its content presume that their thinking largely operates at a pre-reflective level (levels 1–3).

Inasmuch as they do not challenge this presumption one can only conclude that their research is in itself operating at these levels. In other words the researchers will assume that their own interpretations of teachers' thinking are non-problematic and require little justification. The methodology frequently associated with this form of research supports such a view: namely, a reliance on teachers' introspective accounts. Teachers are viewed as infallible authorities on their own mental processes.

(ii) Researchers who explicate teachers' thinking purely in terms of the justificatory reasons they provide for their interpretative acts, presume that such thinking is largely idiosyncratic (level 4) or contextual (for example, linked to standards of reasoning within the occupational culture) and subjective (i.e. they cannot have a direct knowledge of reality which transcends the social context of their interpretations).

These presumptions locate teacher's thinking as largely operating at Kitchener and Kings' levels 4–5. The possibility that teachers think reflexively about the way they personally construct knowledge is ruled out.

Inasmuch as these presumptions are not in themselves questioned during the research one must conclude that the research process is itself operating at levels 4–5. For example, at level 5 we would expect researchers to justify their interpretations of teachers' interpretations in terms of evidence gathered and analyzed according to a particular set of methodological rules enshrined in a particular discipline or tradition of inquiry. They would acknowledge the possibility of alternative interpretations based on different research traditions and disciplines, but be reluctant to acknowledge that these constitute a challenge. Such researchers will be methodologically tolerant but unwilling to debate the methodological issues posed by different research traditions and disciplines generating very different sorts of interpretations of the same phenomena. They will not be happy with interdisciplinary forms of inquiry or the use of multiple methodologies.

> (iii) Researchers who view teachers' interpretations of their professional world as personally constructed will presume that teachers are not only capable of providing justifications for them but also of understanding how they are personally constructed as objects of consciousness.

The researchers will presume that teachers have a potential for studying their own thinking. The realization of such potential corresponds to levels 6 and 7 in Kitchener and King's model. A researcher's access to relevant data about how teachers personally construct their interpretations of the world implies, at least in part, that teachers can develop their potential for reflexive self-inquiry.

One would expect the presumption that interpretations of the world are personally constructed to be reflected in a researcher's interpretations of evidence. (S)he will not only reflect about evidence in the light of certain standards of inquiry, but also about the ways in which the interpretations and standards are constituted by consciousness. (S)he will reflect about the biases or assumptions which frame his/her interpretations of interpretations, and their formation in consciousness over time. In other words one would expect a high degree of reflexive self-awareness on the part of a researcher who presumes that his/her interpretations of interpretations are personally constructed.

Such level 6 or 7 thinking will imply that interpretations of teachers' personal constructions of meaning are achieved in dialogue with teachers[1]. The latter become active partners into research on their own thinking. But this partnership depends upon the extent to which the research process itself is of a form which will give teachers opportunities to develop their reflexive capacities through it.

I would argue that when research into teachers' thinking itself operates at levels 6–7 it becomes a form of teacher development. We can also stand this claim 'on its head' and argue that when teacher educators enable teachers to develop their reflective potentials at levels 6 or 7, then teachers as 'insider researchers' will want to discuss their interpretations of evidence with their tutors. The tutors become participants in a collaborative research process.

Viewed from the perspective of levels 6 and 7 the terms 'research' and 'development' come to represent not so much different activities as different dimensions of a single unified activity, in which 'the outsider' is both a teacher educator and a researcher and 'the insider' is educated through research. It is this single unified activity which we call action-research. When research into teachers' thinking operates at levels 6 and 7 it constitutes in my view a form of educational action-research. Any division of labour between those who research into teachers' thinking and those who foster teachers' learning is an indication that a rather underdeveloped construct of reflection is being employed.

Note

My own accounts of teacher A and B's thinking can be criticize because I failed to involve A and B in dialogue.

References

CARR, W. and KEMMIS, S. (1983) *Becoming Critical: Knowing Through Action Research*, Victoria, Australia, Deakin University Press.

CARR, W. and KEMMIS, S. (1986) *Becoming Critical: Education, Knowledge, and Action Research*, Lewes, Falmer Press.

DADDS, M. (1991) 'Passionate enquiry: The role of self in teacher action research', paper presented to the Classroom Action Research Network Conference, Nottingham. (See Ch. 16 of this book).

ELLIOTT, J. (1985) 'Educational action-research' in NISBET, J. (Ed.) *World Yearbook of Education 1985: Research, Policy and Practice*, London, Kogan Page.

ELLIOTT, J. (1987) 'Educational theory, practical philosophy and action research', *British Journal of Education Studies*, 25, 2.

ELLIOTT, J. (1991) 'Three perspectives on coherence and continuity in teacher education', paper presented at the annual conference of the British Educational Research Association, Nottingham.

GADAMER, H.G. (1975) *Truth and Method*, New York, Seabury.

KITCHENER, K.S. and KING, P.M. (1991) 'The reflective judgement model: Ten years of research' in COMMONS, M.L. *et al.* (Eds) *Adult Development*, New York, Praeger.

LOUDEN, W. (1991) *Understanding Teaching: Continuity and Change in Teachers' Knowledge*, London, Cassell/New York, Teachers' College Press, Columbia University.

MADISON, G.B. (1990) *The Hermeneutics of Postmodernity*, Bloomington and Indianapolis, Indiana University Press, chapter 1.

O'HANLON, C. (1991) 'Coming out-On becoming political through action research', paper presented at the annual conference of the British Educational Research Association, Nottingham. (See Ch. 17 of this book).

SCHÖN, D. (1983) *The Reflective Practitioner*, London, Temple Smith.

SCHÖN, D. (1987) Educating the Reflective Practioner, London, Jossey-Bass.

STENHOUSE, L. (1975) *An Introduction to Curriculum Development and Research*, London, Heinemann.

Part 4

Portraying Teachers' Development

The Development of Primary School Teachers' Thinking about the Teaching and Learning of Science

Peter Ovens

Introduction

This chapter draws upon my experience of an in-service course which I have been running for ten years. During that time the course has changed considerably as my own understandings and practices have evolved, and more recently, my action research has intensified the evaluation of the course, and has accelerated the changes. Since the overall aim of the research has been to improve my practice and the organization of the course, the desire to know about teachers' thinking has not been to gain knowledge for its own sake, but to understand teachers' professional development in order to foster it more wisely.

Contexts

Professional Context

In 1979, little science was taught in primary schools and only a small proportion of it bore much relationship to the image of primary science which had been advocated by three major curriculum development projects over the previous fifteen years, notably *Science 5–13*, (1972). Whilst the projects had emphasized pupil-centred investigative science, the HMI survey (DES, 1978) suggested that most teachers had little appreciation of science, and that the small amount of science that was being taught tended to be knowledge-centred and didactic in teaching style. Therefore a primary science in-service course which takes the projects' image of primary science as its ideal must aim for two interrelated things:

(i) gains in the teacher's appreciation of science education in the primary curriculum (the kind of aim commonly associated with such in-service courses);

(ii) development of the teacher's ability to teach in a pupil-centred, investigative way (a less usual and slightly controversial kind of aim).

The main features of the course are described next, with indications of my sources of data about the course members' development. At interview, I asked applicants to describe their existing teaching of science to me and to say what they were particularly interested in learning from their participation in the course. At an early stage of the course, the course member group discussed the professional needs they individually recognized in themselves. The course tasks encouraged teachers to observe their pupils during learning activities, to monitor their own teaching and to present accounts of both to each other at regular intervals. Before the half-way point of the course, every course member had received a visit from a tutor to observe their teaching of science and discuss their progress in thinking about and practicing their teaching. During the second half of the course, the teachers' own action research studies got under way, focussing on practical professional questions and problems proposed by them individually, giving oral reports regularly to the small seminar groups of 'critical friends'. The Classroom Based Study (CBS) as it was called, was the subject of a written report which was a major, assessed course assignment. Finally, each course member reflected on their development during the year, using resources such as a private diary, and wrote a short statement of the gains they believed they had made — the Statement of Personal Professional Development.

Conceptual Context

As the course outline suggests, the general method of the course assumes that teachers' professional development is achieved through the strengthening of the teacher's capacities to search for and to draw upon particular knowledge and skills in order to think and act more wisely under those circumstances in which the teacher works and in pursuit of purposes s/he determines. Drawing on Maxwell's (1984) philosophy of wisdom, Elliott (1989) defines wisdom as: '. . . a holistic appreciation of a complex practical activity which enables a person to articulate the problems s/he confronts in realising the aims or values of the activity and to propose appropriate solutions' (p. 84).

Professional development is not merely the accolade reserved for teachers whose in-service course achievements most closely match those of the prespecified course objectives of award-bearing courses, it is the entitlement of all teachers that in-service work should enhance their ability to improve themselves as teachers. In drawing out such powers, it is more truly an educational experience. Therefore the course takes it for granted that both on entry and at completion, each course member has a unique set of professional needs and achievements. There is no illusion that all course members will be targeted towards the same preconceived course outcome. The course has in this sense a similar philosophy about teacher professional learning to that offered by the Nuffield Junior Science curriculum development project organizer in 1968 for science learning by primary school pupils. It is reproduced here with my changes in wording shown in italics:

> We concluded, and believe very strongly, that a *teacher* should raise his/her own (*professional*) problems, partly because isolating a problem

Figure 15.1: Summary of the methodology of the part of my action research which is relevant to this chapter

COURSE EVENTS:

interview discussion	course sessions	tutor's visit to the course member's classroom	seminar discussion of action research	course work
↓	↓	↓	↓	↓

DATA:

my observational notes;	audio tape transcripts;	course members' scripts;
↓	↓	↓

ANALYSIS: A case study of each teacher's participation in the course, including the preparation of a *developmental map of the substantive issues* expressed at each stage, and a *diagram of the practice-theory interactions* evident in the course members' action research work.

↓

VALIDATION: Interview with each teacher about the case study and related issues.

↓

FURTHER ANALYSIS: Cross case study themes, for example, issues about teachers' thinking.

is an important part of *professional* thinking, partly because the ever increasing body of knowledge make it increasingly ridiculous to prescribe what any *teacher* should know, but mostly because we do not believe that anyone can ask a completely significant question for someone else. This would demand a complete appreciation of the person's ability, and the extent and quality of previous experience, and only the individual him/herself can ask a question which takes all that into account. (Wastnedge, 1968)

Hence the emphasis of the course on teachers' own professional action inquiry as their process of professional development. I wrote the case studies after the completion of the course and sought clearance by the teacher at a validation interview in which the teacher's views of the study, the course and his/her personal professional development since, were further explored and recorded. Further analysis, of a Gadamerian kind, has taken the form of extracting issues for 'dialectical tacking' (Geertz, 1976, p. 239, in Bernstein, 1983, p. 95) between theory and practice and between context-specific detail (for example, the footnotes used below) and broad aims/ideals.

The Study

The Abbreviated Case Study of Lesley

After five years as a nursery nurse, Lesley took a BEd degree and became a primary school teacher. Having taught for a further nine years, she came on the course 'to become more knowledgeable about science teaching and learning in order to increase my effectiveness in the classroom'. Talking about her own teaching at interview, Lesley said that she liked to 'get pupils to ask their own questions'. She taught at a school in a very poor inner city area.

Lesley described her teaching as based upon small group work with practical tasks and discussion-based learning, using her own work cards with 'a few teaching points on each'.[1] At an early course session, based on 'ice balloons' (Ovens, 1987), I observed Lesley's reaction to my invitation to all course members to explore these large lumps of ice. She was reluctant to handle the ice and seemed inhibited from exploring it in a free and playful manner. However she selected one of the questions or hypotheses about ice which had been brainstormed by the group earlier and began to design a controlled experiment. It was as if Lesley saw this as an opportunity to apply what she knew to be a scientific way of working with an object rather than to 'be scientific', or react more spontaneously and informally as most of the others did.[2] When she used ice balloons in a session with her own pupils at school, Lesley found that they gave a somewhat limited reaction. The younger pupils said very little, which was attributed by Lesley to their limited vocabulary. Several course members, including Lesley, had noticed an absence of pupil questioning about the ice when they tried out 'ice balloons' in their own classrooms.

Lesley volunteered to organize the provision of pupils from her own school for an afternoon course session in college at which the course members supervised and observed pupils using ice balloons as the stimulus. In this context, her pupils gave a much more rewarding response overall, making a range of observations *and raising questions and hypotheses.* Lesley was surprised and delighted by how well they had responded — beyond her expectations.

Lesley's analytic memo at this stage defines her professional need as mainly relating to understanding science teaching and learning. She acknowledges the value of a teacher taking the role of observer to pupils' learning, and she refers positively to the impact of course sessions on her own thinking. In my own reflections at this stage, I felt that Lesley's teaching was less child-centred than had been apparent to me earlier, because she used a much more teacher-set structure and I wondered if this had been having an inhibiting effect on the pupils. There were already indications that Lesley was reviewing her ideas and practice in a critical way.

The Tutor's Visit to Lesley's Classroom

I was not the tutor who visited Lesley's classroom on 2 October 1987. My colleague's report of her visit shows that the lesson had been successful in eliciting pupils' scientific exploration during the making of cardboard spinners, with different groups of pupils being given the freedom to adapt the overall task as they wished. A brief summary of the tutor/teacher discussion of the session suggests that the lesson had achieved 'satisfying progress' in the development of greater responses from the children to Lesley's science teaching.[3] It was agreed that the next step in this development would be 'the encouragement of (pupil) self-organization'. In her report to the course members at a subsequent course session, Lesley told how it was firstly her recognition of the pupils' own ideas and suggestions for the activity, and secondly her expansion of the resource base which had usefully enlarged her own thinking.[4] She said 'I could have let more come from them.' She also said 'I think I put them down a lot.'

This seemed to have been a valuable experience for Lesley. Coming after her experiments with practical problem solving (building spaghetti towers) and other innovations in her teaching, she appeared to have reached a secure basis for reflecting self-critically and constructively about her growing awareness of pupils' independent thinking and her own ability to elicit and support such thinking.[5] So, although my monitoring had detected only one major focus for Lesley's professional development, it seemed to be proceeding on a broader front and very profitably under Lesley's control and in the direction she chose.

Lesley's Participation in the Course

One session about half-way through the course contained discussion of the teachers' evaluations of the course in which there were criticisms of my role in not providing enough explicit assessments and advice to course members. Lesley was not one of the main critics, but joined in the discussion on a couple of occasions, suggesting that she too found this to be a source of frustration.[6] It remains an open question whether the non-prescriptive nature of the course had positively enabled Lesley's progress, in spite of her feelings of frustration, or whether progress would have been enhanced further by more tutor direction of the kind which some of the course members were demanding.

At the beginning of the spring term, Lesley wrote about her 'preoccupation' with her own lack of scientific knowledge and skill,[7] which led her to consider 'a programme of learning for myself over and above what I'm doing on the course'. This is consistent with my data about the classroom visit which showed how Lesley had felt she needed to consider concepts such as inertia and momentum in her preparation, even though the pupils did not need to use them in thinking about spinners. It suggests that although Lesley did not have science qualifications at (for example) GCE Advanced Level, she was working hard to be aware of the science knowledge relevant to her teaching.[8] Lesley's self-assessment disagreed with my assessment of her levels of scientific knowledge and skill. In comparison with other course members I had noticed that she had some relatively advanced scientific ideas (for example, momentum and inertia) and that she could conduct investigative work (for example, with ice balloons) skilfully. I wrote a comment to this effect on Lesley's analytic summary.

Lesley selected 'developing pupils' observational skills' as the focus of her Classroom Based Study (CBS). She wanted to find out:

(i) about pupils' observation skill as a tool for their learning;
(ii) how to offer appropriate experiences and activities to encourage improvements in observation;
(iii) how best to introduce them in the classroom.[9]

I saw this focus as having the potential of yielding a good example of seeking development in understanding and practice interdependently. Lesley regarded observation as a purposeful activity leading to what she referred to as 'development of cognition'. Lesley read about the significance of the learner's existing ideas to his/her selection of things to observe. She inferred that good observation had to serve a purpose in the mind of the learner. This led to a question in Lesley's mind at this stage, which shows the extent of the development of child centredness in her thinking about scientific observation. She said: 'Is it *observing* if they're noticing what the teacher tells them to notice?'[10] In the first stage of her study, Lesley set out to make more 'open' interventions in her discussions with pupils. Her monitoring data suggests that she did this effectively. Her evaluation of the session says that the children's interest in each other's comments had been impressively good, compared with their normal interaction which tended to be argumentative and 'shouting each other down'. In the second phase, Lesley tried to encourage them to observe better by eliciting their questions, predictions and hypotheses. The preliminary discussion about these went well, but it did not lead to better observation as hoped. Lesley attributed this disappointment to there being too many variables for the pupils to cope with. Therefore, in the next phase, where the activity was to perfect a hot air balloon, Lesley felt that she had used a more specific task within which alterations which pupils could make to the balloons would depend upon their observations.

In the fourth phase of the study, Lesley attempted 'to see how children's observations develop when given 'free time' in which to make observations'.[11] She did not impose her own ideas for classifying the collection of things which accumulated in the classroom brought from the environs of the school. Instead, she noticed instances of pupils discussing their own categorizations, and saw examples of strong curiosity, detailed observation and vivid communication, both formal and informal. Lesley provided an impressive summary of her evaluation of this stage of the study.[12] The next stage focussed on the use of models to encourage observation of daisy flowers, and in the final stage, following the environmental theme, Lesley encouraged the children to focus their observations, to see if it enhanced their gain of knowledge. They concentrated on the organisms living on the sycamore tree and learned a great deal about them.

Although her study is organized into sections entitled Action Step 1, Action Step 2, etc. Lesley did not use the term action step in quite the same way that is defined by Elliott's (1981) Working Paper No. 1. For Lesley, a shift in focus to a new action step was justified implicitly (rather than explicitly) by her desire to explore various strategies in turn, rather than by her findings from the previous action step. This raises the question of which should take priority in such circumstances. Should there be a requirement for progressive focussing or should the teacher researcher be free to explore priorities that she/he sets for her/himself?

Figure 15.2:   MAP of progress in substantive aspects of personal professional development as expressed by Lesley

---

A — Interview (June 1987)

I wish to become more knowledgeable about my science teaching and the children's learning, to increase my effectiveness in the classroom. I also want to be able to contribute to the formulation of the school's policy for science.

B — Beginning of the Course (September 1987)

I feel dissatisfied with the amount of science which children gain from my science based topic work. I feel that pupils are relatively unresponsive to the science opportunities. 'How can I understand teaching and learning science?' I am learning to acknowledge the value of the teacher taking the role of observer of pupils' learning. Previous school curriculum development initiatives had *begun* with the formulation of policy and this had not been successful — What shall I do instead?

C — Classroom Visit by the Tutor (Nov–Dec 1987)

I can see progress in the improvement of pupils' responses to science. This has occurred in association with greater flexibility of my organization and teaching, which seems to elicit greater independence in the pupils' thinking.

D — Course Sessions (December 1987–May 1988)

I feel 'preoccupied' with my own lack of scientific knowledge and skill. In this sense particularly, I am becoming more analytical about my own teaching. How do I use more open types of teacher interventions? How do I get pupils' questions and hypotheses to improve their observation?

E — Statement of Personal Professional Development (June 1988)

My ways of presenting work to pupils and my ways of encouraging them have both changed, to give pupils more control over the content and structure of the work. I recognize pupils as more resourceful and creative than I had previously given them credit for. I have greater confidence to be critical about how and what I teach. I am providing for colleagues at school advice and collections of ideas and resources, to support the development of science within cross curricular topic work. I have greater confidence to perform this role, which has been enhanced over the year.

Overall, I felt that Lesley's study was an impressive and interesting one because of the enlightened way in which observation was dealt with, integrating it with the wholeness of the children's scientific inquiry learning. It was conducted in a systematic and organized way, and it showed valuable developments in Lesley's teaching.

An Overview of Lesley's Professional Development

Her own statement of professional progress clearly shows that her self-confidence and self-criticism have grown during the year as she has made important developments in her teaching.[13] She goes on to describe the changes in her teaching which

Figure 15.3:   DIAGRAM of practice — Theory interactions in Lesley's development

Professional practices and experiences	**Professional assessments, reflections and analysis**
	Lesley saw her teaching as 'getting pupils to ask their own questions, to discuss how to get answers'.
Trying out 'ice balloons' with her pupils in her classroom, she did not see their response as particularly good.	
	This was attributed to limitations in their own ability to be scientific, including difficulty with asking their own questions.
The same pupils, brought into college for an observation of teaching and learning, responded very differently to the 'ice balloons'. They not only made a range of observations but also raised questions and hypotheses.	Lesley was surprised and delighted at the time. She continued to express concern about the limited response the pupils showed in the classroom, however she began to experiment with new ideas in her teaching.
During the tutor's visit to Lesley's classroom, there were encouraging signs of pupils' scientific exploration with 'spinners', which Lesley saw as improvements in their response.	Reporting back to course members about the visit, Lesley said that improvements had come because she had begun to recognize pupils' own ideas for activities, and had expanded their resource base. She also said: 'I could have let more come from them — I think I put them down a lot.'

LESLEY'S CLASSROOM BASED STUDY

	Lesley chose to develop her teaching of scientific observation.
In work on air, she monitored her attempts to make her questions to the pupils more open-ended, and felt there was an increase in the pupils' interest and enthusiasm.	Lesley thought this may have been due to her increased interest in them. She considered that she was noticing more things about the pupils' own ideas.
	Next, she took action steps to help the pupils to formulate questions, predictions and hypotheses.
In work on aeroplanes, a marked gender bias emerged in their responses, boys 'played' and girls 'switched off'.	Lesley saw the cause as too many variables for the pupils to control, so she made another attempt to encourage a clear focus for observing, but this time with a narrower task.
In making a hot air balloon, the responses were encouraging overall, however they appeared not to 'see' significance in the unstable behaviour of the balloon, until Lesley's intervention.	The need to intervene was seen by Lesley as a lack of knowledge about how air behaves.
	Next, more time for free exploratory work was allocated.
In environmental work, they devised their own categories and schedules for observation and the collection of specimens, and made inventive use of various methods such as models to show what they knew about the objects from their observations.	Lesley was bringing to bear several new strategies during this stage, and felt that this was the most successful example of the children's observational abilities.

have resulted from the realization that pupils are 'more resourceful and more creative than I have previously given them credit for'. The concluding passage refers to the recent discovery from course members that the image they had formed of her initially was that of a confident teacher of science, at a time when Lesley had not felt confident within herself, admitting that it must have been a bluff! By contrast, at the end of the course, Lesley felt 'I am much more confident of being critical of what I teach.'[14]

During the validation interview, Lesley demonstrated her awareness of the action research approach of the course and the dilemma she had experienced between trying to follow what she understood to be its correct methodology, and following her own interests and preferences for her own professional development. She argued that the teacher should exercise control over her/his inquiry methodology, if conditions are favourable, that is the teacher understands the point of action research, and has the critical community support for the discussion of both methodological problems and substantive issues.

Issues Arising from Lesley's Case Study

Saying what you mean and meaning what you say

A difficulty arises within teachers' communication of their thought and practice from the ambiguity of educational language such as Lesley's declaration at interview that 'I like to get the pupils to ask their own questions'. Another teacher in Lesley's seminar group was acutely aware of the apparent lack of scientific curiosity in her pupils who never seemed to ask questions, and it was her inquiry into the practice of other teachers which revealed Lesley's meaning. This turned out to be that she would usually require the performance of a series of fairly structured activities by the pupils, after which Lesley would elicit their spoken accounts. In saying that 'pupils raise their own questions', Lesley meant that her routine practice involved the children recognizing or taking on questions in a way which was coherent with the understanding which Lesley then held about the scientific abilities which those pupils possessed. Since she doubted that they were able to question and hypothesize *in a mature way*, she did not mean that her pupils freely and independently were doing those things, but could do them within a framework or structure of some kind which Lesley supplied, to take account of their perceived limitations. Their responses were closely tied to Lesley's structured work cards but had been sufficiently different from the 'input' of the card to count, for Lesley, as 'asking their own questions'. By the end of the course Lesley had come to believe that her own pupils did, after all, have a much greater ability freely to question and hypothesize, therefore her practice had changed to recognize this. It became a form of practice which no longer included the structures or frameworks which had been intended to compensate for a pupil need which was no longer in evidence, but which had unwittingly contributed to the apparent absence of the pupil abilities in question.

This manifestation of the difficulty of communication points to the advantages of basing professional discussion on accounts of practice which contain detailed description of specific events combined with expressions of the teacher's espoused theory (Argyris and Schon, 1974), including the practicality ethic (Schwab, 1969). Also, the context in which teachers probed each others' thinking and practice interdependently was that of their own professional inquiry, seeking access to each others' repertoire of cases and reflections on them. As course tutor conducting action research into their learning process in order to enable it more fully, I monitored such discussions and joined them in a similar version of the role of critical friend.

Action research for personal professional development

Lesley did not use the term action step in quite the same way that is defined in Elliott's TIQL Project Working Paper No 1 (1981) because the shifts in focus from one episode of her monitoring and reflection to the next were not logically related to each other in an obviously linear and progressive way. But they nevertheless *were* related to Lesley's own tacit exploration of those facets of the overall subject which enabled her to develop her own theory-in-use more fully, albeit in an apparently less rational way. In an attempt to clarify my own understandings and test them out, I sought Lesley's view of the action researcher's dilemma between following a methodological rule and exercising freedom to act upon a tacit personal preference. The course had offered Elliott's model and requested teachers to logically ground action steps in data from the previous cycle. Lesley strongly expressed her position on this during the validation interview: 'I found that very very difficult to do.' She was dissatisfied, not only in failing to meet Elliott's criterion of action research, but also in feeling a sense of lacking tight intellectual progression in her study. However, she was also equivocal about the solution to this problem. On one hand she said:

> I didn't feel I was stepping through this study progressively. It just became blurred. I felt we could have had more preparation to do with this particular model.

Lesley had said she did not find the Elliott model of action research difficult to understand, so she was wishing she had received closer direction as to how to put it into practice. But on the other hand, she rejected imposition and defended the individual's right to control their research, expressing her uncompromising view of the rigidity of the model:

> I mean I would have thrown John Elliott out of the window (laughs) if I thought it was going to prevent me from following the lines that I'd decided were important to me. As long as I can show within my own model that I'm progressing then I don't see any problem.

Lesley's action step in stage 2 of her study, which was to structure her participation in the discussion with pupils to support the setting of the tasks, was not logically derived from specific observations during the monitoring of stage 1, but was a sensible experiment in her teaching which could easily have been stimulated by the insight into pupils' capacity to be scientific which the stage 1 monitoring contained. For example, the favourable impression she had of the pupils' interest in each others' observational comments, as compared with their usual tendency to be argumentative, inspired her confidence to try a joint discussion about the planning of the next piece of work. The action step can also be seen as another facet of the adaptation of her theory-in-use away from preplanned work cards.

The next action step, to use an investigational opportunity which would not have the disadvantageous aspects of the investigation into paper planes, did follow logically, and yielded confirmation of the improvements in the teacher's involvement with the pupils in the planning stage.

Then came the break between themes, moving from 'air' to 'the environment'. Lesley began with the action step of giving more time to the activities of collecting and displaying objects from the school environment to begin the topic. Lesley does not give any logical connections with the preceding work, and reports her dissatisfaction in feeling the she was 'starting all over again at this point'. But major factors in the situation had changed. A much more open range of possibilities for pupil interest existed within the school grounds, and a different way of working was being tried out accordingly. The collection included pieces of rotting fence, branches, twigs, roots, pebbles, stone chippings, live wood lice, a dead honey bee, worms, an insect pupa, and so on. I believe that it had been her monitoring of the three previous stages of her study which enabled Lesley to feel sufficiently confident in the children's abilities to select such an open opportunity for them, and to resist the wish to impose her categories for sorting, so as to give the pupils more time to develop their own. Therefore it was tacit knowledge of the whole situation and a gestalt grasp of how to develop her teaching further which determined her action step rather than logical justification grounded in evidence. 'By the end of the second week, the pupils' sorting and classifying of items far outstretched my expectations.'[15] Groupings of objects were reorganized, and labels changed and grew in number 'as the children's observations and knowledge increased' (p. 17). I believe that if Lesley had taught the environment topic before the others, and therefore was at her earlier stage of getting used to not using work cards, and also without as much experience of the pupil's successful independent learning, then the action step 'to give them more time to observe', had she still taken it, would have been something quite different both conceptually and in its practical expression. My hypothesis is that being at the earlier stage of development of her pedagogy, Lesley would have assumed a greater need by the pupils for her direction, and consequently this would have largely precluded the response from them which was in fact obtained. Understood in this way, the full meaning of an action step is not adequately described by a short propositional statement in which it is usually expressed, but needs to be grasped through knowing the full context of Lesley's longer term and immediate purposes, experiences and professional opportunities. The short statement of an action step represents only one facet of a multifaceted kind of development.

Brenda's Development

In order to convey something of the similarities and differences between the case studies, another example is reproduced next, in the form of the diagram of practice-theory interaction for Brenda's development. Brenda taught in a prosperous residential area where parents showed much interest in the infants school. She was a little quicker to develop her ideas and practice than Lesley, appearing to be a more self-directed person with more confidence in her capacity to analyze situations for herself. A significant early event was dealing with the interpretation of pupils' exploratory play with a range of resources. When these 5 and 6-year-olds switched rapidly from handling one object to a different one or from doing one

Figure 15.4: *Diagram of practice — Theory interactions in Brenda's development*

| **Professional practices and experiences** | **Professional assessments, reflections and analysis** |

1 ASPECTS OF HER INTEREST IN THE CHILDREN'S SCIENTIFIC LEARNING

By Brenda's own description (given later in the course) her previous teaching had tended to be 'party tricks and prompts' i.e.: set demonstrations followed by pat explanations.

Brenda's own observations of the children's science prior to the start of the course

The children's responses to small group activities assigned to them tended to be stereotyped. Children showed 'skimming' behaviour (rapid movement from one object or way of manipulating objects to another, which Brenda did not see as learning.

Brenda and I jointly observed children exploring a wide range of 'shiny things'. My interpretation of 'skimming' was that the children were gathering a lot of experiences to develop and test their ideas about reflection etc. I called it 'pattern seeking' and claimed that it was scientific learning.

Brenda reconsidered her idea of 'skimming' and looked for evidence to choose between her interpretation and mine.

Brenda gathered examples of the same kind of apparently superficial pupil behaviour, and satisfied herself that it led to worthwhile learning.

Brenda accepted the value of 'skimming' as playful, inventive exploratory learning.

2 SOME OTHER DEVELOPMENTS SUBSEQUENTLY

Brenda felt under pressure for the pupils to achieve something every lesson. She had aimed for a very specific knowledge outcome in the work on 'shiny things' — she wanted pupils to produce a scientific kind of definition of a good reflective surface.

At first, her disappoinment with this not being achieved, she did not see any value in pupils' 'skimming' behaviour. They said a good reflective surface was one which gave funny or unexpected reflections. And they discovered much more besides.

She acknowledged that when the teacher has a narrowly conceived learning objective, it can prevent a recognition or appreciation of other kinds of worthwhile pupil responses.

She began to look for examples of pupils' worthwhile scientific learning in a more open minded way, and with less emphasis on preconceived knowledge outcomes.

She had rejected pupil directed inquiry as an appropriate teaching strategy, and was asking how best to ask children questions to develop their thinking.

She observed situations in which the best learning was shown by those children for whom the activity generated a strong personal interest to inquire in a wholistic way.

This led to a growing appreciation of the child's own inquiry as a superior basis for learning than observing a demonstration or following a set activity involving prescribed scientific skills.

She observed situations in which her own repeated prompts did not necessarily lead to good pupil responses.

Brenda grew less anxious about having to 'feed' the children prompts and information, but still felt that she should 'give' all of the pupils the same experience, despite the organizational difficulties.

?
?

She started to allow more time for children to work through the inquiry processes within their own investigations.

thing with it to another, their activity appeared to Brenda to be purposeless and shallow, with little learning value, and she called it 'frippering about' or 'just skimming'. During my visit, I observed an instance of this and offered Brenda the hypothesis that this kind of activity could be interpreted as scientific learning in which pupils' unspoken questions were being answered and hypotheses tested at the very simple level of thinking which an adult may find it difficult to appreciate due to its speed and the lack of verbal cues. She agreed to test this idea over subsequent sessions and came to revise her assessments in the light of events.

> Children have done and said things in the past few weeks which perhaps
> I wouldn't have noticed earlier, or I wouldn't have given the value that I
> now ascribe to them, that this course has made me aware of. (Brenda)

Brenda's study was more systematic than Lesley's in that there were clearer and more regular reviews of the practical gains made by reflection on her monitoring and critical friend discussion. Also the progression was justified in more explicitly logical ways. In her Statement of Personal Professional Development, Brenda wrote:

> This course has been like no other I have attended with its emphasis on
> the process of professional development. At times it has been difficult to
> appreciate *in which direction we were being led,* (my emphasis) but, on
> reflection, I appreciate that my attitude to and understanding of the teach-
> ing of science have undergone great change since September '87

This ambiguity about direction in this quotation surprised me because I had seen Brenda as one of the most professionally autonomous members of the course, but I now think that it was partly a reflection of a slightly erratic tentativeness in my leadership of the course and partly an indication of how easy it is for tutors to underestimate their impact on the teachers' participation in the course.

An issue arising from Brenda's case: 'They're only playing'

There is a real problem for professional development posed by a double-bind situation such as when Brenda interpreted her pupils' behaviour as 'frippering around' or 'just skimming'. If the teacher relinquishes the tight control needed to ensure that pupils get to see what they're supposed to see (in order to be able to prove to the teacher they have learned the right answer) then this is how the pupils may appear to behave. Not only infants but juniors also will show this 'play' type of apparently aimless behaviour without any apparent control or develop-mental sequence. The teacher's attempt to teach science through investigation may coincide with an improvement in the usual resource provision and a greater amount of freedom for the pupils to move around. If pupils are suddenly given a decent range of resources and the chance for direct experience, it would take a cast iron will to remain controlled! Teachers in this situation are faced with the feeling of losing control both behaviourally and intellectually, they can no longer feel secure in their predictions about what the pupils will do or ask next. The cost-benefit ratio of the pedagogic experiment (Doyle and Ponder, 1976) looks disastrous! It is not at all obvious what, if anything, the pupils are learning with regard to their inves-tigative abilities, and they seem at first to learn very little orthodox science know-ledge, so there is an incentive for the teacher to abandon this risky situation. But this means a return to a pedagogy which the teacher recognizes to be failing to support the learning of investigative attitudes and skills. This is surely a Catch 22 situation for teachers.

Curriculum development projects in primary science successively claimed that teachers' failure to develop the investigative pedagogy was due to inadequate support in the classroom. Nuffield Junior Science had presented its philosophy through mini-case studies of teachers' investigative teaching, and wanted to expand the *personal* support to teachers through in-service courses. But during the 1970s, the Schools Council initially interpreted the problem rationalistically, and set up successive projects to give increased support mainly as technological innovations rather than support to the process of reflective self development by teachers. There were teachers' books of investigative ideas (Science 5–13, 1972), a standard checklist for assessing pupils' development of investigative skills, attitudes and concepts, albeit through the medium of a course rather than only through published material (Match and Mismatch, 1977), a plan for policy development and pupils' work cards (Learning Through Science, 1980). But what teachers really need for pedagogic development is personal support through their personal struggle with the Catch 22 of adopting investigative teaching.

Returning to Brenda, there was an important question for me about my diagnosis of pupils' 'frippering' and 'skimming' as science learning. Was I selling a new dogma in place of the old? Does it require a conversion type of experience for teachers to 'see the light'? I put my faith in Brenda's intellectual independence and asked her to treat my diagnosis as a hypothesis for testing. As Brenda's case study describes in detail, the session I observed was one of several which inspired pupil inquiry for several weeks afterwards during which the pupils continued to find new things they could make and do and talk about, with 'shiny things'. The richness of their store of knowledge at the end, derived from the growth of confidence in their own inquisitive capacities was convincing enough for Brenda to believe in a child-centred interpretation of 'frippering and skimming' and make the breakthrough to an investigative pedagogy. This was *an* ending but not of course *the* ending, because new questions and problems were thrown up, in Brenda's case, how to organize it for sixty pupils!

A Reflective Review

The maps and diagrams of practice-theory interaction I have developed may appear to be comprehensive and authoritative accounts of an individual's professional development, but I am acutely conscious of their relative superficiality and the implied oversimplification of reality, failing to indicate the personal and social dimensions of the learning. However they do give some insight into the progressive nature of professional development. The importance of what Brenda learned about 'skimming' and 'frippering' was that she learned it for herself, by looking critically at her own direct experience, when it was highly relevant for her to do so, i.e.: when it related both to her own immediate concern and also the wider contextual problems she was wrestling with. Given the collaborative nature of the course, it is likely that Brenda's reassessment was partly a response to similar reassessments being made and reported by other course members. Equally, Brenda's own presentation to her group of the data and analysis of the tutor's classroom visit, during which 'skimming' and 'frippering' took place was probably a stimulus to other course members to reassess *their* pupils' behaviour.

The diagrams are simply intended to show something of the qualities and characteristics of teachers' professional achievements. Bearing in mind that they came about through their own self-directed, independent inquiry, using self-monitoring methods and professional seminar presentations, the achievements have resulted from the use of those capacities which are necessary for continuation of the professional development process. Examined collectively, the maps show the similarities and differences between course members' achievements. Their value is limited, however, by the process of abstraction, which prevents the reader from appreciating what has been involved in the professional development process which has occurred. Maps convey little of the personal, historical and contextual influences upon the inquiry and tell nothing of the emotional and ethical commitments of the course member. Presenting a series of statements unfortunately resembles the format of propositional knowledge, which it is not, and thus may distort and diminish the professional enterprise involved.

The general image of the process of personal professional development which emerges can be summarized under the following four dimensions.

Personal

The teachers have a strong sense of ownership of their inquiries. They recognize ways in which professional changes involve alterations not only to ideas they held dispassionately, but also to parts of the persona such as values, beliefs, attitudes and subtle kinds of knowledge which they often referred to as 'awareness'. Given the personal nature of teaching as an individualized form of activity with the heavy involvement in total relationships (not just intellectual ones) with many pupils, there is usually considerable person to person commitment, if not over-commitment. As a result, changes in routines of practice and their forms of understanding are inevitably far reaching.

Social

The importance of critical friendship relationships was almost always cited by course members as being *the* most important single factor in promoting their own development. The dominant role was apparently that of enabler or counsellor rather than expert, but also as an assistant evaluator of critical parts of another person's development. The seminar groups became important reference groups for the teachers' re-evaluations of thought and practice. The giving and receiving of support and reassurance about the similarities of personal reactions to the course or to classroom event was very common. Also, visits to classrooms helped to reduce the social isolation of classroom teaching which otherwise drastically impoverishes teachers' assessments of each other, and in turn the visits helped to support self-assessment (and cast doubt on the otherwise certain knowledge that every other teacher is better at teaching science than you.)

Emotional

There are very clear indications of the feelings of threat to personal and professional self-image experienced by most of the teachers in the early stages which tended to encourage reactions of defensiveness, which were usually short-lived.

Adjustment to this was important to enable self-disclosure within critical friendship discourse, and naturally, some adjusted more rapidly than others. The adjustment stage was usually accompanied by expressions of relief of the emotional strain of keeping self doubts and apprehensions undisclosed until the teachers found that they had many of them in common with each other. Other powerful feelings were experienced and expressed during seminars, such as excitement at witnessing pupils' responses which constituted significant improvements in the quality of their learning, frustration at appearing to be 'deskilled' by attempts to improve practice, elation at having made a breakthrough in insight and/or practical achievement, humiliation at realizing a contradiction between one's own theory and practice, guilt about failure to fulfil real or imagined commitments to the pupils particularly during the early-middle stages when there was deepening awareness of unintended effects of one's actions on the pupils.

Intellectual and Practical

The nature of the knowledge being developed is primarily tacit, characterized by its initial apparent absence from self-awareness, and with the slow, gradual appearance of conscious and explicit forms of recognition by the teacher of her/his knowledge, through communication with others and under the general guidance of the teacher's image of the value of the teaching and learning to which s/he aspired. It did not show many characteristics of an incremental, linear, cumulative or logically controlled form of intellectual progression. Consequently it was inappropriate to pre-specify intentions or outcomes with precision for more than the immediate future. Similarly, developments in practice did not follow a systematically planned scheme of skill development, but consisted of repeatedly taking actions which were justified by the needs of the situation, some of the actions being creative responses to those needs, which constituted separate, small advances in practical technique which *retrospectively* were recognized to be progressive. The kinds of changes in thought and action interdependently usually included a 'perspective transformation' (Holly, 1989) which involved change in a large number of interrelated items of belief, knowledge, action, perception, value and awareness which overall constituted something of a professional paradigm shift in many cases. The significance of published materials to development was not very great for some, but was more to others, who used insights and conceptual frames as learning resources. Although at first they were reluctant to write reflectively, as the course required, they later credited some of the revealed appreciation of improvements to being able to refer back to reflections made at earlier stages, particularly at the beginning, and the task of reformulating them.

Pedagogical Implications for the In-service Course

The major thrust of my research has been to increase the educational value of the course through, among other things, the improvement of my teaching of it. This has included many changes, not least of which has been the move away from dealing with central issues of teaching and learning in decontextualized, tutor-structured presentations, to a structure in which teachers meet them afresh in each context of study of the data from someone's classroom. As in Philip Boxer's conjectural paradigm, (Boxer, 1985) each action research seminar provided repeated opportunities to consider wholistically course members' immediate problems within the contexts of specific practical manifestations in their practice, and the group members helped each other to find analytical frames through their attempts to interpret events. Since the immediate problems were often an expression of the deeper problems and dilemmas of teaching and learning, a course member could encounter the same kind of difficulty, for example 'the Catch 22 of investigative teaching', in many guises, and have experience of working out the ends and means interdependently and differently in each context.

Notes

1 My observational notes from the course session on 1 October 1987.
2 This is based on my observational notes of the course session on 29 September 1987. At the case study validation interview, Lesley wrote the following comment on her copy of the study: 'Not being used to working in this way I saw the activity as somewhat demeaning to my self-image as a teacher. However, experimentation is now a part of my preparation for classroom work'
3 Lesley's and Pat's joint evaluation of the lesson was: 'Would restrict language to "friction" in future, which would allow more time for children to participate in discussion (and less time for teacher introductory talk). Instead of allocating tasks, would allow the children to investigate their own interest, with support for those unsure in this situation.' (my addition)
4 Notes from Lesley's talk (about the visit) to the course session show that Lesley had used concepts like inertia and momentum in her pre-lesson planning, and had anticipated that fair testing of spinners might be possible. The task set (make the best spinner: ie: the one which spins for the longest time) was clearly understood and yielded a variety of ideas and practical tests. After the lesson, Lesley saw that friction was the only relevant concept for the children, and that the phenomenon had been too complex for the application of fair testing procedures to apply.
5 This interpretation was endorsed by Lesley at the case study validation interview. In this part of the copy of the case study which Lesley had read, she wrote the following: 'I was imposing my ideas of what the children should get out of the activity rather than allowing children more freedom to experiment initially.'
6 There had been some confusion about the purposes and outcomes of writing the analytic memo, and Lesley seemed to be probing into my ambivalence about how to operate this (new) part of the course. During the course session, Lesley's comment was: 'I think you've modelled yourself on Jesus Christ and always answer a question with a question.' Later, she said (about this aspect of the course principles), 'Presumably you've modelled this course on previous courses. You've changed it.'
Peter: Yes
Lesley: So had it moved away from a more prescriptive approach to this?
Peter: Yes
Lesley: But why has it?
From the transcript of the session on 23 November 1987. At the case study validation interview, Lesley justified her position by writing: 'To me it seemed that you did not wish to elucidate on this new aspect of the course in relation to previous courses — presumably you wanted to add a dimension that was not there before, and I wanted to know why in order to "react" to it in the "right" way.'
7 Analytic summary 11 February 1988.
8 On 11 January 1988 Lesley wrote: 'A lack of knowledge and/or experience of particular aspects of science teaching can lead to a lack of confidence in presenting such aspects in the classroom therefore leading to an imbalance of scientific learning

on the part of the children.' and later, 'I am much more aware of the analytical aspects of my science teaching now. The first analytic summary was concerned with very practical aspects re the nature table, topics I had introduced, whereas now I am much more concerned with what I need to know in order to achieve a balance of science presentation in my classroom.'

9   Lesley's CBS, p. 3 — paraphrased by me.
10 CBS, p. 10.
11 CBS, p. 16.
12 'Given time in which to observe, the children showed an evolutionary development in their ideas of sorting and classifying' (CBS, p. 19).
13 'What now emerges is that I am much more confident of being critical of how and what I teach!' Course session 27 June 1988.
14 *Brenda*: 'That just shows how much you've changed because you were quite confident about what you were doing. Now you're questioning.'
    Lesley: 'I'm more openminded now.'
    (Laughter)
    Pat: 'The confidence to question what you do is tremendous.' (20 June 1988)
15 Lesley's CBS, p. 17.

References

Argyris, C. and Schon, D. (1974) Theory and Practice: increasing professional effectiveness. London, Jossey-Bass.

Bernstein, R. (1983) Beyond Objectivism and Relativism. Blackwell, Oxford.

Boxer, P. (1985) 'Judging the Quality of Development', in Boud, D. *et al.* (Eds) *Reflection: Turning Experience into Learning.* London, Kogan Page.

Department of Education and Science (1978) Primary education in England — a survey by Her Majesty's Inspectorate, London, HMSO.

Doyle, W. and Ponder, G.A. (1976) The Practicality Ethic in Teacher Decision-making, Texas, North Texas State University.

Elliott, J. (1981) Action-research: a framework for self-evaluation in schools, Cambridge, Schools' Council TIQL Project Working Paper No. 1.

Elliott, J. (1989) Why put case study at the heart of police training curriculum?, New Directions in Police Training, in Southgate, P. (Ed.) *New Directions in Police Training*, London, HMSO, pp. 148–169.

Elliott, J. (1991) Action Research for Educational Change, Buckingham, Open University Press.

Geertz, C. (1976) From the native's point of view: on the nature of anthropological understanding, in Rabinow, P. and Sullivan, W. (Eds) *Interpretive Social Science: a reader.* Berkeley, University of California Press.

Holly, M. (1989) Reflective writing and the spirit of inquiry. Cambridge *Journal of Education*, 19, 1, pp. 71–80.

Learning Through Science (1980) Learning through science: Formulating a school policy. London, Macdonald Educational.

Match and Mismatch (1977) Raising questions; Finding answers. Edinburgh, Oliver & Boyd.

Maxwell, N. (1984) From knowledge to wisdom. Oxford, Blackwell.

Ovens. P. (1987) Ice Balloons, *Primary Science Review*, No. 3, pp. 5–6.

Schwab, J. (1969) The Practical: A Language for Curriculum, *School Review*, 78, pp. 1–24.

Science 5–13 series (1972–1975) Teachers guides. (26 titles) London, Macdonald Educational.

Wastnedge, E. (1968) Nuffield junior science in primary schools, *School Science Review*, 61, 217, pp. 639–647.

Chapter 16

Thinking and Being in Teacher Action Research

Marion Dadds

Small-scale teacher action research has distinctive differences from other forms of research. That almost goes without saying. Yet some of these differences need to be articulated in order to explore the main idea of this chapter. I wish to propose that it is a misconceived enterprise to try to separate teachers' thinking in action research from their feelings, beliefs, attitudes, their being and their sense of self. To do so is to create difficulties in attempting to understand how and why worthwhile change evolves as a result of the teacher's systematic, reflective enquiries.

First, action research is what Kemmis (1989) has called 'first person research' in which the researcher studies his or her own work. This contrasts with second or third person research in which the researcher looks from the outside on to someone else's work. When professionals engage in action research they are entering into a study of their own work and their own working circumstances (Webb, 1990; Hustler, 1986; Nixon, 1981). Self is, thus, more publicly central to the research enterprise than in other more traditional forms of research. For at the heart of the teacher action research agenda is a personally focussed concern (Stenhouse, 1975, Elliott, 1981), one that is close to the management of one's self as a professional and one that is an integral part of one's daily work. This first person focus is what demarcates insider teacher action research from more traditional outsider, second or third person (Kemmis, 1989) research, in which the research agenda will most certainly be emotionally removed from the researcher's daily life concerns. Teacher action researchers own the research agenda. They have close professional involvement with, and attachment, to it. Much of their identity, is, thus, locked into the research focus and the consequent research process.

Nias (1990) suggests that the 'attitudes and actions of all teachers are rooted in their ways of perceiving the world. In this sense teaching cannot be otherwise than personal' (p. 3). Nor, thus, can teacher action research be other than personal. For to be a teacher action researcher is to bring the existing self as teacher into the research process. And with it comes all the attendant wisdom, knowledge, beliefs, values, attitudes, prejudices, loves and hates, of the professional and personal self. In practice, the two roles of teacher and researcher are inseparable. The teacher lives inside the being of the researcher. The researcher lives inside the being of the teacher. They influence each other in a mutually symbiotic way, each informing and shaping the other. There will be forces within the researcher beyond the mere cerebral which, thus, will be drawn in, as research processes touch on 'basic assumptions' (Abercrombie, 1960) and pre-conceptions that have previously been organizing schema for controlling the teacher action researcher's work.

Yet aspects of the action research literature have tended to emphasize iconic and mechanistic views of the action research process as a personally problem-free experience. There are action research steps to be followed, it suggests, in some logical progression that will lead to cognitive enlightenment, and recognition of necessary change (Elliott, 1981; Kemmis and MacTaggart, 1988). This suggests the action research experience to be inevitably systematic, linear, cerebral and behavioristic. Whilst this might be a skeletal description of several of the acts which the action researcher performs, it also leaves much unexplored and unsaid. Evidence from my own action research experience and from work with teacher action researchers in award-bearing INSET (Dadds, 1991) has never quite been adequately accounted for in these essentially cognitive conceptions of the action research process.

The second special charactistic of action research which distinguishes it from second and third person research is, by implication, its commitment to action. Research and its usage are not conceptualized separately in action research. They are interdependent and integrated. Thus, in action oriented research, there are paradigm specific issues to be explored about the links between research and implementation of change. For example, the links between data and action may be more relevant to understanding validity of action oriented research than the links between data and theory (Dadds, 1991). Because of this, action research must be treated as a paradigm in its own right with its own particular commitment to practical rather than purist views of knowledge. Its main purpose is the betterment of educational provision. It is not therefore value-free research either in concep-tion, execution or application. And because it is not value-free it will not be free of the ideological and affective self of the teacher action researcher. Her sense of caring and concern — for principles and people — will be woven into the fabric of her research. Indeed, the emotional bonds which exist between teacher re-searchers and their pupils often offer the motivation to undertake the research in the first place. A drive to improve things for children, to strive for 'a more equitable world' (Lather, 1986) is often an integral part of the action researcher's work. Emotional commitment is, thus, entirely congruent with the action research para-digm. This emotional commitment may strengthen rather than weaken the action research mission. To quote Chisholm (1990),

the integration of emotionality is not weakness, but enrichment. (p. 253)

Thus we cannot draw a false distinction between affect and cognition nor between the purposes of the research and the professional motivations of the researcher in considering action research. The lines between them are but 'dissolving bounda-ries' (Grumet, 1990). Action research challenges the teacher to call upon relevant passions and commitments, to explicate and understand them and to utilize them wisely in the creation and application of new research knowledge. It challenges the teacher to bring the head, heart and spur to action into full and effective play. It seems more appropriate, therefore, in action research to call for 'a rejection of . . . deceptive rational coolness in favour of explicit commitment . . . in favour of passionate scholarship' (Chisholm, 1990, p. 253).

In addition, we misconceptualize the nature of theory in action research if we attempt to objectify and disembody it from our understanding of the teacher action researcher as a person, in exploring the theory practice relationship. Theory has no autonomous existence from the theory user (Dadds, 1991). Theory exists only within people, and only informs action by virtue of the people using it. Gollop (1989) reminds us that 'insight will neither feed the hungry nor clothe the naked nor heal the hurt' (p. 101). Theory alone does not change the world. People do. Well grounded theories may be useful indicators to the teacher action researcher of where and how life could be improved. Well grounded theories may even change the people who change the world. But ideological drive, some passionate commitment to fuel action and appropriate personal and interpersonal skills may be more important for bringing about theoretically-based practical improvement. Warm hearts, commitment, altruistic tendencies, and the ability to persuade and manage people through change may be as equally important as clear ideas in putting the action into teacher action research theories. Indeed these qualities cannot be separated from the cognitive processes which teacher action researchers undergo.

This is not to deny the valuable theoretical contribution which the existing literature has made. Rather, it is to seek to raise an additional and complementary, rather than competing discourse, to help us to account for the personally-driven and often emotionally taxing zones that may lie between the lines, circles, spirals and boxes of action research models. It is an attempt also to account more fully for the often emotionally, or autobiographically charged, starting points of commitment that bring teachers to their research and, subsequently, help them to change their practical worlds.

Putting one's research to practical use in the classroom or the institution places heavy demands on the personal and interpersonal skills of the teacher. Action researchers do not encase themselves in the epistemological isolation of library study. If they are to do something worthwhile with their research, they will also be working in the interactive cut-and-thrust of demanding classrooms and demanding schools, using their nerve endings to seek for the time and opportunity to put their research theories to practical tests. This requires far more of their 'being' than cool, detached, ponderous reflection on field data.

These relationships between 'being' and cognition through action research were witnessed through the work of teachers such as Vicki. Vicki was one of twenty-seven students who became the focus of a more extensive research project which looked at award-bearing action research in an INSET context (Dadds, 1991). Studying her research experience with her has helped to realize the organic interplay between mind and heart in the action research enterprise.

Vicki was a middle school teacher on an action research-based two-year part-time Advanced Diploma course. Here we will consider her personal experience of two of her major action research projects.

One of these projects focussed upon two handicapped pupils in her class. It started from an autobiographical position of cognitive insecurity and it proved to be an emotionally powerful experience.

From the outset Vicki's feelings about having the children in her class were mixed, vacillating from a slight ego trip, 'because the powers that be decided that I could cope', she wrote, to a sense of inadequacy at 'the realization that my knowledge and experience in dealing with handicapped children was very limited'.

She remembered some painful experiences in early adulthood when she took a holiday job in a school for mentally handicapped children. The job was made almost totally unrewarding for 'lack of understanding and immaturity', and from an absence of help and support from the qualified staff at the school. She left with bad memories and a hole in her arm, inflicted by 'one large boy' who 'attempted to bite chunks whilst professing his love' for her.

Neither did her formal education help. She was educated to be sympathetic to the handicapped in a distant kind of way, a sympathy which led her to 'occasionally buying a flag for some charity'. But, on the whole, her grammar school education left her with a very segregationist view of the handicapped. As she explained in her research report, 'we were of the "does he take sugar" era'.

Vicki had 'nagging doubts and worries' about her own limited understanding. Her level of self-confidence was thus tied in with her level of knowledge. This uncertainty was a way into the research. It 'persuaded [her] to take these two children as subjects for a study' with a view to 'trying to reach some conclusions concerning their lives as handicapped children in mainstream school'.

Vicki entered into multiple perspective research, gathering data from parents, the ancillary helper, other teachers and the children themselves. She met a number of ethical challenges during this enquiry as she sought to draw in these other voices to compare with, and contrast to, her own. For example, Vicki wanted 'to get some reactions to the children's ideas of being handicapped and what it meant to take that handicap into a normal school'. But she recognized that this could mean wandering into some 'delicate' issues with the children, issues which she would 'back off' if they appeared in any way to upset the children. One of the children did, indeed, show signs of discomfort, so Vicki decided not to 'probe too deeply'. It seems clear that her feelings for the children and her consideration of their welfare was her prime consideration. They were more important than the planned direction of the research. If compromises had to be made they were not to be made with children's feelings. In a similar vein, her concern for the children's well-being was brought into play when the mainstream children exhibited some jealousy as Vicki took photographs of the handicapped children. The mainstream children may not have felt that the selective attention was quite fair, so Vicki 'overcame this by doing rather more general photographs, in order to include, in the research process, children who otherwise may have felt excluded'. The cost of a few extra, if unnecessary photographs, may have felt small compared to the feelings of her pupils. Here we see teacher professional judgment influencing researcher judgment. Both are informed by the nature of the interpersonal relationships between Vicki and her pupils, and by her sense of caring for them.

Vicki tried to separate thought from feeling in reflecting upon her data, but found this difficult. She sought a more 'objectified' picture, as she called it, of the children. She felt she had to try 'to avoid sentimentality, which is an easy trap to fall into in such an emotive area of education'. But she was not sure that she had succeeded in that detachment. The problematics of this are obvious since, as their class teacher, she was closely involved with these two handicapped children on a day to day basis. She was sharing enough of the daily high and lows, worries, achievements, hopes and fears to find detachment for the purposes of the research difficult. A personal and emotional bond already existed and could not be broken for the epistemological purposes of the research.

Where such teacher emotion comes to cloud judgment in research analysis this clearly can be a research problem. On the other hand, the knowledge that is generated by this emotional bonding may offer unique insights which could do no other than enrich the research, when balanced by clear analysis and theorizing. In addition, such bonding may be the natural basis for an emergent ethical code for the research. Vicki had a 'feeling' for the point at which research ethics were being transgressed because the sensitivities of the children made that point of transgression obvious to her.

As the research project progressed, Vicki was able to see her way through these feelings into new areas of understanding. For example, an interview with the mother of one of the children drew inevitably on affective and heavily biased parental data. The knowledge which Vicki gained from this interview had a significant effect on her perceptions of the child and, subsequently, on her personal and professional attitudes to him. She claimed that it helped her 'to try to understand some of the problems [he] has been faced with in the last two years and how he has tried to come to terms with them'. The developed knowledge paralleled a developed bonding. Vicki's understanding of, and personal regard for, the child grew as a result of this journey into her data.

Also, the positive attitudinal and perceptual changes may, in their developmental importance to Vicki, have transcended the knowledge or arguments generated in the research. It seems that the study opened up a new realm of understanding that challenged and radically modified her initial preconceptions and attitudes towards the handicapped. In its wake, it seems that Vicki's personal regard for the children was considerably enhanced bringing an interpersonal validity to the study. At the end of the text Vicki wrote,

> In carrying out this research, I feel I have laid some of the ghosts of my youth. In becoming so involved in two such admirable children one cannot but feel humbled by their attitudes and achievements. The 'personal tragedy theory' of disability which I had before I experienced David and Janet is no longer with me. I have enjoyed the study and the learning process has involved not only different methods of study but a beginning in understanding such children.

Thus, the growth in understanding for Vicki seems to have flourished on a number of levels. Her feelings, particularly her sense of regard, respect and empathy took on a different quality. Her sense of knowing was a personal concoction of thoughts and emotions, of attitudes and theoretical insights. Theory was not simply a cognitive act but had warm, passionate underpinnings. Ideas and emotions were the integrated warp and weft of her theoretical fabric. And they informed each other.

It would be nonsense to deny that these passionate elements were as important to professional growth as development of cognition. For it seems clear from Vicki's concluding remarks that this had definitely been the case. Her heart seems to have moved as much as her head. And, so, one could argue, it should be, if the research is to make an integrated contribution to professional growth. For the 'self' of the teacher is much more than a personalized set of ideas. Nias (1986) suggests that love lives at the centre of the being of many primary teachers. For Vicki, this inevitably meant that love lived at the heart of the researcher, the researcher whose self was, like a Russian doll, bound inside the teacher.

In the process of doing the research and developing her understanding, there was evidence that a professional conviction had grown, a conviction that was not in evidence at the outset. To this end, the earlier worry about over-sentimentalized data was counteracted by a vibrant, almost passionate plea, in Vicki's concluding words to the study, that these children should be accorded their just deserts of high teacher expectations. For example, the research suggested that affectionate over compensation for the children may also be leading to an underestimation of their abilities. Vicki wrote,

> ... Both children are low academic achievers. I would conclude from the evidence that it may be that the children are not being encouraged to reach their full potential. Experience and research have shown that children respond to teachers who expect them to succeed. We are not stretching them enough. Because they have a disability, because they have problems, and because we sympathize with them, we don't want to upset them more than is necessary. Both children it was reported, are frequently spoken to in the corridors by members of staff. How many of the other 380 children can boast the same treatment. We make allowances for them, a very natural attitude to adopt. But we must make sure that the pressures remain on them to achieve to the best of their ability. We owe it to them as we do to the other twenty-nine in the class.

This overtly passionate appeal to action seems not to be rooted in cool researcher detachment from these children. It draws research insight together with a personal and professional belief in the entitlement of the handicapped. It is ideological, as well as epistemological. It is emotive and attached, not coolly logical and detached. Vicki wanted more for the children.

An extract from the edited tape which accompanied a set of slides embedded in the research, gives, perhaps, the clearest insight into the inseparable nature of thought and feeling in the action research process. It also gives some insight into the significant developmental purposes which the work achieved and some sense of the professional mastery which it brought. Here is Vicki, speaking on the audio material accompanying the written text, reading an extract from her field diary which she kept throughout the research process. She says,

> One evening, last year, when I got home, I wrote this — It's Monday the twelfth, eleven forty, and I had to deal with my first fit. Jean was not around, and it was an event which I knew I would eventually have to cope with. It was not a bad one and David did not flail. The first indication was that one of the children called out, Please Miss, David's having a fit. His arm had become oddly shaped and he began to work his mouth, and his eyes stared. I knew the object was to get him into the recovery position. But he's heavy and I can feel my heart racing. I feel flushed. The children are watching to see how I am going to cope. Actually getting him down is a great physical effort. I eventually do it with the help of the children who help me with his legs. I know I must remember to keep his air passage clear and his head to one side. I talk to him all the time, I'm half kneeling on one side of him with his weight on my other leg. He is out, gurgling rhythmically to himself for about three-quarters of a minute. It seems to be much longer. He begins to come round, and immediately

he wants to get up. This is a struggle because he is still very unsteady. After a fit I knew that David generally likes to sleep. Another member of staff relieves me and takes him away. I immediately feel exhausted. I feel a weakness in one of my legs after the weight of David on it. But I am a little elated. I've got through the first one and it felt like a hurdle I knew I would have to take. He had come out of it okay. I felt a bit pleased with myself and relieved. I knew that if it happened again, I could do it again.

It does not take a systematic content analysis to show that this is emotionally charged data, rising powerfully from the self of the researcher as teacher, the researcher as professional, the researcher as person. This is professional development through research in the making, a clear example of reflection-in-action (Schon, 1983). We see the teacher researcher applying her new professional knowledge to an immediate and urgent practical problem. But it is not detached thought and knowledge that are brought into play in solving this problem reflectively. The heart pounds. The child's well being is at stake. Self-regard is on the line. Professional and personal self-actualization are waiting to fill the minutes ahead. Emotion and knowledge drive Vicki along. This is the feeling of reflective thought.

This then gives us some insight into the interplay of thought and feeling which Vicki experienced in doing the research for her own individual professional benefit. She also had a further purpose. She wished to link her study to the needs of those colleagues who would subsequently be involved in the education of the two handicapped children. She explained,

> One of the reasons I did it originally, my ideas were that it should help the people who were going to have the children next to begin to understand them.

So, beyond the personal, individual purpose, the study also carried a more altruistic, collegial professional motive. Vicki identified the roots of this motive in a general sense of accountability, and a general sense of debt felt in response to being awarded the privilege of day release for further study.

But whilst her first purpose seems to have been well served by the study, this second, more altruistic purpose seems to have been thwarted. According to Vicki's data there appears to have been two reasons for this. On the one hand, Vicki was pleased with the value inherent in the end product of her study for herself, but on the other, she was diffident about the quality being adequate enough for other audiences. In interview she confessed that she felt that the tape slide sequence which she constructed to accompany the research report, 'wasn't technically brilliant, I didn't think anyway'. And she also admitted,

> To actually show that, I would have opened myself up to criticism for the way I did it.

It cannot be assumed that sharing and dissemination of research in the cause of school improvement is a straightforward and unproblematic task for the teacher. Laying one's work open and public for others' benefit is an act of personal and professional exposure. Feelings about oneself are in that work, and in the textual products of that work. The researcher risks judgment on many levels when their work becomes public. And it cannot be assumed that all teacher action researchers feel comfortable and confident in that position. There may be attitudes and feelings to be mastered which do not come readily and easily to all. Where self-identity is closely bound into the research and its products, public judgment and critique affects that sense of self. Work made public is self made public. Work under scrutiny is self under scrutiny. The personal capacity for dealing with this will vary from one researcher to another. But for many, such evaluative exposure is emotionally taxing, and, often, threatening (Dadds, 1986a).

There was a further reason for the sharing and dissemination purpose not being fulfilled. Vicki was not ultimately sure that her views of the children were coincidental with those of their next teacher. To share her own views may have been revealing in a way which she did not want. She said,

> the person who then had Janet and David had very different ideas about Janet and one of the reasons I didn't show it was to show a different opinion.

Why would she not want to do that, we might wonder. Surely sharing differences of perception can be a stimulus to collaborative learning and improved teaching. Vicki may not have been confident enough in the relationship with her colleague for that joint growth in understanding to be an outcome of sharing. She said,

> It might have caused some sort of conflict. And that was not the idea. The whole idea of the tape was to help people to understand and be aware.

It is not clear whether the judgment about conflict avoidance was also a form of self-protection, but it does seem clear that Vicki was motivated at least by some principle of institutional protection.

But the effect of sharing could have been quite the opposite of what was intended. Sensitive to the possible negative effect on the health of the relationship and the institution, Vicki decided against sharing the study with her colleague, and also decided, in retrospect, that this had been the right decision. There was also something of both modesty and a characteristic self-doubt attached to her decision, a modesty and self-doubt that inhibited her from expressing her ideas more overtly with her colleague. She doubted the status and wisdom of her own knowledge and understanding. She explained,

> and I thought, who am I to show [my view] as being the one that is right. So all these things played against me actually forcing the tape on anybody in the end.

Once more, we see a link between Vicki's felt self-confidence in her knowledge, and her behaviour as a researcher. On this occasion, her feelings affected further potential practical outcomes. Uncertainty and a certain lack of self-confidence prevailed over aspiration or, one could say, wisdom prevailed over ambition. Vicki also continued to feel some guilt at not being able to create some institutional capital from her own professional capital. Feelings, thus, were not simplistically resolved, as uncertainty gave way to guilt. One form of self-negation was replaced by another. Either way, Vicki remained in an emotional state of disequilibrium, despite the positive feelings that the research had also generated.

We can, here, see the teacher action researcher at the nexus of a sharing ecology, trying to make sense of various demands, constraints and circumstances in order to make a wise and appropriate judgment about further purposes and audiences for her work. A high level of 'situational understanding' (Elliott, 1991) is required. She is required to read and understand the institutional environment and culture, made up of roles, relationships, attitudes and practices of colleagues, as a basis for further professional usage of her work. This seems no mean task, given that she has already invested much time, energy, commitment, thought and feeling in the process of the research and the consequent textual construction. If she misreads this institutional context, sharing may not be helpful to either side. If she reads it well, her work could either make additional contributions to institutional growth, in however small a way, or remain a limited, if valid study at the level of personal, professional development.

Further, Vicki's own sense of self is necessarily implicated here. Confidence in her own knowledge and certainties is being tested. Her work, if shared more widely, may accrue judgments and consequences which may ultimately prove to have a bearing on Vicki's sense of professional self worth, for good or for ill. How her work is received may prove to affect her feelings, attitudes and ideas abut her own competencies and judgment.

That this action research involved Vicki's emotional as well as cognitive being is, thus, clear. There is much evidence of anxiety, uncertainty, affection, worry, joy, caring as the research caused her to interact with colleagues, pupils and her own emotionally based philosophy and as she made self-judgments about the quality of the work and her capacity to offer a worthwhile point of view. We have a clear sense of the committed and emotionally attached teacher living inside the researcher role, putting people first where methodological dilemmas were presented. The learning process which the research generated was, thus, emotionally as well as cognitively taxing as Vicki came to understand that the floundering and the struggle were necessary elements in that learning process.

There were differing experiences of self-esteem. This was high as a result of the important learning and mastery which she achieved but low at the point of institutional implementation, for we did see Vicki, for a range of reasons, exercising judgment and discretion in keeping the research from more public scrutiny. Whether or not it was the most appropriate judgment, we will never know. But for Vicki it was, perhaps, the best she could manage at the time. It is a pity that she came to see this as a failure, rather than a good and wise judgment.

In contrast, her following research on the gendered nature of schooling and the curriculum had long-term and wide institutional impact. The starting point had been latent in an evolving personal and gendered history. In her childhood, Vicki's parents had tried to avoid gender stereotyping between brothers and sisters, and Vicki had received much encouragement to achieve. But her experiences in adult life had been different. She had been the victim of unequal pay opportunities as a student, had married into a partnership where the traditional domestic role was expected of her, and had later been turned down for a relief teaching role because she had two young children. Elements of her history fostered a strong determination to improve the gendered world of schooling for children, a determination which surfaced in this major action research study which she undertook for her Advanced Diploma. It seems to have been accompanied all the way with a personal confidence which helped to engage the interest of many of her school colleagues. When the work was in progress she told me,

> I'm absolutely determined that I'm going to do a report on it because everybody is interested when they keep saying, how is it going, what are the results.

The research did, indeed, impact on the institution. Vicki negotiated to study a wide range of gender practices in the school, including the use of curricular materials, the structure of class registers, use of computers, competitive games, children's reading habits and preferences, literature images, language interaction between pupils and teachers.

Field work processes raised critical self-awareness of teachers and children, generated critical discussions and caused modification to some practices and some language forms. When the study was completed, Vicki was invited to give feed-back to a staff meeting. From this, she mounted a staff development event which took place on half of a Baker Day. A corporate draft gender policy statement emerged from the intense personal and professional analysis which the day had generated. Much subsequent practice was also affected.

One colleague said of the discussion that led to the policy,

> It felt very constructive. It felt as if you were doing the things that mattered.

The changes generated from Vicki's research and its employment for staff develop-ment were maintained. Over time, the staff in general felt that the changes to perception, attitudes and behaviour had helped to change the staff culture. Also, gender attitudes and beliefs that had lain dormant in the culture of the school had been activated by Vicki's research and staff development work. There was clear indication that institutional maturing had taken place and that Vicki had been an effective agent in this.

Vicki's manner and personality as well as her research insights seem to have made possible the institutional success of the day. Vicki was seen by colleagues as a caring person, one who did not present a personal, emotional threat even though she presented colleagues with challenging ideas.

> 'I think what is good about the way Vicki does it', a colleague said, 'is that she does it with sympathy.'

It was recognized that her gentle and non-confrontational manner was equally well matched with her gendered ideology.

> 'Her person was exactly right for it', he continued. '. . . . if anyone had come to it at a 100 miles an hour it would have met with resistance. But because she came at it with her personality — strong views gently put — I think it was exactly right.'

Another colleague believed that Vicki's sense of purpose and mission in what she was doing had provided the all important driving force. This driving force probably put the action into the ideas which started, and developed, the research. This colleague saw Vicki as,

> A fighter, fighting for an ideal ... A definite quest in life and a quest in her educational philosophy — this won't do, we need to do something about it.

This perception of Vicki was shared by the head. He was in no doubt that this personal and professional commitment was a key factor in the changes that had occurred from the research. Of significance was,

> Vicki's commitment and involvement and willingness to try to make something happen as the result of the time she spent.

She needed to believe that she could actively shape the destiny of her small corner of the world in some way. She needed a belief in herself as change agent — not the heroine innovator, but the gentle, if determined, reformer. Her thinking about gender opportunities could not be divorced from these beliefs nor passion. The beliefs *were* the thinking. The beliefs were the passion. The passion was in the thinking.

This is not to suggest that the mission embedded in Vicki's autobiography, ideology and affect totally overtook her cognitive and discursive self. On the contrary, her calls to action were well grounded in clear arguments, which, in turn, were grounded in institutional data and the wider discourses of gender literature and larger scale gender research. Rather, it is to suggest that good arguments alone may not have been sufficient for stimulating the action that the school saw. The point, here, is that Vicki's ideas and research insights alone were not sufficient for fostering wider dissemination and practical outcomes. The power and drive for change came from deeper autobiographical and affective sources, without which the research knowledge may have lived a life of dust. Also Vicki's personal qualities were vital ingredients in the catalysis that brought about wider change.

Nor was the language of Vicki's research the language of unemotional research and unemotional argumentation. Interwoven with the language of fact and analysis was the language of personal and emotional response, and interwined with a language of affective response was the language of purpose and aspiration. On describing the predominance of male characters in text books around the school, for example, she wrote,

> this is ... alarming when considering that reading was the main pastime on which girls spent their time.

In addition to alarm, she felt worried about some of her data. She wrote,

> I think of all the observations and research I embarked upon the one I found most worrying was ...

She wrote of sadness at what she saw as girls' limited self-aspirations.

> It does seem to me very sad that instead of seeing their future as a development of themselves, they see their own role purely in connection with a husband or a child.

Vicki referred to a sense of 'shock' felt when analyzing gender stereotype images in the comics which, her data revealed, were most commonly read by the children in her survey. She admitted,

I was even more shocked than I thought I would be.

Alarm, worry, sadness, shock. One could argue that this is not the usual language of research. Yet if the role of emotion is to be explicated and understood in teacher action research, it is difficult to see how much more honest and authentic a research text could possibly be in laying such feelings out for inspection. And we may have to acknowledge that these feelings contributed to the driving force that caused Vicki to see, or feel, the need for action, for change.

Vicki was well aware of the personal bias she brought to this research, just as she had been in her previous research with her handicapped pupils. It was a concern that continued to worry her throughout, for she still had a conceptual attachment to a positivist notion of objectivity. She was aware that her passions and biases would influence the construction of the research and the gathering of data, even though the structure of both research studies had generated multiple perspective data. Vicki had drawn these plural data into her analysis and generation of insight. Reflection upon the perspectives of others had developed her understandings. New aspects of the cognitive self had emerged through these processes. There had been much intellectual 'self-transcendence' (Winter, 1989) based upon extending her perceptions of the world through data. In this sense, the research was far from cognitively egocentric nor overly personalized. Even so, Vicki was unable to remain comfortable with the notion that her personalized influence could be the cause of celebration in the research and that it could be a major legitimate determinant of action outcomes rather than a methodological pecularity. She never quite came to terms with the value of personal affective bias in the research process. She partly remained a historical victim of 'research paradigms [which] face so frankly in other directions' (Goodson, 1991, 41).

Concluding Comments

We need to be wary of inferring too much from case study and falling into the trap of theoretical generalizations. Yet Vicki's story was typical of many others in my research project (Dadds, 1991). Here we have seen the historical, autobiographical self of the researcher being brought into play in raising a research agenda. We have seen the professional self clarifying those agenda into worthwhile and developmental research projects for herself, her pupils and colleagues. During the processes of the research we saw the ethical, caring self determining the gathering and use of research data. And we saw the transformation of both the cognitive and affective self taking place as perceptions, understandings and attitudes took on new shape and form. New forms of caring and regard developed. At many points, therefore, and at many levels, the teacher researcher's feelings, attitudes and beliefs were significant factors in conceptualization, execution and implementation of the research. But thought and feeling did not remain static and in these processes, a new 'architecture of self' (Pinar, 1988) emerged. Some of these developmental processes also gave rise to new institutional identities as the research changed the gendered culture of the school.

The demands on the teacher researcher that all this entails can be psychologically and emotionally extensive. Nias and Groundwater-Smith (1988) suggest that

> To gather evidence about, to reflect on and perhaps to change one's professional practice requires self-awareness, self-evaluation, self-revelation and probably creates self-doubt. (p. 3)

In addition to these taxes on one's sense of self, and, therefore, one's emotionality, the demands of implementation of research may bring one into interpersonal challenges and exchanges of a new and different kind.

Lest we worry that these taxations bring nothing but hardship to the teacher action researcher, there were positive concomitants for Vicki in the form of improved self-confidence, as self was confirmed by the learning climate of the collegial staff group and as mastery was achieved in new professional areas. In the gender research Vicki's interests and concerns became the serious interests and concerns of her colleagues. Her passions became legitimized through the corporate curriculum development that emerged from the research. And her skills and credibility as an affective change agent in the school were greatly enhanced. This, of course, is not the lot of all action researchers. Many work in less fertile institutional climates and continue to feel that their research is marginalized, rejected even, by the school culture (Dadds, 1986b; Holly, 1984). These teachers may achieve some success in putting the action into their action research within their classrooms. But they will experience neither the demands, nor delights, of seeing their work generating greater practical benefits to the school. Their emotional and, therefore, their cognitive experiences of action research may be quite different from Vicki's.

Any attempt to explicate and understand the role of the emotional and autobiographical self in the epistemology of the research can thus, only serve to give a more complete or extensive sense of the meaning that the research may have for the researcher. For other interested audiences, it may give an understanding of the internal validity of the research. It is consonant, too, with a methodological desire 'to extend naturalistic forms of enquiry by bracketing in the researcher' (MacLure and Stronach, 1989, p. 4). And it is consonant with a research paradigm that seeks to 'move from being a science that only seeks to represent reality' into becoming 'a discipline that makes explicit our interpretative sides' (*ibid*, p. 5).

And I would also argue that the greater benefit in understanding and explicating aspects of the teacher action researcher's self, both affect and cognition, is towards understanding the processes by which teacher research becomes transformed into professional action and practical change. Such insights may help those supporting teacher action researchers especially within the demands of award-bearing INSET. For if we cannot understand the complexities of what it *feels* like to be a teacher action researcher, we are disabled from providing the most supportive learning climate and the most supportive research relationship that we can offer.

References

ABERCROMBIE, J. (1960) *The Anatomy of Judgement*, London, Penguin.
CHISHOLM, L. (1990) 'Action research: Some methodological and political considerations', *British Educational Research Journal*, 16, 3.

Dadds, M. (1986a) 'Group support for self-directed teacher research', *Forum*, 28, 2.

Dadds, M. (1986b) 'The school, the teacher researcher and the in-service tutor', *C.A.R.N. Bulletin*, No. 7.

Dadds, M. (1991) 'Validity in award-bearing teacher action research', Norwich, Centre for Applied Research in Education, University of East Anglia.

Elliott, J. (1981) *Action Research: A Framework for Self evaluation in Schools*, Cambridge, Cambridge Institute of Education.

Elliott, J. (1991) *Action Research for Educational Change*, Milton Keynes, Open University Press.

Gollop, S. (1989) 'Becoming a teacher: A study of change as a personal process in mature women students', MA dissertation, Norwich, Centre for Applied Research in Education, University of East Anglia.

Goodson, I.F. (1991) 'Sponsoring the teacher's voice: Teachers' lives and teacher development', *Cambridge Journal of Education*, 21, 1.

Grumet, M.R. (1990) 'Autobiography and reconceptualisation', *Journal of Curriculum Theorising*, 2, 2, summer.

Holly, P.J. (1984) 'Beyond the cult of the individual' in Nias, J. (Ed.) *Teaching Enquiry Based Course*, Cambridge, Cambridge Institute of Education.

Hustler, D. (Ed.) (1986) *Action Research in Classroom and Schools*, Lewes, Falmer Press.

Kemmis, S. and McTaggart, R. (1988) *The Action Research Planner* (3rd edn) Geelong, Deakin University Press.

Kemmis, S. (1989) *Metatheory and Metapractice in Educational Theorising and Research*, Geelong, Deakin University Press.

Lather, P. (1986) 'Research as praxis', *Harvard Educational Review*, 56, 3.

MacLure, M. and Stronach, I. (1989) 'Seeing through the self: Contemporary biography and some implications for educational research', paper presented to the annual meeting of the American Educational Research Association, San Francisco.

Nias, J. (1986) 'What is it to feel like a teacher? The subjective reality of primary teaching', paper presented to the annual meeting of the British Educational Research Association, Bristol.

Nias, J. (1990) Changing Times, Changing Identities: Grieving for a Lost Self, Cambridge, Cambridge Institute of Education.

Nias, J. and Groundwater-Smith, S. (1988) *The Enquiring Teacher*, Lewes, Falmer Press.

Nixon, J. (Ed.) (1981) *A Teacher's Guide to Action Research*, London, Grant McIntyre.

Pinar, W.F. (1988) 'Autobiography and the architecture of self', *Journal of Curriculum Theorising*, 8, 1.

Schon, D. (1983) *The Reflective Practitioner*, New York, Basic Books.

Stenhouse, L. (1975) *An Introduction to Curriculum Research and Development*, London, Heinemann.

Webb, R. (1990) *Practitioner Research in the Primary School*, Lewes, Falmer Press.

Winter, R. (1989) *Learning from Experience: Principles and Practice in Action Research*, Lewes, Falmer Press.

Chapter 17

The Importance of an Articulated Personal Theory of Professional Development

Christine O'Hanlon

Personal and Professional Theories

People become teachers for a variety of reasons but mainly because teaching is viewed as a career, and a profession which is personally satisfying. There have been, however, many teachers in schools in the United Kingdom in recent years who have found that the stress of the changes taking place in schools far outweighs the personal satisfaction they were gaining from the job. Many have found the pace and the nature of change too much, they have become disillusioned, found new careers or have taken early retirement (Lodge, 1991). Yet the majority of teachers committed to a career in teaching take their role seriously as all professionals do, and put themselves under a great deal of pressure to behave in line with professional values, even if these values are not always explicit. The role of the 'teacher' once accepted is performed in a personal way. How one carries out the role is always a matter of personal choice, therefore decisions about change in practice are professional decisions based on personal preferences and values. A professional's life is overridden by the need to make quick decisions intuitively in practice. Choosing between several alternatives related to life choices, personal problems, and professional encounters are just some of the decision areas which might arise in the course of a day. Professional decisions made in the practical busy milieu of practice are influenced by personal factors more than we would like to admit. Professionals dealing with personal problems may be less effective, or respond differently in their professional context because of their own paramount personal needs. Professional actions too may be heavily influenced by personal values. Is there a difference between personal and professional needs and values?

How do personal circumstances, experience and characteristics impinge on a professional's development and understanding?

A person who undertakes legitimate professional practice is accepting a professional role. A teacher assumes the role of educator, instructor, director of anothers' learning. She/he is undertaking a role which commits him/her in a professional situation to work within certain boundaries or guidelines. The guidelines which underlie the professional practice are accepted by the person as appropriate in that kind of situation. A person acting in a particular situation is not showing the whole range of his/her attitudes, values, skills and knowledge. In role-taking the professional consciously decides or selects the attitudes, values, skills and knowledge appropriate to the action. Action is being taken spontaneously and intuitively in the classroom and school — deliberate and conscious actions. However, although there is awareness of the action, there may not be a conscious theory of action. Conscious action is not the same as a conscious theory of action. We can act consciously without reflecting on underlying assumptions.

One of the prime criteria for a good theory is that it has to be useful. Yet, many practising teachers and professionals seem to question the efficacy of using theory in their day to day work.

The reason for this may be that many of the presently constructed theories of teaching and learning are not useful to all professionals; it may be that many of our theories are nothing more than descriptive in nature with no implications for action; or it may be that teachers simply have not understood the theories as presented.

Teachers and educational professionals in order to experience professional growth must begin to ask themselves pertinent questions. Firstly they must ask:

(i)   What is the fundamental purpose of what I am doing?
(ii) What are the means to realize that purpose and how are these means different to what other people/professionals do?

In finding the means to realize our primary purpose we need to know what assumptions we are making about human nature and its development. We need to build knowledge and test it by enquiring systematically into experience, making some generalizations about it, and then testing those generalizations to see if our explanations are accurate and help us to understand what is happening. We need to learn through knowing before we 'do', otherwise we perpetuate repetitive action that is based on hidden values, personal experiences and characteristics of which we are unaware.

In order to act confidently in the many situations which present themselves in our lives we must act on our previous learning which is embodied in our assumptions about social/professional situations and our actions within them and upon them. Yet we don't have the time to examine our hidden assumptions within our actions every time we decide to take action. However, our assumptions should be clearly visible to our understanding of our actions and practice. We need to work from an *explicit* rather than an implicit theory. Without an explicit theoretical orientation, action is vulnerable to oversimplification and imitation. When a theory is made explicit a professional has a better opportunity to test and evolve a personal theory based on experiences or on deliberate personal investigation. All teachers have the potential for developing their own personal teaching theory or their own individual professional theory which enables them to become aware of their values and understand action in a situation which demands flexible and individual responses.

A personal or individual professional theory enables the teacher to make systematic observations about his/her teaching experiences; it encourages bringing together various concepts in teaching, and it helps the teacher in the areas of prediction, evaluation of performance and the improvement of actions.

The building of personal theory inevitably implies a form of self-evaluation. An aware examination of personal practice which usually takes place retrospectively

Table 17.1 Model of teacher professional development

Stage one	Stage two		Stage three
Prevailing educational trends and philosophies	Existing theories of education	↔ Info and feedback from trainer/tutor	Personal theory of teaching Personal reflection and re-evaluation
Chronological/ historical time	Observations in classrooms	↔ Reflection	Deliberate action
Personal needs and values	Personal influences about relationships between teaching and learning behaviours	↔ Info and feedback from peers	Personal characteristics of teacher
Personal experience	Personal hypotheses about classroom behaviour and learning	↔ Self-awareness in the professional situation	Teaching pedagogy Pupil learning

with the aim of improving the action in the context. Self-evaluation involves developing reflective qualities as well as a social identity perspective. The social or professional identity emerges from the synthesis of personal and professional values.

The personal needs and values become enmeshed in the professional need and value system and often appear to be indistinguishable to the professional who is making decisions in action. In the facilitation of all teachers' professional development it is essential that teachers are encouraged to develop their own personal or individual theory and that they become aware of the manner in which their personal values influence, contradict or merge with the existing values within the professional culture. The model of professional development which follows emerges from my view of how teachers become professionals in their initial training and subsequently in their further professional development. All students or teachers who seek professional accreditation in the first stage or who seek further qualifications after their initial training, come to the situation with their own existing knowledge about teaching and learning, and their own personal needs and values. The model is developed from my observations, experience, practice, and investigations of the acculturation of students in initial training and their further professional development over a number of years.

In a model of teacher professional development, a process of change and transformation is occurring (illustrated in table 17.1) which combines both personal and professional values into theories of action.

To begin with we need to distinguish between a *'professional'* theory of education and a *personal* theory.

A professional theory is a theory which is created and perpetuated within the professional culture. It is a theory which is widely known and understood like the developmental stages of Piaget. Professional theories are generally transmitted via teacher/professional training in colleges, polytechnics and universities. Professional theories form the basis of a shared knowledge and understanding about the 'culture' of teaching and provide the opportunity to develop discourse on the implicit and explicit educational issues raised by these theoretical perspectives.

A personal theory on the other hand, is an individual theory unique to each person, which is individually developed through the experience of putting professional theories to the test in the practical situation. How each person interprets and adapts their previous learning particularly their reading, understanding and identification of professional theories while they are on the job is potentially their own personal theory. I use the word potentially because it depends to a large extent on reflection and evaluation and on feedback from pupils, colleagues and others.

In this model professionals begin with personal needs and values which become transformed through their professional acculturation and exposure to professional theories into a professional value system. In subsequent action and adaptation of ideas the professional is aware of acting in 'role' and is able to develop a more personal view of him/herself in the professional context. Personal characteristics combine with professional actions to form a pedagogy which may become a conscious theory of action, or a personal pedagogic theory.

Stage one indicates that a person decides at a particular period in their life with their own unique personal needs and values, to become a professional teacher or to gain further professional development or in-service training.

In stage two existing professional theories of education are studied, teaching is practised in the school and through these two variants the person starts to understand themselves in action and to form personal hypotheses about teaching and learning. These constructs or hypotheses become firm, modified or are rejected in their validation within the situation with feedback and evaluation from pupils, colleagues and others.

In stage three the person develops as a professional through accreditation of their work and study, and becomes a practitioner or reflects further on their professional role. The practice is personal in the sense that the individual values and characteristics of the person influence their practice in many complex ways. The teaching pedagogy is adapted to suit the person and the situation and action is undertaken in daily practice. As the person attempts to evaluate or improve the situation they must reflect on their own actions. Their own self-investigatory activities and attempts to understand their practice by means of increased awareness then becomes their own personal theory of teaching. The professionals on reflection become aware of why they are acting as they do and what values underpin their everyday practice. They become professionally acculturated through personalizing the professional theories handed on to them within the professional culture. As a result of rigorous thinking, analysis of inferences and the development of personal constructs or hypotheses, a personal theory of teaching/professionalism emerges. A personal theory is an informed theory which forms the basis of professional confidence with its confirmation in action. The process could be viewed as a perpetuating cycle of stages which continue to renew professional practice through the personal re-evaluation of action in practice.

Jo: A Case Study

Jo is a young teacher who has readily accepted the professional theories passed on to her in her recent training. She has, however, now found that her basic training does not give her ready answers to many of the problems and dilemmas she faces in her teaching in a large mixed ability secondary school. In embarking on an In-service BEd course she is introduced to a form of practitioner research or investigation and reflection into her own teaching. She proceeds from stage one to stage three in her investigatory progress with the help of pupils, colleagues and tutor. Jo uses her diary/journal as a basis for her emergent personal theory of teaching. She articulates her teaching theories in two ways. She writes in her journal/diary and she writes her assignment for the institutional purpose of accreditation. She writes in her journal of her personal evolution and changed awareness, which contrasts with her public account of her professional understanding which is recorded in her writing of the formal assignment.

In the assignment Jo writes more impersonally than she does in the journal. She uses her journal to explain her personal understanding of her teaching purposes and intentions, and she uses her assignment to validate her personal theories by integrating personal and professional theories of teaching. She uses her diary/journal for a personal reflection and re-evaluation of her present professional situation, however, she justifies this publicly by using references and citations from the professional literature.

Jo keeps a detailed diary/journal in which she records her thoughts, ideas and feelings during a twelve week period of her investigation of 'Interprofessional practice in special educational needs'. Teachers are required to investigate the meaning of this phrase through their own practice and then to take action to improve this interprofessional practice.

Jo begins by writing in her assignment that she understands her professional task is to improve her knowledge and practice with the SENs (special educational needs) pupils by forming a better relationship with the Head of the Special Unit in her school. Jo writes formally in her assignment that:

> This assignment is concerned with my inter-professional relationship with Jean Marks, the Head of the Special Educational Needs Unit at Whiteabbey Junior High School. Concern has arisen in this area because of my involvement with the special educational needs pupils in my role as music teacher. I believe that an improvement in my relationship with Jean, at a professional level, would lead to an improvement in my classroom practice with the needs of each pupil being more adequately and effectively met. (assignment)

Jo writes previously, before she writes her assignment, in her journal of her real feelings about Jean's and her own shortcomings:

> 'As usual Jean asked me how my course at the University was going today. I feel uneasy about raising the issue and Jean is such a lovely person always enquiring how my course is going, how am I feeling etc., but never ever does she discuss anything of relevance with regard to the children in the unit.
>
> How on earth am I going to bring up the subject of inter-professional practice in a subtle way?
>
> I know there is so much room for improvement but its approaching this subject with tact! Hold on a minute. What am I 'going on' about Jean's

so called failings for? What about my failings? What have I done to better the situation? Why did I expect Jean to come to me? Should I not have gone to her? Okay, so I initiated a few conversations about how well some of the pupils were doing in music but I never took it any further. (diary/journal)

Jo is becoming conscious of her motives but she has not yet developed a conscious theory of action from her reflection on her own role in investigating the situation.

Jo is reflecting on the purposes of what she is doing in this excerpt. She is becoming aware of the assumptions she is making about pupils in education. She proceeds to show her ability to evaluate herself consciously in the classroom situation;

Again, I'm caught in this awful process of examining my motives and reasons as to why certain situations are the way they are.

When it comes to my lack of communication with Jean about pupils with special educational needs — is it a case of where my priorities lie as opposed to lack of time to discuss things with Jean etc.

There I've written it! What I've been churning over in my mind for some time now but never wanted to admit. After all I had time to test Daniel's musical ability etc. when I was required to do so for my special needs assignment! Yes!

What sort of a teacher am I that would teach a kid like Julie for five whole years and never actually ask or know her age? Never know why she shakes so violently? Never know if she really read the words of the songs we sing!

I'm not only an awful teacher, I'm an awful person — I don't care enough about these children!

They are an *extra* on my timetable, something to be tolerated. No that's not true, I don't mind having them in my classes but they are an extra. My main stream pupils are my main job!! (diary/journal)

Jo is involved in self-confrontation, and an awareness and admission of the real value of pupils within the curriculum. She hasn't tested Daniel's musical ability. She knows nothing of Julie and her problems beyond the obvious in the classroom. There is resentment about having to teach 'these' pupils who are an extra burden for a subject specialist like herself.

Jo continues with the realization that confronting yourself in this way — shakes your belief in your own values — but once written are visible, therefore they must be accepted as real. The diary records,

When Julie came to me for music it was the only time she got out of the unit during the week.

Now I accept that Julie had severe special educational needs but that meant she was too big an inconvenience for the teachers of main stream, low ability classes, so gradually one by one they asked Jean not to send her to their class any more. In the end I was the only teacher who took Julie with a mainstream class.

You know I've written this information about Julie to comfort myself as I feel so ashamed about the way I have felt in the past about the unit children. I feel as if I'm almost inhuman!

Have I led myself to believe boundaries exist which is why I haven't tried to discover information about the unit pupils or is it that they weren't important enough to bother about? I don't want to write any more. I wish I hadn't written any of this — it's so horrible and now it is on paper I can't push it into the back of my mind anymore! (diary/journal)

Jo writes in her professional account now of her realization:

Having accepted that meeting Special Needs had not been my prime concern, the question now arose, WHY was this the case? (assignment)

This self-questioning occurs between two citations from 'Special Needs in the Ordinary School' and 'The Special Child'. The excerpt from 'The Special Child' relates to teachers being well informed about pupils with SENs. This leads Jo to further reflect in her diary on the role of management in the values and actions of the school which she has herself accepted.

I can't believe the way the unit pupils have been timetabled for music as a whole class this year and not been integrated into main stream classes as was the case in other years.

What annoys me is that this has just suddenly happened, out of the blue, no discussion, no planning, no reasoning or consideration if this is really the best thing for these pupils. Jean has absolutely no idea why this has happened. No one even thought to ask her in her role as Head of the Unit what she felt about this.

This no one I've referred to is our senior management. I believe this problem really begins at senior management level. They do not understand the needs of the unit children, consequently they are not even trying to cater for these children when it comes to timetabling.

In her parallel assignment, Jo proceeds with more citations from the literature to back up her realization that ignorance on the part of mainstream class teachers about SENs pupils is widespread and related to management's lack of communication on the issue.

Jo then decides on an action step which includes a case study of a special needs pupil. She dispenses questionnaires to other teachers who teach the pupils in mainstream classes. The return of the questionnaire confirms that these teachers were ill informed about the pupils' problems and educational difficulties, so Jo resolves to share this information at a meeting with management. Management asked for a basic outline of Jo's research in written form. Jo now reflects on Jean's helpful suggestions for better communication strategies in her journal;

Do you know it was a 'good idea' of Jean's to ask me to give her written details about my research as I have spent this last four hours going through a process of really sorting out the situation and how I require Jean's help. Writing, or in this case, typing to Jean has been a bit like writing in my diary — as I wrote I reflected and I actually sorted my thoughts out. I presented my thoughts more precisely and coherently in written form than I would have done orally and I was able to type things that I know I couldn't have said to Jean face-to-face.

I mean there's nothing blunt or offensive in what I've typed — it's just more concise and straightforward, whereas when I start to talk, I get away off the subject and could lose my train of thought. Using this method, information is clear and simple although I hope it doesn't seem too blunt.

I basically told Jean about the other teachers being ill-informed and then said I felt, after much examination and reflection, that our professional relationship could be improved. I blamed *myself* totally for any flaw in our relationship and ended my letter by asking Jean for suggestions about how our interprofessional relationship could be improved. (diary/journal)

She then outlines the research evidence and publicly writes that:

Jean confirmed that she was most willing to assist me with regard to an improvement in our interprofessional relationship and requested that I provide her with my proposals for improvement in this area for consideration. (assignment)

The diary however shows the strain on Jo:

I'm slightly disappointed by Jean's response as although she agrees with me and has opened the way ahead for me — all the push and shove is coming from me.

Jo realizes now that she is the person who is searching for some change in the situation. Jean sees the problem too but does not know how to change things. Jo is taking the lead — which is a new experience for her. She is a junior member of the teaching staff and finds this position uncomfortable at first, but she still reflects, investigates and takes further action.

The professional values implicit in the professional account are accepting and confident — in the diary the personal reflection is more disappointment tinged with resentment. The style of self-expression is very different and contrasts Jo's different views on the purposes of the diary/journal and the assignment. However, she continues to write in a dispassionate way in her professional account;

As requested I constructed a list of suggestions which I then forwarded to Jean and we arranged to meet to discuss them. After the deliberations:
 (i) I had access to all the information and records on SEN pupils.
 (ii) Assessment would now take place on a more regular basis and in a more detailed form from this date onwards.
 (iii) Jean would be available for informal discussion at any time and would be most willing to provide any relevant or helpful information that I require which is not available in pupils' official files. (assignment)

However the underlying feelings that Jo has behind all this negotiation of access is that she feels empathy with Jean now and wishes that Jean had more push to do the things that she sees are necessary. Jo determines to support her in these changes.

> Our discussion ended with me pledging my full support with regard to any changes she wished to make, but I feel great sympathy for Jean as I can identify so closely with what she is feeling.
>
> Jean has got herself into a situation that may prove very hard to get out of. What is required is a combination of *tact* and *forcefulness*. Jean is like me, she pre-judges the outcome of a situation and examines all the negative outcomes that may occur. By this stage she is so worried that she *cannot* go ahead. My present hope is that an 'experienced' special needs teacher gets the post in charge of the proposed second special educational needs unit and gives Jean the support, advice and confidence which she so badly needs.
>
> I feel sad at the end of this interview. I have much more understanding of Jean's problems. However, I feel that our discussion has opened up a two-way communication system between us. She now knows I care, I am interested and that she has my full support with regard to improvement.
>
> Wasn't Jean so open and honest when she admitted her own short-comings or how she feels she has failed? How I wish I had the confidence to implement the changes required!

Jo has now convinced Jean of her commitment to the pupils with special educational needs and has offered her support for further improvement in professional communication. In terms of action Jo turns to the development of a pupil profile form to provide her and other teachers with accurate and relevant information about SEN pupils. There is more successful liaison with Jean on this action.

The assignment or the professional account concludes with a summary of insights gained in doing the research.

(i) I discovered that bias was prominent in my understanding of the unsatisfactory interprofessional relationship that existed between the Head of the Special Educational Needs Unit and I placed full responsibility for the situation with her.

(ii) When addressing the question concerning why I had not done more to improve my interprofessional relationship with the Head of Special Needs, I became aware that this was because the situation did concern me but it was not a prime concern.

(iii) Lack of understanding, not enough careful planning and the passing on of relevant information were contributing factors to the question of special needs not being my prime concern.

(iv) According to relevant literature, remediation with regard to this situation would involve more care in planning, extended consultation and more detailed assessment of how pupils needs could best be met. Consequently, improved communication was required in order to improve practice.

However, the personal account is much more revealing and real and details more explicitly the thoughts ideas and emotions embodied in the transformation of the situation. Apart from making her progressive understanding clear through the explicit journal writing which provides Jo's conscious awareness, she also in the end makes a distinction between acting in a professional as opposed to, a personal manner. The personal aspects of the changed relationship enable Jo to cope with the complexity of the role in a more effective manner. Jo and Jean have become friends and subsequently are *not* now acting in a 'professional manner'. They have broken barriers put in place at a 'professional' level. Values which appear personal rather than professional surface in the situation, for example, the recognition of the personal qualities of each Jo and Jean. Jo discovers that Jean is 'very caring'.

> It is with absolute honesty that I conclude that this has been my most challenging assignment so far but it has also been the most rewarding.
> Jean and I have finally broken down those barriers that have existed for five years at a professional level. I am now her friend, in the sense that I can come and ask anything about any SEN pupil, and know that I am not 'tramping on toes'.
> I have already read all the information available on the Special Needs pupils. By the way, it was most disappointing and told me very little about what I really wanted to know!
> That is why the progress that Jean and I have made as two professionals is so important, as she can help me far more than all that information which is kept under lock and key, as Jean works closely with those kids day in and day out. She is very caring, has their best interests at heart, so ultimately it is to her I will turn in my times of need and questioning. (diary/journal)

> (Jo's diary extracts are the genuine writings of a comprehensive school teacher who prefers to remain anonymous)

Jo has built up her own personal theory of teaching by seeking out the assumptions in her thinking and understanding. Through enquiry and systematic testing she has become aware of hidden values, and the weight she gives to her own personal experiences and characteristics. She has become more professionally competent and confident in the making of her own explicit theory through its articulation in the diary/journal and its more public emergence in the assignment. Jo has been self-critical which has deepened her reflexivity. She has integrated her personal and professional values in the deliberate taking of action to improve her professional role. In so doing her social/professional identity has been strengthened. Jo is now more conscious of herself in her acting through the teaching role.

Self-understanding and Personal Change

All actions taken by teachers and professionals can be seen as role behaviour. But within the role taking is the identity of self. Identity is a conscious awareness of 'who' we are. It evolves and changes with time. Identity varies within the different roles that people play in their lives. It is our identity which forms our awareness and our actions in 'any' or 'many' roles in life including the professional role of teaching. Berger (1966) states that:

Every act of affiliation entails a choice of identity.

Becoming a teacher, or developing into a more proficient teacher entails a commitment to the professional values of the culture of teaching and education. The act of teaching therefore confers that professional identity of role upon the incumbent. This may only be one of many individual roles. The person is perceived as a repertory of roles each one properly equipped with a certain identity. The teaching role identifies us to ourselves as teachers, which subsequently affects our behaviour as we attempt to perform in 'role'. Goffman's (1961) view is that one's identity is formed by one's role. Although both writers express the crucial nature of personal identification within the role, however, Berger sees identity influencing the action within the role, while Goffman sees the role and its actions as forming the person's identity.

Both views from Berger and Goffman are not mutually exclusive. A newcomer to a 'role' will decide on the identity of the role to suit his/her individual personal characteristics, once the role is learned and practised then the role may become more and more part of the person through its practice. The professional identity may in time become the person's predominant identity. A person's identity is continually being constructed, but it may not be understood or discovered until one becomes self-aware, or conscious of the values inspiring our actions. One way of developing this self-awareness is by the encouragement of fully articulated theories of reflection on action.

The development of personal autonomy is a consequence of a conscious theory of action, because in the deeper understanding of one's actions one becomes more self knowledgeable and self-aware. It is with this increased self-understanding that self-confidence grows.

Both Berger and Goffman also share the aspiration of wishing to enlarge the scope for personal autonomy within society. Much of Goffman's work can be seen as descriptions of personal identities expressing themselves in many devious ways within the impositions of institutions. But personal identity or the self, although it exists within all humans is not discovered until we find self-awareness. As Mead (1934) says;

> The reflective character of self-consciousness enables the individual to contemplate himself [sic] as a whole.

The individual in becoming reflexive also becomes capable of total self-understanding. S/he may understand the distinction between the inner person (I) and the person we want the world to see (me). Mead makes a distinction between the 'I' and the 'me' in self. The 'I' is the response we make to the attitudes of others, the 'me' is the organized set of attitudes of others which we assume for ourselves. The 'I' is safe from the outside world. The 'me' can be assessed by others in the social world. The 'I' however, often interferes with the 'me'. Professionals in schools often experience a dissonance between the 'I' and the 'me', they are torn between their personal and their professional values in action, for example, empathizing with the child or with a colleague in a moral dilemma which challenges one to accept one person's view and in so doing to take one' 'truth' as opposed to another. The 'I' prompts support of the child, but the 'me' expects support for the colleague to uphold the professional values of collegiality and solidarity. Our actions are autonomous in one sense, and, in another determined by values imposed in the professional role.

In the understanding of professional practice we can see human action not only as pushed from behind, as deterministically caused, but as action which is intentional and has a future reference. Psychologists like Maslow (1954) see self-actualization as the ultimate need for the self to find expression. This height of human endeavour is based on personal values. A characteristic of Maslow's self-actualization is the factor of self-acceptance. Self-acceptance involves becoming reconciled to oneself and to adverse circumstances and events in one's life (Jung, 1960). In the development of adults in educational contexts self-acceptance/ awareness/evaluation and self-actualization are integral functions of professional development which must be fostered in the facilitation of teachers in professional contexts.

Jourand (1964) carries the thesis further with his view that a person does violence to his/her own needs through failing to be aware of them and to give them expression. The way that an adult performs the professional role has been recognized as a critical index of the satisfactory functions of the role. Jourand describes stereotyped role-behaviour which involves the suppression of one's spontaneous self as damaging the professional even more than the client. He believes that success is increased and personal growth is facilitated when persons/ professionals perform their roles spontaneously, according to the demands of the situation and the needs of the client. This can only be successfully achieved by the confidence gained through greater self-awareness and understanding of our action in making our theories of action explicit.

In initial teacher training or the professional development of teachers we cannot take anything for granted, especially, in the latter case, the false belief that adults because they are professionals are all wise. Therefore the teaching of professional adults is often a form of 'mixed ability' teaching. The professionals have various professional needs which are made more complex through the in-trusion of the self or the 'I' in everyday encounters.

In the educational development of professionals we aspire to lead them to-wards wisdom, to deepen the knowledge that they already possess and to new knowledge and understanding.

Kitchener and Brenner (1990) view wisdom as having four aspects:

(i) A recognition of the presence of unavoidably difficult and inherently thorny problems that confront all adults.
(ii) A comprehensive grasp of knowledge that is characterized by both breadth and depth of understanding.
(iii) A recognition that knowledge is uncertain and that it is not possible for truth to be absolutely knowable at any given time.
(iv) A willingness and exceptional ability to formulate sound, executable judgments in the face of life's uncertainties.

Wisdom therefore in this context, involves facing pragmatic life problems and making decisions about actions taken. In fact Dixon and Baltes (1986) suggest that wisdom is activated when problems with no clear solution are presented to one. The implications for professionals are that ambiguity and doubt are facts of existence and that resolving crises in daily professional activities may be short-lived. The successful professional tolerates such ambiguities.

Kitchener and Brenner's view runs parallel to Rogers' (1967) 'fully functioning person' which consists of the following:

(i)   Openness to experience — has self-awareness and self-acceptance.
(ii) Existential living — living fully each moment.
(iii) Organismic trusting — making spontaneous decisions rather than using rigid preconceived categories.
(iv) Experiential freedom — experiences freedom of choice.
(v) Creativity — the ability to produce new and effective thoughts and actions.

Both Kitchener and Brenner's and Rogers' models for a wise and fully functioning person accentuate the openness and tolerance to experience and ambiguity in life. They suggest the need to feel confident in making decisions and in taking action without too much self-doubt. At the core of the process of professional development is the teachers'/professionals' action towards bringing about improvement and change. Discussion can take place about hypothetical change in a professional situation but actually taking action to bring about change is often resisted, even when the change is seen as an improvement. Marris (1974) identified people's tendency to accept only those things which could be taken into their existing perceptual structure, and to avoid, redefine or reject anything that could not be assimilated. In a basic sense our survival depends on our ability to understand, interpret and to predict events.

However, the consequences of events are only predictable if they fit into the person's own perceptions and interpretations. The interpretations we make can only be understood in terms of our own purposes, preferences, antipathies and our learned experience of the world. Each person copes with the uncertainties of life by trying to conserve the basic structure of the meanings they have constructed for themselves. Change inevitably causes some uncertainty because change involves loss. What we have lost is the existing structure which we created to ensure our understanding and prediction in our lives. In professional development the loss may be a former, routine way of acting and teaching in the classroom or the loss of status associated with teaching certain pupils rather than pupils who bring a higher status, or a changed relationship with a colleague. Each loss is difficult to measure and requires a period of adaptation. It takes time for a person to find a reorientation of thinking and feeling which will integrate the new situation into his/her structure of perceiving and understanding the world. We can use our habitual behaviour and action in professional situations until we discover that they no longer work well. The impetus to change them for what we believe to be a better course of action is both challenging and disquieting. The challenge is to articulate a personal theory within a process of professional development.

Professional development once it is initiated in a manner which promotes autonomy through better self-understanding will perpetuate new ways of understanding and acting in practice. Sharing and developing our new awareness and confidence is possible without formal and hierarchical support structures. In the articulation of teachers' personal theories there are opportunities to hear and share our understanding of what it means to be a professional in the ever changing school culture. In this shared consciousness lies the basis for further improved practice in education which is owned by the practitioners themselves.

Christine O'Hanlon

References

BERGER, P. (1966) *Invitation to Sociology*, Penguin.

DIXON, R.A. and BALTES, P.B. (1986) *Towards Life Span Research on the Function & Pragmatics of Intelligence*, in R.J. STERNBERG and R.K. WAGNER (Eds), Practical Intelligence. Cambridge, Cambridge University Press.

GOFFMANN, E. (1961) *Encounters*, Indianapolis, Bobbs-Merrill.

JOURARD, S.M. (1964) *The Transparent Self: Self Disclosure & Well Being*, Princeton, Van Nostrand.

JUNG, C.G. (1960) T*he Stages of Life* in H. READ., M. FORDHAM, G. ADLER, and W. McGUIRE (Eds), The Collected Works of C.G. Jung. (Vol 8) Princeton, NJ. Princeton University Press.

KITCHENER, K. and BRENNER, H. (1990) *Wisdom & Reflective Judgement; Knowing in the face of uncertainty* in Wisdom. Its nature origins and development STERNBERG, R.J. (Ed.), Cambridge University Press

LODGE B. (1991) *Early Escapes May Be On The Way Out*, Times Educational Supplement, August 23 1991.

MASLOW A.H. (1954) *Motivation & Personality*, New York, Harper & Row.

MARRIS, P. (1974) *Loss & Change,* London, Routledge & Kegan Paul.

MEAD, G.H. (1934) *Mind, Self and society*, Chicago, University of Chicago Press.

ROGERS, C.R. (1967) *A Therapists View of the Good Life: The Fully Functioning Person On Becoming A Person*, London, Constable Publishers.

List of Contributors

Marion Dadds is a Lecturer in Educational Studies at the University of Cambridge Institute of Education. Her research focusses predominantly on enquiry based teacher professional development. She has promoted the use of action-research within the context of award-bearing INSET and is continually interested to understand how teachers use this work to improve classrooms and schools.

Richard Davies is currently working as a Senior Research Associate at the Centre for Applied Research in Education. Until February 1992 he was closely involved in the PALM Project, working with IT advisory teams adopting action-research approaches to IT development in the classroom.

Christopher Day is Professor of Education at Nottingham University. Prior to this he worked as a teacher, lecturer and Local Authority Adviser. He has researched and written extensively in the field of leadership, professional development, teacher thinking and action-research, Current publications include Developing Teachers and Teaching (an edited series for the Open University Press), *Insight into Teachers' Thinking and Action* (1990 Falmer Press), *Managing Primary Schools in the 1990s* (1990 Paul Chapman Ltd.).

John Elliott is Professor of Education in the Centre for Applied Research in Education and Dean of the School of Education at the University of East Anglia. For over two decades he has played a leading role in action-research approaches to teacher education, and more recently in the education of public service professionals generally.

He began his academic career as a central team member of Stenhouse's Humanities Project (1967–72) and then designed and directed the Ford Teaching Project (1972–75). Both projects are now widely recognized to have made seminal contributions to the development of the action-research movement internationally. In 1976 he founded the Classroom Action Research Network (CARN) which has an international membership, and he is currently a consultant to the OECD on action-research approaches to the development of environmental education curricula in member countries.

In addition to numerous articles in books and journals on the theory and practice of action-research John Elliott is the author of *La investigación-acción en educatión* (1990) Madrid: Ediciones Morata, and Action *Research for Educational Change* (1991) Milton Keynes & Philadelphia: Open University Press.

David H. Hargreaves is Professor of Education in the University of Cambridge and Fellow of Wolfson College. His latest book (with David Hopkins) is *The Empowered School: the management and practice of development planning*, 1991.

Saville Kushner is a lecturer in applied research at the Centre for Applied Research in Education. He is a specialist in educational evaluation.

Rae George Munro is Honorary Research Fellow at the University of Auckland and immediate past Director of the School of Secondary Teacher Education at Auckland College of Education. He has completed action-research in curriculum evaluation, enquiry-based learning, and school-based teacher training. He is at present researching into the 'Achievement Initiative' of the New Zealand Ministry of Education.

Nigel Norris is a Lecturer in the Centre for Applied Research in Education, University of East Anglia. His teaching and research interests include social research methodology and evaluation. He has worked on a variety of project, programme and policy evaluations since 1979 and is currently directing a study of social and political conditions of applied research and evaluation.

Dr Christine O'Hanlon is a Lecturer in Special Education and Educational Psychology in the School of Education of the University of Birmingham. She has worked for many years in action-research based teacher education helping teachers to design and develop their curriculum. She has published widely in the field of teacher education particularly in relation to the education and training of teachers of pupils with special needs. She has recently extended this work into the wider European context.

Peter Ovens is Principal Lecturer in Professional and Curriculum Development at the Faculty of Education, Nottingham University, where he teaches science education and action-research on the BEd and MEd courses. His BSc and PGCE qualifications originally took him into secondary science teaching. Then he became a College of Education tutor increasingly involved in primary school work. He initiated the in-service course which is the subject of this paper and began to explore the use of action research by the course members to encourage them to develop their teaching practice. He then carried out his own action-research into his teaching of the course which led to the submission of a Doctoral thesis. His paper in this book draws on one part of the thesis.

Michael Schratz is Associate Professor of Education at the University of Innsbruck, Austria. His main interests are in educational innovation and change with a particular focus on qualitative research methodology. He taught in Austria and Great Britain, did research at the University of California, San Diego (USA), and worked at Deakin University (Australia). Amongst his publications are *Bildung für ein unbekanntes Morgen: Auf der Suche nach einer neuen Lernkultur (Education for an Unknown Tomorrow: In Search of a New Learning Culture*, 1991) and

Teaching Teenagers (1993 with Herbert Puchta). He edited *Gehen Bildung, Ausbildung und Wissenschaft an der Lebenswelt vorbei* (1988), a collection exploring whether everyday knowledge and formal education/scientific knowledge contradict one another, and *Qualitative Voices in Educational Research* (1993) and co-authored *Schulen machen Schule* (1991), a book on school autonomy and development.

Les Tickle is senior lecturer in the School of Education at the University of East Anglia. He has published widely in the field of arts education and teacher education. Recent research has focused on new teacher's induction and professional education. Books include *Learning Teaching, Teaching Teaching* (1987) and *Design and Technology in Primary Classrooms: Developing Teachers' Perspectives and Practices* (1990) both published by Falmer Press.

Index